ACCLAIM FOR Fouad Ajami's

THE DREAM PALACE OF THE ARABS

"Mr. Ajami is deeply schooled in his subject. His writing is smooth, evocative, richly cadenced. . . . One reads on, grateful for the intimacy of Mr. Ajami's portrait, which could only have been drawn by a figure who is himself a kind of bridge between the two worlds of Arabia and the West."
—*The New York Times*

"A remarkable mix of the lyrical and the analytical."
—*The New Republic*

"Mr. Ajami never flinches from judgment, but *The Dream Palace of the Arabs* is more a eulogy for an enlightened intellectual movement than a rebuke of Arab society. . . . Mr. Ajami tells his story masterfully." —*The Wall Street Journal*

"This richly textured, informative and discursive book examines the fit—or misfit—between ideas and politics in the Arab world of recent years. . . . Ironic and insightful, this work is vintage Ajami." —*Foreign Affairs*

"A compassionate survey of the intellectual movements of the post–World War II Arab world. . . . There are great [Arab] writers still living, Ajami points out, who can transcend the stilted confines of current Arab thought. As long as they and Mr. Ajami continue to write, there is hope." —*The Washington Times*

"[A] bold, imaginative and sure-to-be controversial book. . . . A vivid and often moving account of Arab thought today against the background of the lost era of progressive pan-Arab nationalism and high hopes." —*The New York Times Book Review*

THE MASTER-KEY OF OPINION LAY IN THE COMMON
LANGUAGE: WHERE ALSO LAY THE KEY OF IMAGINATION.
THEIR HERITAGE OF THE KORAN AND CLASSICAL LITERATURE
HELD THE ARAB-SPEAKING PEOPLES TOGETHER. PATRIOTISM,
ORDINARILY OF SOIL OR RACE, WAS WARPED TO A LANGUAGE.
—T. E. LAWRENCE, *Seven Pillars of Wisdom*

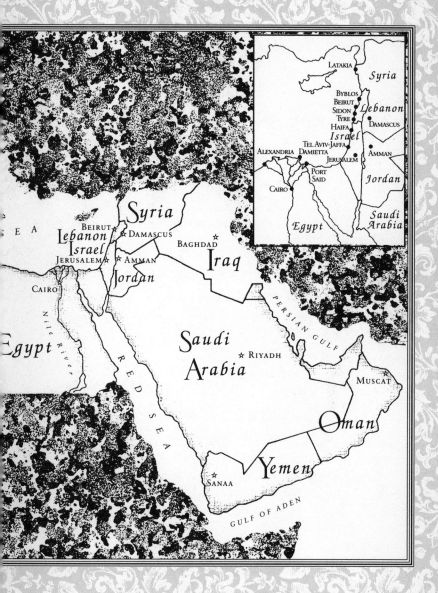

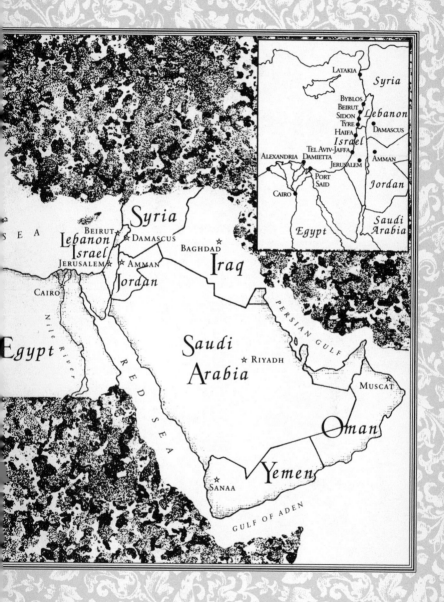

Fouad Ajami

THE DREAM PALACE
OF THE ARABS

Fouad Ajami is the Majid Khadduri Professor of Middle Eastern Studies at The Paul H. Nitze School of Advanced International Studies at Johns Hopkins University. Born in the south of Lebanon and raised in Beirut, he is a contributing editor for *The New Republic* and *U.S. News and World Report* and a member of the editorial board of *Foreign Affairs*. He is the author of *The Vanished Imam; Beirut: City of Regrets;* and *The Arab Predicament*. He has received a MacArthur Fellowship for his work on Middle Eastern politics and culture. He lives in New York City.

THE DREAM PALACE
OF THE ARABS

A Generation's Odyssey

FOUAD AJAMI

VINTAGE BOOKS

A Division of Random House, Inc.

New York

FIRST VINTAGE BOOKS EDITION, JULY 1999

Copyright © 1998 by Fouad Ajami

All rights reserved under International and Pan-American Copyright Conventions. Published in the United States by Vintage Books, a division of Random House, Inc., New York, and simultaneously in Canada by Random House of Canada Limited, Toronto. Originally published in hardcover in the United States by Pantheon Books, a division of Random House, Inc., New York, in 1998.

Vintage Books and colophon are registered trademarks of Random House, Inc.

Grateful acknowledgment is made to the following for permission to reprint previously published material: *Penguin Books Ltd.*: Excerpts from *Thus Spoke Zarathustra* by Friedrich Nietzsche, translated by R. J. Hollingdale (London: Penguin Classics, 1961). Copyright © 1961, 1969 by R. J. Hollingdale. Reprinted by permission of Penguin Books Ltd. *Lynne Rienner Publishers, Inc.*: "The Cave" and "Lazarus 1962" from *Naked in Exile: Khalil Hawi's The Threshing Floors of Hunger* by Khalil Hawi, translated and with extensive interpretive material by Adnan Haydar and Michael Beard. Copyright © 1984 by Adnan Haydar and Michael Beard. Reprinted by permission of Lynne Rienner Publishers, Inc. *Saqi Books:* "The Desert" from *Victims of a Map* by Adonis, translated by Abdullah al-Udhari (London: Saqi Books, 1984). Reprinted by permission of Saqi Books.

The Library of Congress has cataloged the Pantheon edition as follows:
Ajami, Fouad
The dream palace of the Arabs / Fouad Ajami.
p.   cm.
Includes index.
ISBN 0-375-40150-4
1. Intellectuals—Arab countries.
2. Arab countries—Politics and government—1945–
3. Nationalism—Arab countries. I. Title
DS36.88.A4   1998
956.04—dc21   97-24418 CIP

Vintage ISBN: 0-375-70474-4

www.vintagebooks.com

Printed in the United States of America
10   9   8   7   6   5   4   3

For Tahseen Basheer

There was room enough there to place any story, depth enough there for any passion, variety enough there for any setting, darkness enough to bury . . . millions of lives.

—Joseph Conrad

CONTENTS

Preface • xi

A Note on Sources and Translation • xix

1. Prologue: • 3
   THE INHERITANCE

2. The Suicide of Khalil Hawi: • 26
   REQUIEM FOR A GENERATION

3. In the Shape of the Ancestors • 111

4. In the Land of Egypt: • 193
   THE SAINTS AND THE WORLDLINESS

5. The Orphaned Peace • 253

Source Notes • 313

Acknowledgments • 323

Index • 325

THE DREAM PALACE
OF THE ARABS

A Generation's Odyssey

FOUAD AJAMI

VINTAGE BOOKS

A Division of Random House, Inc.

New York

FIRST VINTAGE BOOKS EDITION, JULY 1999

Grateful acknowledgment is made to the following for permission to reprint
previously published material: *Penguin Books Ltd.*: Excerpts from *Thus Spoke
Zarathustra* by Friedrich Nietzsche, translated by R. J. Hollingdale (London:
Penguin Classics, 1961). Copyright © 1961, 1969 by R. J. Hollingdale. Reprinted by
permission of Penguin Books Ltd. *Lynne Rienner Publishers, Inc.*: "The Cave"
and "Lazarus 1962" from *Naked in Exile: Khalil Hawi's The Threshing Floors of
Hunger* by Khalil Hawi, translated and with extensive interpretive material by
Adnan Haydar and Michael Beard. Copyright © 1984 by Adnan Haydar and
Michael Beard. Reprinted by permission of Lynne Rienner Publishers, Inc.
Saqi Books: "The Desert" from *Victims of a Map* by Adonis, translated
by Abdullah al-Udhari (London: Saqi Books, 1984).
Reprinted by permission of Saqi Books.

The Library of Congress has cataloged the Pantheon edition as follows:
Ajami, Fouad
The dream palace of the Arabs / Fouad Ajami.
p.   cm.
Includes index.
ISBN 0-375-40150-4
1. Intellectuals—Arab countries.
2. Arab countries—Politics and government—1945–
3. Nationalism—Arab countries. I. Title
DS36.88.A4   1998
956.04—dc21   97-24418 CIP

Vintage ISBN: 0-375-70474-4

www.vintagebooks.com

Printed in the United States of America
10   9   8   7   6   5   4   3

For Tahseen Basheer

self to dramatize the ordeal of his country. But no sooner had I begun to look into the life and the death of Khalil Hawi than a more textured, a richer narrative emerged. From Hawi's life, I could look into the world of Mount Lebanon where he was born, into his family life, and into the world of Beirut where the poet made his mark. Though Hawi was a quarter-century older than myself, I had no difficulty entering into his world. And in some proprietary way I felt I was picking up fragments of my own life as I looked into his.

I am not sure if I ever saw Hawi in my boyhood, but our city, Beirut, his and mine, was small, and a poem of his, "The Bridge" published in the late 1950s, when I was in my mid-teens, was a poem I memorized by heart. Into Hawi's life, and around that life, I read what had befallen a generation of Arabs: the cultural tide that carried them into the 1950s and 1960s and the ebbing of that tide in the mid-1980s. In these pages, I try as best I can to be true to the man himself and the journey he made from poverty and manual labor to professional fame and success and, finally, to individual despair. An "emblematic" life? Yes and no; in this narrative of Hawi's life I try to capture both the personal ordeal and the wider generational themes.

Straddling the boundaries of Arab politics and letters of the 1980s and 1990s, "In the Shape of the Ancestors" has a tighter time period for its focus than the preceding material about Hawi's life, which led back to the interwar years and even further back into the late years of the nineteenth century and the time of an Arab awakening in politics and letters. In this chapter we are in the world of the theocratic politics of the 1980s. A nativist revolution had erupted in Iran; an avenger, Ayatollah Ruhollah Khomeini, not only had summoned the downtrodden of the Arab world but had glamorized theocratic politics as well. At the heart of this extended narrative is the impasse, the generational fault-line, between secular parents and their theocratic children. The writers I deal with here—Adonis, Nizar Qabbani, Abdelrahman Munif, Sadiq al-Azm—are household names in the Arab republic of letters. Their material, their con-

PREFACE

MY TITLE IS borrowed from T. E. Lawrence's *Seven Pillars of Wisdom*. "I meant to make a new nation, to restore a lost influence, to give twenty millions of Semites the foundations on which to build an inspired dream palace of their national thoughts," Lawrence wrote. But the legend of Lawrence aside—a legend to which Arabs are indifferent—the gifted and tormented Lawrence was on the fringe of modern Arab history. His campaign in the desert was a sideshow. And though *Seven Pillars* is a work of heartbreaking beauty at times, it is really a tale of an outsider who had wandered into Arab life. Lawrence knew it to be so: "In these pages the history is not of the Arab movement, but of me in it," he wrote.

On their own, in the barracks and in the academies, in the principal cities of the Arab world—Beirut, Baghdad, Damascus, Cairo—Arabs had built their own dream palace—an intellectual edifice of secular nationalism and modernity. In these pages I take up what had become of this edifice in the last quarter-century. The book is at once a book about public matters—a history of a people, the debates of its intellectuals, the fate of its dominant ideas—and a personal inquiry into the kind of world my generation of Arabs, men and women born in the immediate aftermath of the Second World War, was bequeathed.

My first extended narrative is the tale of a suicide, and of the cultural requiem that followed it: a gifted Lebanese poet, Khalil Hawi, killed himself on the evening of June 6, 1982, the day Israel had swept into Lebanon. There was a narrative available of the man, the story of a life, and there was a noble death: a patriot killing him-

cerns, are the central themes of the modern Arabic experience. I
open with them, but my destination, my concern, is really with the
rupturing of the secular tradition in the era now behind us.

That era begot a great paradox: It opened with the politics of
the ancestors and of nativism pronouncing on the Arab and Muslim
present yet closed with a war, the Persian Gulf War of 1990–1991,
which a foreign dispensation, Pax Americana, waged against a
despot who had risen in Baghdad to offer Arabs a conjuror's trick,
a defective dream of historical revisionism. I try to catch the spirit
of nihilism that had overtaken the political world. The truth of that
Arab (and Muslim) time must lie, no doubt, in material circumstances. Theocratic politics had blown in when the economic
growth of a quarter-century (1960–1985) had faltered. After 1973
and the dramatic increase in oil prices, a great windfall had come
the way of the Arabs and of Iran. The region had become increasingly urbanized over the span of three decades; it had tasted prosperity but was living beyond its means. When a great recession hit in
the mid-1980s, owing to the fall in oil prices, the newly urbanized
and their children were trapped in a no-man's-land. They wailed for
themselves, and it was their anguish that shaped the politics and culture of that era. That drive to the gold souk of Kuwait that Saddam
Hussein's soldiers took in August of 1990 was a brigand's gift, an offering to all those who had been taunted and denied by an era of astounding fury.

An imperium of strangers (Pax Americana) could work only at
the margins of a world so distant, so unsympathetic, and so dubious about America's purposes. My narrative moves from the swift
campaign Pax Americana fought in 1990–1991 into the reevaluation
of the foreigners' rescue, which emerged five or six years later even
among Arabs who had first sanctioned or winked at the American-
led campaign.

"In the Land of Egypt" opens with a great, defining episode in
modern Egypt's life: the assassination of Anwar al-Sadat in October
1981, the tension in the Egyptian psyche and in the country's history,

illuminated by Sadat and the young band of assassins who struck him down. Years earlier I had been mesmerized by the tale of that assassination and had acquired and read practically all the court proceedings and police investigations that surrounded the assassination. Something that the principal assassin, a young lieutenant in his early twenties, said always stayed with me. "I shot the Pharaoh," he proclaimed. The narrative here has afforded me a chance to return to that episode.

In the years that separate us from the assassination, Egypt, a land infinitely kind and good and generous to authors, went through a great debate, and a relentless insurgency by rebels who partook of the politics and the beliefs of the assassins of Sadat. It was an odd, subtle landscape that Egypt presented: a place where secularism and modernity and worldliness existed side by side with theocratic politics. It seemed to me that the country was more subtle and deeper than the received wisdom about it. The truth of Egypt had endured, a truth captured by one of its most acute foreign chroniclers, Emil Ludwig, in his moving book *The Nile in Egypt* (1935): "This was the state," Ludwig wrote, that had "made a god of Pharaoh, a necessity of work, an art of the technique of irrigation, a principle of rational and clear thinking. . . . The sun seems to have dried up in this country the will to revolt, just as the Nile, with its world of figures, has swamped the philosophic sense." No revolt by a theocratic fringe has carried Egypt away, although many pundits had predicted it. But the theocratic alternative has seeped into the culture of the land, and Egyptians worry about the modernity they had carved out with such great effort and yearning.

It is Sisyphus that the text on Egypt conjures up—the relentless quest of that country for national deliverance. A sense of the duality of Egypt—the modernity at the core of its national aspirations and the nemesis that stalks it in the form of theocratic politics—came to me on my last trip to Egypt in May 1997. The traveler's luck brought me a gift beyond my expectations. A talented filmmaker; Tawfic Saleh, one of the closest friends of the great novelist Naguib

Mahfuz, made it possible for me to spend four evenings in the presence of Mahfuz. In his eighties; frail, with failing eyesight, recovering from a knifing by religious fanatics that nearly cost him his life
and paralyzed his writing hand, Mahfuz and his ordeal represented
at once the modernity of Egypt and the siege of its secular men and
women of letters. To aid in his recovery and to lift his spirit, Mahfuz's physician had recommended that the writer spend his evenings
away from his apartment in different parts of the city. And the Mahfuz gatherings I was treated to were both occasions of genuine debate and a way of honoring the distinguished man of letters, being
in his presence. Physicians, academics, journalists, a young fashion
designer, a marketing representative, men and women from all
walks of life, found their way into the four gatherings I attended.
The talk flowed freely, although the closer of Mahfuz's friends
looked after him, making sure the evenings came to an end at a reasonably early hour.

The physical frailty of Mahfuz was deceptive: he was alert and
a toughness-of-mind characterized his views. Always there at the
ready were the liberalism and secularism that had landed him in
trouble with the religious extremists. (The preacher convicted in the
bombing of the World Trade Center in 1993, Omar Abdul Rahman,
opined that Salman Rushdie would not have written *Satanic Verses*
had Mahfuz been punished earlier for his own brand of free thinking.) To see him amidst his admirers, to see the devotion these
younger people felt for him, the curiosity they had about the more
open politics of his generation, was to be reminded of that country's
deep attachment to culture and reason. One evening, we walked out
into a gentle breeze in the al-Moqattam hills overlooking the city.
Larger than usual, that group of fifteen or so people had turned over
every subject of interest: the possibility of parliamentary politics,
the state of the country's economy, the depth of its bourgeois politics of the past, the state of its contemporary culture, its peace with
Israel. Later that night, when we all walked out to bid Mahfuz
farewell, we came upon the writer's police escort: a police car, plain-

clothes security men, an armed bodyguard who slipped into the seat next to him.

On my last evening out with Mahfuz's group, I rode with the novelist from his home on a boulevard near the Nile to the outskirts of Cairo, to the hotel where the group always met on that day of the week. The traffic of Cairo being what it is, drivers and passengers in the lanes next to our car were soon recognizing the old man with dark glasses and gentle features in the car next to them. The awe and affection for the man were unmistakable. Some drivers made way for our car; others kept pace as best they could in the adjacent lane. A pedestrian, with a child of eleven or twelve years of age, was startled as he looked into the car and realized who the man in the passenger's seat was. Struck by this rare gift, he stood at the intersection in a state of great enthusiasm, pointing out to the boy, most likely his son, the writer in the car. The menace was never far from this adulation: a young, burly security man in the back seat of the car, with a pistol on his knee, watched the other cars and the pedestrians with caution.

In these pages on Egypt, I return to a country that has always held an endless fascination for me. If the material I present catches some of Egypt's subtlety and some of the pain of its uneven encounter with modernity, the effort will have been worthwhile.

The last part of the book, "The Orphaned Peace," centers on the Arab intellectual encounter with Israel. From the time of Israel's birth as a state, talking about Israel has been, in part, a way that Arabs talk about their own world, take stock of their own condition. Neighbor and enemy, so close yet so far and so distant, the Zionist project has fascinated and repelled and teased Arabs. Israel has been a forbidden land in many ways. And the forbidden is always a tangled matter.

In a way the matter of Israel is bound up with the matter of Arab modernity. For modernity to have a chance, the Arab political imagination will have to go beyond that old enmity. Many of the intellectuals probed in these pages know and acknowledge this. Some are willing to let bygones be bygones, to bury the hatchet. A larger stream is incapable of coming to terms with an historic compromise with Israel. Some of the latter plead that it is not time yet for such reconciliation. Others are more forthright. For them, that conflict, as I make clear in the following pages, is a matter of their own fidelity to the truths of their own world.

A NOTE ON SOURCES
AND TRANSLATION

I DREW ON a fairly large body of Arabic material—fiction, poetry, memoirs, social and political commentaries. Except where otherwise indicated in the text or in the source notes at the end of the book, the translations are mine. It is a cliché that translation is always a betrayal, and I tried to be true to the intent and textual integrity of my sources. Whatever the defects of the Arab political experience, the Arabs are blessed with a massive body of writings, a language of stunning beauty, and authors of unusual gifts. In their fiction, in their poetry, in their social commentaries, Arabs provide penetrating insights into their own world. It has been the besetting sin—and poverty—of a good deal of writing on the Arab world that it is done by many who have no mastery of Arabic. This has always seemed odd to me: To presume so much without hearing a people through their own words. The pleasure of this endeavor was the ability to tell this story through the writings of the Arabs themselves.

There were translations that others did that I found true or rendered in ways I could not hope to match. Where that was the case, the translators and their works are identified in the text or the source notes.

I have tried to keep the text "uncluttered." The fuller documentation I provide at the end of the book, in the source notes.

THE DREAM PALACE
OF THE ARABS

CHAPTER ONE

PROLOGUE:

THE INHERITANCE

———◆———

W HEN THE IRAQI poet Buland Haidari was buried in
London in the summer of 1996, the men and women of
Arabic letters who bade him farewell could not miss the
poignancy of his fate. Haidari, born in Baghdad in 1926, had been
twice exiled: he had fled the autocracy of Iraq to Beirut, and he had
fled the anarchy of Beirut and its drawn-out troubles to London. By
the time of his death a whole world of political journalism, of Arabic letters, had put down roots in exile. A political inheritance had
slipped through the fingers of the generations of Arabs formed on
the ideals of secular enlightenment and modernity. The Iraqi poet
who had taken to the road and was buried in the *ghurba* (the lands
of strangers) was part of a great unsettling of things, a deep Arab
malady. Arabs of Haidari's bent had lost their bearings and their
cultural home.

Haidari started writing his poetry in the 1940s. He belonged to
a special breed of poets who took it upon themselves to revolution-
ize their craft and to modernize the culture of Arabic letters. They
were an audacious lot, with boundless faith in the written word and

in the connection between literary reform and political change. They were rebels against authority, custom and tradition, and the world of their elders. Although he hailed from landed aristocracy, Haidari himself had known some marginality and hardship. He had known the life of the streets of Baghdad and had befriended drifters and misfits. The wealth of the Haidari clan went back to the age of Suleiman the Magnificent, the first half of the sixteenth century. They had accumulated huge tracts of land; they had, in the fashion of the landed elite of Muslim cities, spawned a number of religious judges and scholars, as well as government bureaucrats. They were of Kurdish extraction, but this was before the age of ethnic nationalism, when the world of the elites was still open and fluid enough to make room for them. And although they had seen an erosion of some of their wealth and power in the course of the nineteenth century, when the Ottoman imperial system sought to centralize its domains and to cut down the power of the landed families in its far-flung provinces, the Haidaris had kept intact enough wealth and power to see them through. They were pillars of the *ancien régime,* the Iraqi monarchy, which British power secured in that land in 1921.

We don't know with confidence what set Buland Haidari against the world of his family. In one version of the man's life, his uncle, Daud Pasha Haidari, a big man in the old order, had deprived him of his inheritance after the death of young Buland's father; in another, the boy had taken to the streets and to leftist politics. Either way, in his late teens, Buland Haidari put up a stall as a writer of petitions (it was the practice in front of government ministries in Arab cities to have such scribes to draft petitions for unlettered petitioners) in front of the Ministry of Justice, where his uncle, the pasha, served as minister. "Revolt and exile were in me right from the beginning," Haidari would recall shortly before his death. "My alienation grew particularly after I broke with the dominant order in Iraq."

When the old order in his country was overthrown, on a midsummer day in 1958, amid a frenzy of murderous violence, and the young King Faisal II of Iraq and his family were cut down by a military coup, Buland Haidari and his peers were seized with the delusion that a new world was in the offing. They were done with the power of the landed elites, and of the monarchy, and of the influence of Britain in their society. A poet of Buland Haidari's generation, Abdul al-Wahhab al-Bayati, born in the same year, celebrated the revolution of 1958 as a fulfillment of a generation's dreams:

> *The sun rises in my city*
> *The bells ring out for the heroes.*
> *Awake, my beloved,*
> *We are free.*

It didn't take long for the new order of ideologues and officers to drown in its own blood. On the other side of the exaltation and the new politics, these younger Arabs who had welcomed a new dawn were overwhelmed by a terrible politics of betrayal and bloodletting. In no time, Buland Haidari was imprisoned, as his country succumbed to a new season of cruelty.

Haidari then sought a reprieve from the whirlwind of Iraq's politics in Beirut. In that merciful city, he joined other Arab castaways who had played and lost at the game of politics. He was a peaceful man, it was said of him in this place of exile. He had had his fill of violence and certitude, and he loved the forgiving ways of Beirut. He befriended poets and literati of every persuasion: communists, Arab nationalists, believers in the Mediterranean identity of the lands of Syria and Lebanon. He loved Beirut for the new chance it had given him. He ran a bookstore; he edited a scientific magazine; he did freelance work. He was a man with eclectic interests; he wrote books about the connection between art and culture and about the history of mosque architecture. He put together a new life in a country that left well enough alone. He wrote his poetry, and he partook of the received ideas of Arab nationalism of his time. When he spoke of an "Arab nation," this man meant it; when he called for an "Arab renaissance" in culture and letters, he gave voice to the expectation, current in the 1950s and 1960s, that Arabs would dig out of poverty, backwardness, and dependency. A new life required a new literature, a new style of expression, and Haidari was devoted to that Arab literary effort. If anything, his Kurdish background made him more eager to proclaim an Arab sense of belonging. Not for this man, at that time, were the politics of ethnicity. The Arab cultural container was wide and big enough, it was thought, to take in all religious sects and all minorities. It was Arabic poetry that this man wrote, and it was an Arab dawn that he awaited.

When the ground began to burn in Beirut and the dream of an "Arab awakening" came face to face with the facts of religious and communal hatred, Haidari joined those who fled that city to Paris, London, and North America, to any place that would have them. He paid Beirut a tribute of farewell, an adopted son's sorrow, dedicating a poetic collection to it: "To those in whom Beirut remained, although they left, and to those whom Beirut deserted, although they stayed."

Arabs were on the move. There were Arabic magazines, newspapers, and publishing houses; there were restaurants that took their old names and recipes to distant places. There were writers and journalists and storytellers who took the memory of simpler times and places and worked over these memories in new, alien settings. The inheritance—the secular political idea and the dream of progress and modernity—had worn thin. The compact of the generations, that subtle pact between one generation and its successor about what to retain, discard, or amend, had been torn up. In the privacy of their own language, when Westerners, Israelis, "enemies," and "Orientalists" were not listening in, Arabs spoke with candor, and in code. They did not need much detail; they could speak in shorthand of what had befallen their world. The trajectory of their modern history was known to them. An Arab of Buland Haidari's age and awareness would have been through great political and cultural ruptures. He would have seen the coming of a cultural and political tide in the 1950s—growing literacy, the political confidence of mass nationalism, the greater emancipation of women, a new literature

and poetry that remade a popular and revered art form—and its ebb. They would have lived through the Suez War in 1956—the peak of Arab nationalist delirium—and the shattering of that confidence a decade later in the Six Day War of 1967. By the mid-1980s, the men and women of Haidari's generation no longer recognized themselves in the young men and women of the Arab world. In the simplified interpretation we have of that civilization, the young had taken to theocratic politics; they had broken with the secular politics of their elders. They had done that, but there was more at stake in that great cultural and political drama. Home and memory, the ways of an inheritance, the confidence in unexamined political and social truths, had been lost. Consider this simple passage written in the mid-1980s by a man of the Arab elite, of Buland Haidari's time and certainties. Palestinian-Jordanian diplomat and author Hazem Nusseibah was speaking of the Arab nationalists of his time: "They believed in the blending of what was best in the newly discovered Arab heritage and in contemporary Western civilization and culture, and they foresaw no serious problem which might impair the process of amalgamation." No Arab in the 1990s could speak in such terms. The borders between things and people Arab and the civilization of the West had become permeable—today I can pick up a paper my father used to read in the early 1950s in Beirut a block or two from my apartment on the Upper West Side of New York City—but the encounter has become one of great unease, rage, and violence. A great unsettling of things had been unleashed on Arab lands, and they had not been ready for it. What Arabs had said about themselves, the history they had written, and the truths they had transmitted to their progeny had led down a blind alley.

Haidari could speak in that familiar shorthand about Arab history. He knew that his readers would understand him. The Arabs were amid an "ocean of terror," he wrote. Terror had nearly overwhelmed intellectual life. There was, he said, the terror of those who anoint themselves as interpreters of God's law, of heaven's command on earth: the religious fundamentalists. There was the terror of political regimes monopolizing the symbols of national-

ism and loyalty. There was the terror of tribalism, ethnic warfare, and national chauvinism. "Anyone who violates this political trinity is destined to be killed or to be charged with heresy and apostasy." Daily, he added, there were reports of the murders of men and women of letters all over that "Arab homeland." The knife and the violence spared no one, not even a figure as old and celebrated as the Egyptian novelist Naguib Mahfuz, who was attacked by young fanatics in Cairo in 1994. Haidari wrote in despair that there was little that thinkers and writers could do amid this "ocean of terror." To survive, they had to hear no evil, speak no evil, see no evil.

In the way that writers always speak to an audience specific in time, place, and knowledge, Haidari did not have to elaborate on the meaning of tribal wars and chauvinism. By then the large pan-Arab truth that a century of nationalism had preached had cracked. Haidari was a Kurd, as no doubt a good percentage of his readers were aware; they knew what had happened in the hill country of Kurdistan only a few years earlier. In the summer of 1988, between August 25 and 27, to be exact, the Iraqi regime used chemical weapons against its own Kurdish citizens and thousands perished. The regime had hatched a monstrous "resettlement" scheme, creating a vast free-fire zone and razing hundreds of hamlets and towns to the ground. The relationship between the Kurds and the Iraqi state that had arisen in the aftermath of the First World War and the diplomatic settlement that followed that war had never been easy. Intermittent rebellions had erupted in Kurdish lands, but this kind of state violence, and its scale and audacity, were new. Prohibitions and limits had been transgressed, it seemed, in many realms of Arab life, and what had happened in the hills of Kurdistan in the summer of 1988 was of a piece with this eerie change in Arab life.

The violence in the Kurdish hills—a subtext to Haidari's words—was hardly unique. Haidari's readers possessed other memories, other pieces of knowledge, stark evidence that their world had come apart. They had seen the communal wars of Lebanon and the sectarian battles in Syria. No consoling tale offered by nationalist apologists or by "foreign friends" eager to hide the warts could have

hid those terrible tales. A ruinous war passed off by its promoters as a "racial" war between Arab and Persian had been fought for eight long years between Iran and Iraq. The identity of millions of Shia Arabs had become a burden during those years. And in the summer of 1996, when Haidari, the innovative poet who worked at the altar of Arab cultural renovation, was buried on foreign soil, his read-ers—they had been reading him, in his final years, in a London-based Arabic weekly, al-Majalla—could grasp the loaded meaning of where he was buried.

HAIDARI'S GENERATION IS not mine. Born in 1945, in Lebanon, I and Arabs of my age were their heirs. The edifice of Arab nationalism, a secular inheritance into which politicized men and women of the generation that preceded mine had poured their hopes and dreams—and evasions—was in place when I came into my own. Mine was an obedient generation: On one side, there were our elders, the Haidaris and others I have come to chronicle in writ-ing this work; on the other, younger men and women who have come to greater grief amid the breakdown of the Arab world in re-cent years. Nowadays when outsiders come calling on Arab lands, it is easy for them to say that a theocratic wind carried that world. They would not recognize, those outsiders eager to judge, what hopes and what labor went into that inheritance. Arriving after a terrible storm, those who come to the Arab world today can scarcely know what stood there or what was true when that world was intact and whole. A fire brigade that rushes in to put out a fire cannot de-scribe what was there before the fire wreaked its vengeance. Places where I once lived—places now doubly removed from me across time and distance, places of my childhood in Lebanon—became po-litical material for journalists who covered the pandemonium of that country. In the wars of Lebanon in the 1980s, the Commodore Hotel in West Beirut came to great fame as a haunt for foreign re-porters. Dispatches were filed from the Commodore. Fixers, militia leaders, diplomats, and spies worked out of the Commodore. There was a parrot by the bar that imitated the whistle of the incoming

shellfire, there was Fat Tommy, the cat that slept wedged between the Reuters and the Associated Press news tickers, and there were the resourceful staff, who welcomed foreign reporters checking in with a suave question: "Sniper side or car bomb side?" The stories of the Commodore were the stories of a people setting their country on fire, but doing it in style. Before its fame, the Commodore was just a place near my aunt's house, a short walk from my secondary school, where I often went at midday for my lunch break. On sunny, warm days, from my aunt's balcony, I could take in the sun-bathers and swimmers at the Commodore pool. What we knew of the Commodore was what a cousin of mine who pretended to be in the know about such things claimed: It was where stewardesses from foreign airlines hung around.

I was born at the foot of a Crusader castle, the Beaufort, in a small village in the south of Lebanon, near the Israeli–Lebanese border. In the early 1980s, Beaufort was always in the news: An Israeli–Palestinian war was fought over Beaufort and its location. The Palestinians overran the castle and the village below; the Israelis came to move them and their guns from the heights and the castle. I knew Beaufort for its wonder; I possessed of it a more intimate history. I had a child's knowledge of it. It stood on the ridge near my village, near my grandfather's land and vineyard, a castle long ruined but majestic and solitary, hanging at the edge of a rocky precipice, above the bristling rapids of the Litani River, which flowed some fifteen hundred feet below. From the ruined walls of Beaufort—like dragon's teeth these walls seemed from a distance— you could see the snow-covered peaks of Mount Hermon and into Galilee in northern Israel—in my childhood a forbidden land across a frontier of barbed wire. From the parapets of Beaufort, the chroniclers say, the signalers could send their messages to the slopes of Mount Hermon, to the Castle of Toron, to Sidon by the coast, some thirty kilometers away. The Crusader Kingdom had built a chain of fortresses on the likeliest invasion route from Damascus, a long route, a hundred or so kilometers as the crow flies, and Beaufort was

one of these great castles. I had a proprietary claim to Beaufort as a schoolboy. When I read of the Templars, a fierce order of monks and warriors repairing the fortress and building a Gothic hall in its central courtyard, I viewed that history with a certain possessiveness. I loved the tale of one Reginald of Sidon, an "Orientalized Frank," who once held sway in Beaufort and endured a year-long siege by Muslim forces. Wounded and taken prisoner, outside the castle walls Reginald urged the defenders not to give way. Tied to a tree, he exhorted his men inside while they shot arrows at him to put an end to his ordeal. A different kind of history came to Beaufort in our time—more history than the village at its foot had ever bargained for. My grandfather, a big man in this small place, died before the troubles and the outsiders intruded into his world.

My village was a stern place, a rocky hamlet that grew stunted tobacco plants. The writers who celebrated the Arab awakening in letters and politics never ventured there. My family, landed people, tobacco growers, belonged to the minority Shia sect of Islam, but the cultural tide had brought us to Beirut in the late 1940s, when I was four years of age. My family had made an earlier passage to Beirut, in the mid-1930s; my uncles and aunts had needed more schooling, but their confidence had given way in Beirut, and they had retreated to the familiarity of their world in the southern hinterland of the country. The second passage, more urgent, had worked. Growing up, I came into the politics and culture of Beirut of the 1950s. These politics and the culture belonged to me in a way they did not to my elders.

I was eleven when the Suez War erupted in 1956. I was some months short of my thirteenth year when the civil war flared up in Lebanon in 1958 and the U.S. marines hit the beaches of Beirut. We came into politics early: It was the city, the time, and the passion of nationalism. I braved the fury of my elders once, not so long after that hot summer of 1958, and went to Damascus, aboard a bus with my friends, to attend a rally for the Egyptian leader Gamal Abdul Nasser. We caught a glimpse of the hero-leader of Arab nationalism as he made an appearance on the balcony of a guest-palace. It was a time of innocence. Around the corner, it was believed, lay a great Arab project, and this leader from Egypt would bring it about.

I knew little of religion. My family were Shia Muslims, that I knew: It was a piece of self-knowledge that our divided homeland, some sixteen or seventeen religious communities, transmitted to us all. But the religious rituals were an entirely different matter. A mosque, a Shia mosque, had been built in the Armenian–Shia neighborhood of northeastern Beirut, where my father had bought land and built a house. An enterprising mullah had taken the initiative in building the mosque. There had been no money to spare for the mosque: the cleric had traveled far for the new money. He had gone to West Africa, where there were Shia traders from the villages of south Lebanon, and they had given what they could. He had gone to Iran and gotten some help from the Shah, Muhammad Reza Pahlavi, the only Shia sovereign in the lands of Islam. A plaque at the entrance acknowledged the help of the Shah of Shahs. The mosque was built in installments, whenever new money came in. It was the mosque of a people suddenly released from the land and the countryside, a people without money and without deep roots in the city. None of my peers, I recall, observed religious ritual or went to the mosque for Friday prayers. We were not a religious breed. Our lodestar was the secular political and cultural world.

I bobbed back and forth—we were good at such things, the children of the Levant—between the world of my elders and kinsmen and the culture of the city. Our modernity was like that: it lay side by side with ancestral prohibitions and phobias. It looked away from the past and hoped to be released from the grip of its ways. The world of my elders was a world of private concerns: the land my grandfather owned; the price of tobacco paid out each year by the tobacco monopoly; the money to be made by my uncles and aunts in Liberia and Sierra Leone, by my father in Saudi Arabia. My concerns were public; my world was easier: it was the gift of that older generation to me. Where my mother was born and raised, a stone's throw from Palestine, she had not paid the drama that un-

folded there between Arab and Jew much attention. She had her
world and the stark sensibility of her world. *Al-dahr ghaddar*, Fate
is vengeful. Fate had played with the lives of men and women, and
it had dealt the Palestinians what it had. This sensibility could not
be mine or my generation's as a whole.

Nationalism remade that world in a hurry and renamed things.
Our village and the town of my mother's large clan, so close to
Galilee and to the Jewish settlements there, had had their own traffic with the Jews across the Lebanon–Palestine frontier. Smugglers
would slip across the border and return with tales of the *Yahud* (the
Jews) and their settlements. (The smugglers did their best to stay
at their work after 1948 and the war that gave birth to Israel, but
the work grew more hazardous and difficult.) In the open, barren
country near the border, that land could be seen and the chatter
of its people heard across the barbed wire. At night, a searchlight
from the Jewish settlement of Metullah could be seen from the high
ridge on which my village lay. The searchlight was from the town of
the Jews, my grandfather said. The oral history transmitted to me
by my grandfather—we possessed no written records, no diaries—
was of places now on the other side of a great barrier: Acre, Safad,
Tiberias, the marshes and swamps of Huleh Lake, so thick with vegetation that riders had to lie flat on the necks of their horses for
more than an hour at a time. There had been older tales in our villages of the Jewish settlements, of the women who worked the fields
side by side with the men, the sorts of tales peasants and riders
brought of unfamiliar things they had seen on their wanderings. By
the time I had come to some political awareness in the late 1950s, the
die was cast, and there was in place a simple enmity. The burden of
Palestine would write so much of the politics of the years to come,
a great, consuming issue.

I was formed by an amorphous Arab nationalist sensibility. The
shadow of the Egyptian Gamal Abdul Nasser lay over the Muslims
of Lebanon. I partook of the politics of Muslim West Beirut. In that
summer of 1958 when the Iraqi monarchy was overthrown and the
American forces rushed in to Lebanon, dispatched there by Eisen-

hower to check Arab radicalism, I had not grieved for the Iraqi monarch. In the way of an impressionable boy, I partook of that enthusiasm for a new dawn. Across the line, a cable car ride away, in Christian East Beirut, there was an entirely different sensibility: the Maronite community, with its ethos of independence and its sense of being set apart from the Muslim Arab world around it. The Maronites had a strong sense of themselves; they had their formidable clergy, their own schools, traffic with Europe, special ties to France. They possessed a special history: the flight of their ancestors from the oppressed plains of Syria to the freedom of Mount Lebanon. I could not share the history of the Maronites; it could not have spoken to me.

In my family we possessed a special mark. My great-grandfather had come from Tabriz in Iran to our ancestral village sometime in the mid-1850s. The years had covered the trail my great-grandfather had traveled. The Persian connection was given away in the name by which he was known in his new home: Dahir Ajami, or Dahir the Persian. None of his descendants bothered to look into that Persian past. The generation preceding mine had its hands full mastering the ways of the city, or making their way in West Africa and remitting money for the extended family. My own generation could not have been bothered with ancestral tales. What culture we needed was there: the politics of nationalism, the call of Arab modernity, the American pop culture that was flooding our world in the 1950s.

We can come into a cultural inheritance without fully understanding it. I took for granted the modernity of Beirut, which I took to mean the high heels my aunts wore, the Western (French and American) schools we attended, the Egyptian fiction my younger aunts read behind the backs of their older siblings, the glitter of Beirut. There were *madani* (city) ways, and my uncles and aunts, newcomers to the city, yearned to make these ways theirs. I could not have known that the modernity I took for granted had been earned the hard way, secured by a generation that had fought for every little gain. It was only in 1928—only a few years before my family's first passage to the city—that a younger Muslim woman of Beirut,

dependent comment is no longer accepted on its merits but welcomed or frowned upon if it upholds or denies the wishes and
contentions of a particular party. Ever since I came back to
Egypt last winter I have been moving from one field of contemporary study to another, but only to find, sooner or later, that
each of them impinged on some aspect or another of high politics which it would be wiser not to touch upon at present if one
intends to move about freely in Egypt and continue to have access to people and enjoy their confidence. You may be surprised
to hear that that applies also to questions of purely cultural
character. But it does. Not only is the cultural factor at the root
of Arabic-speaking nationalism; it also plays an important part
in the Moslem religious revival. And both those forces are so
much more self-assertive than they were one or two years ago
that people are as ready to take offense or quarrel about cultural
programmes as they are on purely political issues. As a result I
have felt disoriented and at times seriously discouraged.

The outbreak of the Second World War had made it almost impossible for Antonius to go on with his itinerant life—travel restrictions, censorship. For a man who lived on motion and on the reports
he filed for the institute that subsidized him, this was a great loss.
And in February 1939, his patron, Charles Crane, died, which deprived him of a powerful backer. He pleaded with the officers and
trustees of the institute for time and understanding. In a note he
wrote in April 1940 from Cairo, he spoke of the "drying up of the
normal sources of knowledge" and of the difficulty of sending regular mail and reports. Although he offered his services to the American consular missions in Beirut and Cairo, it was decided that a
fellow of a research institute who did no reporting from the field
was expendable. An American in the Levant, who was associated
with the Byzantine Institute, reported in a letter in May 1941 that he
had seen Antonius, who "seemed very much at sea in regard to his
work" and was excruciatingly aware of his patrons' dissatisfaction

For the task which I have set myself, which is to draw a narrative picture of aspects of this awakening, I have not even the qualification of being a Moslem. My only claims are two. One is that the circumstance of a Western education superimposed upon my Arab descent has given me, by comparison, a natural readiness to see something of the two sides of questions affecting the relations of the East with the West. The other is that, as I say, my official duties have, over a period of sixteen years, placed me here and there in a position of vantage to see for myself and sometimes, in a small way to act.

Antonius had given the struggle over Palestine between Arab and Jew all his loyalty. He had assigned the issue of Palestine pride of place in his narrative of the political history of the Arabs. He had poured into the Palestine question his sense of disappointment with the British mandatory government he had served, which denied him the promotions and the acceptance he craved. But no sooner had he written his book than his life began to come apart. He had staked a great deal on the book, but it found modest success in England and the United States. He had to do a lot of traveling for Crane and the institute, travels that took him from his base in Jerusalem to Beirut, Damascus, Amman, Cairo, with occasional trips to the Arabian Peninsula. Life on the road took its toll on both his marriage and on his health. And the larger life of the Arab lands held increasing disappointments and frustrations for him.

In a note in August 1938 from Alexandria, to the director of the ICWA, Walter Rogers, he wrote of the difficulty of finding new material and of writing freely on issues that mattered. He sensed growing obstacles to speaking openly, constraints on freedom of expression.

There is always room for an infinite variety of writing on an infinite selection of topics, so long as one is careful to avoid going to the root of things. But such work is outside the sphere of my predilections. . . . What I mean is that national partisanship is becoming so acute and party differences so embittered that in-our land: the final years of Ottoman rule, the First World War, the dream of Arab self-rule that followed the war, the era of French ascendancy in Syria and Lebanon. In the 1950s, his son Saeb towered over the city's politics. He was always a minister or a prime minister or a member of parliament. To me, the Salams seemed safe in their power, secure in their city ways, but in a memoir by Saeb Salam's older sister, Anbara, I learned that the Salams had fought to push the cultural frontiers for their family and their city. Anbara herself had gone behind the veil as a girl of ten. It had taken a great struggle for her to shed her veil some years later. When Anbara's and Saeb's mother went for her dental check-ups, the dentist worked on her teeth while she remained veiled. Only her mouth was uncovered for the dental work. In the memoir, Anbara tells of a sea voyage in her early youth, in 1912, to Egypt. On that passage she was bedazzled by the modernity, the large stores and the lights of Egypt. The trip was her first exposure to electricity, which came to Beirut two years later. In the Beirut of my days, we were confident that we were years ahead of the Egyptians, that we were more hip and Westernized, but that knowledge was defective. It was our hubris, the things we took for granted, that gave us that defective knowledge. To be seen and appreciated, an inheritance has to be looked at with a cold eye and with patience.

Ten years after Nazira Zayn al-Din had written her book, there appeared another book by George Antonius, *The Arab Awakening.* This was to be the manifesto of the Arab national movement. The man who wrote it was true to the spirit of that age: He was a Greek Orthodox, a son of a trading family from Dayr al-Qamar, one of the principal market towns in Mount Lebanon. Born in 1891, he was raised there, then taken to Alexandria and its polyglot world at age eleven. He was educated at Cambridge, where he took a degree in engineering at King's College. He savored the streets and the life of Alexandria (Alex to the smart set) with E. M. Forster when Forster spent three years in Alexandria in the First World War as a volunteer for the Red Cross. A work by Forster (published in 1922), *Alexandria: A History and a Guide*, acknowledged a debt to "Mr. George

Nazira Zayn al-Din, had written a devastating book, learned, heavy, and brave, on veiling and unveiling that had staked out the right of women to shed the veil yet remain within the faith. Nazira's background is familiar to me. She was the daughter of a judge, a child of the upper bourgeoisie of Beirut. I can summon up her and her world with ease. In my mind I can see her in the garden of a large house (this was Beirut before the high-rise buildings and the urban sprawl) behind a wrought-iron gate in the midst of a family gathering at dusk, being indulged and listened to by an attentive father. She had made an offering of her book, *al-Sufur wa al-Hijab* (Unveiling and the Veil) to her father, head of the appeals court, Said Zayn al-Din, presented it to him as a "reflection of the light" of his knowledge and his belief in freedom. She had not given an inch to the religious obscurantists. There were four veils in the land, she had written: a veil of cloth, a veil of ignorance, a veil of hypocrisy, and a veil of stagnation. She asked for no favors: she was born free and wanted for her land and for the women in her land the freedom of "civilized nations." Muslim men had begun to give up the fez; Muslim women had an equal right, she asserted, to shed their veils. That liberty I saw in the Beirut of my time, the liberty my aunts had taken to, had been a relatively recent innovation and had not been easy to secure. It was in that time, the time when Nazira wrote her controversial book, that another daring Muslim woman, Saniyya Habboub, took the cable car to Bliss Street, to the campus of the American University of Beirut—the same cable car I took all over the city almost daily—and entered the university through its main gate. There, inside the sanctuary of the university, she took off her veil and set out on her university studies.

In the 1950s, when I began to learn the social and political facts of Beirut, the Salam family was probably the preeminent family in Muslim West Beirut. They were philanthropists and educators, and they were active in the political arena. In the early years of this century, Salim Ali Salam had been mayor of Beirut, one of its leading merchants and public citizens. He had served in the Ottoman parliament and taken part in all the great issues that had played out in with the "scanty work" he had been doing. From Beirut, another American wrote to the Institute of Current World Affairs on July 22, 1941, that "Antonius seemed apathetic . . . found him living well and comfortable at the home of the wife of a former president of Lebanon as I recall."

A week later the Institute of Current World Affairs terminated Antonius's contract, notifying him of its action in a letter in care of the American Consul-General in Beirut. Antonius tried to stay the decision. From Beirut he cabled the ICWA's director: "Fully understand trustees dissatisfaction. Am profoundly dissatisfied myself but suggest that they await my letter before unilaterally terminating agreement for causes outside my control. Anyhow overdue installments cannot be affected retrospectively by notice to terminate. Delay places me in very embarrassing indebtedness."

Four days later, there was another letter, in the same vein:

Beirut, November 25, 1941

Dear Mr. Rogers:

Far from being satisfied, I am depressed and demoralized by my present impotency. In the first place there is not enough to keep me sufficiently occupied and to provide my mental energy and needs with the outlet of expression; and even such studies as I can carry out are often necessarily incomplete in the sense that they do not satisfy my ideas of thoroughness. In the second place, I find it irksome and extremely disagreeable to have to depend on Institute funds for my maintenance, at a time when I am precluded from making an adequate return. . . . I have offered my services in turn to the French, the British and the American authorities in my area, and I offered them without restriction as to locality or scope save for two stipulations, namely (1) that the work entrusted to me should be in my area, to enable me to continue to watch current affairs for Institute purposes, and (2) that it should be constructive work in the public service and not merely propaganda.

It was time for Antonius to return to Jerusalem and his wife and daughter. His battle with cancer was nearing its end. He wrote from Jerusalem to Charles Crane's son, John, on February 12, 1942:

> To John Crane
>
> > Karm al-Mufti
> > Jerusalem, February 12, 1942
>
> Dear John:
>
> I left Beirut a week ago bound for Cairo, and have had to stop a few days here, having been laid up with a recurrence of my intestinal trouble. I had a long spell in hospital in Beirut at the beginning of the summer, and shall probably have to have another spell there on my return from Egypt. I was in hospital at the American University during the whole of the British campaign in Syria. . . . Shortly after my persecution by the Vichy French and the Italian Commission began. At first they wanted to expel me, and later to put me in a concentration camp. It was only my illness in hospital and the intervention of the American Consul-General that saved me from the worst effects of the persecution.
>
> > Yours ever,
> > George (Antonius)

There was to be no passage to Cairo. Antonius died in Jerusalem on May 21, 1942. John Crane reported the author's death to the ICWA's director three days later.

> From Chicago
>
> > Sunday May 24, 1942
>
> John Crane to Walter
>
> In case it does not see print, I wanted to tell you that I got word this morning that George Antonius died last Thursday in Jerusalem. No details accompanied the message. . . . Incidentally I do not see anyone to whom we might send condolences. I have of course no idea how Dr. Nimr feels about him these days.

A cable came from Katy Antonius on May 27: "George died here suddenly on twenty-first. Please inform press." A year later Katy wrote to John Crane. It was a candid note: it had an estranged wife's pain and the grief of a nationalist writing of a public life. It was written on an aerogram of the period. When I picked it up in Hanover, I had a feeling I was being served history up close: intimate, plaintive, pained.

> Karm al-Mufti
> Jerusalem, June 13, 1943

Katy Antonius to John Crane.

I still feel *very sore* about the way the Institute wrote to George those last months before his death. . . . You know he had a flat in Beyrouth for the past two years and came here and to Cairo. You see, George died and left *absolutely* nothing to his child—except for that insurance. My father provides me, that is true. Still after George working here for 16 years, and then with you for 11 years. . . . it seems sad to think the little he had just paid his bills.

She returned to the book. She felt deeply about it.

Here and in Egypt not a single copy are [*sic*] available which is shocking—there has been a great demand. . . . I have been approached several times here and in Cairo for an Arabic translation of the book. I do not think of it as a financial proposition. But I am desperately keen on its being read and I feel that it's the best and clearest thing ever written about the Arab cause and God knows "we" need some help and some clearing. George's death is felt more and more. His loss cannot be replaced. I feel we're like a drifting ship at present. If nothing else he was at least a rudder.

Antonius was buried in Jerusalem on Mount Zion in the Greek Orthodox cemetery, the oldest of that city's Christian cemeteries. The Israeli writer (and former deputy mayor of Jerusalem) Meron

Benvenisti, who knows his city like the palm of his hand and who, in one of his many books, chronicled Jerusalem through its cemeteries, had happened onto Antonius's burial site in his researches. Benvenisti had told me of his own visit to that gravesite: a son of the Zionist enterprise paying homage to a chronicler of the Arab awakening. On a day when I had wearied of reading his archives (he was diligent, he kept records of all his activities and his correspondence), I sought his grave. The groundskeeper took me straight to the location—it was under a tall pine tree in the shadow of the abbey of the Dormition: a solitary grave with rough-hewn stone. Nearby there were large vaults where members of leading Jerusalem families were buried together. Antonius had lived and died and was buried a loner. On the headstone someone had placed a red flower, several days old. I had the distinct feeling that the groundskeeper had led many others there before me. On the headstone, in Arabic and English, were Antonius's name and the dates of his birth and death. In Arabic alone, there was an ode that had served as an epigraph for *The Arab Awakening,* an ode that a nineteenth-century Lebanese literary figure, Ibrahim al-Yaziji, had written: "Arise, ye Arabs and awake." It was a Friday, the groundskeeper was alone, and the cemetery was deserted. He allowed himself a note of irony as he left me at the grave: The Arabs had not yet risen, he said, and the hopes of Antonius remain unfulfilled.

HOME COMES AND speaks in prose and exile in poetry, it has been said. Today in the Arab world—I left for America a day or two short of my eighteenth birthday, in 1963—I am a stranger, but no distance could wash me clean of that inheritance. In 1980, in an earlier book, *The Arab Predicament,* I was younger and approached my material more eager to judge. In my haste and my dissatisfaction with what the modern experience in the Arab world had brought forth, I did not appreciate what had gone into the edifice that Arabs had built. I grew more curious about that history in the intervening years and came to realize how little one really knows of the things that are all around us. In a New York library, I came across a faded, worn-out

book about the small corner of Lebanon where I was born; it had been written by a prolific religious scholar from our hinterland who knew and traveled into the larger worlds of Iran and Iraq. In that book, private and public history came together, and the scant knowledge we have of matters we presume to know came into sharp focus for me. I read that before my great-grandfather made his way to our ancestral village, he broke his journey, as it were, in a larger town not far from our village. There he married the widow of a religious scholar and fathered children. He came to Arnoun, our ancestral village, only after the death of his first wife and in Arnoun he wed the woman who was to be my grandfather's mother.

Two narratives were available to me. I could have written of my private, family inheritance, but Arabs are reared to tread carefully on private family matters. We are taught not to air family matters that we glimpse. And besides, the public inheritance was more important, having been played upon for the last two decades. Its concerns have been tugging at me, and it is of these concerns that I thought I should write.

THE SUICIDE OF KHALIL HAWI:

REQUIEM FOR A GENERATION

———◆———

K HALIL HAWI, A poet of renown and professor at the American University of Beirut (the AUB), educated at that university and at Cambridge, killed himself in the late evening on June 6, 1982, at the age of sixty-two, on the balcony of his home in West Beirut. A troubled and sensitive man of great literary talent, he had picked a dramatic occasion for his death: Earlier in the day, in midmorning, Israeli armor had struck into Lebanon. Israel had come to put an end to the Palestinian sanctuary in Lebanon, to be rid of the running war on its northern border with the forces of the Palestine Liberation Organization, which it had fought over the preceding decade. "Where are the Arabs?" Hawi had asked his colleagues on the university campus before he went home and shot himself. "Who shall remove the stain of shame from my forehead?"

For over a decade, Hawi had lived a solitary and angry life, quarreling with his colleagues and at odds with the literary world in his city. A Christian from Mount Lebanon, he had anguished over the

fate of his country, which had succumbed to an endless season of troubles. In an intellectual journey that spanned four decades, he had arrived at a reconciliation between his fidelity to the earth and mythology of Lebanon and his political belief in a wider Arab nation; with the undoing of Lebanon and the indifference of the Arabs to Lebanon's fate, Hawi was forced to reckon with his beliefs. There was peace between Egypt and Israel, and there was a benign world of wealth on the Arabian Peninsula; the patriotic poet who shot himself in Beirut was sure to be seen as the sacrificial lamb for an Arab world that had fragmented. The private pain and personal idiosyncrasies and demons that led him to this end were to be brushed aside. In Hawi's death, the world of Arabic letters saw a judgment on the Arab political condition.

Born in 1919, Hawi belonged to a distinct world. He was an innovator in the world of poetry and an Arab nationalist obsessed with the main themes that held the men and women of his time: the reform of the Arab political world, the terms of the encounter with the West, the struggle between the weight of custom and tradition, and the yearning for political and cultural change. When Hawi's contemporary, Nizar Qabbani, the popular poet of romance, was still writing about what "the brunette" told him in the evening and about love and languid affairs (Qabbani and his poetry were politicized by the Arab defeat in the Six Day War of 1967), Hawi was writing with great force of the Arabs' desperate struggle to give birth to a new political and cultural world. His most celebrated poem, "The Bridge," published in 1957 in a collection, *Nahr al-Ramad* (River of Ashes), was to become a document of that time, a poem of singular truth and beauty. At once a work of deep sorrow for what ails "the East," it held out hope for what was to come and for the young. The rhythm of the poem, the spare, haunting imagery, and the subject matter all came together in a virtually hypnotic, unforgettable piece of writing that fused the power and form of the classical poems of old with a deeply personal voice and the indelible mark of a great, restless talent. This is from a translation by Issa Boulatta of McGill University.

It suffices me that I have the children of my contemporaries,
that of their love I have wine and bread.

*　　　*　*　*

They cross the bridge blithely in the morning
My ribs are stretched out as a firm bridge for them
From the caves of the East, from the swamps of the East
To the New East
My ribs are stretched out as a firm bridge for them.
They will go and you will remain
Empty-handed, crucified, lonely
In the snowy nights while the horizon is ashes
Of fire, and the bread is dust;
You will remain with frozen tears in a sleepless night
The mail will come to you with the morning:
The news page. . . . How often you ruminate its contents,
Scrutinize it. . . . Reread it!
They will go and you will remain
Empty-handed, crucified, lonely. . . .

Khalil Hawi's eulogists saw in his suicide the end of an era in the modern political life of the Arabs. Arab culture, with its emphasis on what is owed the clan, the family, and the religious sect, is not given to sanctioning suicide, but the eulogies for the poet were tributes to the sorrow he had felt for the collective Arab condition. Writing from Paris in *Le monde,* the North African writer Tahar Ben Jalloun said that Hawi, a man alone and broken over the wounds of the Arabs, had chosen "supreme silence." Palestinian poet Mahmoud Darwish, an Israeli Arab who had left Israel and settled in Beirut, said that Hawi had foreseen "the fall of everything" and had fixed a date for his own end. "Hawi took a hunting rifle and hunted himself, not only because he wanted not to give evidence against anything but because he wanted not to be a witness for or against anything. He was weary of the state of decay, weary of looking over a bottomless abyss."

Munah al-Sulh, a fellow Lebanese and classmate of Hawi, who

had known him from his student days at the university in the late 1940s and early 1950s, placed the poet in the culture and politics of his generation. Both men had belonged to a political-literary society formed in 1918, al-Urwa al-Wuthqa, the Close Bond, a gathering of students and teachers drawn from the full range of Arab countries at the American University of Beirut. "We had a severe standard" in that society, the eulogist said. "We lived in the shadow of the 1948 war and of the Arab defeat in that war." Political matters and political thought were bifurcated for this group: everything associated with the "disaster" of 1948 was condemned and rejected; everything had to be new in politics and letters. Khalil Hawi was a product of this era of Arab life, Munah al-Sulh wrote. From his beginnings as a mountain village youth, he had delved into the depths of Arabic literature and the Arab heritage, and Islamic philosophy. He had studied Hebrew on the side, and he was fond, his friend said, of comparing the "poverty of Hebrew with the wealth of the Arabic language." To this poet had come a measure of national pride, a belief that the Arabs were called upon to take their place "on the highest levels of world civilization." This belief in "the special destiny" of the Arabs existed side by side with the poet's keen, merciless eye for the defects of Arab public life. "I can say that I have never seen love and hate so closely bound up together as I did in Khalil Hawi's view of the Arab condition. He loved the Arabs greatly, but he hated their contemporary impotence and weakness. It is perhaps this ambivalence which lies at the root of Khalil Hawi's genius." The Arabs lived a "singular collective history" in the 1950s, and Khalil Hawi was "a poet of that moment" in the life of the Arabs. He lived and he died, this eulogist added, in a state of conscious agitation and anxiety, *qalaq*, over that spirit of innovation in his own work and in the life of the Arabs.

A hypochondriac, an angry and troubled man who never married, Hawi nevertheless led a life that was a fair reflection of his time and the intellectual possibilities open to his generation. A village boy from Mount Lebanon, raised in the hill country at the foot of the majestic Mount Sannin, Hawi had traveled far beyond his village and the difficult circumstances of a family of limited means. He was the beneficiary of an age of secular education and enlightenment. He did not hail from the *haute bourgeoisie* that dominated the intellectual life of the American University of Beirut and the Arab nationalist movement. He willed himself into the university and literary-political world. His journey out of poverty and the possibilities that Protestant missionary schools and the American University opened up to men (and women) of his generation are part of a special history among the eastern Arabs—an age and its undeniable accomplishments and, then, the heart-rending disappointment when Arab nationalism ended in failure and frustration.

The eulogists told an uncomplicated tale: a nationalist hero against the background of a dark night. But there was more to the patriotic death than met the eye, and more to Khalil Hawi than the cut-out that the political narrative had turned him into. The life of the poet had unraveled over a number of years. There had been a suicide attempt a year earlier, when Hawi had tried to kill himself with sleeping pills. And there had been a painful personal climb out of poverty and family hardship.

The main corrective to the political legend was supplied by Khalil Hawi's younger brother, Iliya, a literary man with an exquisite ability to tell a story. Four years after Khalil's death, Iliya published a masterful biography of the poet. It was an unusual work given the premium the culture sets on family devotion and discretion. *Ya rabb ya suttar,* an appeal to God has it, Oh God Thou who veilest. In this world, "honor," privacy, and public decorum are rarely breached. Family secrets are taken to the grave, and the lives of mothers, sisters, and stepmothers are sacred, forbidden matters. Even lesser concerns—the hard times endured by families on their way out of poverty—are handled with care. Fiction enabled modern Arabs to enter emotional territory that biography had not traversed, but the biographies remained stilted, polite, and opaque. In the autobiographies, fathers were invariably strict but well intentioned, mothers devout and patient, and the sisters stayed out of trouble.

Set against this cultural background, the work that Iliya Hawi wrote was a brave undertaking.

Although some sibling rivalry is given away in the book, Iliya Hawi did not write a debunking work. He demystified his brother; he gave voice to a measure of guilt that he had not been able to fathom the depth of his brother's despair and anger. The promptings of the book would appear to be the timeless promptings of the writing vocation; the younger man (they were separated by ten years) had always lived in the shadow of a judgmental and talented older brother. Although he had been a prolific literary critic, he never thought he measured up to Khalil's standards. He had always looked for "material" of his own; he admits that he never felt confident or at ease in the presence of his brother. In the aftermath of the poet's suicide, the material was there and Iliya Hawi owned it—the family background, the ancestral village, the private man and his neurosis. Out of the family life, out of what the younger man had seen, he wrote a work of his own, a sprawling book of some seven hundred pages, at once his brother's chronicle and his own personal and family history.

This family history, rendered with great skill and delicacy, was not all that Iliya Hawi did with his brother's haunting legacy. The same year the book was released, Iliya also published a huge, dazzling novel, *Nabhan,* which treated the same material but set it in the context of Lebanon's history in the late nineteenth century. Nabhan, the hero—clearly Iliya's brother, Khalil—is a tragic figure consumed by a manly ideal he cannot match, a tormented, austere man who both reveres and pities his land, a man at odds with power, property, family, and social custom.

Then a brave and candid Iraqi woman, a short story writer, Daisy al-Amir, who had been Khalil Hawi's fiancée (a marriage had been planned, but he had not gone through with it), came forth to say what the political eulogists did not know or wouldn't say. Khalil had been in the grip of a deep, long depression. He had never recovered from that earlier suicide attempt. The thought of suicide—

and the talk of it—had never left him. He was convinced that the literary world in his city had become the domain of hucksters determined to deny him and his poetry the place and acclaim he had earned. True, he had celebrated in the poetry of his youth the coming of an Arab dawn, but he was a man of Lebanon, and he had been grieving for his land and for what had become of it in the course of a drawn-out, dirty war. The mastery of that suicide on the sixth of June had been perfect timing for the deed: the loner dying for an "Arab nation" that had lost its way.

If Hawi had been worried about his place in Arabic letters and Arab memory, he made sure that he would never be forgotten. The great, defining poem in the late 1950s and the dark, despairing deed in 1982: He had provided the bookends for a special time in Arab life. Whatever literate and politically conscious Arabs would do in the years to come, they would never recapture the texture and intimacy of those years. Beirut would forever change, the Arabs would go separate ways (even as they insisted that nothing had changed, even as they shouted to the heavens that the old fidelities were still intact), and a generation would be left holding in its hands an inheritance it could not pass on to its sons and daughters. There would be work here for the eulogists and the memorialists, but that period of history would be irretrievably lost and Hawi would emerge as its stern, brooding prophet.

KHALIL HAWI WAS born to a Greek Orthodox family. His was a special community of Christians. The Greek Orthodox of Syria, Lebanon, and Palestine left a powerful mark on the secular ideologies of Syrian and Arab nationalism that swept through the lands of Greater Syria over the preceding century. Of all Christian communities in the checkered world of Lebanon, Syria, and Palestine, the Greek Orthodox was the first to throw itself into the secular political currents of Syrian and Arab nationalism. The Maronites, quintessential children of the mountain and of Lebanon proper, savored their ties with the Holy See and with France and looked to the French for protection, and the Protestant churches were nineteenth-century creatures of the European and American missions in the Levant, but the Greek Orthodox placed themselves at the head of the secular nationalist movement. True, they had their own protector, their own foreign connection, Russia and the Russian Orthodox church, but that connection had been severed by the Bolshevik revolution in 1917. There had been a time, before that great event, when Russia had intruded into the lives of the Orthodox and posed as their defender against the encroachment of the Protestant missions and against the Ottoman overlords of the lands of Greater Syria. Under Tsar Alexander II (1855–1881), Russia developed a strong sense of religious mission. The tsar styled himself the "Orthodox tsar," and his country as the heir to Byzantium, the "Third Rome." There was heady talk of the recovery of Constantinople, restoring to the church of Saint Sophia the worship of the "true God." An Oriental project played on the Russian imagination; a bid was made to position Russia as the protector of all the Orthodox of the Ottoman empire. The building of a vast Russian compound in Jerusalem, with its Church of the Holy Trinity, in the 1860s grew out of this religious and political calling. Ships now came to Jaffa from Odessa bearing Russia's pilgrims. Some fifteen to twenty thousand pilgrims made the religious journey every year. Impoverished, helped by small contributions, drawn from Russia's vast peasantry, these pilgrims made their way from Jaffa to Jerusalem on foot. They were a zealous lot: In 1884, under the autocrat Alexander III, the pilgrims pulled a twelve-thousand-pound bell cast in Russia from Jaffa to Jerusalem. It took them three weeks. They sang their hymns as they dragged their bell to the seven-domed Church of Mary Magdalene on the slopes of the Mount of Olives.

But this Russian project in the Middle East fizzled out a decade or so before the Bolshevik revolution, however. Russia was no match for the British and French or for the American religious and educational missions. The share of the Orthodox among Palestine's Christians fell as the ranks of the Catholics and Anglicans rose. The Greek Orthodox in Syria, Lebanon, Palestine flocked to secular nationalist movements of every kind. A fault line ran through that church between the Greek priesthood and the Arab laity; it was easy for the bold of spirit to break with the church and take the plunge into the secular, political world. George Antonius, the celebrated author of *The Arab Awakening*, once belonged to the Orthodox church. Michel Aflaq, the French-educated Damascus schoolteacher who founded the Ba'th party, was another, and so was an influential academic historian at the AUB, the Syrian Constantine Zurayk, a tireless advocate of Arab nationalism. The list goes on. When Hawi made his ideological home within the world of Arab nationalism, he followed a time-honored tradition among his community.

Although Hawi took no interest in his church, he remained a devoted man of his village of Shweir, a hamlet of clay tile roofs and church steeples at the foot of Mount Sannin, with its snow-covered peaks. Some twenty-five kilometers east of Beirut, the hill country around Shweir was God's country; the devotees of these hills near the Mediterranean swore they could see faraway Cyprus on a clear day. It was this bewitching corner of Lebanon that the Song of Solomon celebrated: "A fountain of gardens, a well of living waters, and streams from Lebanon." From its sources high in the hills, directly beneath Mount Sannin, the mountain's fullest stream, Dog River, made its way to the sea a few miles north of Beirut, through a grand, wild gorge. The river issued from two vast fountains, the Fountain of Milk (Naba' al-Laban) and the Fountain of Honey (Naba' al-Asal). To the north, by the town of Byblos, the Adonis River snaked its way through the hills to the sea from a grotto in the mountain. Clinging to the cliffs, idyllic villages with terraced vineyards ascended to a clear blue sky. The solitude of this "goodly" mountain and the rhythm of its seasons—the harsh, snowy winters, the lush, sudden springs, the mist blowing into the valleys from the peaks of Mount Sannin—and the mythology of death and resurrection that sprang up in the hills shaped the people of this land and their self-image and marked their poetry and literature. They were keenly proud of their land, the people of the mountain. They forever dwelled on its beauty and bliss, taught their children and reminded themselves that the hills of Lebanon were mentioned in the

Bible seventy-five times, that "God had laid His gracious hand on their land." They listed, with evident vanity, the armies of the world that had come through the place over the ages and left their monuments as they made a bid for this special land.

The beauty of the land was the other side of a spare, hard existence. Those idyllic villages had known intermittent periods of hunger; these splendid hills, a kind of desolation. The land lay fallow as the men took off to distant places: the New World, Africa, and Australia. An uncle of Khalil Hawi had died at an early age in Boston, where he had gone to make his fortune. Khalil Hawi's grandfather made his way to Australia and went back and forth between Australia and Lebanon three times between 1890 and 1914. To be raised in these mountain villages, as Hawi was in the interwar years, was to grow up a step removed from a time of hunger and famine in Mount Lebanon. Hawi knew that history and the terrible swath that deprivation had left behind. His mother was a good storyteller and passed on to her son the narrative of what had befallen the land in the decade prior to his birth.

Silk, and the mulberry trees that fed the silkworms, had been the mainstay of the mountain. Silk and the commerce of silk with Lyons and Marseilles had led to Beirut's rise from a small, walled town at the beginning of the nineteenth century to a thriving city of international commerce by the 1870s, an emporium serving Damascus and the Syrian interior. Silk and the silkworms pushed aside other agricultural pursuits. By the latter part of the nineteenth century, half the cultivated land in the mountain was covered with mulberry trees; the majority of the population lived off the silk industry. The feeding and care of the silkworms set the rhythm of the mountain's life. Schools shut down at the height of the season in the spring and turned into warehouses for the silkworm. Families made do with cramped corners of their homes to make way for the shelves of bamboo canes and large, flat trays on which the mulberry leaves were spread. The mountain knew a time of prosperity. Some eight thousand people a year, it was estimated, traveled from Beirut, the port city of the mountain, to Marseilles on the boats of a French company, Messageries Maritimes, for vacations in France. It was hard booking space on the French steamer ships at the height of the travel season. It was a time of bliss and plenty, but the bubble burst. Between the 1890s and the outbreak of the First World War, the silk industry was virtually wiped out. The Japanese were producing better and cheaper thread. The small sheds in the mountain where the cocoons were spun had been unable to compete. Many people gave up on silk and cut down the mulberry trees: The land was needed to grow food for a desperate population. In this time of panic, tens of thousands fled the land. The Ottoman rulers—proud and brittle, eager to hide the warts of their empire—tried to stem the tide and keep people from leaving for the New World, but to no avail.

A calamitous event is said to have taken place in the Hawi family shortly after the First World War erupted. The money that the poet's grandfather had earned in his time in Australia was stolen from a box that had been hidden under the steps of the family home. There is no way to judge the reliability of this account. The hills were full of such tales: There had been a time of splendor but we were robbed of it; there had been noble Arabian horses, but they were spirited off by brigands to faraway Damascus; there had been exquisite deadly muskets in this house, but they were confiscated by the gendarmes. What we know is the greater calamity that befell the land during the years of the war. In distant Constantinople, the Young Turks took their country to war on the side of Germany and Austria. The Ottoman realm was a crumbling empire, but the Young Turks who seized the machinery of government threw caution to the wind. Turkish rulers brought to an end the autonomy of Mount Lebanon, a special regime that had governed the land of the mountain since the 1860s under European eyes and tutelage. Turkish troops occupied the mountain, bringing great sorrow and terror to the land. The troops that came to the mountain and passed through Hawi's village had been decimated by a fierce storm. They were a pitiable lot. The survivors made it to Shweir, but they tore through the place, confiscating what little supplies and livestock the villagers had. They requisitioned pack animals and moved into village homes as soldiers and villagers alike wrestled with a harsh winter.

A reign of terror came to the mountain. Informers were everywhere as brother betrayed brother to the Turks. Famine was not far behind. It is estimated that three hundred thousand people starved to death in Syria. Bayard Dodge, a "blue blood" of the American missionary presence in Lebanon, a future president of the American University of Beirut, and a son-in-law of a past president of the same institution, who spent his summer months in Shweir, recorded the ordeal of the land:

> The air was filled with the sound of bells tolling for funerals and children crying for crusts of bread. . . . Clothing was so scarce that the Americans turned in their suits and the women used curtains to make dresses. . . . Kerosene was so scarce that the people used olive oil lamps, as their Phoenician forefathers had done. Poor people fought over garbage pails. And many mountain houses became vacant, their occupants dead and their doors used to make coffins.

The mountain that had given its land to the mulberry trees was unable to feed itself. It was cut off from the Bekaa Valley, the granary of the country, and from Hawran, the wheat-growing lands of Syria. And it was treated with particular severity by the Turks, who saw traitors everywhere among the Christians and knew that the people of Mount Lebanon were praying for the downfall of the empire and the victory of France.

The land was cursed, it seemed. In the spring of 1915, misfortune blew in from the sea. Waves of locusts swept in, devouring everything in their way. The locusts covered the face of the sun, and their roar could be heard as they swarmed up the hills from the sea. From the rooftops the town criers summoned people to work: By order of the state, the locusts' eggs were to be hauled off and dumped in the sea. Every man, woman, and child was put to work clearing the locusts' eggs. What could not be carried to the sea was buried in ditches in the fields. Men did what they could. Fires were lit to consume the locusts. But the locusts kept coming. It took a "mysterious wind" (the words are Iliya Hawi's) blowing in at night to carry the locusts to the sea. The predators disappeared as suddenly as they had turned up.

Then the circle of misfortune closed. A Turkish commander, Ahmad Jamal Pasha (given the name of al-Saffah, the Bloodshedder), minister of marine of the Young Turk regime in Constantinople, turned up to torment the lands of Syria, Lebanon, and Palestine. A military man in his early forties, Jamal Pasha had played high imperial politics; he had done his share to plunge his country into war. In early 1915, he took to the field as a commander of the empire's Fourth Army. He led a badly trained army to the banks of the Suez Canal to take on the British. His campaign ended in disaster, and he fell back on Syria, Lebanon, and Palestine. These lands became his private turf. It was a poor consolation prize: The world that mattered to this merciless plotter was in Constantinople. He ruled his turf with an iron hand, sniffing conspiracies everywhere. He had a particular animus toward the Christians of the mountain; he was sure that their loyalty belonged to France. (Jamal Pasha knew intrigue; he himself had his channels to the French, probing them at every turn, promising accommodation in return for French support against the masters of the regime in Constantinople, his partners in this ruinous war.)

It was a treacherous time. A military tribunal in the hills spared no one suspected of sedition. Jamal Pasha was lucky; the dragoman of the French consulate had betrayed his employers and turned over to the Turks the French records—the petitions and appeals for French help against the Turks, the professions of loyalty to France that the notables of this land had written to the French, the pleas for Syrian independence. With the records available to it, Jamal Pasha's tribunal went to work. There were public hangings in a Beirut square, that was later renamed Martyrs' Square in honor of the condemned men. Jamal Pasha's brand of justice was imperial justice—blind to religious affiliation, taking in Muslims and Christians alike.

In one episode, sixteen men, nine Christians and seven Muslims, were sentenced to die. A priest was given permission to pray with the men the night before they were sent to the gallows, and he stayed with them late into the night. He spoke to them in an ecumenical way of homeland and sacrifice. He told them that they were dying for their country in the same manner that Christ had died for the salvation of man. The condemned then recited a poem in tribute to their land and to its independence.

Jamal Pasha paid the village of Shweir a brief visit. Khalil Hawi's mother retained the memory of this brush with the dreaded ruler. The villagers were assembled in Shweir's square, in front of the serai, the government headquarters, to greet their visitor. The Pasha, as he was known, did not live up to his legend: He had a large head and a round, heavy face and was shorter than his terrified subjects had expected him to be. A local man fluent in Turkish was chosen to speak for his village. The man proved unusually brave: He professed the loyalty of the village but spoke of the hunger and misery of the people and pleaded for help. Jamal Pasha rebuked him: "Is there any mother among you who has eaten her own child?" the commander asked. The village speaker said that this had not happened in Shweir. Jamal Pasha then named villages where mothers had done so. "You are better off here and you had better keep quiet."

Khalil Hawi's mother, Salima Ataya, barely survived the war. Left in Shweir with two younger brothers after her father went to work as a stonemason in Jabal Druze (the Druze mountain), in the southeastern corner of the Syrian interior, she kept going by working for the Turks, knitting and mending socks for the soldiers. It was barter work; for her labor she was given a ration of wheat and barley. Frightened by the hunger all around her, she hired a muleteer and took her brothers to Jabal Druze, across a landscape of desolation and banditry, joining those who had come to wait out the war in the districts of Jabal Druze and the wheat-growing lands of Hawran, where the hand of Turkish power was lighter than it was in Mount Lebanon. No sooner had Salima Ataya made her way to

Jabal Druze than her father died of typhus, which had been devastating to the people of Mount Lebanon. The people of Mount Lebanon were not used to the acrid water of their new surroundings. They were buried where they fell, far from their ancestral land, denied the comfort of their priests and the ceremonies of farewell.

It was in Jabal Druze that Khalil Hawi was born in December 1919. This was a harsh, forbidding landscape: hillsides of black basalt, scrub oak, and thorn, a dry, solemn wilderness that a secretive religious sect had made its own. Khalil Hawi's father, a stonemason, had been in that part of Syria since the war erupted. Salim Hawi and Salima Ataya had married in Jabal Druze; the future bride's mother had nursed Salim Hawi back to health after he came down with what seemed to be a deadly fever. It took forty days for the fever to break. Salim Hawi woke up one morning to tell his future mother-in-law of a dream that had come to him before dawn. In his dream he was back in his village in springtime. The sun was brilliant and the hills covered with flowers. "Rejoice, the dream means that you shall survive and go back to your land," she told him. He was to do this with his wife and his first-born son, Khalil, right after the boy's birth.

Khalil Hawi "possessed" this cruel history. The paralyzing fear that was part of this history was always an affront to him. "You were chickens and rabbits," he told his mother. "You should have rebelled and fought and killed." During the years of the Second World War, when the privations of that war hit his village, Hawi led a demonstration of village youth and gave a stirring speech: "We don't want to die like our grandfathers did, as rabbits and chickens, on deserted roads and in distant lands without uttering a word." Life was hard and uncertain. Four of Khalil's siblings, three brothers and a sister he had grown particularly attached to, died in infancy.

To grow up in Shweir in the 1920s was to awaken in a place digging out of a calamity: broken men and women; houses run down by neglect and abandonment; families waiting for money to be sent by the men who had gone to Africa and the New World, waiting for

news and money from the stonemasons and bricklayers scouring the towns of Syria and Palestine for work. The building trade and the work of the stonemasons were hazardous endeavors. There was a dreaded scene in Shweir. Hired cars would turn up in the village square bearing the coffins of the unlucky stonemasons and bricklayers who had met their fate in the Golan Heights or Hawran or Jabal Druze. The villagers knew what became of the progeny of the dead, the poverty and defeat that awaited their orphans and widows.

Shweir was a "very pious village," Bayard Dodge's daughter, Grace Dodge Guthrie, wrote in her book, *Legacy to Lebanon.* Shweir was Grace Dodge's summer home as a child. From this village her father would ride his thoroughbred, Sudan, to his work in Beirut. Grace Dodge was a few years older than Khalil Hawi; she was writing of his time and place:

> Our maids go to various services at different places, as the monks and priests are fond of varying their performance. Bells ring out for feast days continually, as the sects hold their feasts at different times. All about the village are monasteries, one which contains the first printing press to be brought to Syria. It has black type like the presses of Luther's time.

The rituals that Grace Dodge saw were less religious devotion than the immemorial customs of a mountain people. The Shweir of Hawi's childhood had churches and sects aplenty: a Presbyterian church (we know this from Grace Dodge's memoir; this was the church her family attended); Hawi's Greek Orthodox people; Maronites and Catholics. A monastery on the outskirts of town, up a hillside of pine trees, Mar Elias, had two adjoining churches, one Maronite, the other Greek Orthodox. A foreign traveler, Ethel Stefana Drower, rendered this monastery as she saw it in 1925 and described it in her book of travel, *Cedars, Saints and Sinners in Syria:*

> The Maronite building is the more modern of the two, having been rebuilt lately on the old foundations. The Greek Orthodox

monks, less prosperous perhaps, still use their old church, very attractive with its sunny courtyards and outside stairway leading to the roof, from which there is a side view of the country beneath. . . . These dark little Greek churches, with their icons and semi-pagan traditions are more congenial to me than the somewhat tawdry Maronite churches with their conventional, blue-clad Madonnas and gaudy Sacred Hearts.

Religion was as practical and hard as the land. There were Protestant missionaries in Shweir, but their writ was a measure of the wealth they had and the services they could render. In these lands it was said that the Gospel and the hymns could be heard as long as the money and the patronage of the missions lasted. The luck of Shweir was the intense competition among the churches, which had given rise to a number of good schools sponsored by the churches and missions. A trail led from Shweir all the way to Scotland and the University of Glasgow: Scottish missionaries and teachers had been coming to Shweir since the 1850s. Daniel Oliver, a tireless Scotsman from the northern highlands of his own country, had started a school in this village (he had a string of them in neighboring villages) that Khalil Hawi would attend in due course. The Americans were there as well. There was a Jesuit school, and there was, of course, that "Muscovite" school for the Orthodox (Moskobiyya School, the people called it) that the Great Tsar and his church had patronized prior to the Bolshevik revolution.

A cultural and literary awakening came to Mount Lebanon in the latter years of the nineteenth century, made possible by the silk trade, the foreign missions, and a stable political regime that the European powers had sponsored since the 1860s. In a stunning turn of events, a band of Christian secular writers emerged to give the Arabic language a period of brilliance and creativity. Arabic had not been the language of the mountain; the language of the Christians had been Syriac. There was a Muslim expression: "Arabic has always refused to become Christian." The Christians had been burdened with all the disadvantages of a conquered people using an

alien medium of expression. They had persevered and had injected into their new language their distinct aesthetic sensibility; they had been able, Hawi wrote, to overcome their "sense of isolation." The children of the mountain had an eye for nature, for the beauty of their land, and this feel for landscape found its way into their writings. Ridding themselves of the debased, devotional literature their community had produced in the early and middle centuries of Islam, the Christian secular writers were to play a crucial role, in that time of change and curiosity in the middle years of the nineteenth century, in narrowing the gap between the classical Arabic of letters and the vernacular of daily life.

The translation of the Bible into Arabic in 1865 caused a landmark literary and cultural transformation in the mountain. This endeavor was an amazing feat, a labor of perfectionism and devotion driven by dissatisfaction with the versions of the Bible that were in use at the time. Two American missionaries, Eli Smith and Cornelius Van Dyck, and two of the earliest pioneers of the renaissance in the mountain, Nasif al-Yaziji and Butrus al-Bustani, began the project in 1842, driven by the determination, the missionaries proclaimed, "to give the Word of God to forty millions of perishing sinners." Two decades later, they had a text. It was "the first work," Khalil Hawi wrote, "to shake off the moribund traditions of the age of decadence." The revolt against eloquence and rhetoric had hit its stride. The Jesuits were not far behind. The prestige of the Protestant translation spurred them on. In 1872 they embarked on a new translation of their own, commissioning it to an outstanding linguist, Ibrahim al-Yaziji, whose father had translated the Protestant version. It took the younger Yaziji eight years to come up with the Jesuit version.

A town of artisans free of princely families and *Iqta'* (feudal) landowning elites, Shweir was ready for this new dispensation of schooling and education, which enjoyed great prestige among the people of Shweir. Stonemasons like Khalil Hawi's father, who packed their belongings and equipment in the springtime and traveled in search of work only to return for the winter months, were determined to spare their children the harshness of their own lives. Schooling offered a way out. The lore of the village, the tales told in the village square, by the 'ayn (the village spring and well), exalted the physicians, lawyers, and teachers who had come out of Shweir and gone on to glory in the city or in distant lands.

These tales kept people going and steeled their will. The Shweiris prided themselves on the historian Asad Rustum, who had risen from humble origins to become one of the leading scholars in the land; they kept track of one of their own, a physician by the name of Khalil Saadah, who had graduated from the American University of Beirut, authored an English-Arabic medical dictionary, and ended up as a pamphleteer and editor in the Lebanese communities of Argentina and Brazil. Another native of Shweir, Nami Jafet, had gone to Brazil penniless and built there a sprawling business empire of maritime companies and factories of every kind. There was a statue of Nami Jafet in front of the municipal building. (Years after he quit the country, in 1952, Jafet's descendants gave the American University of Beirut a large gift that enabled it to establish its first real library, named for him.)

There was nothing unusual about Khalil Hawi, the Greek Orthodox child, beginning his education at a Jesuit school; he would later attend an Anglican school. The denominational schools did what was expected of them to uphold the religious dogmas of their churches, but schooling was what mattered, and the place had a way of discounting the religious dogma the schools taught. In Khalil Hawi's first school, where rote learning was the norm, as it was throughout the land, children who did not know what the words meant were taught about "heretics" and "heresies." It was a standard drill: "Who are the heretics?" And the children would answer: "The heretics are those who violated the teaching of the Church and disobeyed the Pope; they are the Orthodox. . . ." Orthodox children had routinely supplied that answer as they were instructed. The rebellious streak so visible in Hawi's adulthood must have been there in the child: He refused to give back the expected answer and the priest who taught this class lost his patience, caning him for his disobedience.

In the small, intimate setting of Shweir the boy stood out, marked by his teachers and his extended family for things better than the work of stonemasons and builders. He was a gifted student, proud and independent, quick to his hurt, quick to stand up for his rights, and village culture admired these traits. His feel for the language, an ear for rhythm and cadence, announced itself early. That talent, it was believed, had been transmitted to him by a maternal uncle, a bard much admired in Shweir and villages beyond. There was a folk poetry, *zagal,* a medium in which balladeers extolled their heroic deeds, denigrated their opponents, and told of the timeless sufferings and yearnings in these hills. The balladeer was invariably a man's man, a carouser and a rebel, and Khalil's uncle was no exception. He excelled at ringing the heavy church bell in the village (the heaviest, a gift of Russia to the Orthodox church), and he was a womanizer and a heavy drinker. But the bard had had plenty of time for his nephew Khalil. He had taken him under his wing and encouraged what he recognized to be a budding talent with words and images. Death came to Khalil Hawi's uncle early— from tuberculosis—when Khalil was ten. It was a shattering loss for a child who had already seen death steal away three of his siblings, but the impressionable boy had assimilated the inheritance, the love of words, and the "manly" ideal that came with the poetic craft. Khalil's father, a serious man of few words but many family burdens, may not have cared for the balladeer's example, but he accepted the verdict that his first-born would go beyond him, that the world of manual labor was not to be this boy's world.

For Khalil Hawi and his parents, it was a tug-of-war between their desire to have their eldest son (Hawi's parents had five younger children who survived) stay at school and their need to send him out on the road to master the stonemasons' and bricklayers' trade, but misfortune appeared to trail Khalil Hawi's father. No sooner was he done with one setback than another reared its head. One devastat-

ing crisis came his way in 1925, when the Druze homeland, Jabal
Druze, in Syria, was set aflame by a great rebellion against French
rule. Salim Hawi knew the Druze homeland. It had supplied him
with work; he had grown fond of the proud Druze mountaineers
and felt at home among them. This ferocious rebellion raged for two
years and punctured the confidence of the colonial power. The
Druze highlanders raised the standard of revolt to protect the timeless independence of their land; a legendary chieftain, Sultan Pasha
Atrash, summoned them to arms when French interference in the
Druze mountain grew intolerable and French rule had become in-
trusive and heavy-handed. Instead of treading carefully with this
proud and independent population, the French set out to subdue the
Druze homeland. Peasants were encouraged to break with their
tribal lords; forced labor was pressed into public works. The Druze
might have tolerated a subtle "native policy" that let well enough
alone, but the clumsiness of the French triggered this rebellion.

It took the full might of the French colonial armies to put down
the Druze. A humble stonemason, a *Nusrani* (Christian) working
the hill country of Jabal Druze and the adjacent Hawran plains,
happened in the way of a great upheaval. There was no money in
Jabal Druze. A severe drought had impoverished the cultivators.
Brigandage had spread. Rebel bands and French expeditions fought
a bitter war. The Moroccan *spahis* (cavalrymen), the most feared of
France's soldiers, looted and terrorized with abandon. Salim Hawi,
who had known the proud spirit of the Druze, had no fondness for
the French. From Jabal Druze he brought back tales of what the
French had done to the Atrash clan after their army snuffed out the
rebellion. The French had come up with petty, cruel schemes to
humble the leaders of the rebellion. Old men who had led large,
proud clans and who had not known a day of manual labor were
sent out to clear the roads and carry stones for the stonemasons.
Salim Hawi had not been able to bear the spectacle; years of friendship with the Druze notables made it impossible for him to be party
to that kind of violation. The French obliged and threw him out of
Jabal Druze.

A terrible ordeal hit Salim Hawi a few years later, interrupting his eldest son's schooling and sending him to work for a dozen years. An odd ailment afflicted Salim Hawi that kept him in bed, and without work and income, for two years. The stonemason had been on the road and had taken a nap on a cold stone under a tree. When he woke up, he was unable to move his leg. No one knew what to do about his ailment. Village remedies and fortunetellers were of no avail. What modern medicine there was here was no help either. There was no money saved for that "black day," no money for the winter provisions. It fell to Khalil Hawi, then thirteen years of age, to deal with the shopkeepers who wanted their bills paid. Proud and promising, the schoolboy had to grow up in a hurry. Shweir was a place that knew and kept no secrets. The boy, hounded by the shopkeepers for overdue bills, endured public humiliation. The disdain in Hawi's poetry for the "merchants of the temple" and the usurers must have its roots in the injured pride of those formative years.

Schooling for Khalil became a luxury that the Hawis could not afford. The schoolboy of thirteen quit to become a laborer. More than a dozen years would pass before Khalil Hawi would return to school. This was his private wound. It forever set him apart from the pampered children of the bourgeoisie whose company he would come to keep in later years. He knew and experienced the lives of the downtrodden. He drifted in and out of odd jobs; he did manual, physical labor. He worked as an apprentice cobbler in his village; he became a wall plasterer and a bricklayer in Beirut, Jordan, and the Golan Heights; he worked for the British army when it came to Lebanon and evicted the forces of Vichy France in the middle of the Second World War. There came a time, it is true, when praise was given to the *batunji* (bricklayer and builder) who became a professor and a poet, but the pain of that journey was his own wound and mark.

Hawi retained this private memory from his first days as a laborer hauling off stones on a building site in his village as his classmates passed by on their way to school: "What was truly painful was that some of them would stop for a conversation with me, I who

had known a privileged life before." There was no romance in this
land that surrounded the self-made man, and there was no glory for
manual labor. There were the sons of the lady, it was said in this unsentimental land, and there were the sons of the maid. Some men of
means in the city could be heard bragging that the *shirwals* (the
loose, baggy pants that peasants wore) of their fathers were still
hanging from the mulberry trees in the village, but this affinity with
hardship was not something the culture really honored or claimed.
Khalil Hawi slipped into the world of losers. The remarkable thing
about him was his escape a decade later from that world into the
company of those who mattered. Hawi wrote his own life—the deferred dream of education and learning, the difficulty of making
ends meet, and the loss of his boyhood innocence—into these lines
in his collection, *Bayadir al-Ju'* (The Threshing Floors of Hunger).
This is the superb translation of two Hawi scholars, Adnan Haydar
and Michael Beard.

> *When evening haze prevails*
> *Save your maternal tears;*
> *Entreat me not to say:*
> *"Behind the wasted caves*
> *Behind the barren shores*
> *A world of books, a home*
> *A field, a plough, await."*
> *Omnipotent I rule*
> *The genie of the caves.*
> *Manna and quail and wine*
> *Unknown to earthly jars.*

A practical mother who wanted the shopkeepers paid off; a son
who ruled "the genie of the caves": Hawi had wanted to work as a
watchman for the village's vineyards, which had become his refuge
after his father's illness. He loved their solitude and pristine beauty,
but there was no steady work for a watchman. Hawi did the cobbler's work because his parents wanted for him—and for themselves

and the younger children—the safety of a vocation and a trade. But it was never easy for him to get along with the master cobblers he apprenticed for. He waited on tables in the summer months in a cafe owned by a relative in Duhur al-Shweir, on the ridge overlooking his village, a summer resort for the smart, affluent set from the towns of Lebanon, Syria, and Palestine. He abhorred this crowd, grieved that his countrymen had to make their way as servants and hotel keepers. He gave up on shoemaking and on Shweir and settled for the life of a day laborer and wall plasterer on the outskirts of Beirut.

"There can be no doubt that the lowland, urban civilization penetrated to the highland world very imperfectly and at a very slow rate," the great historian Fernand Braudel has written in *The Mediterranean and the Mediterranean World in the Age of Philip II*. "In the mountains then, civilization is never very stable." There is no need to romanticize the mountain sensibility; there was plenty of this romanticism surrounding Mount Lebanon, exalting the freedom of the mountain set against the servitude and tyranny in the plains below. This romance of the mountain was spun by the highlanders themselves and by outsiders who came to visit these mountains. "The steepest places had been at all times the asylum of liberty," the late-eighteenth-century French traveler Baron De Tott wrote of the hill country of Lebanon. There came with this romance an old, inescapable truth: The highlanders brought with them to the coastal plains the nerves and the suspicion of the mountain. The friends in the city who spoke of Hawi as a brittle man, *asabi* (high-strung), had encountered a man who never shed the ways of the hills.

"Always go down, never go up," was a maxim of mountain life in the Mediterranean. Mountaineers had left the mulberry trees and the land and had set sail for the New World and Africa or come down to Beirut. Tens of thousands had made that necessary choice. Khalil Hawi knew both the hold of that mountain on its people and its curse and cruelty. The mountain freedom was both truth and legend; he was under no illusions about the burden of scarcity, custom, and clerical authority in those hills. In his sole book-length work of prose, which he wrote in his late thirties (his dissertation at Cambridge), he took up the political culture of the mountain and of his countrymen:

> The free air of the Mountain, and the dignity of the Mountain itself, leave their impression on their spirit and physique, while a primitive kind of ideal morality is manifested in their conduct. Nevertheless, after their youth is over, the repeated shocks and frustrations which they are fated to receive from the evils inherent in their surroundings, the realization of the tragedies and the futilities in the history of their country, and the practical wisdom which their parents try to teach them, itself learned from frustrations and the futility of idealism, all these combine to keep them from belief in any great cause such as public welfare or the advancement of the nation. Petty egoism and indiscriminating opportunism seem indispensable qualities if they are to adapt themselves to their environment, and become capable of struggling with its political, social and economic conditions. Yet the good qualities developed in their youth do not disappear entirely from their mature character, even though these play no essential part in directing their conduct. Petty feuds, intrigues, and lack of integrity are accepted as normal, while dignity, frankness and open-heartedness are nothing more than an apparent aim, a shield and a mask.

The first journey out of the hard truth of the mountain, and the first attempt to step beyond the hold of home and parents and the psychic injuries of the cobbler's work, came when Khalil Hawi was fifteen years of age. He did not have to travel far: He became a follower of Anton Saadah, an adventurer and Pied Piper, a fellow Greek Orthodox born in Shweir who had returned from Brazil some years earlier after an absence of a dozen years from Lebanon to preach a militant doctrine of Syrian nationalism. For those who came under his spell, Anton Saadah offered a gospel of political redemption. It took Khalil Hawi years, and much anguish, to work his way through and out of the web that Saadah spun for the impressionable young men who came to see him as a political prophet with a magic wand for the ills of the lands of Lebanon, Syria, and Palestine. When Hawi found his way into secular Arab nationalism in the 1950s, he was a man on the rebound. His first ideological home had been in the bizarre political movement, the Parti Populaire Syrien, which Saadah had created, part an underground fascist formation, part a cult that surrounded a man of great charisma.

Anton Saadah turned up in Lebanon in 1930. Before he was put to death by the Lebanese government in 1949, he had ensnared some of the ablest minds among the politicized youth. Saadah was in his mid-twenties when he made his way back to his ancestral land. He returned with empty pockets and no fixed occupation (the emigrants who left this land preferred to get lost in God's lands rather than return without money to show for the years they had spent abroad). He had known a turbulent life. He had joined his father, Dr. Khalil Saadah, in his wanderings. The older Saadah had left his children behind in the old land and led the life of an itinerant political journalist and emigré leader in Egypt and then in Argentina and Brazil. The mountain was too small for Khalil Saadah, who had wanted to bring an end to Turkish sovereignty; the physician had been forced to flee the land. Sixteen years were to pass before Anton saw his father again. In the interim, the boy lost his mother, who died in Egypt in 1913 after joining her husband there. Anton was left with his father's family; his formative years had been the years of famine in the Great War. He survived but took with him the memories of what he had witnessed and suffered when he left the country in 1919 at the end of the war to join his father in Brazil.

A life of political dreams and economic marginality awaited him. Khalil Saadah published an Arabic newspaper for the emigrés, al-Jarida; his son became his typesetter and sole reporter. (A second publication, the monthly al-Majalla, followed after the failure of the first publication.) In that distant South American setting, among the Syrian and Lebanese emigrés, father and son entertained big dreams for their ancestral land and for young Anton's place in its future. They lived in Brazil, but they vicariously fought the campaigns

of the old land, quarreled with the other emigrés, and belittled the
traders who were eager to get on with their lives in South America.
For young Anton, the life of São Paolo was a time in purgatory. The
real world, the things that mattered, were in the old land. A young
man of twenty, Anton was filled with fury that no honest patriot
had assassinated British foreign secretary Lord Balfour on his visit
to Syria in 1925. He wrote endlessly of the struggle in Palestine between Arabs and Jews and blamed the powers that be in Syria,
Lebanon, and Palestine for the growing power of the Jews in Palestine. He was heart-broken when the French put down the Great Rebellion in Syria. He told his fellow Syrians and Lebanese that he had
not come to Brazil to stay or to make a fortune, that he was "a man
on a mission." The longing for home tormented him. "I feel a con-
stant yearning for my country," he wrote in 1929, a year before his
return to Lebanon. "I yearn for the valley and the pine forest and the
spring. How I wish I could return to my birthplace." No letter from
Anton Saadah (and his true believers have assembled and kept his
words) ever described the physical landscape or the social life of
Brazil.

In his South American years, Anton Saadah received little formal education but became a man of great intellectual claims. He
returned to Lebanon an eccentric young man: bearded, intention-
ally enigmatic, claiming knowledge of an amazing number of foreign languages—German, Russian, French, English, Portuguese,
Spanish—and a thorough command of history and philosophy. To
this stubborn land of sects and clerical authority and the big men
who led these sects, Saadah brought his belief in imminent revolution. He came ready to create a Syrian nation within the "natural
frontiers" of historic Syria. Bounded by the Taurus Mountains in
the north, by the Euphrates and the Iraqi desert in the east, the Sinai
Peninsula in the south, and the Mediterranean in the west, these
lands (Syria, Lebanon, Palestine, and Jordan) were the sacred location of Saadah's Syrian nation. There had been a great Syrian *umma*
(nation, community), Saadah preached, that had nothing to do with
the "backward nations" to its east, a nation possessed of an ancient

civilization that had illuminated the cultures of Athens and Rome. That civilization had gone into eclipse, contaminated by the "backwardness of the East," diminished and degraded for centuries. Saadah had come to deliver this Syrian race out of its long night of darkness.

In fact, there had never been a Syrian nation. The lands Saadah claimed had been places of jealous, feuding communities. Two colonial powers ruled over these territories—Britain and France. There were other claims of loyalty as well: the Maronite attachment to an independent Lebanon and the Muslim Sunni sense of belonging to a wider Arab world. Saadah looked past all those obstacles; he offered his own self-confidence and a pseudo-mystical notion of a Syrian race to young men in search of a political order that was better than the order of the oligarchs, merchants, and clerics.

The house of Anton Saadah's family in Shweir had been sold. A man with no property in the village, Anton had made for himself a thatched hut in the hills above the town. This hut, his sanctuary in the summer months, was sanctified: here the man read, meditated, and planned the conquest of political power. For his main base of operations, however, he chose the neighborhood of the AUB campus. This was the right place for a political plotter and stylist. He was a dilettante: he tried his hand at fiction, he played tennis and bridge with the university crowd, he was a good swimmer. He checked out big weighty books from the library. He charmed the university president, Bayard Dodge, whom he met in the village of Shweir, and Dodge made room for him at the university, tutoring German on the side to students whose interest in German had been stirred by the rise of Adolf Hitler. (Dodge, the patrician, was not above dissimulating in the interest of his university; he would deny any connection to Saadah after the latter's rise to political notoriety.) Saadah's audacity seemed to know no limit. He sat in on a course on "Semitic culture" taught by a young teacher, Anis Frayha, trained at the universities of Chicago and Tübingen, but proceeded to take the lecturer to task for misreading the history of Syria and missing the unity at the heart of Syrian history.

It was easy to see that this man was headed for trouble. He mocked all the timeless truths of the place: the belief in property, family, and custom; the claims of the religious sects. A shopkeeper in Shweir who knew the world took Saadah aside for a fatherly bit of advice. "Go to the American University, find some work there; you want to rule the Muslims and they will not be ruled by someone from outside their faith. If you persist, they are sure to kill you. Give this up and head for the university." A similar piece of advice was given him by Anis Frayha, the university instructor Saadah had clashed with over Syrian history. Frayha was a wise young man, a Quaker who had grown up in a nearby Druze village in the mountains; his university education had not dulled his village pragmatism. "With a name like Anton you will not succeed in heading a political movement; this is a [Christian] saint's name. I will grant you any wish you have if the Alis and Abdel Saters of the world [Muslim names] will follow you." But scores of young men were willing to pursue Saadah's dream, and he had no trouble gathering around him a core of true believers. He found them among the Greek Orthodox, the Druze, the Protestants, and the few Shia who had stirred to a world beyond clan and sect. (He was less successful with the Maronites and Sunnis.) He found them among the unsettled young dissatisfied with the inadequacy of their elders' world. He held out to them a promise of reform and a way out of the world of the oligarchs, merchants, and custodians of religious sects. "You are studying the stars," he said to a bright astronomy student at the AUB, "without knowing anything about who owns and dominates the ground you are standing on." The would-be astronomer abandoned his lab to take up the study of economics and philosophy.

Saadah had that sharp "stranger's wakefulness," a gift from his years in South America. (I owe this expression to Leon Wieseltier's essay "Against Identity.") It enabled him to see things that others didn't. He looked at the old medium of poetry produced in the land and saw nothing but the dead weight of the past, imitation, form with no force. He ridiculed the poetic tradition emanating from the land of Syria and Lebanon, with its hills and green valleys, that bowed to the poetic tradition of the Arabian Peninsula and described the flat, desert landscape and adopted that alien landscape for its own. He called on the young, the literati, and the poets to write their own experience, the world of their own senses and surroundings, into their literature and poetry.

Saadah had no interest in the desert world of the Arabian Peninsula; he even dismissed Egypt (then in the midst of a bourgeois awakening in its politics and culture) as a nation of "the East" with little of relevance to the needs of his Syrian nation. "Come with me," he summoned the poets and literati of the lands of his imaginary kingdom. "Let us together light a torch for this Syrian nation battling darkness. Come let us build palaces of love and wisdom and beauty and hope out of the material of its history and its genius and its legends and its teachings," he wrote in a book entitled *al-Sira' al-Fikri fi al-Adab al-Suri* (The Intellectual Struggle in Syrian Literature). He called on the poets to abandon the concerns of the poetry of love and to write of home, politics, and public affairs, to recover from history's darkness the soul and the genius of Syria. This call to a revolution in letters was but an expression of a wider revolt against French rule, the rule of an elite steeped in compromise and collaboration with French rule.

Saadah arrived at an opportune time, the years of economic depression and deepening discontent with French rule in Syria and Lebanon. France had broken the resistance to its power but had not found a workable order of authority. France was reeling at home in the 1930s, unsure of itself, its economic resources too fragile to permit colonial largesse. Between the end of the First World War and 1939, the franc lost nine-tenths of its gold equivalent; the romance for colonies, for a Greater France, became a thing of the past. New notions of collectivist nationalism, assertions that France was a declining power whose moment of ascendancy had passed, came into France's domain in Syria and Lebanon from Mussolini's Italy (and later Germany). Mussolini vowed the undoing of France's empire; the Mediterranean was to become Italian, *mare nostrum,* "our sea." Italy's ships were bigger, her trains faster, her authoritarianism more effective. The Italians knew the lands of the Levant: their clerical missions, the Franciscans in particular, had put down roots here long ago, as had the trading firms of Italy. Mussolini's bravado, his alternative to the liberal doctrines of Britain and France, was seductive. The passion of Anton Saadah was in tune with the restless politics of the 1930s.

Khalil Hawi's parents wanted their son to stay away from Saadah. They needed no book learning to tell them that the *hukuma* (government) was bound to put an end to this trouble. They knew that there was no bread in this kind of sedition. The stonemason and his wife knew their country and its codes; they knew that those who owned and divided up the place were bound to strike. They did not have to wait long: Saadah was in and out of prison, and his followers in the village were rounded up and beaten without mercy in the village square. Mothers and wives with white bundles of food came and went between Shweir and the prisons in Beirut.

But it proved hard to convince Khalil Hawi to choose caution. A young poet with promise and injured pride, a dreamer forced into the demeaning work of shoemaking, he found in Saadah's party a place where his pride could be salvaged. Older men from neighboring villages, Druze mountaineers, sought him out; it was rumored that the poet was trusted by his leader, that he knew his hideouts in the hills. The gendarmes terrorized Shweir at will, but Khalil Hawi was spared. The deportation of Saadah by the authorities in 1938 gave Khalil Hawi and those like him a reprieve. (Saadah would come back in 1947 to an independent Lebanon in yet another bid for his kingdom.)

Politics aside, Khalil Hawi outgrew his village. At age twenty he left Shweir and settled for the life of a laborer in Dawra and Bourj Hammoud, a squalid encampment on the northeastern approaches of Beirut. This gritty industrial wasteland belonged to the unwanted. The sea by Dawra was the city's dump. The Armenian refugees who had survived the horrors inflicted on them by the Young Turks in the Great War and its aftermath had been the first to claim this wilderness on the edges of Beirut. They had camped

there, given the names of their old towns in Anatolia to the alleyways of this squatter settlement: Camp Sis, Camp Adana, Camp
Marash. The Armenians waited here, sustained by the dream of imminent return to their own earth. At first they had refused to learn
Arabic and rioted against the teachers of Arabic assigned them by
the relief agencies. They wanted nothing to do with the Arabic language, no suggestion that they had been banished forever from their
own world. But the Armenians had stayed. And they were joined by
refugees of every variety: Assyrians and Chaldeans, Syriac Orthodox from Turkey, the Shia underclass banished by poverty from the
hinterlands of south Lebanon and the plains of the Bekaa Valley.

Artisans and craftsmen in their former homes in Turkey, the Armenians made this neighborhood a magnet for the unwanted. Some
Armenians still harbored the dream born in the Great War: an independent Armenian state in the eastern half of Anatolia stretching
from the Black Sea to the Mediterranean. They wanted the young
(and the thousands of orphans who had survived the war and the
exodus from Turkish lands) to be educated in literary matters, made
ready to rule an independent Armenia. But the innate practicality of
this nation had prevailed. The Armenian young were taught to be
shoemakers, tinsmiths, weavers, carpenters. In an orphanage where
they were taught the skills they needed for their life, the Armenian
children put up a sign: SWEET IS THE BREAD OF OUR SWEAT.

Khalil Hawi was to see a whole new world of physical and moral
degradation in this urban setting. This was a world on the other
side of the fresh mountain air and the vineyards and the scruples
of Shweir. There were streetwalkers and "night ladies" in Dawra.
There were refugees living out in the open by the sea. They lived by
their wits; they did what they had to do to survive. A young man,
still in his late teens and with a sensitive temperament, Hawi took in
all this desolation. A good many years later, in the smart residential
district of Ras Beirut, the bay or tip of Beirut, near the American
University, where Hawi the academic made his home, he still
dwelled on the squalor and despair he had seen in Dawra and Bourj
Hammoud.

Reading kept the bricklayer and wall plasterer going. He read his countryman Khalil Gibran; he read French poetry, Hugo, and Flaubert; he was fond of the English Romantics. The dream of education and of breaking out from the laborer's world never abandoned him. A break came his way in the Second World War, when the British army evicted the Vichy forces from Lebanon. Hawi secured a job with the British as a labor supervisor and worked for the British army for two years. This was a lucky twist of fate: The followers of Saadah (and young Khalil no doubt among them) were enemies of France and Britain and admirers of the Germans and Italians. There was a great division then in Lebanon, and in the Arab lands beyond, between those whose interests, education, and sympathies inclined them toward the British and the French and those who believed that their future and the future of these lands lay with the Germans and Italians. No one who lived through this period ever shook off the memory of the fall of Paris to the Germans and the response to it in this land. Some wept openly for the French; more celebrated the comeuppance of the colonial power. A popular couplet at the time taunted the French about Hitler's victory:

> *Ya France, hiddi W'irhali*
> *Ijaki Hitler, Abu Ali,*
> Oh France, dismantle and be gone
> After you is Hitler, Abu Ali

"Abu Ali" was the popular name given to neighborhood toughs, an endearing nickname. The German wreaking havoc on Europe was doing to the colonial masters of the Levant, the British and the French, what the people here could not do for themselves. To some Arabs, the victories of the Afrika Korps were but retribution and payback to their European rulers. Those who blew with the wind began to brush up on their German. But Britain held on in the Middle East, and in that summer of 1941, the Allied armies struck into Lebanon and Syria from British strongholds in Palestine and Transjordan and from the sea. The Vichy forces put up token resistance but capitulated. Damascus fell, and then it was Beirut's turn. The fiction of France's power and the "honor" of France were given a fig leaf. A French officer (from the Free French), General Georges Catroux, entered Beirut alongside a British commander. Then Charles de Gaulle himself turned up in Beirut, paid a visit to the AUB campus, and took tea in the garden of the AUB's president's home.

The victory of the Allied armies brought some economic relief to Lebanon. In the preceding two years, grain had practically disappeared from the market; petroleum, sugar, and rice were scarce; and employment was nowhere to be found. This change of foreign rulers was for the good. A million and a half Allied soldiers flooded the region, and they needed local labor and provisions. The British empire was running itself into insolvency, but the wealth of the British and the vast American means poured into the war gave the place an economic lift. Inflation came and hit the poorer classes and the artisans, but the beneficiaries of this windfall were content to take this lucky break. Khalil Hawi was resourceful and lucky, and he knew enough English and was educated enough to do well by this opportunity.

It was with the money saved during this period that Hawi resumed his education in 1946. He chose a preparatory Protestant school in the Beirut suburb of Shwayfat, a demanding feeder school for the American University favored by families of means and property. Boarders came to this school from the established families of Syria, Iraq, and Palestine: the Shawas of Gaza, the Bakris, Barazis, and Azms of Damascus, and so on. A proud family tradition had seen to it that the school at Shwayfat remained an institution of authority and standing. Reverend Taniyus Saad, a minister and educator known for the devotion, zeal, and discipline with which he ran his school, had passed it on to his son, Charles. Khalil Hawi was twenty-six years old when he enrolled at this school for one year prior to his admission to the AUB. There was not much this prep school could teach him; he was a decade older than his classmates and well read. What he needed was the certificate the school handed him, and the green light it gave him to enter the university.

He had pined for the chance to attend the AUB. This dream had sustained him through the years of manual labor and humiliation. The AUB was a piece of a more glamorous world. It exuded the authority of the great, foreign society that had planted it here in the 1860s. Its magic touched those who were lucky to claim it and to belong to it. In the clutter and chaos of Beirut, the AUB campus stood apart—a fifty-two-acre "Garden of Eden" was how Grace Dodge Guthrie described it. The Yankee missionary Daniel Bliss, who had launched this institution, had looked long and hard before he found a location for his college, in 1866, on the northern shore of the Beirut promontory. Bliss had not exaggerated when he described the place as "the finest site in all Beirut if not in all Syria." The plot of land he chose was outside the city walls; a single mule path of red dirt connected the place to the rest of the city. What had been a parched piece of ground where jackals cried behind rocks at night (the description is from an AUB president, Bayard Dodge) became the special "Garden of Eden" that Grace Dodge Guthrie saw: tawny buildings amid lush gardens, a neat and ordered place shaded by pine, eucalyptus, and jacaranda trees, with the mountains in view and the sea below.

Generations of missionaries and educators passed on to their students here a sense of entitlement and a sense of place and public service. A young man like Hawi, who had had his fill of the work of the unwanted, was glad for this chance. His years of university education were destined to be no ordinary years. He and a class of nearly five hundred students entered the university at a time of great political upheaval: the Palestine war between Arab and Jew, a time of deepening radicalization among the young. The self-confidence of the ruling stratum in Arab social and political life was torn asunder in that year, 1948–1949, and the bubble around this American sanctuary in Beirut burst.

In the preceding years it had been relatively easy for the university's American custodians to keep the outside world at bay; a distinct political culture was born here of the marriage between the American missionary impulse and the sensibility of a secularized urban elite that saw the education at this American collegiate insti-

tution and its glamour as an extension of its own primacy and privilege. The Americans walked a fine line; they preached the gospel of
liberty but ran an institution of paternalism and obedience. They
paid homage to the "Arab awakening" but were determined to keep
the politics of the lands around them at bay. They had come to en-
lighten "the East" and prided themselves on their grasp of the "Eastern mentality." "In the Near East, even now, the necessity for rather
strict supervision over student life is greater than it is in America,"
wrote Stephen Penrose, the AUB president in the late 1940s and early
1950s. A physicist who had once served as a special assistant to U.S.
Secretary of Defense James Forrestal, Penrose saw the problem as
stemming from the early childhood of the race:

> There, discipline is apt to be rigid but merely for the sake of dis-
> cipline, rather than for the cultivation of intelligent respect for
> sound principles of behavior. The result is that a Syrian boy, for
> example, turned loose in the comparatively free atmosphere of
> an American college, may misuse his freedom in reckless indul-
> gence simply because he is unaccustomed to lack of restriction.

Penrose wrote this in his book, *That They May Have Life.* The
title came from the motto of the American University inscribed on
the Moorish stone archway of its main gate: "That they shall have
life and have it more abundantly." American and Arab understood
the rules. We have a glimpse of this world from a memoir by Hisham
Sharabi, a Palestinian from Jaffa, a child of the secure bourgeoisie
who graduated from the university in 1947, the year Khalil Hawi
matriculated. Of his social class and his peers at the university,
Sharabi wrote in his book *al-Jamr wa al-Ramad* (Embers and Ashes):

> We were few among the tens of thousands of our people's youth,
> but we never understood that we enjoyed privileges denied oth-
> ers. We lived in big houses, we enjoyed life as we wished, we knew
> no deprivation. We considered happiness our birthright. . . . Our
> leaders and teachers hated the West but loved it at the same time;
> the West was the source of everything they desired and the source

of their misery and self-contempt. It was thus that they implanted in us an inferiority complex toward the West combined with a deification of it.

The poet and laborer who came to study philosophy and Arabic literature had walked into a maelstrom. The war for Palestine had brought into Beirut, and into the sanctuary of this American institution, the sons and daughters of the Palestinian upper orders. The Palestinian world had collapsed, no match for the Zionist enterprise. The upper orders, the urban elite, families of means and property, had been the first to flee the cities of Palestine. In their new surroundings, the children of this calamity vowed to continue the old fight. Political demonstrations became the order of the day. The AUB Student Handbook of 1949 threatened dire measures against those who would meddle in politics, "possibly as severe as expulsion, if the circumstances and the evidence seem to warrant such action." But there was no way of returning to the former habits of political quiescence. By the time Khalil Hawi found his way into *al-Urwa al-Wuthqa* (the Close Bond), a Palestinian medical student from Lydda, a Greek Orthodox, George Habash, had been elected president of this group in 1950. Habash would play a decisive role in shaping the radical political culture of his era; he was to be Yasser Arafat's nemesis in the Palestinian world, his fierce opposition to the ruling Arab regimes and their ties to the West, a source of inspiration to his followers. In a fitting piece of irony, Habash had entered the university on a scholarship provided him by the British Council in Beirut.

For Hawi there still remained his first political romance: the Parti Populaire Syrien and its leader Anton Saadah, who had returned in 1947 after an absence of nine years in South America. This attachment had to play itself out before Hawi could pick up the cause of Arabism. Saadah's themes had not changed; the years had only given him more ammunition and new causes. There was the fight for Palestine, that "southern wing" of Syria, as he called it. The men in power in Syria and Lebanon had not covered themselves with glory in that fight; the ruling regimes seemed ready for the plucking. Saadah had big plans for the conquest of political power. There were paramilitary uniforms for his followers and secret training camps, where an army of the Syrian nation of Saadah would be trained. The plans were much bigger than the man and his followers and their limited means. The army of that Syrian nation was, in the main, a phantom army, but Saadah was confident that his kingdom was just over the horizon.

Khalil Hawi was a man with no margin for error. His devotion to Saadah and the cause of Syrian nationalism had to be balanced against his poverty and limited means. With only a handful of merit tuition scholarships at the university, Hawi, who had excelled and claimed a scholarship enabling him to stay at school, was eager to keep his scholarship. There was his love of poetry, giving him a private world and making a name for him in the literary circles of the university. Although he never broke with Saadah, he kept at a safe distance from the man when the end came for Saadah in 1949.

Saadah never mastered the hard realities of Syria and Lebanon. His time in South America (two decades of his adult life) must have been partly to blame. Brazil and Argentina were new lands, peopled by immigrants, vast spaces to be shaped in the image of those who would possess them, whereas Lebanon was an old, surly land, every inch of its soil captured from the rocks, then fought over, claimed, and jealously protected. The escape into books, fantasy, and a primitive cult of nationalism further eroded Saadah's grasp of the facts of his land. The following he had was no match for the order he wanted to overthrow. He belittled the oligarchs of the place, but the place was theirs. He sought the separation of politics and religion, but the political order in his Lebanese birthplace was anchored in religious sectarianism.

When Saadah's revolution played itself out in the summer of 1949, it was a deed of nullity, a farce, a two-day affair. The state set a trap for Saadah's followers and put down their insurrection with ease. The leader made a run for it to Damascus. A military adventurer, a colonel, Husni al-Za'im, who had pulled off a coup of his own in Syria earlier in the year, promised Saadah help and asylum, but the colonel was not a man of his word, and Saadah was driven to the Syrian–Lebanese border and turned over to the authorities.

The Lebanese government was quick to strike. A military tribunal sentenced Saadah to death, and the two big men of the republic, the Maronite president and the Muslim Sunni prime minister, ordered his swift execution. The details of Saadah's final hours have been preserved for us in Sharabi's *al-Jamr wa al-Ramad* (Embers and Ashes) and in the pages of Beirut's preemiment daily, *an-Nahar*. Saadah did not plead for clemency; he asked to see his wife and three daughters but was turned down. He asked to give one last political testament but was told that since there were no journalists around, there was no use issuing any declarations. He held his ground and insisted on his right to record a final word: "I believe that the Lebanese government committed a wide conspiracy against me and against my movement. I view those who conspired against me and who sentenced me to death and who will execute me with contempt." In the early hours of dawn, on the eighth day of August 1949, Saadah was taken to a firing range by the sea, where he was shot. His body was taken to a Greek Orthodox church, where a priest conducted prayers for him in the presence of the firing squad. The priest did his duty under duress; he wanted nothing to do with this staged, cruel affair. In Saadah's village, the church bells were rung in sorrow for him and in defiance of his executioners.

Saadah died a noble, defiant death. He made sure of that. He knew that his own cult and the cause of his Syrian nation demanded no less. He had walked into the presidential compound of the Syrian colonel on his own, knowing the odds and sending his driver-companion to safety before doing so. Before the tribunal, Saadah was surrounded by soldiers, Sharabi wrote, "but did not look a prisoner. I know what he is thinking of: he wants to have his say, and to depart with his head unbent. . . . It is his last stand of pride." Sharabi loved his leader; a young man of twenty-two, he had an exquisite eye for the smallest details about Saadah. Sharabi was on the run in Amman on his way to Chicago and a new life in America, when he read the papers the day after the execution. Sharabi was spared because his idol was careful to get him out of harm's way. Sharabi recognized the suit Saadah wore before the tribunal: It was the summer beige suit that Saadah had brought with him from Argentina two years earlier. (Life handed out a certain kind of justice. A week after Saadah's execution, a young Syrian lieutenant and his unit fought their way into Husni al-Za'im's residence, carried him off in an armored car, and then murdered him; the lieutenant, it was reported, charged Za'im with betraying Saadah.)

It had to end this way for Saadah because his was no ordinary call. Whether he knew it or not, he had launched an assault on the Arab-Islamic history of the lands of Syria. The Muslim conquest (the *fath*) in the seventh century, a new dispensation, had remade the civilization of Syria. The urban order of orthodox Sunni Islam had prevailed in the plains, the valleys, and the coastal towns. Heterodox Muslim sects and Christian communities had survived but had made their accommodation to the ascendant culture and the language of the ruling order. Saadah's philosophy was a repudiation of all that history.

Writing from Buenos Aires in 1943 in his book of astounding audacity, *al-Sira' al-Fikri fi al-Adab al-Suri* (The Intellectual Struggle in Syrian Literature), Saadah described the history of Syria as a series of "ruinous conquests" that had alienated Syria from its inner core and its "psychological foundations." In his half-learned way, he dispensed with so much history and hacked away at matters of enormous danger and complexity. In his call for that secular nation of Syria, many Muslims saw the phantom of Byzantium that the Muslim conquest had overwhelmed. Natural Syria, Greater Syria, they believed, was but another name for the Patriarchate of Antioch, once a proud center of Syrian Christianity. Lying on the River Orontes, a dozen miles from the Mediterranean, Antioch had been one of the great cities of the Roman empire, the chief city in Rome's Asiatic domain. For the early Christians it was a sacred place: where Saint Peter founded his first bishopric. Antioch had known greatness. The patriarch of the ancient See of Antioch had dismissed the rise of Constantinople as the bid of a peripheral outpost. The city then passed back and forth between Islam and Byzantium. Conquered by Islam in the seventh century, it reverted to Byzantine rule in the tenth century, only to be taken back by Turkish soldiers in the latter years of the eleventh century. There, in Antioch, Greek and Muslim commerce met and Syrian Christianity knew a time of relative tranquillity.

Cut off from the Latin West during the age of European incursions into the Levant and finally rid by the Bolshevik revolution of the false hope of some imaginary brothers in the faith coming to the rescue, the Greek Orthodox raised the banners of secular nationalism. Children of the cities (Beirut, Aleppo, Damascus, and Jerusalem), the Greek Orthodox could boast that theirs was a history of affinity with mainstream Syrian Islam. They had neither welcomed the Crusades in centuries past (as the Maronites were supposed to have done) nor been beneficiaries of the gifts of France, England, Prussia, and the American missions that had come the way of the Catholic and new Protestant denominations since the mid-1800s. One of their own who swam against the current in his church in the 1950s and 1960s, the Lebanese philosopher and diplomatist Charles Malik (a believer in Lebanon and its Western ties and a man at odds with Arab nationalism), described the politics of his sect in a telling way: "Their relation to Islam over the centuries may be characterized, in one word, as existentially chequered, morally subservient, and spiritually tragic, although in the Arab world at least, they worked more closely with their Muslim compatriots on civic, social, cultural and national problems than any other Christian group." The Greek Orthodox had been eager to please and to belong; Byzantium was a relic of the past, a benign ghost. But there was no reasoning away the suspicion that this Syrian nationalism of Saadah and his enthusiasts was Byzantium, the Church of Antioch, dressed up in new secular garb.

For Khalil Hawi this was a time of grief and enormous guilt. He had not been there by Saadah's side. He had come to the university after years of striving for this chance, and he did not want to risk what he had. There was his academic work at the university and perhaps the premonition that the cause was doomed. In the years to come, Hawi never wavered in his conviction that Saadah had been a noble soul who had sacrificed his life for a beaten nation. He mourned him in poems that were circulated by Saadah's followers, who were then on the run. In these poems Hawi came close to calling for a just revenge against the Lebanese rulers who had executed Saadah. Lesser men had inherited Saadah's mantle, however, and it was easy to walk away from them and from the belief in Greater Syria.

By the mid-1950s, during the high tide of Arab nationalism, Hawi made the new political dispensation his own. It had been a mistake on Saadah's part, he was to say, to separate the fate of Syria from the larger Arab world. Hawi was swept up by the current of Arab nationalism. The ideas of Arab nationalism dominated his immediate environment around the university. The new political loyalty came to him in the company of the Iraqis (a strong contingent at the AUB, they were innately pan-Arab in their orientation), Jordanians, Syrians, and Palestinians who were his peers and friends. And there was the common literary medium: Arabic poetry. He mastered a literary form that skipped the boundaries of the Arab states and traveled with ease. It was heady and natural for this young man from the mountain to claim a large dominion for his poetry. Whereas in the past he had experimented with some local (Lebanese) poetic forms, folk poetry, he now wrote the classical *Qasida*, the ode, making that large Arab world his own. He had seen the murder of Saadah; life had heaped in his lap enough sorrow. He no doubt knew the difficulty of regenerating an old order, but he brought to this new dispensation his trademark themes: the fight between old, dead political and cultural forms and the fragile promise of an Arab renewal. He expressed this in his early verse, *al-Nay wa al-Rih* (The Flute and the Wind), published in 1961.

I would have never welcomed the sun,
had I not seen you bathe in the morning
in the Nile and the Jordan and the Euphrates
from the stain of sin.

As for the crocodiles,
they have departed our land,
And our sea has churned with them.
They left some remains
Their skins were flayed
and no new skins
have taken their place.

They belong to a past that is gone
And will never return.
Their names are buried before my eyes,
A mere smoke they are.

Beirut was in the midst of a boom, and the AUB was large and wealthy enough to make room for Khalil Hawi. He lived in the dormitories and devoured the books, eager to make up for lost time. The money he had saved from years working for the British army paid for the first three years of his undergraduate schooling; a relative lent him the money he needed for his fourth undergraduate year. Two of his mentors, who had taught him languages and philosophy, were there for him as he worked his way into this new and alien academic environment. He changed his field of study from philosophy to Arabic literature and became an instructor in Arabic studies, but with great reluctance. He was hooked on Freud, Spinoza, Hegel, and Nietzsche, determined to find in their works some deep metaphysical answers, a system of interpretation that would take him beyond the social conventions of his world. He was typical of his time and his generation of educated Arabs in his enthusiasm for foreign texts and political philosophy. The world outside—the world of the oligarchs and the religious hierarchies, the world of the fathers and of property—was stubborn and could not be fought. The villages in the hills seemed timeless and resigned; rebels and reformers turned up now and then, but the social and political order brushed them aside. Foreign philosophers and foreign texts, the ideas of German Romanticism, were an antidote to the reigning order of things. A young man like Hawi with no property to speak of and no sure prospects read into the books his personal needs and the collective needs of the society around him.

Of all the philosophers Hawi read, he was always partial to Nietzsche. He was sorry that he did not know German, so he could read him in the original, but there was an Arabic translation of Nietzsche and studies of Nietzsche all around. Nietzsche and his *Thus Spake Zarathustra* were the rage among the wing of the intelligentsia in the Levant who came into their own in the 1940s and 1950s. The young who would launch the Ba'th party in Damascus, the followers of Saadah, and the restless types who remained politically unaffiliated but on the lookout for a system of ideas that would bring down the dominant order were all under Nietzsche's spell.

The themes and style of *Thus Spake Zarathustra* were enormously seductive to this breed of young rebels. Anticlericalism, the belief in individual will, and the uncharted territory of the future preached by Nietzsche were ready-made for those who believed in imminent revolution and redemption. When Nietzsche wrote, "I am my own forerunner," he put into words the yearnings of this generation, who had lost faith in the ways of their fathers and the ways of the past:

> But why do I speak where no one has *my* kind of ears? Here it is yet an hour too early for me.
>
> Among this people I am my own forerunner, my own cock-crow through dark lanes.
>
> But *their* hour is coming! And mine too is coming! Hourly will they become smaller, poorer, more barren—poor weeds! poor soil!
>
> And *soon* they shall stand before me like arid grass and

steppe, and truly! weary of themselves—and longing for *fire* rather than for water!

O blessed hour of the lightening! O mystery before noontide! One day I shall turn them into running fire and heralds with tongues—

one day they shall proclaim with tongues of flame: It is coming, it is near, *the great noontide*!

Thus spake Zarathustra.

Or consider this other passage from Nietzsche for its mark on Hawi's own work:

My pity for all that is past is that I see it: It has been handed over—handed over to the favour, the spirit, the madness of every generation that comes and transforms everything that has been into its own bridge!

A great despot could come, a shrewd devil, who with his favour and disfavour could compel and constrain all that is past, until it became his bridge and prognostic and herald and cockcrow.

O my brothers, your nobility shall not gaze backward, but *outward*! You shall be fugitives from all fatherlands and forefatherlands!

You shall love your *children's land:* let this love be your new nobility—the undiscovered land in the furthest sea! I bid your sails seek it and seek it!

You shall *make amends* to your children for being the children of your fathers: *thus* you shall redeem all that is past! This new law-table do I put over you!

The echo of Nietzsche is unmistakable in Hawi's poetry: the sordid present and the promise of an unburdened future. Hawi and his peers despaired of their parents, although they may have been reluctant to say this or explore it in full. There were cultural prohibitions against full-scale repudiation of the authority of the fathers, but the torment with the elders' world overflowed the lives of the men and women of this generation and gave the politics of these years the seething quality of muted rebellion. Family life was tyrannical, stubborn, and hard. Mothers' injunctions were suffused with superstition and pessimism about the world and the ability of men and women to bend it to their will. Fathers insisted on obedience to their writ and put up countless obstacles to youthful rebellion. The custodians of the dominant order may have looked pompous and hopelessly out of date, but the levers of power were still in their hands. Anton Saadah had mocked the political order in Lebanon, but Riad al-Sulh, a wily prime minister with a red fez and as much land and property as the eye could see, had sentenced him to death. (Here, too, as in the case of the Syrian colonel who betrayed Saadah, vengeance was to be exacted. Two years after Saadah's execution, Riad al-Sulh was gunned down in Amman while on a visit to the Jordanian monarch, King Abdullah.) There was a rift in this world between the books of the philosophers and the world of custom, tradition, and parental authority.

For Hawi in this academic world this must have been hard to take: his abiding passion still lay in poetry. Four years would pass before he was to finish a master's thesis on reason and revelation in Islamic philosophy. He was earning a modest living teaching in the Arabic department at the university. In 1954 he met and fell in love with a young aspiring Iraqi writer, Daisy al-Amir, with whom he would carry on an intense but troubled relationship in the years to come. Poetry and literature brought them together after the young woman, the daughter of a prominent figure in the Iraqi Anglican community, fell under Beirut's spell when her widowed father married a Lebanese woman.

Hawi was a realist; he knew that he could not live off poetry. A scholarship took him to Cambridge in 1956 for three years, where he attained a doctorate in literature under the supervision of a noted

Arabist, A. J. Arberry. Hawi had his patrons on the AUB faculty, who had secured for him that opportunity at Cambridge. He had always been close to his teacher, Anis Frayha, who now headed the department of Arabic literature. An earthy, unassuming man from a small village, Frayha had savored the ways of the countryside of Lebanon, had gone to great universities in Europe and America, but had retained an interest in the folk life of the mountain, the proverbs and language of the peasantry. Hawi had had a rougher go of it than his teacher, but he could see in his patron and his patron's career the possibility of his own success.

Although the passage to Cambridge was his break, his one chance to make a permanent place for himself at the AUB, Hawi was to fight the decision. He saw it as another "betrayal," another surrender to the requirements of livelihood, rank, status, and success. He wrote in this vein to Daisy al-Amir before he embarked on his journey. "And what of poetry, shall I let it atrophy and die, shall I abandon it? Perhaps it will dry up and not stir again." He had not cared for the academic work, he admitted; he had felt cheated by the company of the "faded and yellowed old books" he had been reading. This trip to England was another escape, he feared, from the call of poetry.

He was in his mid-thirties when he arrived in England, but he was not a worldly man. He was out of his depth and bereaved by his distance from his birthplace. "I am a total stranger here; there is no face I recognize," he wrote to Daisy from Cambridge in September 1956, two days after his arrival:

It is a total, absolute estrangement. . . . Eat for me, with appetite and pleasure, some clusters of grapes for the grapes here are for display in the windows and not to be eaten. . . . Eat for me some Lebanese food, for food here has no taste and no color and no flavor. . . . Talk to everyone in Shweir, forgive them the mistakes they make, for anything there is better than my cold room and the eyes without expression and the inert, mute things all around me that say nothing to me and tell me of nothing.

A child of the sun and the Mediterranean, Hawi struggled with the weather and the winter of England. The fog overwhelmed and depressed him. There had been mist in his village: It blew into the valley from the peaks of Mount Sannin; it was a mist of many colors, the sun always bursting through to burn it off. In England the fog was dark and impenetrable. He wrote endlessly of this fog and the overcast sky, his village and its landscape a beloved memory.

He protested too much. In time Hawi came to savor the academic culture of Cambridge, the theaters of London, and the great libraries. To the Lebanese literary critic Jamil Jabr, who later wrote a book of his own on him, Hawi wrote in admiration, in a letter in 1957, of the culture of this new place: "How pure is the climate of literature and thought here! Shall we ever approach this in Lebanon?" He had been fed the fascist, anti-British harangues of Saadah, but he could see right away the saving graces of democracy. He was moved by the protests that erupted in England over the country's Suez War. He saw dissent, and the land of the "colonial enemy" became a less threatening place.

Hawi's Cambridge letters to Daisy al-Amir are, alternately, manipulative and tormented. He courts the woman in one letter and takes back his pledges and professions of love in the next. Always he writes of his health: He is at death's door; he does not know what the next X ray will reveal, for he fears all kinds of ailments. He wants her to come to him, but he does not want to be a "thief" laying a cruel claim to her love, robbing her of a chance for happiness and a normal life, taking for himself the "flower of your youth."

She did come to him for lengthy periods during his Cambridge years. It was to her that he dedicated the book that grew out of his Ph.D. dissertation. "To Daisy, the hand that held my hand in the nights of doubt and creation." She made her first visit to him in the spring of 1957. She escorted him back to the old country, to the embracing warmth of his beloved mother and the familiar landscape.

In his earlier academic years, Hawi had written of distant, formal matters: reason and revelation in Islamic philosophy. This time around he would stay closer to home and his own small world in

Mount Lebanon. For his dissertation, Hawi chose the life and career of the Lebanese-American poet Kahlil Gibran. (Christened Gibran Khalil Gibran, the famed writer's name was shortened and its spelling rearranged at the Quincy School he attended in Boston.) He dismissed his choice of Kahlil Gibran as a pragmatic one—it was an easy subject, he would have time to read history and philosophy and to compose his poetry on the side—but there was more to it than that. Kahlil Gibran (1883–1931) lived his entire adult life in America and did his work on the Lower West Side of New York City, but his memory and his themes were cherished in Lebanon. It was a stone's throw from Hawi's village of Shweir to Gibran's village of Bisharri in the northern part of the mountain. All the elements that went into the making of Gibran were in Hawi's life as well: the beauty of the mountain and its poverty; the power of the religious institution and the revulsion against it by the young and free of spirit; the cruel ways of a smug, merciless elite and the doomed efforts to change those ways. Gibran had been born nearly four decades earlier, but the essential facts of Lebanon's social and political life had not changed, and Hawi had no difficulty entering into Gibran's world.

To write of Gibran was to write of a legend. Gibran had been good, Hawi knew, at spinning his own myth, the "Oriental sage," the hermit of the East doing his work in prose, sculpture, and painting, in New York City. The Lebanese had loved the legend of Gibran. In his success in the New World they had been eager to see the distinctive genius of their land. In a desperate flight from her husband and his tyranny, Gibran's mother had taken him and his three siblings to Boston in 1894, when he was a boy of eleven. At home, Gibran's had been a harsh life of poverty, with a cruel overbearing father, a drunkard who bullied his family. In America, in Boston's Chinatown, life had been mean and raw. In a shockingly brief period of time between 1902 and 1903, Gibran lost one of his two sisters, his half-brother, and his mother to tuberculosis. Out of his grief came the aphorisms that made Gibran's book, *The Prophet*, the sensation it became in the 1920s and 1930s. Lebanon

and the Lebanese had worked their will on the tale. The tale of sorrow was turned into a narrative that ennobled the land. It was a time of empire: Europe held the lands of the East in its thrall; Britain and France had carved up the region into colonial spheres of influence. There was no harm in this tale of consolation, the boy of the East, from a small mountain village, becoming a guru for the seekers in the West.

In writing of Gibran, Hawi worked a heavily traveled trail. After his death in 1931, Gibran had had his fawning biographers: Barbara Young, an American author, a devotee of Gibran, had sanctified his memory with a hugely popular book, *This Man from Lebanon,* which she published in 1945. Young peddled the myth that Gibran had fashioned around himself: that he was a boy of "fortunate" birth who grew up in an atmosphere of love and culture, that he was given reproductions of Leonardo da Vinci by his father. Barbara Young held on to this myth even after she had visited the humble village dwelling where he was born. There had been debunking works of Gibran as well: a jealous Lebanese author, Mikhail Naimy, who passed himself off as a friend of Gibran, produced a work of undisguised spleen that depicted Gibran as a schemer who charmed unsuspecting women for his own material needs, a man whose mysticism and aphorisms were a cover for a life of indulgence and self-absorption.

Hawi did Kahlil Gibran a fair measure of justice. He understood his countrymen's need for the consoling legend of the man. He knew why the emigrés from Lebanon to the New World had been so devoted to the memory and cult of Gibran. These emigrés, he wrote, were peddlers and shopkeepers, despised in their new surroundings as a people "whose sole purpose in life was the accumulation of money. Gibran's spiritual writings in English furnished them with proof that they came from a better race and had a higher aim in life."

Gibran's work and sensibility had nurtured Hawi during his years of poverty and manual labor. It was not in the man to demolish Gibran. His was to be, on the whole, a tender and careful assessment of Gibran, a fond farewell perhaps. He gave Gibran his due in Arabic letters and paid homage to his role in the refinement of prose poems. He offered a sober critique of his writings in English. There, the teacher and the prophet in Gibran, he wrote, "overwhelmed the lyrical poet." Gibran had been an outsider to the Western tradition, he added. "Gibran could not challenge the literary world and assert himself in it" with his use of the epigram, the aphoristic style, and the parable; he could only appeal at "a popular level to the late Romantics and seekers after the exotic."

The Cambridge interlude took Hawi in new political directions. He had come to England at the height of the anticolonial movement; there were young people at Cambridge from practically all the lands of Afro-Asia and Arab students aplenty. (It appears to have been his fate to be drawn to Iraqis, and he found them here as he had back in Beirut.) England had just waged its campaign against Egypt, the Suez War, only to discover that a new dispensation now obtained in the world: She had been rebuffed by the United States and threatened by the Soviet Union. Among the Arabs and Africans, the postcolonial age had begun, and it was the natural working out of things for a younger, politicized academic to be given to this new enthusiasm. He was at a distance from the Arab world, and from far away that fragmented world looked whole and its divisions seemed rather easy to overcome.

More important, though, Hawi had been changed by the writing and the research he had done. To fully come to terms with Gibran, he had to situate himself and his writings both in the life of Mount Lebanon and in the literary renaissance of the Arab world and the Arabic language. Hawi had taken that plunge and had arrived at a reassuring verdict about the "Arabism" of the Mountain. The Arabic language and the industry and genius of gifted pioneers, he would come to believe, had irrevocably changed the Mountain in the course of the nineteenth century. Linguistic nationalism had led to "emotional nationalism," and this Christian Mountain, which had paid its literary dues, had put behind it the insularity of its past. Religion remained a divide of no small consequence between Mount Lebanon and the Muslim plains and cities, but the literary revivalists wagered that public life would draw a separation between religion and politics. This was Hawi's wager in the mid-1950s as well.

Through and through, Hawi was an exacting, uncompromising man (he said he owed this to the work of the bricklayer and stonemason, for that craft demanded no less from its practitioners); he needed that reconciliation between his loyalty to his village and to Lebanon and this wider Arab calling if he was to go on. He found it in the Arabic language and in Gibran and the other literary revivalists who came out of that proud country in Mount Lebanon to master—and modernize—the classical Arabic tradition. "I was excessive, nearly violent in my poetry and in my sense of belonging to an Arab renaissance," Khalil Hawi told one interviewer. He was severe and unforgiving, he said, with those in Arab political life who thought that the Muslims were natural claimants to an "Arab calling." He thought of himself as an "authentic Arab"; he conceded Muslims no advantage over him; he pitied some of the educated Muslims who were sure that their Islam gave them a superior claim to the truth of the culture.

Hawi came back from Cambridge to literary fame, secured for him by his first collection, *Nahr al-Ramad* (River of Ashes), and by its centerpiece poem, "The Bridge." His place at the university had been altered by the Cambridge degree; the marginal existence was now behind him. He could look forward to a permanent appointment on the faculty. He had chronicled a literary renaissance in Arabic letters, he had prophesied good tidings for "the East," and he could see in his own life an unfolding of these larger themes. He had worked hard and had been rewarded. He had put together a professional life, and he had the campus, the neighborhood of the university, and the haunts of the intellectual class around the university. His material needs were simple. He moved into a quiet neighborhood off Jeanne d'Arc Street, a short walk from the campus, in Ras

Beriut, the self-styled Anglo-Saxon sector of the city, with its snack bars and Americanized ways. The furniture in his flat was old and basic; he was without telephone or central heating. By the measure of what he lived through and where he had been, this monkish existence was all the comfort he needed. His home was full of books, the gardens of the university were there for him, as was the beach nearby, which he loved.

Hawi was never to marry. This alone would set him apart in a country and a culture that sanctified family life. No doubt this was a choice that pained his parents. He was their eldest, and they were country people, and to them marriage was the rounding out of an adult life. Only "odd" people, it was believed, peculiar people with terrible secrets, chose the single life in the culture of the time. He chose to remain unencumbered and alone. He walked away from his relation with Daisy al-Amir. All he would say now was that the "gossip of women in Beirut" had separated them. He offered as well another lame justification: poetry and the torments of poetry. A poet committed to the cause of a "great cultural renewal," he said, was intrinsically unable to give marriage the attention it deserved. No woman, he added, could compete with the call of his poetry.

The break between Hawi and Daisy al-Amir came in 1962. He sealed it in a letter to her in December of that year. He circled the old, familiar evasions:

> I only decided to sever what was between us when I became convinced that the life of marriage and family is forever denied me. My physician advised a tough regimen for my stomach ailments before I could ever think of marriage. Marriage requires things I do not have—temperament, ambition and money that should be plentiful. . . . I was tempted to lean on you and your strength to go on, but I thought that honor required that I let you go.

A better sense of Khalil's frame of mind was supplied by his brother, Iliya, in *Nabhan,* the novel that he wove out of his brother's life. In the fiction, Nabhan says of himself: "I was not made to be a

ment. The modern defeat of the pan-Arab dispensation that he had
taken to was like falling through trap doors to a bottomless past.

"Let me know if Arab unity is achieved; if I am dead, send someone to my graveside to tell me of it when it is realized," Hawi had
said on one occasion. He must have known that it was idle to build
an edifice as large, as impossible as that. It was the more intimate
ordeal of his country, his city, and his ancestral village that would
engage and torment him in his final years. It was one thing to praise
the dawn of a new era for the people of "the East" but quite another
to deal with the dirty war that played itself out in his land. It was
past poetry and philosophy and texts now: the warlords, militias,
checkpoints, and communal massacres were to become the stuff of
daily life.

Grant Hawi this: He was never taken in by that war or by the
ideological pretenses that draped this dirty war at the beginning. He
remained at odds with the two projects that fought it out over
Lebanon: the Palestinian leftist scheme that sought to push the old
order in Lebanon into its grave; and the "Lebanese," principally
Maronite, defense of the land's sovereignty and of the old order. He
could not be taken in by the Palestinian leftist scheme, being at heart
a man of Shweir and of the hills. A loyal son of the land, he could
not indulge those who were cavalier about Lebanon and its distinct
political culture, who saw Lebanon only as a base for a Palestinian
campaign against Israel. The Palestinian poet Mahmoud Darwish
may have hailed the nobility of Hawi's suicide, but Darwish, who
had come to Lebanon from Israel in the early 1970s, was part of a
new Palestinian bid for power in Lebanon. Darwish did not have to
mourn the fate of this Lebanese earth. It was not his homeland, and
the Palestinian decade in Lebanon (1970–1982) had been good to
him. He was part of the apparatus of the Palestine Liberation Organization. He and others like him—Palestinians and Lebanese
alike, who rode this Palestinian wave until it broke—could look at
that decade as a time of fulfillment and success. Their politics were
ascendant around the AUB and its neighborhood. They had the un-
divided attention of the Arab world and the conviction that some-

known, and intuited plenty along the way. In time, he grew embarrassed by the optimism of his most famous poem, "The Bridge." He
refrained from reading it in public; he wanted it forgotten. That
bridge to the future, he said with great bitterness, turned out to be
a "bridge made of paper." It could not support those who wanted
to cross it and was best burned and forgotten.

A premonition of doom ran through his work. The men and
women hailing him as the voice of a new Arab generation and the
expositor of a different kind of reality should not have missed the
despair. His personal climb had been too high and too steep. He had
arrived, but the journey had broken him. The ride with Anton
Saadah and Syrian nationalism had taken its toll. True, he had conceded that the course of Saadah was impractical, but Saadah had
been his first hero and idol. The uncompromising life Saadah led
and his solitary death for the cause he believed in forever haunted
his followers. In a land of deals and bargains, Saadah had struck no
bargain with the dominant order. Gifted young men who had followed Saadah but had gone on to success and respectability—and
safety—were never free of his memory; his tale stalked them in the
years after his death. "I believed in Saadah with all my senses and
convictions; for me he was the leader and the hero and the ideal
father. I loved and respected no other man. He shall remain thus
to me," Hisham Sharabi wrote of Saadah in a memoir written a
quarter-century after Saadah's execution, after his years in America.
No one who had been at Saadah's side managed to shake free from
the cult of the man. Hawi, we know, had seen Saadah as a Christ-
like figure: the devotion, the mildness of manners, the personal austerity, then the fitting death. It was one thing to give up on the party
that Saadah had left behind, to concede that the political authorities
were determined to snuff it out and that one was safer under the
banners of the pan-Arab national movement, and quite another to
bury the ghost of Saadah once and for all. By the time the Arab national movement ran aground in 1967 with its defeat in the Six Day
War, Hawi had become an old hand at the politics of disappoint-

publications in an orchard near his home. He was lucky, for he was indeed searched on his way down from Shweir.

It was easy for a man with Hawi's intellect to see that this political tug-of-war between a sterile political order and hopeless rebellions was not his world or his cause. Poetry was a nobler calling, truer to his temperament and to his innate pessimism about the human condition in his land. He alternated between periods of great productivity and times when he felt, as he described it, an enmity toward his paper and pen. But he became what he had willed himself to be: a cult poet working at the frontiers of the Arabic ode. A surprisingly keen observer of his poetry, his physician, Nasib Hammam (a relative of his, himself a man of Shweir) said that Hawi's poetic voice was a cross between Isaiah prophesying good tidings, "Arise, shine; for your light has come," and Jeremiah foretelling the fierce anger of the Lord and the ruin of nations.

Although he had emerged into the spotlight with a celebrated poem bearing the promise of an Arab rebirth, jeremiads, it must be said, were truer to Hawi's inner core. Deep down, he was a pessimist and a "warner" of dangers to come. An unforgiving streak of moralism lay at the core of his being. He expected his country and his adopted city to be more "virtuous" than they could afford. His was a country of trade, Beirut a city of a thousand compromises and poses, its ruling passion commerce and the traffic in worldly things. He must have despaired of remaking so wily and burdened a land. This is from his first published collection, *Nahr al-Ramad* (River of Ashes).

> *We are from Beirut, alas, we were born*
> *With borrowed faces and with borrowed minds.*
> *Our thoughts are born whores in the market places,*
> *Then spend their lives pretending to be virgins.*

Hawi wrote this early in his sojourn. Never had there been any triumphalism even in the most optimistic of his work. He had seen, life and a public possession. The new poets were done with the classical form and its hegemony. To the old, honored medium they brought the urgency and restlessness of their time. The *Qasida,* the ode with its familiar meter, gave way to free verse.

The voice and needs of the poet now dominated the work. The poetry was taken, as it were, from the ancestors and claimed by a new breed of poets. In the *Qasida* of old, which had come from the Arabian Peninsula, it had been the standard practice for the poet to begin his work by lamenting the traces of his beloved's encampment in the desert; the new poets would dispose of this former practice. Whereas poetry had once praised princes and patrons, it now yielded to and contained the anxieties of an urbanized generation searching for its own bearings in the world. Innovators like Hawi, Adonis, Qabbani, and Bayati were through with the cultural forms and prohibitions of the past. The spread of literacy and the mass politics of nationalism, the growing role of women in public life and the steady assault on the restrictive sexual mores of the dominant culture, provided the new literature with public space and with protection. Whereas fiction seemed to be the medium of the Egyptians in the late 1950s and 1960s, poetry was the medium of choice in Beirut and the wider lands of the Fertile Crescent.

Hawi gave poetry everything he had. More than a decade after the death of Saadah, he had been released from the political grip of Syrian nationalism and from the political romance of his youth. He had one close brush with disaster. Saadah's followers attempted a hopeless *coup d'état* against the Lebanese state in December 1961. The state and the army crushed the rebellion, and in a familiar drill thousands of the party's members were rounded up and imprisoned. Hawi knew that he was under suspicion, that state security had kept a file on him. He was in his village on the night of upheaval, and he had in his possession party publications that he valued and wanted to keep. Fearing that Shweir was a marked place sure to be searched by the police, he wanted to take the publications to his office at the university. His mother protested, certain that there would be checkpoints on the road to Beirut. Hawi burned the al-Bayati. The Palestinian literati were a case apart. They were in full force here; this had become a home for them: the poets Fayiz Suyyagh and Tawfiq Sayigh, the literary critic and scholar Ihsan Abbas, and so on. There would come, in time, some literary men from the Arabian Peninsula as well, writers who wanted greater cultural and political liberty than their austere land permitted. Beirut made room for them, and they in turn gave the city a bright new role in Arabic letters.

An old political and cultural tradition was under attack in the late 1950s and early 1960s: the authority of the oligarchs and political notables and the dominant style of literary expression—the flowery language, the formal poetry correct in its mechanics but disconnected from the stuff of everyday life, hiding and repressing the writer's spirit and voice. Hawi and his peers hacking away at the literary and political symbols of their elders were confident that the battle over literature was nothing less than a battle for the Arab future. The air was filled with this kind of heady conviction as well as a supreme delusion about the ease with which cultures could be undone and remade. Bands of poets and writers congregated around literary organs that preached all kinds of political attachments. The pan-Arabists wrote their poetry, fiction, and essays in the monthly al-Adab (where Hawi, too, put out a good deal of his work); the literati who saw themselves as children of Lebanon and the Mediterranean set out to write free and experimental verse in a new organ of their own, Shi'r, which the young poets Adonis and Yusuf al-Khal of the Lebanese city of Tripoli had launched in 1957.

Poetry, it has been said, was to the Arabs what philosophy was to the Greeks, law to the Romans, and art to the Persians: the repository and purest expression of their distinctive spirit. Easy to transport, composed to be recited in public, the classical pattern of Arabic poetry had held for centuries. There were set limits on rhyme and rhythmic pattern and limits as well on subject matter. Formal and stylized, the poetry had been less a personal statement of the poet's spirit and temperament than an expression of old ideas in striking new forms, a thoroughly social medium, a creature of court father or a family man. A man begets children and a family if he is a friend of life, but I am life's enemy; there is little in it that appeals to me. I want to turn the world upside down. He who marries gets domesticated. . . . I want to stay on the run, a fugitive."

For Khalil, his parents and his younger siblings were enough family life. He claimed (though this was denied by his brother Iliya) that he was carrying the financial burden of his family, that he was seeing them through, that he even sent them money when he was on his scholarship in England. Whatever the truth, he could see movement, success, and education in his family. (Iliya would make a literary name for himself in time; another brother, Sami, would become a philosophy professor and make his way to an academic career in Milwaukee, Wisconsin.) He had willed himself into a better place, and his example and some material help from him had carried his family out of the world of manual labor.

The Hawis were hardly alone. Their country was doing well. In the 1960s Hawi could see progress around him in his homeland: new money remaking the land, touching the lives, as with a magic wand, of growing numbers of his countrymen. And there was a stirring in the cultural world. Journalism and the life of letters were in ferment. Beirut was the beneficiary of the coming-to-power of the military officer corps and the ideologues in Syria, Iraq, and Egypt. Every time these lands banished a dissident or a daring writer, the dissident turned up in Beirut. This was a house of many doors, as an Iraqi exile who landed in Beirut said of the city of his refuge. Men and women of independent temperament made their way there. From Syria came literary figures who would remake and modernize Arabic verse: Nizar Qabbani, the poet of romance; and Adonis (the pen name of Ali Ahmad Said), a young poet and critic destined to tower over his contemporaries and to write some of the deepest inquiries into the sources of Arabic and Islamic literary traditions. From the whirlwind of Iraqi politics and the violent revolts that hacked at the foundations of that unfortunate land came poets of unmistakable genius: Buland Haidari and Abdul al-Wahhab thing grand was being hatched in this "Arab commune" in West Beirut.

This was not a ride Hawi could take. He felt great pity for his country and its people. In the remembrance of him left by his brother Iliya, the poet had seen in the bread lines and economic hardships that came with this war a replay of what had befallen this land in its calamitous years of famine and hardship shortly before his birth. Hawi's sense of Lebanese patriotism, his brother writes, was offended by the play of things in south Lebanon, by the country's loss of sovereignty over that part of its territory in the escalating fight between Israelis and Palestinians. The injustice was galling to him: his country as the setting for a wider Arab–Israeli conflict that larger Arab powers were determined to spare their own people.

To this conflict, then, he brought the sentiments of a man of Lebanon betrayed by the cynicism of the Arab world toward Lebanon and its ordeal. He could not see his country as a laboratory for the wars of others or sanction a war on its land as a battle for some hazy Arab future. Some intellectuals, writers, and pamphleteers in Beirut spoke in such terms, but he could not partake of their politics. His country and its social peace mattered greatly to him. The fierce moralism at the core of his being was offended by this war in his country. It must have seemed odd to him (there is ample confirmation of this in his brother's biography of him) that this most fragile of Arab countries, a land with a strong Christian presence, had been left to suffer for an Arab fight that other Arabs had lost the willingness to prosecute.

However, Hawi kept his distance as well from the Maronite militias that had taken up arms to defend the independence of Lebanon and its traditional role as a haven for its Christian communities. To Bayati, who saw him in the midst of this war when he came to Beirut for a literary conference (the city maintained this duality of things; the literary conferences and the massacres side by side), Hawi railed against the protagonists, condemned them as mercenaries one and all who had embarked on a grand betrayal of the country. His wrath took in all the armed camps. "Tragedy," he said, "has befallen us; it is everywhere among us, in our cities and our streets, in every nook and cranny." He reserved his deepest anger and scorn for the writers and pundits who threw their support to the combatants. In a country claimed by armed camps, he remained alienated and unconvinced.

Early on in this war, in 1976, he divined the drift of events to come. He looked for a way out of the country, took a one-year leave from the university, and sought a reprieve in distant Wisconsin. His nerves were on edge; he did not take to the city's division along sectarian lines, between predominantly Muslim West Beirut and a Christian enclave in the eastern part of the city. He found it hard to put up with the swagger of the militiamen and their checkpoints. He could never submit to their requests for ID cards and their harassment without drawn-out arguments. He even quarreled with the gunmen of Anton Saadah's party near his home in West Beirut. A band of gunmen had overheard him belittling their leaders while he was using the phone in a shop on his street. It had taken the intervention of those leaders who had known him and known his ties to Saadah to call off the boys with the guns. The journey to Wisconsin offered a temporary escape.

Wisconsin could not heal him, though. The flat land, the long winter, and the frozen landscape chilled his soul. It was of this alienation and of this time and place that he would write in his collection, *al-Ra'd al-Jarih* (The Wounded Thunder).

> *He got used to a solemn, frozen wilderness,*
> *Across the road, he saw impenetrable faces.*
> *With the spring he was greeted with fragile buds*
> *He wept for the scent of the young dark-skinned children.*
> *His tears burned,*
> *And the condemned man gathered himself to return home.*
> *He will not spend his final years in the depths of this exile.*

His country's war—dirtier, crueler, and more disillusioning by the day—would be awaiting him upon his return. Khalil may not have been a dutiful son of the Greek Orthodox church, but something in his dilemma in this civil war bespoke his wider community's dilemma. The wars of Lebanon—at once a civil, communal war between Muslims and Christians, a Palestinian–Lebanese war, and a proxy Arab–Israeli war fought in that most helpless and impossible of countries—had left the Greek Orthodox in no-man's-land. This was a fight the Greek Orthodox could not win. The cause of Lebanon had been claimed by the Maronites; the cause of Palestine and the Arabism of Lebanon was a prescription for the unmaking of Lebanon. The rage of the poet and loner was in part an expression of his community's unease about its fate. The Greek Orthodox had done well by Beirut; it had belonged to them and the Sunnis before the Maronites and the Shia had converged on it in more recent times. The Greek Orthodox had done well by the "ambiguity" of Lebanon at the crossroads of causes, attachments, and larger powers. They could now read the wind: They were destined to lose out in the new order of things, the new world of militias, warlords, and armed boys.

Nor did Hawi feel at one with the university that had given him his chance and a way out of his difficult past. His had been no easy journey; the ways of professional academic life had been hard to assimilate. The campus of this university was open to talent, but this was a city of the Levant, where pedigree and social background were of great importance. He could not fake the ease of his peers or fall back on their sense of entitlement. He was always aware of his *otherness*. Underneath the veneer (and reality) of an American academic institution lay the facts of social and economic class. The university mirrored these old facts: it was a citadel of the Arab bourgeoisie. A child of the poorer classes could slip through the gates, but *nasab*, genealogy, the influence of a man's pedigree on his condition, made no bow to modernity. *Nasab* was one of the great pillars of Arab social life; this alien university could not reinvent the setting in which it was based, nor did it desire to do so. Where Khalil Hawi had come to this university alone, through the unlikeliest of routes, he was surrounded by colleagues who had hailed from easier backgrounds and whose world had always accommodated them.

There were four members of the Jerusalemite Khalidi family (three of them brothers) on the faculty of the university. The three Khalidi brothers were sons of Ahmad Khalidi, an educator with an impeccable reputation who in the 1930s and 1940s had headed Al-Kulliyah al-Arabiyya, the Arab College, an elite collegiate institution in Jerusalem. A pioneer of modern education and himself a graduate of the AUB who translated the works of Freud, Ahmad Khalidi had been an exemplary member of the Jerusalem aristocracy: noblesse oblige, a life of public service, an insatiable love of knowledge and research. The best and brightest of Palestinian youth had passed through Ahmad Khalidi's college; his students revered him for his rectitude and devotion to his work. When he succumbed to premature death in Lebanon, shortly after the 1948 war and the loss of his world in Jerusalem, he was busy laying the foundations of a charitable school for the Palestinian refugees in Lebanon. To his sons had passed this legacy and the confidence that came with it.

The maternal lineage of two of the Khalidi brothers (the eldest was born to an earlier marriage) closed the circle. Their mother, Anbara Salam, belonged to Muslim Beirut's leading aristocratic merchant family; she had translated works of Virgil and Homer and had been an outspoken advocate of education and enhanced social and political rights for women. She had known an unusually cultured life. The Salam household in West Beirut was for all practical purposes a court of Beiruti public life. Anbara's father, Salim Ali Salam, had been a mayor of Beirut, perhaps the dominant Muslim politician and philanthropist of the city in the interwar years. Anbara's younger brother, Saeb, had risen to the heights of political power, serving several times as prime minister of the country and with an unbroken record of primacy in Beirut's politics. He was the Egyptian leader Gamal Abdul Nasser's man in Lebanon and a political figure of great poise and authority. The administrators who ran the affairs of the AUB needed and courted his goodwill. They called on him when student strikes got out of hand and when lecturers landed in trouble for running afoul of religious or political strictures. His nephews on the faculty of the university were the inheritors of a secure sense of place.

The Khalidis were exceptionally privileged, to be sure, but there were others, including the two Khalafs, Samir and Nadim, twin brothers, one a professor of sociology and the other of economics. Also on the faculty of his department was a distinguished historian of Lebanon, Kamal Salibi. Three generations of Salibis, converts to Protestantism, had been associated with the university. Kamal Salibi's grandfather had been in the medical school of the university back in 1882 and had taken part in a student rebellion dubbed the "Darwin affair," which had pitted the students of the medical department and a handful of liberal-minded teachers against the custodians of the university. A storm had broken out over creationism when a band of students mourned the death of Charles Darwin and hailed him in a scientific journal as the "most learned of this age and the most famous of its men." The evangelical missionaries who financed and ran the place drew the line: Darwin and his theories were intolerable in an institution of theirs. The medical students persevered; a copy of the Ottoman state medical certificate awarded Kamal Salibi's grandfather hung on the wall of his grandson's study. Three decades later, another Salibi, Kamal's father, served as assistant college physician. An outsider, a stonemason's son, was never fully at ease here.

Some months before his death, Hawi was appointed to a prestigious chair in Arabic, the Jewett chair, which a Harvard Arabist, James R. Jewett, had endowed in 1929 in honor of his wife, but this vindication did not console him. He had to be talked into accepting the appointment. The honor had come too late in his career and in his life. He made a point—vintage Khalil Hawi—of refusing a ceremony to invest him with the chair. After the death and retirement of colleagues and mentors he had known in better days, after the depletion of the faculty's ranks since the outbreak of the war in the country in 1975, he had drifted away from the university. He had nothing but scorn for the clique that ran it, had not cared for the courses he was assigned, and had even talked of suing the university over his pay. The tormenting pride he had carried into this new setting never left him. A man who told the university administrators that he would always be known for his poetry and that university teaching would be only a footnote to his life in poetry was destined to be an outsider who never took to the placid ways of the professional life and never made his peace with the culture and privilege of the AUB.

Written sources are discreet and polite on this matter, but a fault line had opened and grown wider by the day between the Lebanese and the Palestinians at this American institution. We glimpse this in the memoirs of Hawi's colleague and contemporary in the Arabic department, the Palestinian scholar Ihsan Abbas. An appointment to a chair in Semitic languages—the old chair of Hawi's mentor, Anis Frayha—became the occasion for a battle between the "Lebanonists" and the Palestinians. The latter prevailed and brought one of their own from England for this chair. The poet railing about his standing in the university was at once a man of perpetual marginality and a son of the land, a nativist, who had wanted Lebanon for its own. Gone were the heady days of an Arab renaissance and the poetry about children of the Nile and the Euphrates cleansing themselves from the sins of the past. His country was aflame, and he wailed for it.

Again, it is Iliya Hawi's work of fiction that takes us into this territory. Nabhan is above all a man of his birthplace; he wants Lebanon for its own, as a sovereign, final homeland. "I want a country and a homeland which belongs to itself from the beginning to the end," Nabhan says in defining his creed, as he battles the powers and takes to the road, a rebel determined to awaken his people. His was a hard battle, Nabhan knew. His country had always been a land for hire, its people had bent with the wind, foreign armies and foreign consulates and lords had toyed with its destiny. Such a land was hard to liberate. In a despairing moment, Nabhan sees into his people's dependence and into the ruinous way in which they have brought outsiders into their lives:

> You cannot avenge *ahl al-balad,* the people of the country; they died of their own free will, no one killed them. Cowardly and selfish, a people of small gains and horizons who hide behind the shutters of their windows, who close their eyes when they should look, who speak only to gossip. Such people cannot be avenged. The revenge I seek is for my own soul, so that I do not fall into the depths of despair, so that I could cleanse myself of my sins and my compromises.

In the retrospective of Hawi, it came to light that he had been teaching on the side at the state-run Lebanese University, a world removed from the privilege of the AUB. He had taught there for no remuneration and had quarreled with AUB's administrators, who wanted him to sever his connection with the other institution. He felt at home with the students of the Lebanese University, an affinity of social and economic class. They gave of themselves freely to education and knowledge, he said of the students of modest means who attended the Lebanese University; he welcomed them at his home in the presence of his aged mother with her village ways. He rid this small circle of disciples of the awe they felt for the American University, of the sense of inadequacy with which they approached it. "With Khalil," one of them wrote, "we began to enter the university with confidence; we would join him there in the cafeteria or the classroom or the library or for a walk in the gardens; we would read to him what we had written, and we would take in what he had to say."

A cultural tide had carried Hawi from his village and his manual labor to university life in Beirut and Cambridge. A vast world had opened up to him. In his early years as an academic, he wrote of that cultural tide, of the educational awakening among Arabs, with painstaking detail and veritable awe. He had been attentive and respectful, perhaps bedazzled, by what the pioneers in Arabic letters and thought had accomplished, but this faith deserted him toward the end. The tradition that had sustained him—the literary tradition he had chronicled, the Islamic philosophy he had come to master—had been unable to prevent the culture's descent into hell; he became increasingly dismissive of what the preceding century in Arabic culture and political thought had produced. He had exalted the modernists in Arabic letters and politics and had labored in their shadow. He now wrote off what they had brought from the West and tried to graft onto indigenous culture as nothing but mimicry, the stale effort of those who had carried from the West only "those things that were superficial and easy to carry." That whole Arab awakening, he was to write in an essay two years before his death, had been a pretense that had "covered up the total backwardness of Arab society." The modernists, he said, had not understood the West itself, let alone laid the foundations for a viable Arab renaissance. From distant Western shores these claimants had brought only those "colored empty sea-shells that the tide brings to shore." The society had traded its old forms of backwardness for new ones. Old habits of domination, old ways of political thinking, had simply donned new masks. And political men and women had become good at *taqiyya*, dissimulation, hiding what they really thought, in the process hiding their society from genuine scrutiny and assessment. In the "modern" political movements littering the landscape, he saw nothing but the hold of old "tribal, sectarian, and clannish loyalties."

As Hawi grew severe in his judgment of the age of Arab enlightenment, he fell back on a metaphor from the building trade and his days as a bricklayer. It was harder, he had learned, to build on the foundations of an old house than to build a new one from scratch. The cultural and political order was stubborn and had proven impossible to repair. The dream of doing away with the old foundations—the dream that must have been imparted to him in his youth by his hero, Anton Saadah, and the dream that had played on the minds of many of his peers in the intellectual world—was shown to be the unrealistic idea it had been all along.

Private shame, public shame. Hawi brought them together, the shame of his country made into his own, the shame of the Arab world turned into something deeply personal. It was hubris and pride in part, and personal escape into public politics as well. A level-headed friend (his physician) told him that his personal share of this great Arab shame was a trifle, that the shame covered everyone, but this modesty was not in him. Iliya Hawi's fictional hero, Nabhan, speaks for the poet when he addresses a fickle crowd of his countrymen: "I want to tell you that public shame is more searing than private shame. You feel shame if your houses were not adequately furnished, if you lacked proper clothes, but you feel no shame when a ruler comes your way with a different language and different features, when your leaders watch every breath you take."

In his sober moments, this Nabhan knows the folly of this pretense, the hubris of this claim. "I am Nabhan, I am only responsible for my private shame; as for the shame of my country, they are all, out there, responsible for it. . . . My share of this public shame is only a millionth of it." But the modesty does not prevail. "Revenge," Nabhan says in fatalism and self-flagellation, "is not a natural thing, it is like love and hate, it forms in the soul, of its own free will."

Writing of Kahlil Gibran, Hawi observed: "He is one of those figures in the history of literature who, for one reason or another, invite more comments on their lives than on their achievements." This was to become true of Khalil Hawi as well. The modern Arab condition was to be read into his journey. The distinguished Iraqi poet Abdul al-Wahhab al-Bayati, who first met Hawi in the mid-1950s and remained close to him, exalted Hawi's suicide as a heroic deed. When a nation is unable to repel its invaders, "the source of its misery," it is fitting, he wrote, that a great poet become a "sacrificial lamb." For Bayati, this death was but a "signal" that this dark Arab time had begun to change, that a "new Arab people" were about to be born. In a prose poem written from exile in Madrid in early 1983, Bayati mourned his friend:

When the poet killed himself
his great journey began
And his vision
shone bright in the sea
when his cry penetrated
the kingdom of exile
The people
coming from the Desert
have stepped forth,
Destroying the gods of clay
Building the kingdom of God.

"He died and took his secret with him," Daisy al-Amir wrote of Hawi. She had no desire to settle old scores with him, but in a remembrance of him at once serene, forgiving, and honest, she stepped away from the political eulogies to illuminate the man himself. A man who had been a finicky dresser, careful about his looks and attire, had begun to let himself go. He had loved his cigarettes, was addicted to smoking, but had given it up toward the end: another small deed of self-punishment and denial. He had grown increasingly embittered about his place in the world of letters, convinced that the world of letters had forgotten him, that his signature poem, "The Bridge," no longer moved or held his readers. "When I think back on the poem, I feel great sadness. I gave them my life, but they left me behind. If they still remembered the poem, they only did so in passing," he had said of his readers. A proud man, he had insisted that he had no interest in fame or public acclaim, but she knew him and she knew better.

Before his deep depression set in, Daisy al-Amir invited him for a reading of his poetry at the Iraqi Cultural Center in Beirut. He had begun to stay away from all literary gatherings and conferences, but she gave it a try and was surprised when he agreed. The reading was a brilliant success; a vast crowd turned out for this evening dedicated to his poetry, overflowing the hall in which he read, and he was thrilled by the enthusiasm of his audience. All was well in the world, he told Daisy, and he was glad to be reminded of that. She had hoped that the success of that evening might turn him around, but he slipped back into his depression and loneliness.

Khalil was a creature of habit, Daisy al-Amir wrote. The civil war, in full fury since 1975, had robbed him of the comfort of familiar things: "The restaurants he knew had shut down, so had the barber who cut his hair, as had the man who ironed and cleaned his clothes. . . . Beirut had become a city of frightening ghosts." More important, the war, the checkpoints, and the turfs that came with the war denied him access to his beloved village. Khalil had bounced back from his first suicide attempt, or so it seemed; he claimed that he had been surprised by the love of his family and friends. But he had not found his way and he had cracked. "They now attribute his suicide to the accumulation of Arab defeats and setbacks. Yes, Khalil was a faithful poet and a patriot, but was he not human, did he not have a personal life? Has any Arab official killed himself or tried to? Why should Khalil have taken it upon himself to bear the burden of these officials?" Not for this independent woman were the comforts of nationalism. Every man, she said, was "his own planet" with his own concerns. Khalil was perhaps right, she added, when he wrote that he had fed the birds from his threshing floors. There now hovered around him "birds" of every kind: They had come to feed off the legacy he left behind.

In the months preceding his death, Khalil Hawi spoke of his loss of faith in the written word and in poetry. He had given up on writing: "What can we write about this time of decline in culture and politics in our Arab world today?" There was nothing to say; the sycophants and hucksters in politics and letters were multiplying day by day. "Manhood" and honor had been lost, he told a colleague, Najib Saab, who saw him the day before he died. Over and over again he spoke of suicide as a sane response to the ills of his city, his land, and his craft. He spoke of a dramatic suicide and said that he had been tempted to kill himself in the middle of Hamra

Street, West Beirut's smart shopping street, not far from his home, a short walk from the campus of his university, to express his rage at the swindle that was Lebanon's public life and at the cynicism of the other Arabs feeding the flames of Beirut. He had held back because he feared that his deed was sure to be dismissed as the "exhibitionism" of a man who needed and craved attention. He found a perfect occasion for his death: he would depart as his people's tribune. He awed his peers, the men and women of the secular enlightenment, and left them mourning him and grieving for their world. They had hailed him when their world looked open and full of promise; they now conceded him the truth and nobility of his silence. He broke his mother's heart (she would survive him for eight long years), but it was, the eulogists said, for something larger than a mother's grief.

Hawi's had been an Odyssean journey. "When I first knew him," the critic Jamil Jabr wrote in appreciation, "he was a laborer in the building trade and a balladeer, *zaggal,* with plaster on his shoes. Then he came to see me in the mid-1950s, a university instructor preparing a dissertation on Gibran, and I provided him with some documents." Hawi had known manual labor and Cambridge, public acclaim and solitude. In his ear he could hear his mother's wisdom right alongside all those books he had crammed. He had fallen for Syrian nationalism, for pan-Arabism, only to return to his love of Lebanon. He had foretold glad tidings, then warned of terrible calamities. Along the way, he had found a sheltering cove, but he could not take to the peace of this shelter. He loved the image of his own doom, lived with it, and brought about its fulfillment. Iliya Hawi's Nabhan is again the tragic hero's true reflection. He toys with normalcy, with the idea of living "like the others," prospering "like the others," but that safe outcome is not for him. A lover who knows and understands this tormented Nabhan well tells him of his destiny: "You will not be like the others. You are cursed. Demons rage within you, you shall be marked for sorrow, there is no escape for you."

Hawi went far only to find a great darkness. No wonder a large number of literate Arabs read into him the torments of Arab modernity. On the other side of the manual labor of his father, the desolation that his aged and wise mother had seen during those years of famine and calamity, on the other side of a public Arab history given to moments of exaltation, he found a brand-new hell. He (and many others of his generation) read all those books, but to no avail. A nemesis lay in wait for them. The world was not to be found in those foreign texts after all. Their modernity had been a false promise. That dawn—Hawi wrote in one of his darker volumes of verse, *Wounded Thunder* (1979)—ushered in a "strange morning." The sun had reversed its orbit and risen in the West. He wept for himself and for that "Arab nation" whose salvation he had so much wanted to see:

> *How heavy is the shame,*
> *do I bear it alone?*
> *Am I the only one to cover my face with ashes?*
> *The funerals that the morning announces*
> *echo in the funerals at dusk.*
> *There is nothing over the horizon,*
> *save for the smoke of black embers.*

"This Arab age is not an age of poetry. It is no wonder the poet killed himself," Samira Khouri, a colleague of Hawi, wrote in tribute to him. This was the kind of eulogy he would have wanted for himself. "You remained pure and unsullied by this era of expulsions and the whip and the assassinations and the hired word," she said addressing him. There, too, this eulogist was close to where this son of the Mountain had placed himself in the decade of senseless bloodletting unleashed on his homeland.

In "Lazarus 1962," a poem that broke with the optimism of his old signature poem, "The Bridge," Hawi gave voice to a great despair from which there was no escape. (This translation is Adnan

Haydar's and Michael Beard's; Tyrian red is a Phoenician dye that was adopted and used extensively by the Romans.)

> *The damned vision shall not fade*
> *Even if masked with veils of "Tyrian red."*
> *I cried; I was a walking corpse*
> *Adrift in city streets.*
> *The thronging crowds are chewed by flaming wheels.*
> *Who am I to protect them from the rage*
> *of fitful eddies and of gulping flames?*
> *Deepen the pit, gravedigger,*
> *Deepen it to bottomless depths.*

In the years to come there were endless testimonies from the many who had seen him in his final days. They recalled, preserved, worked over, and squeezed every word and gesture of the man—a handsome man of medium build and broad shoulders, with dark wavy hair on the sides, a man pacing the gardens of his university, politely warding off offers of companionship and uttering dire predictions of greater ruin to come. His students recalled him as an exacting, intense teacher, his trademark worry beads in hand, meticulously going through his favorite literary and philosophical texts. They said of him that his good graces never left him, even toward the end of his life. A chronicler who came forth to speak of him more than a dozen years after his suicide (in a book in Arabic, published in Sweden, written by an author living in France), the young Palestinian journalist Mahmoud Shurayh, said that the poet had interrupted one of his angry monologues about the end of everything Arab to tell him to take better care of himself and had offered to help him with some money to get his teeth fixed.

One of Hawi's students, Jihad al-Turk, recalled that it was he, in the gardens of the university in the early evening hours of June 6, who had told the poet of Israel's invasion and that Hawi had covered his face in despair, bade him farewell after inquiring of the few details about the invasion that were known at that time of day. Two old friends of Hawi ran into the poet after that, and they talked of the big news of the day. Hawi was angry and bitter, these two men said. For him, the invasion was a "stain of shame on the country's being." Then, by their accounts, he left the university through its main gate, heading in the direction of Bliss Street, "alone and broken."

The man's trail was then picked up by a fellow poet, a relative on his maternal side, Shafiq Ataya, who invited Hawi to his place. On the way to Ataya's home, Hawi recited some lines of his poem "Lazarus"—he knew the poem by heart—and said, in elaboration, that he had found it impossible to "awaken the Arabs from their deep sleep." He then listened to the evening broadcast and railed once more about the Arab state of affairs and about the homeland. The two poets then walked the streets of their neighborhood for another hour before parting company.

We know what happened next. All those details have been preserved as well in the account of the journalist Mahmoud Shurayh and in countless other renditions of Hawi's last days. Some ninety minutes later, at 10:30 at night, Khalil Hawi took his hunting rifle and shot himself in the head on his balcony, which overlooked the sea and the AUB clock tower. He fell beside a favorite jasmine plant. No neighbor bothered with the sound of the shotgun: Bullets and explosives had been Beirut's standard noise for more than seven years, and this was an evening of war.

Hawi's body was discovered in the morning. His neighbors had seen it from balconies overlooking his. Umm Khalil, Khalil's mother, was the first to arrive at the scene of sorrow. When she saw her *bikr* (first-born), the old mother, one chronicler writes, let out a "shriek of horror that tore through a sky covered with planes overhead attacking Beirut." Two men of the literary vocation, friends of old, one of them the poet with whom Hawi had walked the streets of the neighborhood the night before, rushed there as well. One of them thought he saw a little deed of grace, a final act of thoughtfulness from Khalil toward his mother: He shot himself, this friend said, in a corner of the balcony, by the drain, making sure that his mother would be spared the grim task of cleaning up her beloved son's blood.

Postscript: *The Murder of Malcolm Kerr*

Eighteen months after the suicide of Khalil Hawi, death touched the campus of the AUB again; this time, it was an American Arabist, Malcolm Kerr, the president of the university. He was shot and killed on January 18, 1984. Unknown assailants shot him in the head while he was on his way to his office. This was no ordinary American visitor or someone passing through; he was born in Beirut in 1931, in the very hospital where he was pronounced dead. He was an intimate stranger, this city a home of sorts for him. His father, Stanley Kerr, had served as a professor of biochemistry at the AUB, his mother, Elsa, as the university's dean of women. Stanley and Elsa Kerr had stayed in Lebanon for nearly forty years. And it was in Lebanon that Malcolm met his future wife, Ann Zwicker of California, a co-ed who had come to Beirut in 1954, wide-eyed and full of wonder, for her junior year abroad.

For Kerr, the child of Presbyterian educators, the AUB presidency had been the stuff of dreams. It was his fate that this gift had come his way in 1982, in the midst of a terrible Israeli–Palestinian war fought in Lebanon in the summer of that year, after seven years of ruin and bloodletting in the country. He had come into that dream appointment when the American presence in Lebanon had become a matter of great controversy. Guilt for the "green light" America had given Israel's campaign of 1982 had brought American forces into the country on a "peace-keeping mission." This was a hasty decision, another case of American innocence abroad. A token multinational force of five thousand men—U.S., British, French, and Italian forces—were sent into Lebanon in September of 1982. Once on the ground the distant superpower had become party to the sectarian wars of Lebanon, and to the fight over that country among Syria, Iran, and Israel. The affair ended in heartbreak. In April of 1983 the U.S. Embassy in West Beirut had been blown up. And in October of that year there was that unforgettable scene of carnage when a suicide driver had crashed into the U.S. marine headquarters on the southern approaches of Beirut, an explosion that took the lives of some 240 Americans. The university and the Arabist who came to lead it were caught up in larger struggles beyond their control.

Kerr had not needed that appointment: he had a successful career at UCLA, he had risen through the academic ranks, and he had carved out a place for himself as one of his country's leading Arabists. From 1979 to 1981 he had lived and worked as a visiting professor at the American University in Cairo. But Cairo was not for him, and the American University in that city meant little to him. It was the dialect of Lebanon that he loved and responded to. His memories lay in Beirut and in the hill country beyond the city. His feel for that land and for its varied sects and communities had come to him from his parents. His father, Stanley, a clinical biochemist, had left his work at Walter Reed Hospital and had come to the Levant in 1919 as a volunteer for Near East Relief, the humanitarian corps that the American Board of Commissioners for Foreign Missions had established in 1915. He started his work in Aleppo amid the Armenian refugees, a jack-of-all-trades: a photographer, a "gatherer of Armenian waifs" from the Kurdish and Turkoman families they had been forced into, a medical and sanitary officer and laboratory worker. He fought the spread of malaria and fever relapse among the refugees; he tested the water supplies; he prepared sterile solutions for intravenous injections. Fearless and driven, he went out into the surrounding countryside to retrieve Armenian children from the tribesmen and villagers who had picked up the children from scattered and frightened bands of refugees fleeing Turkish lands.

In the autumn of 1919 Stanley Kerr was transferred to Marash in southeastern Turkey. Marash had had an ancient Armenian community, by most estimates a community of some eighty thousand people. By 1923 after the events of the Great War, the massacres of the Armenians and the fight over Turkey's borders that followed the war, all of Marash's Armenians were killed or exiled. In Marash the slender, bespectacled young volunteer, Stanley Kerr, had entered into a lifelong relationship with the Armenians. He did relief work, he served as an intermediary with the Turkish authorities, and he left that city for Beirut with the last caravan of Armenian orphans. (It was in Marash that Stanley Kerr met his future wife, Elsa, a young Ohio woman who was teaching at a Marash school for girls. He chronicled that remarkable story in a book he published in 1973, *The Lions of Marash*.) The attachment to the Armenians and the romance for Beirut had cast their spell on Stanley Kerr. He left Lebanon for Pennsylvania for three years, but no sooner had he finished his Ph.D. than he returned to Beirut for a career that saw him through retirement in 1960. Malcolm, the Arabist, was the inheritor of all that, and though he had written of Egyptian and pan-Arab matters, it was the smaller history of Lebanon—the ways, the cuisine, and the culture of its people—that held him. In a memoir that she wrote ten years after her husband's murder, *Come with Me from Lebanon*, Ann Zwicker Kerr writes that Malcolm had quipped that there was a "25 percent chance that I'll get knocked off and that it will happen early on," but the AUB appointment was irresistible. He would merge with the history of the place. He would return to that familiar "garden of Eden" by the Mediterranean, to Marquand House, the presidential residence amidst the pine and jacaranda trees, to the president's office at College Hall. These were hallowed grounds for him: Revered figures had lived and worked there, missionaries and educators whose lives and legacies were known to him since his childhood years.

Kerr knew the risks: In July 1982 David Dodge, acting president of the university—a son of a former president and a descendant on his maternal side of the AUB's founder, Daniel Bliss—had been kidnapped on the campus of the university. Dodge had been a childhood friend of Kerr's; it was known that he had been taken to Iran through Syria and held there for more than a year. The city and the Arab world that Kerr had known in his childhood and in his youth were now a benign memory. He was no stranger to what had unfolded in the intervening years. In a piece written in 1983 eulogizing a Jordanian friend of those years, he spoke in sorrowful tones of an irretrievable age of simplicity when the sacred texts (*The Arab Awakening* by George Antonius) and the heroes and the villains came in dramatic, unambiguous colors. The world was changing, he wrote, and our "small cast of heroes and villains was being crowded out by a new mass of faceless participants, too numerous and too amorphous to be either controlled or held accountable. Mass politics and mass consumer culture had arrived." He grieved over what had been lost, the security and intimacy of that elite tradition—and over the crassness of the new Arab–American encounter. He was a patrician; he had put years into the study of Arabic and of the Arabs. "The foreigners coming into the Arab world are a different lot than before, and they are in much larger numbers," he wrote in that eulogy to his Jordanian friend. "They come with less interest in the country and its people, with less desire to stay, and with a greater devotion to making quick money. Many of them are working-class people who know or care little about Islamic cultural norms regarding female modesty or the consumption of alcohol. The encounters of such people with the local population can bear more resemblance to highway collisions than to social introductions."

In an earlier essay written in 1981, "Rich and Poor in the Arab Order," perhaps the best of his essays, he caught the despair and breakdown of the Arab world. He set aside the sardonic, bemused tone of some of his previous writings to say grim things about the Arab reality of that period. There were "two joint ventures" in the Arab world: the "scandalous expenditure of billions of dollars" in the Gulf and the "unceasing orgy of killing and destruction in Lebanon." These ventures had outside participants as well, "fellow builders, as it were, of the New Arab Order." The Arabs who had once designated Lebanon as a playground and a convenient "haven of sanity" had now turned that country into "a preserve in which to unleash their demons of madness, while transferring their instincts for tolerance and mutual advantage to Saudi Arabia and the Gulf." There were rumors that this article had come up when Kerr was being considered for the presidency, fears that this sort of writing would diminish his capacity for fund-raising for the beleaguered university. He had made it through the search and made his way to Lebanon.

I knew Kerr but not intimately or well. We had a professional relationship. I saw him in Cairo once or twice; our paths crossed in Washington and New York. When I began to write of contemporary Arab politics in the late 1970s, I was venturing into material that he had established as his own intellectual territory. He was a leading authority; he was the benevolent outsider, more patient with the follies of the Arab world; I was *of* that world and I wrote of it in a different way. We never pushed our disagreements; we did not know each other well enough for passionate disagreements. The last time I saw him was in New York at the Waldorf Astoria in mid-November 1983, two months before his murder. There was a reception in his honor and in support of the AUB; I had come to accompany a visiting Lebanese politician from the Bekaa Valley, a Shia patrician whose family was connected through marriage to my own family. Kerr, of course, knew of the man, but the two of them had never met. They had something in common: Sons of theirs were classmates in their freshman year at the University of Arizona. They promised to see each other back in Beirut. Kerr was eager, he said, to know more about the Shia. That community, now Lebanon's largest, had been on the fringe of social and political life in the Lebanon he had known in his younger years. The men and women he knew were the Palestinian bourgeoisie and the Beirut patricians, Sunni Muslims and Christians alike who dominated the culture and the world of those years. The Shia were among that "new mass of faceless participants" he now saw overrunning the intimate world he had known. The shadow of the dark politics of Beirut and of the new Shia militancy were there in that glitzy affair at the Waldorf: David Dodge, Malcolm's predecessor, acting president of the AUB, was in attendance. This was shortly after his release from his Iranian captivity. Dodge was introduced; he acknowledged a standing ovation, then sat down without saying a word. He had been released on condition that nothing be said of his captivity, and he had honored that deal. The torments he had just endured remained his alone.

There was no way of knowing who had struck Kerr down on that day in January of 1984. Leading men of Lebanon had begun to fall to assassins; the identity of their killers was at best guesswork. A group by the name of *al-Jihad al-Islami* (Islamic Holy War) claimed "credit" for the murder; no one knew if that organization existed. The day after Kerr's murder, Walid Junblatt, the young chieftain of the Druze whose father, Kamal, was gunned down by an assassin back in 1977, said that the right-wing Phalange Party was to blame and that a decent man had been killed because he "refused to be dragged down the current of Phalange rule but desired to maintain the university's academic message." Junblatt and his community were in the throes of a bloody struggle against the Maronites and their leading military formation, the Phalange Party. It was in the nature of things for Junblatt to charge his enemies with Kerr's murder.

If Kerr's murderers had intended their deed as an assault on the American presence in the land, they had not been off the mark. America was done with Lebanon: American officials talked bravely of not walking away from Lebanon and "allowing the forces of radicalism to prevail," but the countdown for American withdrawal had begun after the attack on the marines' headquarters. Kerr's murder had accelerated that withdrawal. It had underlined the follies of that American expedition and served notice that Beirut was lost to a new reign of cruelty. A Lebanese friend of Malcolm Kerr said that Lebanon did not deserve Malcolm at this time. That friend was right but told only a partial truth. The traffic that had brought the likes of Kerr's parents to the Levant issued out of a world that "modernity" and change had blown away.

TWO YOUNG GRADUATES of Andover Theological Seminary, Levi Parsons and Pliny Fisk, the sources say, were the first to make the passage to Beirut. Their destination was the Holy Land; they set out from Boston Harbor in November 1819, ready "for angels great, in early youth/To lead whole nations in the walks of truth." Parsons, who helped found a mission in Jerusalem, later reported that it was hard work carrying the Gospel to "people living heedless in the land where it was first proclaimed."

Other missionaries followed, young men from Amherst and Yale and, in time, young women from Mount Holyoke. While English missionaries favored Jerusalem, Beirut remained a special preserve of the Americans. The Beirut that early missionaries found was a small port town with a history of neglect behind it, a township with gates that closed at night, with a belt of outer watchtowers, and a scattering of people who lived beyond the city walls. Here is a portrait of Beirut supplied by one William Goodell, a missionary from Templeton, Massachusetts, in a letter he sent home in early 1824:

> The place in which providence has cast our lot is pleasantly situated on the western side of a large bay. On the south is a large and beautiful plain, varied by hills covered with olive, palm, orange, lemon, pine and mulberry trees. From the terrace we occupy we can see without the walls of the city no less than 200 cottages, scattered here and there in the fields of mulberry trees.

A fuller sense of the place endures in the pages of what is no doubt the most stunning and popular of the missionary works of the period, *The Land and the Book* by W. M. Thomson, which was published in 1872. A man of the great American Midwest, "thirty years missionary in Syria and Palestine," Reverend Thomson meant his book, packed with illustrations of the flora and fauna of the land, to be a "guide to the manners and customs, the scenes and scenery of the Holy Land." Thomson was always there in the pages of his book: alternately curious and haughty, knowing of the most amazing of details, impatient with the people of the land. He was a man of enormous learning and self-confidence. He wrote the book, he said, because much that had been written about the biblical landscape was shown to be "incorrect or rendered superfluous" by biblical researches. A large part of his pages, he assured his readers, was written "in the open country—on sea shore or sacred lake, on hillside or mountain top, under the olive, or the oak, or the shadow of a great rock: There the author lived, thought, felt, and wrote; and, no doubt, place and circumstance have given color and character to many parts of the work."

Thomson had not exaggerated. His passion for that "good land" yielded a work of beauty. The life of the land and its people, the scenery, the origins of the place-names, are all there in vivid detail. In his pages I found the majestic Beaufort castle near my village, and he named and described what I had seen. "Look, now, across the profound gorge of the Litani, and you can see that fine old fort hanging on the very edge of the precipice. I have often visited it, and have spent several nights encamped in its ample fosse. The view from the top is magnificent, and the gulf, down to the river beneath, is frightful. I never visit it without playing the boy by rolling stones from the tip of the castle, and watching their gigantic leaps from point to point until they are lost in the bushes or the river at the bottom." Thomson's writing, always true and always clear: The rolling of stones to the river was the thrill of our play as children during the summer months in my ancestral village at the foot of Beaufort.

The portrait of Beirut that Thomson left was of a town between seasons: its past yielding to demography and change. Hitherto the walled town was shut down at dusk, its gates locked for the night, and movement through its streets at dark monitored by the city guard and conditional on carrying a lantern. "The city-guard creeps safely about in utter darkness, and apprehends all found walking the streets without a light. Remember, and act accordingly, or you may get locked up in quarters not very comfortable. Beirut is gradually departing from some of these customs, but enough remains to afford a type of all you will see elsewhere except at Damascus," Thomson wrote. Now the city was spilling beyond the old walls, and "no city in Syria," he added, "perhaps none in the Turkish empire has had so rapid an expansion. And it must continue to grow and prosper. . . . This is Beirut, with the glorious Mediterranean all around, and ships and boats of various nations and picturesque patterns sailing or at rest. You will travel far ere you find a prospect of equal variety, beauty or magnificence."

It was during this time of growth and this movement beyond the city walls that Daniel Bliss, a missionary from Vermont's Champlain Valley, had launched the college that was to become the AUB. It opened in 1866; its first entering class, sixteen students, were to study under Bliss himself, two other missionaries, and a Lebanese tutor in mathematics. This was the inheritance of Kerr, and this was the setting in which he was born and raised. When his future wife, Ann Zwicker, came to Beirut in 1954, after a seventeen-day journey from New York on a Dutch freighter, she could still behold a small colonial city of walled sprawling houses, with bougainvillea over the walls and lush gardens and narrow alleyways. The young graduate student who was courting her, showing her the sights of the place, and deciphering its ways, had the best of all possible worlds: He stood at the crossroads between this land and the American inheritance that was fully his. It must have been a time touched with wonder. In the summer months, Stanley and Elsa Kerr would retreat to the hills, to a quaint town in the mountains, to a house of stones amid a grove of pine trees with a majestic view of the valleys and the hills. On the land around them, on the same hilltop, there were houses of four other American professors, and a vineyard where Stanley Kerr, the inventive biochemist, tried his hand at grafting different sorts of grapes and fruits. Strictly speaking, the political and class certainties of the world in this city and the country were not Malcolm Kerr's, but he partook of them; he had high hopes for Arab nationalism and faith in the social class that dominated that movement. The surprises the world held in store for the Arabs of his generation would be there waiting for him when his professional dream was fulfilled. He became "lord of the manor" (his words in a letter to his wife), but the house was aflame.

IN THE YEARS that followed Malcolm Kerr's murder, thoughts of him and of his father, Stanley, have come to me now and then in the most surprising of ways: a son of Malcolm, Steve, the boy I had heard of in 1983 as a freshman at the University of Arizona, had become a basketball player, drafted into the NBA. He played for the Cleveland Cavaliers and then for the Chicago Bulls. I knew little of the NBA, but I kept track of Steve Kerr, and always looked for him and for his stats in the box-score. I learned that he was a good spot-up shooter; he was one of the very best at taking the three-point shot from "beyond the arc." In the 1997 championship season, he lived out his own dream. In the deciding sixth game of the NBA finals against the Utah Jazz, he sank the winning shot, after a pass from his teammate, Michael Jordan. Two games earlier he had missed an open shot, another pass from Jordan, and he was inconsolable over it. I watched him on ESPN (the sports channel) the day after he had missed that open shot while he did a long interview from Salt Lake City with a reporter who waded, toward the end, into the matter of his father's murder. It was easy to see that the interviewer had taken the blond, boyish-looking player into a territory Steve Kerr did not want to revisit. Yes, he said, he missed his father, he thinks of him every day, and he knows that his NBA career was an accomplishment his father would have been proud of. He then returned to more mundane matters: the open shot he missed. A few days later in Chicago in that deciding game, he had the same open shot and sank it for the title.

In the dispatches of the Chicago Bulls, it was reported that Kerr had once had a scuffle with Jordan and that he had stood his ground against "His Airness." That reporter had filed the dispatch as something wondrous and unexpected. But for the grandson of a man who went into the hills around Aleppo and Marash with a pistol at his side to retrieve Armenian waifs and take them on a caravan to

Beirut, a boy who had endured his father's loss, the struggles of the NBA must seem quaint in the extreme. A trail has ended and the east has been left to its people. The spot-up shooter for the Chicago Bulls, born in Beirut in 1965, lives in a world where the missionary zeal and the quaint places are faint memories that no voyage and no effort could ever hope to retrieve.

CHAPTER THREE

IN THE SHAPE OF THE ANCESTORS

THE FAILURE OF the written word convinced Khalil Hawi that the battle of his generation of Arabs had been lost. The text had sustained the men and women of the Arab nationalist tradition. Sweeping out all that stood in its way, the language of secular nationalism had been heady and sure of itself. It had wished away great timeless truths that were everywhere in Arab life: the truths of the clans and the religious sects; the split between the thin layer of literary and political culture and the popular traditions below that mocked the optimism and bravado of the written word. Hawi was ahead of his time in his despair of writing and the written word. In the years to come, the problems of writing, the difficulty of matching Arabic words and Arab things, became a steady lament in the world of letters. Arab men and women of this century escaped into the word, and the word failed them.

Not long after Hawi's death, two celebrated peers of Khalil Hawi, the romantic poet Nizar Qabbani and the poet and literary critic Adonis (the first born in 1923, the second in 1930), offered their own autopsies of the written word and the Arabic political text. For these men, both Syrian born but living in Beirut for some years, the crisis of letters was but a reflection of the Arab political condition. The Arabic word was ailing, the two poets said in different ways and different settings. It had become harder to write. There was a disquieting fit between the written language of politics and poetry and the world Arabs confronted each day. "I can't write," Qabbani told a Kuwaiti daily in May 1985:

> I don't write because I can't say something that equals the sorrow of this Arab nation. I can't open any of the countless dungeons in this large prison. The poet is made of flesh and blood: you can't make him speak when he loses his appetite for words; you can't ask him to entertain and enthrall when there is nothing in the Arab world that entertains or enthralls. When we were secondary schoolchildren our history teacher used to call the Ottoman empire "the sick man." What is the history teacher to call these mini-empires of the Arab world being devoured by disease? What are we to call these mini-empires with broken doors and shattered windows and blown-away roofs? What can the writer say and write in this large Arab hospital?

Qabbani borrowed the term *jahiliyya,* meaning pre-Islamic ignorance, to describe the Arab reality of today. In that original time of darkness the poet had had a function: The poet was his tribe's "lawyer," chronicler, and scribe. The new *jahiliyya* is darker than the old. It has annulled the role of the poet because it wants people on their knees; it wants them to crawl. The "sultans of today" want only supporters and sycophants, and this has had the effect of emasculating the language. They fear the word because the word is "intrinsically an instrument of opposition": the enmity between the word and *al-sulta,* authority, is classical and inevitable.

Qabbani, who lost his wife in one of Beirut's daily episodes of violence (a bombing of the Iraqi embassy in 1981), was asked about the fate of the city that had nurtured him and been home for him. Beirut, he said, was a "ball of fire that has burned my hands. But I still hold onto it, just like the child who puts in the palm of his hand poisonous insects, who holds onto a scorpion without being afraid of being stung." The Beirut of the 1950s and 1960s—the enchanted city of his youth, the city of poetry and pleasures—was a "thing of the past." You can't bring it back to life, as you can't bring back the old glories of Rome and Athens. "History is a river that never flows backward. . . . We must have the courage to admit that the war in Lebanon has overturned the old Lebanon. Some of us may dream of young Beirut, of the playful city that enthralled millions of men, but we must be realistic and consider the city before us. Nothing remains of old Beirut except the scent of it that blows from old notebooks."

Qabbani's lament—that words have been rendered futile by the course of history—was foreshadowed in "Balqees," a long poem named for his wife and written in grief after her murder. It was published in 1982 in the magazine *al-Mostaqbal*; the translation is by an outstanding former student of mine, Lisa Buttenheim.

Balqees, don't be absent from me,
After you, the sun doesn't shine on the shore.
I will say in my inquiry that the thief has come to wear a fighter's
*   clothes,*
I will say in my inquiry that the gifted leader is now an agent,
I will say that the tale of enlightenment is the most ludicrous joke
*   ever told,*
And that we are a tribe among tribes.
This is history . . . oh Balqees.
How do people distinguish between gardens and dunghills?
Balqees . . . oh princess,
You burn, caught between tribal wars,
What will I write about the departure of my queen?
Indeed, words are my scandal. . . .
Here we look through piles of victims
For a star that fell, for a body strewn like fragments of a mirror.
Here we ask, oh my love:
Was this your grave

Or the grave of Arab nationalism?
I won't read history after today,
My fingers are burned, my clothes bedecked with blood,
Here we are entering the stone age. . . .
Each day we regress a thousand years.
What does poetry say in this era, Balqees?
What does poetry say in the cowardly era . . . ?
The Arab world is crushed, repressed, its tongue cut. . . .
We are crime personified. . . .
Balqees . . .
I beg your forgiveness.
Perhaps your life was the ransom of my own,
Indeed I know well
That the purpose of those who were entangled in murder was to kill
*   my words!*
Rest in God's care, oh beautiful one,
Poetry, after you, is impossible. . . .

Adonis's account of his predicament, given in a provocative book of literary criticism, *al-Shi'riyya al-Arabiyya* (Arabic Poetics), which was published in Beirut in 1985, went beyond the grief of Qabbani. Here we have a sustained analysis of what Adonis calls the "dual siege" of the Arab writer, who is caught between Western thought on the one hand and the hold of Islamic tradition on the other. Adonis's is not the common concern that has bedeviled Arab thought since its encounter with the West, the frequently false anxiety about reconciling "tradition" and "modernity." We are way past that here. What we have, rather, is an obituary for *asr al-nahda,* the age of the enlightenment, or what Albert Hourani called the Liberal Age in Arab history, which began in the early 1800s.

Adonis's argument is that the marriage between the West, or the kind of modernity that the Arabs imported from the West, and *turath* (tradition), or the dominant political and cultural order to which men and women in the Arab world must adhere, has produced a monstrous and arid world. A "vast desert of imports and consumption" has created a false image of modernity—in fact, "a large swindle," a world in trappings that have nothing to do with either the Arab world as it really is or with the West. "Our contemporary modernity is a mirage." Intellectuals and writers who succumb to the temptations of this false modernity are doomed from the start. Trying to emulate the style and forms of an alien civilization, they produce dead works, replicas of one culture in another. As long as the Arabs fail to understand that there is more to the West than what they have so far found in it—its spirit of curiosity, its appetite for knowledge, its courage before dogma—the "Western" modernity of the Arab world will be a "hired" form of modernity, brought to Arab lands through "trick" or "theft."

But then there is that other false option that paralyzes Arab thought, that offers to rescue it from the assault of the foreigner: unquestioned adherence to the world of the ancestors. Indeed, the authority of the ancestor increases as the cultural seduction of foreign models grows more intense and their intrusion more relentless. Surely, says Adonis, "authenticity" and "fidelity" do not require either a slavish imitation of the ways of the elders or a willful insistence in the face of reality that inherited ways hold all the answers: "Authenticity is not a specific point in the past; identity does not require a return to a particular position in our history." Fidelity is more a matter of creativity, of retaining and applying the spirit that moved Arabic and Islamic civilization in its more creative eras. It is making sure that the "new" emerges out of the past, that there are no "false discontinuities," no contrived breakthroughs.

Adonis admonished his readers that the opposition of "Muslim–Arab society" to the "European–American West" is not a "human or philosophical or poetic opposition." It is merely a "political" opposition:

> Our opposition to the West should not mean its total and generic rejection. It should entail our rejection only of its colonial-ideological formation. Thus when we reject its machines and technology, this should not mean that we reject the

intellectual process that produced these machines. It should mean only that we oppose the way this technology is dumped on us, the way it turns us into mere consumers, the way it turns our country into a large flea-market.

Care must be exercised lest this false dichotomy between an "Islamic–Arab East" and an "advanced European–American West" become a warrant for Arab backwardness and Islamic retrogression. Strictly speaking, he wrote, there is no East or West. Each of these worlds has many worlds within it. In the West there are forms of life that are more backward than anything in the East. Moreover, "small worlds of creativity and progress" exist within the East. Like it or not, something of a "world civilization" encompasses us all. Modernity is no longer the property of a given place or a given people; and it is no longer possible to avoid.

Real modernity is born, says Adonis, when the "dual dependence" upon the contrived world of the foreigner and the contrived world of the ancestor is transcended. Modernity—real and living—will have a chance when the repressed yearnings of this large and silent Arab civilization are released, when people write new things, when they are bold in the face of prohibitions. Then the Arabic language, free from the hold of the past and from attempts to imitate European and American models, might give expression to something vital and decent. Until now, Arab thought has been timid; insecure and on the run, it has been marred by a kind of "awe of magic," either the magic of the foreigner or the magic of the past. Authority, al-sulta, has always paid homage to the magic of the ancestor and persecuted those who questioned it, even as it was itself falling under the sway of foreign powers.

"Something in the Arab world has died," Adonis said to me in a conversation in 1986, shortly before he left Beirut for France. He was struggling with a hard decision: to give up on Beirut and settle in France. Adonis was fifty-six then. He had endured Beirut's carnage and breakdown for more than a decade. He was reluctant to leave, to let go of the material of his art. He knew the sad fate of exiled writers, their alienation from new surroundings, their nostalgia for an old country that grows more distant and more abstract. And he was worried about his distance from the Arabic language.

A child of the Syrian hinterland, born in 1930 in a small mountain village midway between the towns of Tartus and Latakia on the Syrian coast, Adonis came to Lebanon in 1956. He arrived a broken man. The Syrian regime had imprisoned him for one year and then had let him go. No charges were filed against him, and no trial was held. Syrian politics were a volatile, unpredictable affair, one military *coup d'état* after another, numerous political parties and cabals in a raw struggle for power. The young Adonis had been hauled off to prison after his graduation from the University of Damascus. Like so many of the best of his generation, Adonis had joined the movement of Anton Saadah and he had paid for that choice.

"A gap had opened," he wrote, recalling that time, "between me and the reality around me. A feeling took hold in me that I was living on the edge of the place, on the verge of falling. I began to notice that language was like man himself, that it had calamities of its own, and that its biggest calamity is the book which is born a corpse, nothing but a pile of words." He was desperate to break out of the hold of the dead language and the dead books. He had a superficial knowledge of French; he had studied it at a French school in Tartus, but the school had shut down with the coming of Syrian independence. He was not deterred and took to reading Baudelaire. He read a French translation of the German poet Rilke, French-Arabic dictionary in hand, staying with the reading, marking up the books with Arabic-French translations. An "inner voice" guided him, warned him against falling deeper into a void.

Lebanon, a more forgiving country, seemed the proper place for the aspiring poet and writer to heal his wounds and build a new life. When Adonis crossed the Syrian border into Lebanon in 1956, he came in the month of October, during the Suez War. He always remembered the timing of his passage. The world looked boundless and open-ended for his generation of Arabs, and change was in the offing. British and French prestige and primacy were going up in flames in a doomed colonial experiment. The military regime in Egypt was already fashioning out of this episode the material of a new nationalist legend: the "new Arab" was defying Europe and putting to an end its mastery in Arab lands. It was fitting that Adonis chose this country as his home—he would eventually acquire Lebanese citizenship—for the hills and the mythology of this land supplied him with his pen name. The cult of Adonis, the shepherd-god, emerged out of these hills. The mouth of the Adonis River was on the coast of Lebanon, near the town of Byblos, its source in a grotto in the mountains above the sea. The origins of the legend may have been Sumerian, but the Phoenicians partook of its symbolism of death and annual resurrection. In the legend, Adonis is fought over by Aphrodite, queen of the light, and Persephone, queen of the shadows. Zeus orders him to live half the year in the world of light and the other half in the world of shadows. On a hunting expedition, Adonis is cut down by Aphrodite's husband, Ares, the god of war, who had turned himself into a wild boar. From the underworld into which his spirit descended, the tears of Aphrodite summon Adonis back to life each spring. Her tears and the blood of Adonis celebrate the cycle of nature: the winter yielding to a brief spring, when the barren hills come to life with crimson anemone and every kind of wildflower, before the sun scorches the earth again.

Layers of civilizations could be found in these lands: Sumerian, Phoenician, Greco-Roman, Arab, and Turkish. By choosing the pen name of Adonis, the Syrian poet defined himself as a son of the Mediterranean and of Syria's polyglot inheritance.

Pan-Arabists, who viewed Syria and Lebanon as but a fragment of a wider Arab space, drew their sources from the Arabian Peninsula and took in the lands of Egypt and North Africa; they had never cared for that pre-Islamic mythology. A new dispensation in the Fertile Crescent dating from the seventh century onward, Islam had been self-consciously new and revolutionary, consigning that pagan past to oblivion. The Arab political idea rested on that Islamic narrative. In the pen name he chose for himself, Adonis picked a political and cultural identity: He loved the poetry and the history of the Arabian Peninsula and of Islam, but he looked back further in history to the pre-Islamic sources of Syria's civilization.

Beirut adopted the young Syrian, and he embraced it with the devotion of a newcomer who savored its liberties and understood how precious these liberties were. "I got to know Beirut street by street, from all directions, particularly from the direction of the sea, the same sea that I seldom noticed in Tartus and Latakia, where I was born and where I grew up." This was a "neutral city," he wrote of Beirut; it took no position on the great questions of the heritage versus modernity, and allowed the protagonists to have their say. It was hard to know where Beirut's indifference to these great questions ended and its genuine tolerance began; the modernity of the city may have been a "storefront with little on the inside." But men and women were permitted a greater latitude than they were in other Arab settings; he was lucky to be there, he said, when Beirut was slowly emerging as the capital of Arabic letters and the city of the Arab enlightenment. That role had been Cairo's from the late 1800s until the 1950s. Then military rule in Egypt had hemmed in the life of the mind, politicized the written word, and begun to persecute intellectuals. Beirut won by default. The world around it, it seemed, needed a free, emancipated city, and the Lebanese obliged. By his own account, the Beirut that Adonis found was a jumbled world of extremes and contradictions: extreme wealth and extreme poverty, religiosity and modernity side by side, loyalty to the past and unfettered attention to the imported goods, positions, and ideas of the West.

This tumult nurtured Adonis. He came from a minority background, that of Shia; the literary and political world in which he rose had not bothered with the matter of his religious background. He himself had volunteered his Shia ancestry in a passing remark in 1968 in a public lecture he gave before the *Cénacle Libanais* (al-Nadwa al-Lubnaniyya), that city's vibrant forum of public debate of those years. "I come from a Shia home," he said. "And every Shia home inherits tragedy while it awaits a coming deliverance." This was offered as a rhetorical flourish, an insight into his temperament. It was not a statement of sectarian loyalty; the man was larger than that, and the moment was not a moment of sectarian ascendancy. His uncluttered prose and haunting poetry secured him a preeminent place in the literary life of the city. In his boyhood, he had been tutored by his father in the Quran and Islamic mysticism and history, but he had a deep interest in Christian symbolism and thought as well, and Lebanon was an ideal place for him. He made his way to St. Joseph University in East Beirut, an educational institution established by the Jesuits in 1875. (This university was the Jesuits' and Francophiles' answer to the American University of Beirut and its blend of Anglo-Saxon education and Arab nationalism.) From there, a scholarship took him to the Sorbonne, where he indulged his passion for French letters and culture. He saw no contradiction between his lifelong interest in Islamic sources and tradition and his love of French culture. He had never been biased against Western thought, he was to write in a literary autobiography. As a student leader in the 1940s in the secondary schools of Tartus and Latakia, he had participated in anti-French demonstrations but never took part in the burnings of French books that were a standard feature of these demonstrations. "Did I make, even then, an instinctive separation between my political attitude toward the foreigner and my cultural-literary commitments?" For this man the politics of nationalism were never enough. He ventured beyond the truth of sects and political parties and the narrow call of nationalism. He dug deep into the sources of Arabic culture and poetry but did so from a decidedly humanist tradition. He dismissed "race and blood" as the defining forces in Arab and Islamic history and as the sources of Arab identity. He was a child of the catacombs, a minoritarian; he would not indulge a narrow, radical definition of home, culture, and hearth.

The pan-Arabists never trusted Adonis. They took his pen name as proof of an attachment to the Phoenician and Greco-Roman sources of Lebanese and Syrian culture. They held against him his early fling with the ideas of Anton Saadah and Syrian nationalism. His genius carried him through, however, and he thrived. Beirut's journalism sustained him as he wrote his poetry and literary criticism. He met a soulmate, a Lebanese poet, Yusuf al-Khal, with whom he launched a literary magazine, *Shi'r*, devoted to new poetic forms in the late 1950s; he launched another literary venture, perhaps the Arab world's most innovative and daring literary magazine, *Mawaqif*, in the aftermath of the Six Day War of 1967. In the wreckage of that war, in the enormity of the Arab defeat and the lightning speed with which Israel devastated the armies of Jordan, Egypt, and Syria, Adonis and his colleagues at *Mawaqif* saw the charred ruins of the edifice of radical Arab nationalism. For them, that defeat was the spur for a brave reassessment of the dominant political style of the 1950s and 1960s and of the very language and vocabulary of politics. But there had been endless surprises in store for him and for his peers, and he was leaving Beirut in the mid-1980s during a time of ruin. Like Qabbani, he spoke of the death of Arab civilization. There comes a time, he said, when people can no longer give. In Beirut's wars, he had seen all the grand ideas and all the ideologies issue in slaughter, and the return of the Lebanese and other Arabs in Lebanon to a primitive tribalism. Adonis no longer recognized his city. And for a poet, he possessed a marked reluctance to name things, to describe what he had seen. Had he intuited that it would end like this? In "Lamentations for Our Present Times," one of his most haunting poems, written in the late 1960s, Adonis wrote of tyranny, silence, and exile:

> *The chariots of exile pass the walls*
> *between the chants of exile,*
> *and the flames of fire.*
> *And the poems have departed*
> *with the chariots of exile.*
> *The wind is merciless toward us*
> *and the ashes of our days are on the ground.*

We see our soul in the flash of a knife,
or atop a helmet.
And the autumn of salt
spreads over our wounds
and in sight, there is no budding tree or spring.

A more recent poem, "The Desert," written in 1982 and translated by Abdullah al-'Udhari, caught the despair of a generation that had seen Beirut, the city of Arab enlightenment, slip into a new world on the other side of civility, routine, and familiar things.

> . . .
> *Whatever will come it will be old*
> > *So take with you anything other than this*
> > > *madness—get ready*
> > > > *To stay a stranger. . . .*
>
> *They found people in sacks:*
> > *One without a head*
> > *One without a tongue or hands*
> > *One squashed*
> > *The rest without names.*
> > *Have you gone mad? Please,*
> > *Do not write about these things.*
>
> *Darkness.*
> *The earth's trees have become tears on*
> *heaven's cheeks.*
> *An eclipse in this place.*
> *Death snapped the city's branch and the*
> *friends departed.*
>
> *The flower that tempted the wind to carry its*
> *perfume*
> > *Died yesterday.*
>
> *The sun no longer rises*
> *It covers its feet with straw*
> *And slips away. . . .*

Reality had outpaced the poet's bleak vision. Is it any wonder that many of those in the Arab world who traffic in words felt that they had so little to say? From its very beginning in the late 1800s, Arab nationalism had been a project of the intellectuals, an idea flung in the face of a political order that was always torn by all sorts of conflicts. But a deep political crisis had set in by the early 1980s, and it had become difficult for even the most devoted to persist. Arab society had run through most of its myths, and what remained in the wake of the word, of the many proud statements people had made about themselves and their history, was a new world of cruelty, waste, and confusion.

Arab politics had been a roller-coaster ride: from the October War of 1973 and the "windfall society" that oil wealth had spawned to the summer of 1982 and the solitary stand of Beirut when Israel struck against the Palestinians. A Kuwaiti academic who came of age during the ascendancy of the Arab nationalist era (the years between the Suez War of 1956 and the Six Day War of 1967) described the bewildering ride of his contemporaries in clear terms: "I cheered in 1956," he said, remembering the hopes that surrounded the radical Arab nationalism of the time. "I cried in 1967 after the Six Day War. I cheered again in 1973 when I was told that a new world beckoned the Arabs. Now in the summer of 1982, after a decade that began with such promise closes with a bitter taste of defeat, I am too shocked for words, for tears or even for anger."

There was wealth in the Arabian Peninsula, communal massacres in Beirut, and peace between Egypt and Israel. The stubborn assertion that a collective Arab condition prevailed from one end of that Arab world to the other was shattered. It was not just that the Arabs had been reminded of the borders of different states they inhabited. Beyond that powerful truth, there had come into their world, since the early 1970s, new temptations that the windfall fortune of oil had made possible. It had become harder to maintain that a singular fate awaited the Arabs; money dug a fault line between those classes that could partake of this new dispensation of wealth and the "modernity" that came with it and those broad sectors of the population on the fringe of this new order of things. The petro era unsettled the place, and Arabs (and Iranians) were thrown into an unfamiliar world.

Whatever its shortcomings, the old world (which ruptured after 1967 and was broken with a fury after 1973) had been whole: It had its ways and its rhythms. At least people knew who they were and had some solid ground to stand on. The winners may have been a little uppity or cruel, but they could not fly too high: There were things that people were ashamed to do, limits that marked out the moral boundaries of their deeds. The permissible *(halal)* was distinguishable from the impermissible *(haram)*. Scoundrels and bullies knew what they could and could not get away with. There was, in sum, a moral order. Then all this was blown away. The continuity of a culture was shattered. All attempts to reconstitute the wholeness, to ignore the great rupture by means of cultural chauvinism or a hyperauthentic traditionalism, brought only greater confusion and breakdown.

The new wealth shifted the center of Arab political life toward the "desert Arabs" and the oil lands of the Peninsula, but the luminaries in the republic of letters had never taken to the oil regimes of the Persian Gulf and the Arabian Peninsula. Austere and envied, the desert world distrusted the intellectual class and their product: the written word. In turn, the intellectuals could never grant these dynastic states credit for what they had built. It was the prevailing assumption among the intellectual class of the "city Arabs" that these regimes would be swept aside and their fortunes put to use in the service of a pan-Arab project. Little more than a decade after the new oil fortune remade the social and economic landscape of the Arab world, Cassandras were prophesying an end to the great hopes pinned on the new fortune. It was a time of economic downturn and recession for the oil producers, but the Cassandras saw more than a mere economic downturn. They spoke of the future in apocalyptic terms. On the horizon they saw the unmaking of the world that oil had built.

The great themes of oil—the sudden wealth, the ruling dynasties, the foreign protectors of sparsely populated oil lands, and the coming calamity—found their most powerful (and polemical) chronicler in Abdelrahman Munif. In a sprawling cycle of novels, *Cities of Salt,* Munif attempted nothing less than the grand oil novel of the lands in the Gulf. (The novels have been superbly translated into English by an American writer, Peter Theroux.) Born in 1933 in Jordan to a trading family of Saudi Arabian origin, Munif was an Arab nationalist through and through, true to all the strictures of radical Arab nationalism. Stripped of his Saudi citizenship in 1963, at the height of the struggle between radical Arab nationalism and the pro-Western regimes, and educated in Cairo, Baghdad, and Belgrade with a doctorate in oil economics, Munif poured into his fiction the politics of a generation of radical nationalism. He came to the work of fiction in his late thirties, opting for literature, he declared, when he realized that the Arab political game was a cruel hoax, a "big trick," and a realm of perpetual failure and betrayal. His political opinions were the vogue of the 1980s. At his best he was a captivating storyteller capable of summoning the desert world and its distinct rhythm, texture, and solitude, of taking his readers back to the desert world as it existed before the coming of oil. He had, as well, the advantage of depicting a political and cultural landscape unknown to his readers in Cairo, Beirut, and Tunis. In the cities of the Levant and North Africa, there was precious little knowledge of and little curiosity about the lands of the Gulf and Peninsula. The "city Arabs" had been immune to the romances of the desert that had gripped British travelers, explorers, and diarists. What knowledge there was of these oil lands consisted of a jumble of stereotypes and no small measure of condescension.

There was little ambiguity in Munif's world. The arrival of the British and the Americans into the oil lands was like the sweeping in of a yellow wind bringing ruin in its train. The whole moral and political outlook of Munif is set early in the first volume of *Cities of Salt,* when the peace of an oasis town, Wadi al-Uyoun, is shattered by the arrival of three American prospectors searching for oil. After the arrival of "those devils," nothing stays the same. Children turn on their elders. A man of the oasis town turns into a phantom and haunts the place. Nearby an American-built town grows taller, more spacious, more alien by the day. A world "buried in sand and oblivion" is stirred to life. It trades its old, timeless harshness for a hybrid world.

For Munif, the fiction was made to carry the politics. He was forthright about his intentions and loyalties. "Before the oil," he told a Beirut weekly in an interview in 1985,

> the desert man was as thin as a stick, now he is as round as a barrel of oil. This is against the law of nature. Man in that desert world used to follow his camel all day long and be content with a little bit of milk and dates. He would stay strong and lean, able to handle the adversity of the physical world around him. This enabled him to survive and adapt. How are we to compare that man of days past with what we have today?

This world of oil, Munif observed, was a world of desolation, *kharab*. Its wealth was "temporary," easily depleted; it built a "dependent world," a "consumer culture," which altered the psychology of Arabs, their relation to one another. "People have become mere passengers on a train, thrown together by accident and chance. . . . This Arab oil has corrupted the Arab condition not only in the oil lands, but in the Arab world as a whole." Where the Arabs of old "journeyed on caravans in search of water and food, the Arabs of today are searching for some liberty and security and for their right to have their say."

Munif knew about wandering and exile. He had made a home in Paris. (He would eventually settle in Damascus.) The "oxygen of liberty," he said, had been depleted in the Arab world. "That's why someone observed that Paris is the only place that resembles a capital of the Arabs." The exiles owed it to those forced into silence to speak the truth "before the final curtain comes down." This was a desolate Arab reality, but many in the intellectual class, Munif said, were caught between the "ruler's sword and his gold." When this oil wealth dried up, Arabs would become "lost and bewildered," and these "cities of salt" that oil wealth built "will perish and die unlamented, and leave no trace behind them."

The desert Arabs who had known the harshness of their world before oil were, in the main, immune to any nostalgia for that old world. They knew its cruelty—the famines and the drought. But a powerful current of nostalgia suffuses Munif's work. In *Cities of Salt,* the opening volume of the cycle of novels, Munif explores why the sons of the desert world in his fictitious principality of Mooran journey to the ends of the earth only to be drawn back to the desert. This is from Peter Theroux's translation into English:

> Despite the greenery, water and abundant wealth of the towns they lived in, they felt suddenly beset by sorrows whose origin they could not understand. . . . Strange, even mad ideas contended in their minds. They must have been mad to leave Mooran, falsely swearing that they would never come back, because of the restrictions and hardships there. Though Mooran seemed to be gone, it slumbered in their depths, only to explode later on, with the same unreasoned force that had moved them to leave it, and it was this force that brought them home again.

Munif was no stranger to the cruelty of what had come before the age of oil. In the same novel, his narrative opened with a calamitous event before the age of oil: a drought that came howling through the principality of Mooran: "The first year brought drought. It was a long, dark year for animals and crops, and the people moaned with hunger. Livestock perished, the desert blew in to the edge of the cities, bringing hunger and other menaces with it, and everything appeared to be on the brink of collapse and death. The ground shook and seemed ready to overturn." The plague was not far behind. Old and young alike perished. Death did not stop at the gates of the ruler's modest palace, "but went through them and invaded." It had not been pretty, that old world, and it had not been merciful, but it was whole. This was Munif's play of worlds, the choice he offered,

the world of age-old ways versus the cities of cement; the spare, uncluttered world of the ancestors traded for a littered landscape of
industrial machines and imports. This nostalgia for that vanished
desert world was odd, and strange to the culture. It had something in
it of the sensibility of the great, foreign desert explorers and writers,
men and women like Gertrude Bell, Freya Stark, and Wilfred Thesiger. There is in Munif the same sorrow for what befell the land and
the desert world that Thesiger expressed in his great work, *Arabian
Sands* (1959). Here is perhaps Thesiger's most memorable paragraph
of sorrow, as he catches the twilight of the desert world and reflects
on his last exploration of the Empty Quarter, which he made in 1946.
(I quote it at some length for its singular beauty and for its affinity
with Munif's sensibility.)

> I went to Southern Arabia only just in time. Others will go there
> to study geology and archeology, the birds and plants and ani-
> mals, even to study the Arabs themselves, but they will move
> about in cars and will keep in touch with the outside world by
> wireless. They will bring back results far more interesting than
> mine, but they will never know the spirit of the land nor the
> greatness of the Arabs. If anyone goes there now looking for the
> life I led they will not find it, for technicians have been there
> since, prospecting for oil. Today the desert where I travelled is
> scarred with the tracks of lorries and littered with discarded
> junk imported from Europe and America. But this material des-
> ecration is unimportant compared with the demoralization
> which has resulted among the Bedu themselves. While I was with
> them they had no thought of a world other than their own. They
> were not ignorant savages; on the contrary, they were the lineal
> heirs of a very ancient civilization, who found within the frame-
> work of their society the personal freedom and self-discipline
> for which they craved. Now they are being driven out of the
> desert into towns where the qualities which once gave them mas-
> tery are no longer sufficient. Forces as uncontrollable as the
> droughts which so often killed them in the past have destroyed

the economy of their lives. Now it is not death but degradation which faces them.

Here is Munif's rendition of the desert world that oil obliterated:

Mooran was, in those years following midcentury, still a desolate and forgotten settlement: more than a village but not quite a city, much like the little towns strewn along the trade routes or in the larger oases. The people there lived humble, even rough lives. Fathers inherited from their forefathers a simple view of life and death; and because they did not expect much of life or fear death during the years they spent on earth, toiling for a crust of bread, and though the crust was hard or remote most of the time, they did find ample time to contemplate their surroundings, and took delight in memorizing poetry, verses from the Koran and old folktales. On the long summer nights they found their spirits departing beyond life and death and their eyes wandering the heavens to locate the stars and planets or trying to read in the wind the signs of dust storms, locusts and catastrophes.

This is what replaces the harshness of Mooran: the oil town of Harran and its alienation, an arid workshop on which the flotsam of the world descended:

Once, Harran had been a city of fishermen and travelers coming home, but now it belonged to no one; its people were featureless, of all varieties and yet strangely unvaried. They were all of humanity and yet no one at all, an assemblage of languages, accents, colors and religions. The riches in the city, and underneath it, were unique in the world, yet no one in Harran was rich or had any hope of becoming so. All of them were in a race, but none knew where to or for how long. It was like a beehive, like a graveyard. They even greeted one another differently from people in any other place—a man greeted others and then looked searchingly in their faces, as if afraid that something might happen between his greeting and their reply.

Munif's literary license dispensed with the subtlety of social and political life in the Gulf and the Peninsula. He offered his readers (and they all came to his fiction ready to believe the worst of what he had to say about the princes and their British and American protectors) a one-dimensional world: caricatures of princes drawn from the Arabian Nights and their foreign handlers. Of the emir, the prince of Harran, he wrote: "And the emir, was he their emir, there to defend and protect them, or was he the Americans' emir? He had been a different man when he first came to Harran. He used to stroll through the market and invite townsfolk to his house to drink coffee, but he changed abruptly." The emir of Harran was taken in by the sycophants who came into his court from distant lands, and he grew enthralled with the gadgets of the Americans. He was convinced "with absolute certainty that the Americans thought of everything." He had no need of his people; foreign protection took him beyond the verities and bonds of his old world.

A generation earlier, in the immediate aftermath of the Six Day War of 1967, Arabs came together to mourn what had become of the edifice of Arab nationalism, of the work of Nasserism, the Ba'th party, and Arab socialism. Power, said the Egyptian pundit Mohamed Heikal in a clever play on words, had shifted from the Arab *thawra* (revolution) to the Arab *tharwa* (fortune). But fortune had not altered the place of the Arabs in the world; it had not made them more united than they had been; it had not delivered the Palestinians a state, as the extravagant hopes after October 1973 had held. Wealth had touched, unsettled, and tempted the world, spawning dreams of a golden political revival for the Arab world. The intellectual class had caught the bug. During the preceding decade they had entertained bold, fanciful ideas about a grand "Arab project" that would harness the wealth of the oil states to a pan-Arab political project, but these great ideas of deliverance had not come to pass.

The world that emerged in the shadow of the new wealth triggered a ferocious rebellion. We were to give this storm an Islamic label, "Islamic fundamentalism." In Lebanon and the Gulf we were to hear the claims and noises of a radical Shi'ism. But although Islam was indeed the banner that was unfurled, we spent too much time speaking of "Islam" and not enough of the sentiments and furies that gave political Islam its modern relevance.

A grim fight broke out between the heights of Arab society and its depths. The fight destroyed countless lives—and many political constructs. Politically, the principal casualty was Arab nationalism, a fragile edifice that looked past anything it did not wish to see. It was contemptuous of the hinterland and virtually silent about popular culture. It never really had a theory of practical action, having inherited the remains of the old Ottoman political tradition. An easy leap was made from Ottomanism to Arabism; the new idea relied roughly on the same social base as the old, the universe of urban elites, merchants, and army officers. Some of pan-Arabism's most passionate advocates were Christian Arabs, who were searching for a place in a largely Muslim world, but its principal social glue was the political and cultural ascendancy of urban, orthodox (Sunni) Islam, and for decades its most frequently proclaimed cause—pursued now with cynicism, now with conviction—was Palestine.

The political capitals of this idea were Beirut, Damascus, and Baghdad. Cairo was a latecomer to Arabism. Qaddafi's Tripoli followed suit, but it remained a place of little consequence in the pan-Arab scheme of things. Cairo under Nasser gave the pan-Arab movement its moment of power, but Cairo under Sadat was the first to exit, leaving the Levant and the Gulf to their own feuds and disorders. The great Egyptian revolt against the West, and the great venture into the Arab–Israeli War, ended in futility and defeat—and then in dependence on America. Pride can be a heavy burden; under Sadat and Mubarak, Egypt put pride aside for the purpose of coming to terms with the world.

Three attempts were made to reconstitute Arab political life in the aftermath of the defeat of 1967 and of the defection of the Egyptian state from Arab politics. First was the Palestinian movement, which enjoyed a brief moment of ascendancy after 1967. Second was the recovery of the dominant political order in the war of

1973 and in the petro era, which gave power to the conservative oil states in the affairs of the Arab world. Third was the revolt of Shi'ism. The last had greater intensity and greater depth than its predecessors, but its predecessors also had their moments of delusion. Those, too, were times of a belief in the quick fix, in the promise that there was a bright new world in the making.

When it rode high in the aftermath of 1967, the Palestinian movement insisted that it had the answers not only to the problems of the Palestinians but also to broader Arab ailments. It was the Palestinian belief that "guerrilla warfare" or "wars of national liberation" or "revolution" would deliver Arab society from its superstitions and weaknesses, that the Palestinian movement would create a new, emancipated society. The pamphleteers went to work, and so did the gunmen, proclaiming an era of daring and defiance. But it was all delirium.

It turned out that the order of Arab states had found room for the Palestinians only because of its own weakness in the aftermath of 1967. When the order of Arab states bounced back in 1970, the Jordanian army shattered the Palestinian sanctuary and its illusions. Roughly the same story played itself out in Lebanon, although there, slightly more than a decade after the debacle of Jordan, the Arab world left the task of dealing with the Palestinians to Israel's defense minister, Ariel Sharon. By then the Palestinian movement had been stripped of any sense of mission—except keeping what it had in Beirut. In Beirut there were perquisites to be had: checkpoints that humbled the Lebanese who had to cross them; contraband trade; the spectacle of press conferences, officials, and cadres; and, more generally, the semblance of politics. A Levantine movement in a Levantine city.

The petro era was a different time. Its assumptions were simple: The Arab would be a consumer; the Arab world would be deradicalized; there would be a solution to the Palestinian dilemma. By one reckoning, this was to be a time of restoration, a triumph of the old order, a shift in the balance of power from the radical cities of Cairo and Damascus to the conservative states of the Gulf. But restoration required discipline, which was nowhere to be found in the windfall society of the oil era. Finally, in 1979 and 1980, the Iranian revolution served notice on that period of plunder and confusion. It was ironic but apt that the era of wealth, pretension, and contrived Westernism spawned a season of Islamic wrath. The petro era experimented with an impossible combination, paying homage to the *turath*, the tradition, while throwing the doors of the Arab-Islamic order wide open to the Americans. It tried to have it both ways, and it failed.

In the third movement of restoration, restraint was cast to the wind. Khomeini's revolution marked the revenge of the *turath*. The Mahdi, the Messiah, appeared in full force. There was no secular cover, no Western discourse. That the new rebellion originated not in the Arab world—not in Beirut, Baghdad, Damascus, or Cairo—but in Iran says a great deal about the paralysis of Arab politics. The Mahdi found it easy to make himself a party to the politics of the Arab world. The power of Khomeini's millenarianism was its ability to rally those excluded from Arab politics and to expose the great weakness, the forbidden secret, of Arab nationalism: It was Sunni dominion dressed in secular garb.

Arab nationalism had left large populations in the Arab world unclaimed and unincorporated. In earlier times, unable to walk undetected into decent "secular" company, these marginal individuals and groups had been forced to submit and to petition. The Khomeini revolt gave them the self-confidence and material assistance to put an end to their subservience. Borrowing a page from the old urban elites whose order he was undermining, Khomeini, too, concealed the sectarian edge of his rebellion. The revolt of Shi'ism for which he had to settle—he could not get the Sunni Arabs to accept his call—was to be, in his words, a revolt of the oppressed and the faithful against privilege. There were wrongs to be righted and hidden resentments: that the modern Iraqi state had been, since its inception in the 1920s, nothing but a minority dominion of Sunni officers and ideologues; that the Shia in Lebanon had been the dregs of the country; that the Shia in the Gulf had never quite been able to break through the subtle and not-so-subtle barriers between themselves and the ruling order.

True, a decade before the Shia revolt, the city of Damascus had fallen to a minority sect of Alawi soldiers from the Syrian country-side, to country boys with memories of persecution and poverty. But the loss of Damascus was devoid of any great ideological meaning; it was merely another tale of sectarian revenge by an exotic sect be-yond the bounds of Islam, of the soldier laying claim to rule. More-over, the conquest of political power in Damascus left the Alawis in a rule-or-die situation. They couldn't push their victory too far. There were too few of them, and they were a community only of Syria itself, with no presence in other parts of the Arab world.

The Shia challenge, however, was different. This rebellion laid claim to nothing less than the Prophet's mantle, to the full legacy of Islam. It had going for it, too, the demographic weight of the Shia of Lebanon and Iraq (where the Shia constitute the majority of the population) and of the substantial Shia communities in the Gulf states. Where the Alawis had asserted their right to a share of the spoils of power, the Shia underclass and its clerical tribunes came with trumpets and scripture to offer what mainstream society every-where has always dreaded: redemption and deliverance. They came to settle an account that was in many ways as old as Islam itself. It was the rebels against those who had acquired an earthly political kingdom, the children of the millennium against the settled classes. This was a clash of two rival historical temperaments: the "saints" versus the merchants.

It was easy to placate the Alawis. The Shia were far less trac-table. Placating them would have required nothing short of redraw-ing the social contract of the Arab world. It would have required people to shed their phobias and their obsessions, to set aside old accounts and ancient hatreds. The gatekeepers would have had to be generous. Those who clamored at the gates would have had to be patient and well mannered. Even in the best of times, this would have been a hellishly difficult undertaking in a world where triumph rarely comes with mercy or moderation. Thus Sunni panic intersected with Shia triumph. The die was cast.

In Lebanon, the battle for West Beirut was decided in favor of the Shia squatters, the newly urbanized and their children. Conquering their self-contempt, the Shia finally made their bid for power in February 1984 and overran West Beirut. They emerged as the dominant power in that part of the city—but challenged by the Palestinians, loathed by those who remembered Beirut as a city of grace and culture, and resented as intruders by the Sunnis for whom West Beirut had been home. And they were the masters of a gutted city. During the preceding decade, the notables and the eminent families of West Beirut had surrendered much of their power to Palestinian gunmen. Thus, when the Shia struck in 1984, the old order in the Muslim sector of the city was helpless to defend itself. Its prior subservience to Palestinian gunmen and street gangs had sealed its fate.

Passion, demography, and chance took the Shia of Lebanon beyond the insularity and fears of the past and gave them unbridled new confidence. They were the country's largest religious community, but they had been its "hewers of wood and drawers of water." Deep-seated traditions of quiescence and timidity had governed their lives. They had been a people of the countryside, but poverty in their ancestral villages in the Bekaa Valley (bordering Syria) and in Jabal Amil, the hill country on Israel's northern border, had hurled them in growing numbers into a Greater Beirut. Per capita income in Beirut was five times higher than it was in the countryside. The city was a magnet for a population anxious to dig out of the poverty and cruelty of the past. Once within the world of Greater Beirut, there came to these people new needs—and resentments. Their political rise in the 1980s was due to the accumulated resentments and achievements of a quarter-century.

The midwife of this Shia awakening was none other than Israel, which swept into Lebanon in June 1982 both to shatter Palestinian dominion in West Beirut and the south and also to restore Maronite hegemony. The first mission was relatively easy to achieve, but the second mission was not to be fulfilled. The moment of Maronite hegemony had passed. The beneficiaries of Israel's Lebanon war and of its subsequent occupation of parts of the south were the Shia. By shattering Palestinian dominion, Israel did for the Shia what they were unable to do for themselves. Israel's occupation of the Shia patrimony in the south closed the circle; it gave a people awakening to their own power the material out of which militant myths are made.

The powers of self-delusion and make-believe being what they are, there were many now grieving sentimentally for the charmed city of the past, skipping over a decade of Palestinian bravado and caprice. In their enthusiasm, the Shia of Lebanon assumed that the credits earned in their fight with Israel would give them a place of honor in the Arab world. After all, they had fought an Arab fight, with ferocity and zeal. Their "martyrs," young children who hurled themselves at Israeli checkpoints and installations in suicide operations, had driven Israel to a sliver of territory on the border. They pointed out that they had done better against Israel than had the Palestinians. But the gatekeepers in the Arab world and their pamphleteers could not embrace the truck bombers or the Shia militancy that generated them. By then the fight over turf and symbols within the Arab world had become far more urgent than the old struggle against Israel.

The Palestinian–Shia war that broke out in West Beirut in May 1985—the so-called war of the camps—provided a measure of relief to those in the Arab world worried about Shia militancy. Determined to put an end to virtual Palestinian rule in Muslim West Beirut, the Shia laid siege to the Palestinian refugee camps. It was a cruel fight over the wreckage of what remained of that part of the city. This time the anti-Shia feeling could be indulged with abandon. Nobody in the Arab world was asking how, or to what end, the Palestinian refugee camps were rearmed. In the period 1982–1983, it was the conventional wisdom in the Arab world that the Palestinian interlude in Lebanon had been a disaster, but now things had changed. West Beirut was overrun by the Shia; the hope for the status quo in Lebanon had been in vain. The carnage in and around the camps made it easier once again to have the Shia on the defensive.

For all its drama, the battle in Beirut and southern Lebanon was really an extension of the battle raging farther east between the Iranian revolution and the Iraqi regime. It was there that the Arab political order would make its stand. The "Persian state" had to be kept at bay and the Iranian revolution quarantined if the familiar order of things in the Arab world was to have a chance. Just as it was no accident that Khomeini named his military campaigns for Karbala, the great Shia shrine to the martyrdom of Hussein, the grandson of the Prophet Muhammad, it was also no accident that Saddam Hussein of Iraq labeled his campaign Qadisiyyat Saddam. (Qadisiyya was the seventh-century battle in which the Arabs conquered Persia and converted the Persian realm to Islam.) The Iraqi campaign was to be phrased in the simple and crude language of race: Arab versus Persian. Since the 1920s and 1930s, Arab nationalism had fallen under the spell of Germanic theories of nationalism—the unity of the "folk," the bonds of race, the entire baggage of German populism. This strain of nationalism found particularly fertile soil in Iraq. It was natural for Saddam Hussein to fall back on the call of the race and the nation. The tribe was threatened, so the tribe struck back.

The modern state of Iraq was a patchwork of Sunni and Shia Arabs, Kurds, Jews, and Assyrians. The Jews and the Assyrians were easy to ruin, overwhelm, and expel. The Kurds in the northeast highlands proved more intractable. The Shia majority in the southern, rural part of the country could not be expelled; instead it was politically intimidated and bullied into submission. Its identity was assailed, its schools and institutions subordinated to the state apparatus. But the course of urbanization that brought the Shia to the cities, and then the reverberations of the Iranian revolution, began to threaten the elaborate Iraqi system of control. Habits of quiescence were shed. A year before he went to war against Iran, Saddam Hussein declared that the Iranian province of Khuzistan might be

Iraq's best line of defense against a Shia revolt within Iraq itself. Launching Qadisiyyat Saddam in 1980, he presented it to the wealthier states of the Gulf as their campaign as well: the "eastern flank" of the Arab world.

In Saddam's reckoning, the custodians of wealth and power in the Gulf states were "secret sharers" of his anti-Shia and anti-Iranian drive. Of course, he was a bully and an upstart. They were not. His means were violent. Theirs were not. But for both, a job had to be done. The work of defending the familiar order of things, of preempting the potential rebellion of the Shia stepchildren in the Arab world, fell to Saddam Hussein. The conservative custodians of Arab wealth and power would subsidize his endeavor. And soon— the tale is familiar—they were throwing good money after bad. A line could not be drawn for the Iraqis; the greater their despair and their need, the more the Gulf states had to pay.

Saddam Hussein was no Wellington on the battlefield, but he was of the clan. Besides, he was buying time for Saudi Arabia and the smaller states of the Gulf. The Iranian revolution's moment of enthusiasm was bound to pass, and after the Iranian clerics discovered that "revolutionary happiness" could not be exported, a deal might be struck with them. The mullah's zeal might give way to the merchant's cunning. The states of the Gulf would survive the upheaval of the Iranian revolution as they had survived the turmoil of the Nasserite revolt. Just as Nasser and Sadat abandoned those in Jordan and Lebanon, and those among the Palestinians, who had really believed in the revolution, so in Iran, reasons of state would prevail, and the enthusiasm of the true believers would be checked.

The custodians of power in the Gulf states understood that the Iranian revolution was a greater tempest than Nasser's; it was closer to home and used more explosive material. For their part, the Iranians made no secret of what they wanted: an Iraqi regime made in Iran's clerical image. In the Shia shrine towns of Najaf and Karbala, in Iraq, and in exile in Iran, Iraqi clerics waited for the moment of their revenge. And in the terrified, silent country over which Saddam

Hussein presided, it was assumed that there were multitudes of men and women waiting to say at last what the Ba'th socialism of Saddam Hussein meant to them.

In the Gulf, the assignment of taking on the Shia revolt fell to Saddam Hussein. In the Levant, there was the curious spectacle of Yasser Arafat and the remnants of the Palestine Liberation Organization offering themselves as a praetorian guard for the enfeebled old order, as those who would do battle for the Sunni structures of power against the Shia. In Syria, sitting astride this divide between the old order and its challengers, was the enigmatic Hafez al-Assad, himself part gendarme of the old order, part rebel. The wily ruler in Damascus could switch camps and loyalties, telling the men of the old order that he shared their aversion to chaos and that the turmoil of Lebanon was beyond his writ and power. And just as insistently, he let the rebels know that he was one of them, that he could be nothing else, after all, himself a heterodox stepchild from the impoverished Alawi mountains of Syria, the quintessential outsider.

Sending his army into West Beirut in February 1987, Assad drew a line. The chaos of West Beirut—the extremism of the Party of God (Hizbollah) zealots and the return of Yasser Arafat's men to the city—had to be checked. The Syrians let it be known that two senior commanders of the Syrian expedition had performed the grim task of snuffing out the rebellion of the Muslim Brotherhood in the Syrian city Hama early in 1982. The rebellion in Hama had been put down without mercy or qualms. Since then, Hama has become a code name for official repression, a promise of the extent to which the regime in Damascus is prepared to go in dealing with those who get in its way. With the outright butchery of twenty-two members of the Party of God so soon after the arrival of Syrian armor into West Beirut, the Syrians announced a new regime for the city. "We don't want the great Syrian prison," a Lebanese leader, the Druze chieftain Kamal Junblatt, had said a decade earlier as Syria began its campaign to dominate Lebanon, but that was where the Lebanese ended up after a ruinous decade. (The shape of things to come was foreshadowed by Junblatt's assassination early in Lebanon's ordeal; he was struck down in 1977. There was no room in the new order for independent leaders of his kind.)

The struggle between the dominant Arab political order and the Iranian revolution and its tributaries led down a blind alley. The Shia challengers pushed on, driven by a spirit of revenge and the promise of the millennium. Their revolt—to borrow the words of Victor Hugo, who described another time and place of revolt and vengeance—carried away "great and sickly spirits alike, strong men and weaklings, the tree-trunk and the wisp of straw. Woe to those it carries away no less than to those it seeks to destroy." Although there was no evidence that this revolt could succeed where its predecessors had failed, that it could add new skills to a civilization falling behind the rest of the world in technique and productive capacity, the fury would not subside. None of this fury had anything to do with the repair and nurturing of a decent political and cultural order.

They were "sons without fathers," a Lebanese sociologist, Waddah Chrara, wrote of the Party of God cadres who inherited the ruins of West Beirut. That sector of the city—home of the American University of Beirut, the Western embassies, and the beachfront hotels—had been the repository of a special urban culture and a political sensibility that came with it: Arab nationalism, with its familiar mix of Western airs and anti-Western politics. The new claimants to West Beirut, sons of peasants newly urbanized, were the bearers of a new dispensation. In a city that had been good at parody of Western ways, the new breed staged their own parody of what had transpired in Khomeini's Iran. Their call to an Islamic millennium, their campaign to extirpate the roots of the American presence, doubled up an undisguised rebellion against the old order of Arab nationalism and its custodians in the upper order. In the authority of a religious scholar in a distant Iranian realm and in the material help his state offered its adherents in Lebanon, the sons of peasants and their clerical leaders, young *mujtahids* (religious schol-

ars), who seemed to emerge overnight, found the warrant for audacious acts.

With lightning speed, in 1983 and 1984, the young men of Ayatollah Khomeini's crusade and a new breed of wholesalers of terror
who did Iran's and Syria's bidding proceeded to demolish the American presence in Beirut. A hasty American decision had been made
in September 1982 to dispatch American forces to Lebanon. This
was an open-ended, ambiguous errand to a place America did not
fully know or understand. America had indulged great hopes that
an American era had begun in Lebanon, but the Americans would
not stay the course in Lebanon; there was no taste in America for
tribal wars in places with tangled histories. It took several car
bombs and a few willing young "martyrs" to drive the U.S. Marines
out of Lebanon, to frighten off the great power from afar. The old
secular nationalists had railed against the power of the West; the
children of this new theocratic upheaval took this encounter with
the West in a grim, new direction. They offered their deeds and their
"martyrs" as ample proof that their time had come, that the old
bourgeois order of secular nationalism had been emptied of force
and meaning.

Around the corner lay redemptionism's nemesis: the ways of a
cynical, materialist city like Beirut that knew how to tame ferocious
revolutions; the impact of corruption and new money that a distant
Iranian state had made available to its operatives in Lebanon; the
resilience of older classes who waited for this revolt to blow over
and to make its peace with hierarchy and property. But that lay in
the future. In its moment of enthusiasm, this revolution had the
sanction of an armed imam and the strength of an underclass's rage
and resentments. The men, militia leaders, and clerical tribunes who
sacked the old order in Beirut were a generation removed from the
land, the countryside, and the peasant world of the south and the
Bekaa Valley. Half a century earlier, when the parents of the new
Shia claimants began their timid migration to the city, the dead
among the Shia had to be taken back to be buried in their ancestral

villages because there were no Shia cemeteries in the city. There were no Shia mosques either. Beirut belonged, for the most part, to the Sunni Muslims and Greek Orthodox. These new warlords and foot soldiers of the Shia movements could hardly grieve for the ruin that had befallen West Beirut: In its charmed days, it had not been theirs. They had made their home on the southern approaches of the city beyond the sand dunes that fringed the city, and they had made their homes alongside the Armenian refugees in a large squatter settlement north of the city. Their exaltation in a city now ruined by its feuds is no mystery. Long ago, John Milton's *Paradise Lost* described for us euphoria at a time of ruin:

> *Here we reign secure, and in my choice*
> *To reign is worth ambition, though in Hell:*
> *Better to reign in Hell than serve in Heav'n*

In its aftermath, the Iranian revolution and its Islamic sources became a subject of endless commentary. It fell to the poet Adonis to divine early on the destination of that revolution in essays he wrote in 1979 and 1980; the first of these essays was published in February 1979, the month of Khomeini's return home from his long exile. "Beware the oppressors, beware the liberators," the great Russian writer and exile Alexander Herzen (1812–1870) had written of the European and Russian revolutionaries of his time. There was something of this spirit in Adonis's view of Iran's upheaval. He welcomed the storm, but he had a premonition that it would end in failure. He knew its ultimate destination. Just as the nationalism of the preceding era had given rise to the officer class, he saw the harvest of this new revolt giving rise to a new phenomenon: *al-faqih al-askari,* the armed jurist. He was reluctant to sit in judgment on this revolution; he would not raise his voice against it or join its critics. The true judges of this revolt, he said, were the excluded, the poor, and the disinherited, for whom this revolt was the "first promise" of justice made them in a long time.

The secularists were on the run, and an Iranian Shia *mujtahid* had made himself party to the affairs of the Arabs. The sympathy of Adonis for this theocratic revolt put him at odds with some of the writers who had been his peers and collaborators during the preceding decade. He came in for a particularly scathing attack from a fellow Syrian writer, the philosopher and Yale-educated academic Sadiq al-Azm, whose influential autopsies of Arab society in the aftermath of the 1967 war, *Self-Criticism after the Defeat* and *Criticism of Religious Thought,* published in the late 1960s, were among the most celebrated and influential works of that era. Contemporaries, the two men spanned the full spectrum of Arab (and Syrian) society: Adonis, a child of the hinterland and a mountain village; Azm, a son of one of Bilad al-Sham's (Greater Syria's) aristocratic, landowning families, a Damascus family with two centuries of political power behind it. Adonis combined his mastery of Arabic and Islamic material with a deep interest in French letters and essays; Azm was a product of Anglo-Saxon training and empirical philosophy. In Adonis's sympathy for the Iranian revolt, Sadiq al-Azm saw nothing but betrayal of secular politics and the secular tradition. Adonis, he said, had fallen under the spell of charismatic authority and had joined the ranks of the Islamists. A modern man, a "former secularist" and "former socialist," Adonis had wandered into the thicket of religious controversy, his critic claimed. He had done so out of despair, out of a defective romance for that religious impulse at work in the history of "the East." Having given in to the idea that religion was the moving force of Islamic history, Adonis was bound, Sadiq al-Azm said, to end up where he did, in a political world where religion absorbed everything and made small and insignificant all other matters, such as "economics, oil, class struggle, ideology, progress, and decline."

The attack against Adonis was true to Azm's style and commitments. In the preceding decade, he had lost his professorship at the American University of Beirut for running afoul of the Muslim religious establishment. He had angered the Left and the Palestinians with cool and merciless studies of their exaggerations and writings. But Adonis had other critics who worked with more pernicious material. In the able poet whose imagination and literacy embraced wide Islamic and Western concerns, they saw the sectarian, the child of the Syrian hinterland. In this poet's sympathy for Iran's upheaval, they could hear the call of the minoritarian sect from which he had hailed. An urban truth was in retreat, and those old, buried atavisms of the sect and the clan had begun to reappear.

Adonis had no patience for the doubters or for those in the Arab intellectual class who dismissed Iran's revolt as a theocratic under-taking. Everywhere around these intellectuals, he said, were arid structures of cultural and political oppression. They could not cast stones because the world around them was a wasteland; the Arabs talked of unity but were divided. They paid homage to secularism, but that secularism was a cover for sectarian loyalties. They talked of socialism, but their experiments in socialism had given birth to the rise of "new plundering classes." Even the pride of modern Arabs, *asr al-nahda,* the age of the enlightenment, had turned the intellectuals and their work into instruments of autocratic regimes. Arabs were in "a cave"; their path was blocked. He would venture out with the new revolt, even if there were no sure and safe lands beyond.

Few if any other writers of his generation had Adonis's interest in religious thought or in the connection between the authority of texts and literary and poetic traditions on the one hand and politi-cal hegemony on the other. Five years before the onset of the Iranian revolution, Adonis published his magnum opus on these matters, a brilliant multivolume work, *al-Thabit wa al-Mutahawwil* (The Fixed and the Changing), on the struggle between religious literary orthodoxy and creativity in Islamic history. In it, he inquired into the very roots of Islamic and Arab history. He followed the philosophies and arguments of the dominant order and its defenders, poets and religious authorities alike, and the dissidents who had risen in inter-mittent rebellions against the powers-that-be. It was no secret where Adonis himself belonged. He was an innovator. He aligned himself with the poets, the writers, and the dissidents who stood alone and against power. In a long journey through Arab-Islamic history, from

Islam's rise in the Peninsula in the seventh century to the present, Adonis was guided by a singular zeal: a passion for liberty, innovation, and daring. His vision was steady and without illusions, unsparing in its perception of rulers, commanders, and courts and their appropriation of poetry, religious texts, and traditions as their props of power. Once a new revelation and a rebellion, Islam had ruled, and its arsenal, Adonis wrote, had been deployed against the dissident and the rebel. The powers had been shrewd. They had played on the instinctive human fear of anything new and untried; orthodoxy became something to be "preserved and defended." Hegemony, property, and inequality acquired the sanction of revered texts and traditions. "Knowledge becomes authority and authority a kind of truth; truth varies with hegemony," he wrote. It was against this background that the Iranian revolution had to be viewed. The authority of the religious interpretation, historically on the side of power, the courts, the merchants, and the magistrates, was now providing a writ for rebellion.

The success of this revolt, Adonis warned, was not ensured. He had studied the history of Islamic revolts and seen the liberators turn enforcers of new structures of oppression. In this new revolt, too, he saw the possibility of disappointment. Khomeini, the destroyer of old structures, was sure to establish a new realm. Like other religious-political leaders before him, this new imam was destined to merge the realms of power and knowledge, to claim for his dominion religious sanction and authority. Would there be a place under the new dispensation for freedom of inquiry and dissent? Adonis warned the Arabs in proximity to this revolt of special dangers. In Iran's revolt, the Arab masses could come to experience, vicariously, their own release from oppression. The Arabs might become spectators, ignore the specificity of their own condition, defer their own quest as they became entranced with the daring and spectacle of Iran's revolt.

But the specter haunting the revolution was that of the armed jurist, *al-faqih al-askari*. Just as the old revolts of the 1950s and 1960s had been usurped by a military caste, this new revolt could end in failure and oppression, Adonis warned. The language—and the banners—could change, but men and women could emerge empty-handed from this revolt. Although there would be a new language, the dilemmas of the society—its backwardness, its inability to see and define its malady—would persist. Arabism would replace Islam, the vocabulary of politics would change, and the Islamic public would replace the Arab public, but the dominant ways of the culture would survive. Political thought would remain an instrument for "fighting the other rather than a means of self-criticism and self-discovery." The culture would have made another detour. It would have headed right back to its stagnant past, right into the arms of a religious-political leader, to do his bidding and to surrender to him its judgment and freedom, only to end up as yet another unrealized dream in an Arab-Muslim history littered with betrayed promises.

The moment of reckoning for the revolution of the "armed imam" came in the summer of 1988, when Ayatollah Khomeini told the believers of the Iranian revolution that his campaign against Iraq would have to be written off. During the preceding decade, Khomeini had been a stern and remote figure. With his revolution on the ropes, he spoke to his "revolutionary children" in a different voice. He would drink the "poisoned chalice" of accepting the peace; he was "ashamed," he said, before his nation and its sacrifices. It was hard for them, he knew, to accept what had come to pass. "But then, is it not hard for your old father?"

The sorrow of that moment in the summer of 1988 evoked memories of another summer two decades earlier: the summer of 1967, when the hero-leader of pan-Arabism, Gamal Abdul Nasser, told his faithful that their dream of power had ended in bitter disappointment and defeat. Different men working with different material, the secular soldier in Cairo and the turbaned leader from Qom had promised more than they could deliver.

Khomeini's revolution embarrassed and bloodied the status quo by appealing to the nativism and "authenticity" of traditionalists bent upon retaining their ways, but it did not prevail. The Iraqi state withstood the buffeting of war, and the conservative states of the Gulf dug in and waited out the revolution's moment of enthusiasm. The revolution had claimed a universal message, a broad Islamic mandate; its rivals had depicted its unbounded claims as a cloak for Iranian hegemony, a bid for the mantle of the Prophet by a minoritarian Shia sect at odds with the ways of orthodox Islam. The revolutionary state had promised utopia, a revenge against the mighty and the pampered, a social order more pure and authentic. To the numb and the jaded and those sitting on the fence, however, the conservative rivals of the revolution offered the safety of routine, the comfort of what men knew and lived with.

Perhaps the shrewdest among the guardians and tribunes of the Iranian revolution knew it all along, that a "sister republic," to borrow the language of the French revolution, or "potential capitals of our revolution," in Ayatollah Khomeini's words, would be elusive. Even the Jacobins in their time knew that foreign revolutionaries were fickle friends, that foreign adventures were expensive endeavors, and that the world outside the borders of the revolutionary republic was a stubborn place. "We think of ourselves as primarily responsible and bound defenders of Iran, which is our place of birth," Khomeini's first prime minister, Mehdi Bazargan, wrote to him in a celebrated "open letter" in 1986. "Our concern with the world outside our home and homeland and nation is clearly secondary." But this was the voice of the "loyal opposition"; Bazargan had been forced out of power less than a year after the revolution's triumph. A different impulse prevailed in the conduct of Iran's affairs.

The pan-Islamic millennium was not to be. The revolution did not catch on in the dynastic states of the Persian Gulf and the Arabian Peninsula. These states had been in the way of the Mahdi's wrath, special targets of his revolt, but the material for social revolution was missing in these states. There was a greater "fit" between the ruling dynasties of the Gulf and their citizen-populations than there could be in a vast realm like Iran. The Saudis and the small dynastic states of the Gulf drew the right lessons from the fall of the

Shah. They avoided the chaos that beset Iran in the 1970s, trimmed down their pretensions, sought ideological cover.

The basic themes of Khomeini's revolution and the patterns of the religious-radical alliance, the partnership of mosque and bazaar, were particular to Iran, a society known for both its long periods of submission to despotism and its recurrent rebellions. These large themes found no echo in the Arab realms nearby. The states of the Gulf were too small, their politics confined to the competition of clan, family, and faction. Temperamentally, Iran has been a land susceptible to the power of ideas, to political and philosophical abstraction, to the pamphleteer. It has been described by one of its known foreign admirers, E. G. Browne, the British scholar, as a "hotbed of philosophical systems." The culture of the Arabian Peninsula and the Gulf states has in contrast always been thoroughly empirical and raw, its politics the struggles of clans and determined men, tribal affairs to the core. The conservative Arab states of the Gulf had known no struggle between the religious class and the regime. Where the Shah had sought to decimate the mullahs, the Saudi state co-opted the clerics, left them niches in the social order where they were supreme: religious ritual and observance, education, the judiciary. The Saudi realm rested on a partnership: the dynasty has enjoyed an unquestioned monopoly in matters of "high policy," such as defense, oil, finance, and foreign affairs. But the religious functionaries have always had their prerogatives—and their compensation. They have been allowed access to the airwaves and to the printed media. There was no campaign here to remake the political culture of the place, no fight between a "modernizing" state and a popular culture trying to stay alive. The Iranian clerical leaders had hoped to overturn the secular dictatorship in Iraq, but these hopes must have been tempered by sober calculations. Iranian religious leaders knew Iraq's shrine cities and Iraq's social situation. They knew the deep-seated pessimism and quiescence of the Shia of Iraq. Khomeini himself, after nearly fifteen years of exile in Iraq, must have fully understood Iraqi politics. The Iranian revolutionaries had sponsored Iraqi Shia dissidents, but these dissidents could not overturn the "Sunni ascendancy" in Iraq. The Shia clerical estate was too weak to mount a challenge to the Iraqi regime. The Shia of Iraq had a beloved leader of their own, Ayatollah Muhammad Baqir al-Sadr, a brilliant jurist and writer, the "Khomeini of Iraq." But he (along with his sister) was put to death by Saddam Hussein shortly before the Iraqi ruler launched his war against Iran. The war put the Shia of Iraq in an impossible situation. The Iraqi despot had closed up the political universe in his terrified land.

In retrospect, it is easy to see that the Iranian revolutionaries overestimated the centrality of their realm to the wider world of Islam. There was a time, in the high Middle Ages, when Persian civilization and language served as the elite culture of the Muslim world from Indonesia to Morocco, but in the modern world this is no longer the case. For all the sound and fury of a revolution that asserted its relevance to others, its right to guide them, Iran remains a solitary society with a strong national and cultural tradition. Shi'ism, which the Iranian state adopted in the sixteenth century, is one factor in this isolation, and the country's unique cultural traditions have compounded this sense of separateness.

The Iranian revolutionaries did not really know the Arab society they sought to change. After a long fight with the Shah, they had their revolt; they came to show the path to redemption and deliverance. But in the Fertile Crescent and Egypt, men had already experienced their moments of elation, their outbursts that passed for revolutions—the politics of the Ba'th and Nasserism—and they had seen these detours end in defeat, futility, or sterile dictatorship. It was a cynical, weary region that the Iranians set out to transform. Arab society turned the new revolution into something very old and familiar, something it knew how to handle: the feud between sect and clan.

Adonis was proven right by the course of that great civil war in Islam between the Iranian revolution and its enemies. For the Arabs who had seen the Iranian upheaval as their own, who had known satisfaction from its fury and power, the "redemption" blowing their way from the east was a false promise. The theocracy that crushed liberty at home could not extend it to others. "A good man can save a country, whereas a bad man can destroy it," Ayatollah Khomeini had once observed. He had been both avenger and builder of a new realm. Thrown up by chaos, he had provided a cruel kind of "solution" for his country: clerical rule, obedience, a state that stitched together the interests of the bazaar and the urban underclass. In 1988 he issued a remarkable ruling: "Our government," he pronounced, "has priority over all other Islamic tenets, even over prayer, fasting and the pilgrimage to Mecca." Politics was clearly in command; religion its handmaiden. The redeemer was a turbaned shah. What work he did, what power he unleashed, what "solution" he offered, were in the end an affair of Iran. The specificity of the Iranian revolution could not be wished away.

The Arab Shia could not win. In their minority status, their vulnerability to power, and their need to tread carefully, they were true to the ethos of Shi'ism itself and to its historic predicament. In the beginning of Shia history, at the heart of the faith, there was the tale of Imam Hussein, the grandson of the Prophet Muhammad whose lonely death in a seventh-century battle in southern Iraq lies at the heart of the Shia faith. Khomeini had adopted this tale, claiming the beloved, saintly man as his inspiration. "I am a Husseini not a Hassani," he had said of himself. It was after Hussein's solitary stand at Karbala in southern Iraq that Khomeini named his military offensive against the regime of Saddam Hussein. (Hassan, the older of the two brothers, the two imams, had accepted the logic of power. In A.D. 661, when his father the Caliph Ali was struck down and power passed from Hijaz to Damascus, Hassan acknowledged what he could not reverse. He offered the founder of the Umayyad dynasty in Damascus a grudging acceptance.) It had fallen to Hussein to challenge the new Damascus regime. In 680, he rode from his home in Hijaz to southern Iraq, where he was cut down. It is around Hussein's martyrdom that Shia history revolves, and it was over his legacy that Khomeini and his more liberal critics at home waged a proxy debate about Iran's future, about the balance in the Shia tradition between zeal and solitude on the one hand and routine and social peace on the other.

In Khomeini's rendition, Hussein Ibn Ali, a grandson of the Prophet and a son of the Prophet's cousin, Imam Ali, rode to a sure death at Karbala. In this manner the hero-martyr of Shia history was turned into a prototype for the suicide driver. But Hussein's was a different journey. Karbala was not his destination. It was where he was trapped on his way to a worldly city, the city of Kufa, whose people had sought him out in their struggle with Damascus, the other center of Arab-Muslim power. "We invite you to come to Kufa as we have no imam to guide us." He had been reluctant to go. He was warned by a shrewd and wise poet that the Kufans were an unreliable lot, that their hearts were with Hussein and their swords with the impious ruler Yazid, who had come to power in Damascus. Assassins had been dispatched by the regime in Damascus to cut him down; he would make the journey with a heavy heart. On the plain of Karbala, cut off from the water of the Euphrates, he and his band of companions were met by a large contingent of the ruler's troops. Hussein and his companions were killed. The imam was beheaded, his body trampled by horses, and his severed head carried from Karbala to the ruler's court in Damascus. For centuries, Karbala had been the material for lament, sorrow, and political withdrawal. In Khomeini's sermons, the pendulum swung to the other extreme. Karbala became a warrant for unrelenting zeal.

In the "open letter" to Khomeini that the liberal and humane Mehdi Bazargan, a leading figure of the "devout bourgeoisie," French-educated but at home with the Shia faith, addressed to Khomeini in 1986, Bazargan aimed at nothing less than recapturing Karbala from Khomeini and from the unforgiving interpretation Khomeini had given it. Khomeini's revolution, he wrote, had made martyrdom a "goal in itself." It had dispatched the believers and the young into doomed military campaigns the same way the horde had been dispatched by the Crusades, "barefoot toward Palestine," oblivious of the fact that they might "die of hunger and thirst along the way." This revolution had thrown caution and reason overboard;

it had acted as though nations were no longer in need of "modern means of warfare and statecraft."

The legacy of Imam Hussein, Bazargan wrote, had been disfigured. "In your message . . . Hussein rushed willingly to his death in Karbala. Therefore, according to you, all of us must either be killed or taken captive in order to free the oppressed from the yoke of their own governments." But Hussein's story was different, Bazargan said. "A realistic glance at the epic of Karbala" leads to different conclusions: Hussein's move did have some "promise and some calculations" behind it. He had been asked to offer allegiance to an unjust ruler and had been unable to do so. He was neither a gambler nor a reckless man. The Arabs of Kufa had petitioned him to take up their leadership; he had waited until 70,000–80,000 people in Kufa had sworn allegiance to him through his emissary. "In the social-geographic context of Iraq in those days, these figures were extraordinary and represented the overwhelming majority of that region," Bazargan wrote. Trapped in Karbala, the saintly man remained a realist to the very end. Told by one of the commanders of the Damascus troops that the Kufans had had a change of heart, Hussein accepted the logic of things: "Now that they have withdrawn their invitation, I will change my destination and return the way I came," Hussein answered, but to no avail.

Whereas Khomeini insisted on "war, war until victory" in his struggle with Iraq, the Hussein of Bazargan's rendition was a leader who did everything he could to avert a clash with his enemies. War was imposed on Hussein; he fought a defensive war and fought it well, until he was "compassionately and God-pleasingly martyred by the transgressors." There is no warrant in Karbala, then, for a war that knows no limits. Khomeini's "war, war until victory," said Bazargan, was the same as "war, war until annihilation." There was no honor in a campaign of endless slaughter that sacrificed "the valuable young generation of the country," that destroyed its "economic installations." Khomeini may have claimed the authority and the Shia tradition, but he had strayed, Bazargan said, from "the objective realities and the lessons of the apostles and the imams."

On its own earth, in Iran, that interpretation of the Shia faith and of Karbala had led to a great incoherence. Its gift to the Shia Arabs was more problematic still. The clerical ruler who declared himself a Husseini not a Hassani presided over a large realm with great strategic and economic assets. He could lend some courage to the Shia Arabs, he could subsidize the cadres and tribunes of the Party of God in Beirut, and he could embolden the Shia of the small principality of Bahrain, but he could not remake the world of the Shia in Arab realms. He could not alter the condition of the Shia in the Saudi kingdom, a vulnerable minority in the eastern oil province of the kingdom, professional and well off, but marked as outsiders and heterodox in a political realm that rested on the foundations of a conservative brand of Sunni Islam. To survive and be left alone, the Shia in the Saudi realm needed the patronage and protection of the monarchy against the zealots of neo-Wahhabism (named for the eighteenth-century preacher, Muhammad ibn Abd al-Wahhab, whose partnership with al-Saud had anchored and legitimized the Saudi state ever since). There were Wahhabi extremists, religious and layman alike, some of them schooled in the great universities of the West for that matter, who would lay waste to the world of the Saudi Shia. There were religious agitators who declared the Shia heretics, their property forfeit, the livestock they slaughtered *haram* (impermissible) to eat, traffic with them forbidden. To survive, the Shia of the realm needed some of the attributes of Imam Hassan, the ability to strike a bargain with the dominant world around them, the gift of reading the balance of worldly power.

Although Iran lay just across the waters of the Persian Gulf, the cities and jurists of Iran might as well have been a world away from the Shia of the eastern province of the Saudi realm. In the immense landscape of Arabia, it is hard to escape the uniqueness of the place and its sense of solitude, hard to believe that a foreign people from across the waters with a different language and a different temperament could come to the rescue. The Shia did not govern the realm, nor did they expect to. From the dynasty, they sought and obtained a workable social contract: the protection of the state in return for loyalty, the right to professional life, the sanctity of property and home.

A sense of this came to me on repeated visits to the oasis town of Hofuf in the eastern province, a town with a substantial Shia population. Blessed with artesian wells, Hofuf has a stunningly lush feel to it amidst the scorched landscape all around it: groves of palm trees, open streams, and fruit gardens. When he saw it in the 1920s, Colonel Harold Dickson, one of the Pax Britannica's gifted administrators and chroniclers in the Gulf, described it as "an emerald in a setting of yellow sand," adding that the town reminded him of Damascus—the desert yielding to sudden, unexpected vegetation. On my first visit there, I made my way to the *Husseiniyya* (a house of religious observance and mourning obviously named for the beloved Imam Hussein). A merchant whom I had asked for directions led me to a simple, unassuming building at the end of a quiet alleyway. I came back to Hofuf two or three times on subsequent visits.

I befriended a young local merchant in his late thirties and an older man of the professional class. You could see right away in this region the manners and ways of a people at ease with the world outside. One of the great travel writers of the nineteenth century, William Gifford Palgrave, had caught the feel of the place in a dazzling book, *Central and Eastern Arabia* (1871):

> A sea-coast people, looking mainly to foreign lands and the ocean for livelihood and commerce, accustomed to see among them not unfrequently men of dress, manners, and religion differing from their own, many of them themselves travellers or voyagers to Basrah, Bagdad, Bahreyn, 'Oman, and some even farther, they are commonly free from that half-wondering, half-suspicious feeling which the sight of a stranger occasions in the isolated desert-girded centre; in short, experience, that best of masters, has gone far to unteach the lessons of ignorance, intolerance, and national aversion.

In our time, the oil industry and the traffic of the Americans have worked their ways on this worldly region. Trouble had hit Hofuf and its neighboring Shia towns in the 1980s in the war between the Khomeini revolution and the states around it. Riots had erupted in the nearby town of Qatif, portraits of Khomeini had turned up in the eastern province, and the traditional ban on public observance of Shia ceremonies of mourning to honor the memory of Imam Hussein had been challenged. A few had taken to the new politics, but in the shade of the young merchant's lovely sprawling house, on the outskirts of Hofuf, with a garden of lemon trees and little streams everywhere, and the merchant's children and nephews playing about, I was reminded of the older truth of Shi'ism: its suspicion of political power, its view of politics as an activity corrosive of the soul. After Karbala, Imam Hussein's son, Zayn al-Abidin, whose illness during that battle had spared him the fate of his father and his father's companions, turned away from politics, dedicated his life to prayer and religious observance. Yet another saintly figure of Shi'ism, Imam Ja'far al-Sadiq (d. 765), had rescued Shi'ism from the excess of the extremists within its ranks and then codified its laws and jurisprudence. There had been battles in the history of Shi'ism, but there was a warrant in the tradition for those who wanted a reprieve from the politics and the warfare. It was a false gift Khomeini bore the Shia Arabs who lived in a world that required from them tact and subtlety.

THE SEVENTH-CENTURY symbols—Khomeini's millennium and Karbala, Saddam Hussein's battle of Qadisiyya and "Arabism" against "the Persians"—tore asunder the social peace of the Fertile Crescent and the Gulf. Underneath the modern cover there remained the older realities of sects, ethnicity, and the call of the clans. Secular nationalists in the Arab world squirmed when faced with this bleak verdict. Souad al-Sabah, a woman of the ruling family of Kuwait had written poetry in homage to "Iraq's sword" in its war on behalf of the "Arab truth" against the turbaned mullahs across the Gulf. A quarter of the citizen-population of her small city-state of Kuwait was Shia; some had come from Iran generations back; others from Bahrain; still others from the eastern province of Saudi Arabia. Terror had hit Kuwait, there had been Shia attacks against the French and American embassies in 1983, and there had been an attempt on the emir's life in 1985. There was a wind of sectarian antagonism at play. The sects had coexisted in this tolerant principality on the Gulf. There had been little if any intermarriage between the two communities; the Shia merchants had done well but had been kept out of the inner circle of power. Now the old contract had come apart. There were greater limits on the communal and religious life of the Shia. Thousands may have been deported. The strident "Arabism" of Kuwait, the poetry in praise of the Iraqi despot, were about Kuwait itself. I speak to my daughter-in-law so my neighbor will hear, goes an Arabic proverb. The poetess, a patron of the arts, culture, and literature, while praising the despot in Baghdad, was addressing the Shia at home.

I went to Kuwait in the midst of all this, in the spring of 1985, on a professional assignment that seemed safe and antiseptic. I was there with another American academic as an external examiner for the political science department of Kuwait University. It was my first visit, and I found the place appealing in an odd sort of way. I was quite taken by the landscape and surprised by my response. The starkness of the land, the turquoise waters of the Gulf at the edge of the desert, the immense blue sky: It had a beauty of its own. The place seemed vibrant and open to me. I had found a circle of academics and through them I had no difficulty entering the social life.

The visit remained a simple affair, or so it seemed to me at the time. It was shortly after my American colleague (he was a stranger to the place, his relation to it unburdened by any ties, the perfect innocent abroad) and I submitted our report that I was to see shadows of Kuwait's life. The report, perfectly professional, safe, and sterile, had recommended that some courses in politics were better taught in English, that English was the dominant language of that field, and that young Kuwaitis were part of the modern traffic with the world and would be better served by immersion in the English language. It had been an innocent recommendation; we had endorsed what had been suggested to us by the students and the professors with whom we had talked.

No sooner had the report been submitted than it was greeted by a small controversy. The pretext was the matter of instruction in English; the real issue was my invitation to the university, the very fact that I had been permitted entry to Kuwait. A writer by the name of Baghdadi was furious that I had been let in, angry that the treasure of the country had been spent to bring me there. I had come to Kuwait after an era of extravagance when there had been vast spending on journalists and foreign academics. Baghdadi was not a subtle man; for him I was a servant of American imperial interests (why else would I recommend a seminar or two in English?), I was a friend of Israel and Israelis, and, most damning of all, I was a Shu'ubi. With this last label, Baghdadi went to the heart of the matter. The Shu'ubiyya movement had been a political-literary revolt by non-Arab (mostly Persian) converts to Islam in the early centuries following the rise of Islam. Modernity and secular nationalism had found new usages for the term, flung at every critic of Arab nationalism. In the midst of this terrible time between Sunni and Shia Islam, a Shia and Shu'ubi who had not been deferential to the historiography of Arab nationalism had been allowed entry to the country. Baghdadi knew the power and the meaning of the label. The decent drapery that covered such feuds had been removed. The issue was rendered more transparent by the last names of the protagonists: Baghdadi from the city of Baghdad; Ajami from the country of the Ajam, Persia. It had become that kind of time in Arab political life.

I had not known much of Shi'ism when Baghdadi tried to pin the *Shu'ubi* label on me. I had not (yet) written of Shi'ism. I had grown up as a Shia *assimile* in the secular culture of Beirut. The Shia faith I associated with my mother, who was a believer. She had visited the Shia shrines in Syria and Iraq for solace. The Shia faith had kept her going, but I had kept my distance from it.

My early politics could not have been radically different from Baghdadi's. I was raised on the Arab nationalism of the 1950s and 1960s. I had known the secular politics of Nasserism, and that political culture had sustained me in my early teens. But my critic had seen the (Persian) ancestors clinging to me; in my politics he saw the power of an old sectarian call. It was easy for me to read of his fury from afar; I had a home in America, a society for whom these furies were incomprehensible. But those for whom these Arab lands were home were caught up in no-man's-land. They had traveled far, but right around the corner they were face to face with atavistic feuds that had never gone away.

(There was no safety for the hunter in this kind of world. Eleven years later, Baghdadi himself was at the center of a deadlier controversy. He had received a death threat; a leading Islamist in the country had condemned Baghdadi as a man who belonged to the "doomed secularist nation" and a "bastard child of the Orientalists." Baghdadi had taken on the Islamists in a weekly column he wrote for one of the dailies and in his lectures on a course in Islamic political thought he taught at Kuwait University. His enemies had charged him with *ridda*, apostasy. In his defense, Baghdadi had called upon the governments in the Gulf to face "the threat to civil society" that the political-religious extremists represented, "this cancerous illness." The Islamists, he added, had enormous resources at their disposal but were after him to "cut off my livelihood, perhaps to liquidate me physically." The world had changed and had not changed. This new deadly force of *takfir*—declaring one's enemies apostates and religious deviants—was the old nationalist sensibility of an earlier time, *takhwin*, branding dissidents as traitors in new garb. At the core of both forces lay the dread of "the other," the impatience with difference.)

From the dark alley of this sectarian feud, the secular nationalists were offered the semblance of an escape. It came their way from the West Bank and Gaza, the Intifada, the uprising, which broke out in December 1987. An elemental revolt of the "children of the stones," the uprising doubled as a national revolt against Israeli rule and a revolt of the despised against the upper orders of Palestinian society. The revolt broke out in Jabalya, the largest of the squalid refugee camps of the Gaza Strip. The indigent rose up in a raging protest that echoed through the land, taking both Israel and the Palestine Liberation Organization by surprise. A ferocious "rite of chaos" (the words are those of the able Israeli journalists Ze'ev Schiff and Ehud Ya'ari), a revolt of despair, the uprising of the "children of the stones," was to become the new inspiration, proof that the passions of the Arab world had not yet been spent.

Nizar Qabbani had always been a poet of great occasions, a chronicler of memorable events, and he was to pay that rebellion of youth the homage of an enfeebled older generation. In *The Trilogy of the Children of the Stones,* a work of prose and free verse, he hailed the force of this new anger and saw it as a harbinger of hope:

> *The children of*
> *the stones have scattered our*
> *papers,*
> *spilled ink on our clothes,*
> *mocked the banality of our*
> *old texts. . . .*
> *What matters*
> *about the children of*
> *the stones is that they*
> *have brought us*
> *rain after centuries of*
> *thirst,*
> *brought us the sun after centuries*
> *of darkness,*
> *brought us hope after centuries of*
> *defeat. . . .*
> *The most important*
> *thing about them is*
> *that they have rebelled*

against the authority
of the fathers,
that they have fled the
House of Obedience,
that they have
disobeyed our commands and
our wishes.
It is their luck that they
have decided to fight
as they wish, live as
they wish, die
as they wish.

O children of Gaza,
teach us some of what you know,
Teach us to be men,
for among us men have become
as dough

* * *

O Children of Gaza
Don't mind our broadcasts
Don't listen to us
We are the people of calculations
of addition, of subtraction
Wage your wars and leave us alone
We are dead with no tombs
Orphans with no eyes.
Children of Gaza
Don't refer to our writings
Don't read us
We are your parents
Don't be like us.
We are your idols
Don't worship us

O mad people of Gaza,
a thousand greetings to the mad
The age of political reason
has long departed
so teach us madness

The "children of the stones" were everything the older generation had not been: irreverent, defiant, and bold. They would not run
away as their elders had. Qabbani was not alone in the awe he felt
for the boys of the Intifada. Mahmoud Darwish, the poet of the
Palestinian national movement, saw the stones hurled by the young
building a new world. Darwish, who had lived in Israel and worked
as a journalist in Haifa until 1971, maintained close ties with the Israeli Left and the peace movement. He was to jolt his Israeli friends
with a poem published in early 1988 in *The Seventh Day,* an Arabic
weekly in Paris, "Passing between Passing Words." It was to become
the poem of the Intifada, written in the form of an address to the
Israelis:

O you passing between passing words
Carry your names and go away
Take your hours of our time and go away
Steal what you will from the blue of the sea, and the sand of memory
Take what pictures you will, so that you will understand
How a stone from our land builds the ceiling of the sky. . . .

O you passing between passing words
Pass like the bitter dust, but
Do not pass among us like locusts
For we have what to do in our land
We have wheat to grow and to water with the dew of our bodies
We have things here that will not satisfy you:
A stone or a partridge
So take the past, if you wish, to the antiquities market

And return the bones to the bird, if you wish,
On a tray of clay
We have things here that will not satisfy you: we have the future
And we have what to do in our land.

In time the Intifada was overwhelmed by violence. Three years into the rebellion, the hunt for "collaborators" took a toll of more than four hundred lives, and the uprising wreaked terrible destruction on Palestinian society. The Palestinians had been here before. The Arab Rebellion of 1936–1939, in its time the stuff of legend, had been consumed by its own fury, an act of self-immolation. After the initial euphoria, there had come hunger and deprivation. Then came the "Night of the Long Knives," when Palestinian society turned on itself and began the hunt for collaborators and sacrificial lambs. The same cycle played itself out in this uprising. "The dream of the Intifada has become a nightmare," wrote Adnan Damiri, a figure of the uprising who had paid his dues and done time in Israeli prisons; his work was published in the Palestinian paper *al-Fajr* in mid-1991. By then it was common knowledge that ordinary men and women in Palestinian society feared the boys of the Intifada more than they did Israel's power, but that dark side had to be overlooked by those at some remove who needed victories to celebrate.

The old worshiped at the altar of the young; a thwarted, secular generation saw in the brutality of youth an answer to its own feeble heritage. On one side the dandies of old; on the other the cruel young, undeluded but merciless. There was a replay here, in the Arab setting, of that great theme of generational revolt that played itself out in mid-nineteenth-century Russian history and politics between an old, feeble liberalism and a merciless Jacobin revolt. The classic portrait of that rupture between generations was Ivan Turgenev's *Fathers and Sons,* published in 1862. In Bazarov, the novel's central character, Turgenev sketched a timeless portrait of the confident young, cruel, fanatical, and unbent. Turgenev, we are told by Isaiah Berlin in his celebrated essay "Fathers and Children: Turgenev and the Liberal Predicament," chose and then discarded a fitting epigraph for the novel:

> Young Man to Middle-Aged Man: "You had content but no force."
> Middle-Aged Man to Young Man: "And you have force but no content."

Turgenev was under no illusions about what Bazarov could do. He knew that he would "clear the ground" and then self-destruct. "I conceived him," Turgenev wrote of Bazarov, "as a somber figure, doomed to destruction because he still stands only in the gateway to the future." Bazarov, a young medical researcher, is set against the background of an old but doomed gentry class that treasures civilization and poise but is unable to defend them against autocracy from the right or against the new revolutionism of the young. Bazarov has no use for the civilities of Russian life. The accomplishments that a Westernizing elite fought for against the background of an old despotic tradition and a peasant culture steeped in superstition and custom are of little interest to him. "Aristocratism, liberalism, progress, principles—think of it, what a lot of foreign and useless words! To a Russian they are not worth a straw," Bazarov says to Nikolai Petrovich, a middle-aged provincial notable who treasures the little buds of progress that have sprung up and been nurtured in that Russian landscape. He and his peers do not have to build anything new, Bazarov proclaims. "The ground must be cleared first." There is nothing to save or savor in public life, nothing "which does not call for absolute and ruthless repudiation."

The world sketched by Turgenev bears an uncanny resemblance to the political and cultural landscape of parts of the Arab world (and Iran) in the 1980s. The fanatical young, the Muslim Bazarovs, showed the old nationalist classes the searing contempt of those convinced that nothing before them had worked. As the suicide drivers in Beirut and masked boys in Gaza stepped forth to claim their place in the mid-1980s, they were keenly aware of the self-doubts and self-flagellation of the generation that preceded them. These doubts had been the standard fare and output of the last two decades. The postwar Arab nationalists were on the run. Society had gone beyond the secular nationalists formed on the campus of the American University of Beirut and in the great traditions of the West. A Gaza preacher by the name of Shaykh Ahmad Yassin struck out on his own, in the shadow of the Intifada, and formed a movement of religious-political redemption that would come to notoriety and fame in the years to come, the Hamas movement. The clerical leader and his followers dismissed their predecessors and their secular rivals as a band of "wine drinkers and pork eaters" who had offered nothing but a string of defeats and failure. The Muslim Bazarovs were glad to put the old "modernists" out of their misery.

FIFTEEN YEARS AFTER the death of Khalil Hawi, a generation after the fall of Beirut and the flight of its old intellectual class, and a decade after his departure from the Arab world, Adonis penned these lines:

> How wondrous this snow
> It writes on the earth with warm ink.
>
> Here I see with my two eyes
> How a pond called the future evaporates.
>
> A people bewitched
> with a history written with chalks of illusion
> Its day is raw
> Its night half-cooked.
>
> Understand me, my homeland, understand me
> I cannot defend you
> except with my wings.

The wings were about freedom and about flight and exile. He and so many men and women of his outlook had packed the truth of their world—a whole tradition, the sacred memories, an inheritance—and taken it on the road.

In another passage, in a book written at about the same time and hailed as a breakthrough for the writer, *al-Kitab* (The Book: Yesterday, the Place, Now), Adonis caught the sterility of this new Arab time, its very ignorance of the sacred past it had disfigured and turned into a weapon of combat:

> *The storyteller claims,*
> *that this presence that drapes*
> *itself with the ancestors is*
> *nothing but an absence.*
>
> *It sees nothing of the beauty of the garden,*
> *Except a wilted flower.*
> *Is this a just language?*
>
> *The anger of the earth, the dream of the buds,*
> *the whispers of the desert,*
> *The storyteller said nothing of this.*
> *How? The storyteller has no right to silence.*
> *Here is the sun whispering to the storyteller,*
> *and repeating with pride:*
> *The wisdom of the light is deeper and more durable*
> *than the bloody night of your barren earth.*

"You go not till I set you up a glass, where you may see the inmost part of you," Hamlet says to his mother. From Baghdad, in the summer of 1990, there had come the most peculiar bearer of a glass: the Iraqi ruler Saddam Hussein. He may not have known what he was doing, but he held up a glass to the Arabs all the same. There were deadly ideas and worries floating in the Arab world when Saddam overran Kuwait—ruinous concepts of Arab nationalism that flew in the face of political reality, atavistic resentments along that ancient fault line between Sunni and Shia Islam, resentments toward the West born of the very attraction to it, a recognition that an era of unprecedented Arab wealth had come to an end, and then that desire to place the blame on the Gulf states for everything wrong under the sun. The Iraqi dictator plucked these ideas and resentments and turned them into monstrous instruments.

Souad al-Sabah, a poetess of Kuwait and a member of the ruling family who had written fierce verse in praise of the "Iraqi sword" during Iraq's war with Iran, came forth in 1990 to mourn Iraq's conquest of her birthplace in a poem entitled "Who Killed Kuwait?" Here is an excerpt:

> *Who killed Kuwait?*
> *The Killer did not descend from the sky*
> *or emerge from a world of dreams*
> *Didn't we all take part in the chorus of the Regime?*
>
> *Didn't we all applaud the master of the Regime?*
> *Didn't we all make pretty the mistakes of the rulers*
> *with the sweetest of words, with the most deceitful of words*
> *Didn't we all march like sheep in the caravan of the rulers?*
> *He who killed Kuwait is our own flesh and blood*
> *He is the embodiment of all our ways.*
> *We made him in accord with our own measurements.*
> *No one can say "no."*
> *We all participated in the crime*
> *We all took part in the making of the devil*
> *We all applauded the tyrants and tyranny*
> *We can't complain about our idols.*
> *Was not the making of idols our profession?*

Confessional and evasive in equal measure—the collective "we" assigning guilt to everyone and no one at the same time, editing out the anguish and sorrow of those brave enough to have stood up to Saddam Hussein in the years that preceded the invasion of Kuwait—Souad al-Sabah expressed only the hurt that the "Iraqi sword" had been turned against the folk and the clan. She had not fully assimilated the calamity of having written in praise of that Iraqi sword to begin with. She was hardly alone in the shocked sense of bewilderment at the protector and gendarme of Baghdad, the faithful son of the Arab national project who had turned on his own.

Routine, it turned out, was but a brief interlude between two audacious bids. No sooner had the Arab-Muslim world said farewell to the wrath and passion of the Ayatollah Khomeini's crusade than another contender rose in Baghdad. The new claimant was made of material different from the turbaned savior from Qom: Saddam Hussein was neither a writer of treatises on Islamic government nor a product of high learning in religious seminaries. Not for him the drawn-out ideological struggles for the hearts and minds of the faithful. The new contender was a despot, a ruthless and skilled warden who terrorized his country and turned it into a large prison. With his audacious bid for Kuwait in the summer of 1990, Arab nationalism hatched a monster.

Three years earlier the Kuwaitis had dodged a bullet. The turmoil of the final year of the Iran–Iraq War had come closer to them, and they had turned to the Americans, seeking protection for their oil exports. The Reagan administration was on the rebound then from the fiasco of its arms sales to Iran; it obliged the Kuwaitis, reflagged their tankers, and the danger subsided. But countries cannot be reflagged like ships and tankers. In the summer of 1990, Kuwait was left to the tender mercies of the Iraqis. The Kuwaitis were in the way of a state possessed of considerable power and a sense that the world around it owed it a great debt for the service it had performed in its long struggle against the Iranian revolution. Saddam had been protector and gendarme. He now came to collect what he saw as the fair wages for the work he had done.

He struck in August, dusting off a fraudulent claim to the wealthy principality next door. Before he swept into Kuwait, Saddam went through the motions of negotiating with the Kuwaitis. The single negotiation session, held in Saudi Arabia, lasted two hours. Then came the dash for the loot on August 2, 1990.

The emir of Kuwait never thought it would come to this. In his place of exile, in the Saudi resort town of Taif, awaiting the liberation of his land, he recalled times when he and Saddam Hussein broke bread together. Bedouin-style, Saddam Hussein would pick for the emir choice cuts of lamb and place them on the emir's plate himself. By the ways of the place, the old ways, this was a special demonstration of fidelity and friendship. There were other acts of kindness. Back in 1985, at the height of the Ayatollah Khomeini's campaign of terror, the emir was the target of an assassination attempt by a Shi'ite terrorist; he suffered minor injuries when a suicide driver attacked his motorcade. There were daily calls from brother Saddam inquiring about the health of His Excellency the Emir. There was a division of labor then. A job had to be done. The Persian state and its Shi'ite tributaries in the Arab world had thrown together the ruling Gulf dynasties and the Iraqi dictator.

Not the most articulate of leaders, Saddam Hussein found his themes as he went along. He annexed the dreams and resentments of other Arabs, appealing to their atavistic impulses. Hurriedly he rolled out his own map of a phantom Arab nation and picked up an old weapon. In the barracks and the academies there had once been a vision of Arab history, a memory of a time when the Arab world was supposedly one and whole, a tale of betrayal at the hands of European powers, and the dream of a leader who would set history right again. This was the material that Gamal Abdul Nasser of Egypt had worked with in the 1950s and 1960s, and this was the material that Saddam would try to revive.

With great stridency, Saddam Hussein railed against the "colonial borders" of the Arab world. Those borders were false and contrived, he said, and they placed Arab demographic weight on one side and Arab wealth on the other. In fact, however, he himself ruled a polity that had been put together by British power in the aftermath of the First World War out of the wilderness of Mesopotamia and the fragments of what were three separate provinces of the Ottoman empire: Baghdad, Mosul, and Basra. It was British armor and will that created an "Arab national state" in Iraq and left it with favored borders in the face of superior Turkish claims in the north and Kurdish yearnings for autonomy in the hill country of Kurdistan. The British beat the Shia majority in the south into submission to make way for that Arab national state and its would-be rulers, the Sunni Arab townsmen of the Tigris and Euphrates valleys. But the Iraqi strongman saw no contradiction between the facts of his country's past and his own pan-Arab ambitions. He rolled together the claims of Arab nationalism and the resentments of the more impoverished Arabs.

A Danish traveler and scholar by the name of Carsten Niebuhr, the sources say, was the first to put the name "Kuwait" on a map. The date was 1765; the place a little trading town built in the early years of the eighteenth century. Its people were smugglers, seafarers, pearl divers, and merchants who led their caravans from southern and eastern Arabia to Syria. They lived by their wits and made their way between contending Turkish and British empires. Oil changed their life. The place may not have been the "desert democracy" its rulers and scribes claimed it was, but it was a benign place, a merchant principality. No "visitors of dawn" hauled off dissidents to jail, no cruel utopias were unleashed on it. Saddam and the Arab crowd that rode with him dispensed with that history.

The people of the Gulf and the Peninsula who knew their world before the age of oil have a memory of a time when they marked their history by famines, when the Who's Who of the Najdi elite of the Saudi realm went north to labor in the port city of Basra. Only in 1946 did the emir of Kuwait turn a silver valve wheel on a loading pipe and start the flow of oil, thereby changing the principality by the bay into an object of envy. Before that, the history of that town of pearl divers and fishermen was a steady diet of hardship and deprivation. The lands of the north had the rivers, the agriculture, the advanced cities; those in the Gulf peninsula relied on locusts for their protein. All this now belonged to a vanished past. The states of the Gulf became convenient scapegoats for the failures of the larger Arab world around them.

Timing helped Saddam Hussein pick up the support he managed to rally. He made his move into Kuwait at a time when the Arab world felt it was being passed over by history. The move into Kuwait came right after that *annus mirabilis* of 1989—Europe's Springtime of Nations—left the Arab world on the sidelines. History had gone elsewhere, to Germany and Eastern Europe. There were even celebrated elections in several Latin American settings. It was the season of democracy, but the Arab world's tyrants were still in power. The old Soviet empire was coming apart, and its Arab satrapies were left holding the bag.

"Look at us," said a Jordanian reflecting on the Arab condition in mid-1990. "Our situation is terrible. The whole world is getting democracy except for us. Our economies are a mess, we are weak, we are being left behind. We can't even stop the Russian Jews from immigrating to Israel." In the Iraqi despot, some Arabs would see an instrument of redemption. There was no rival public project in the Arab world. To those who identified with him, Saddam Hussein passed off his conquest of Kuwait as the dawn of a new age. His admirers and those who indulged him said that he was not exactly the right man but that he came at exactly the right time, that it was enough that he had dealt a death blow to the old order.

A decade earlier, Saddam Hussein had posed as a man of order. He had mixed with the dynastic rulers in the Gulf and presented himself as a defender of commerce and orthodoxy against the Persian state and its Shia tributaries in the Arab world. He had befriended the Saudi monarch and the emir of Kuwait. His brutal past, it was said, was surely behind him; he had matured and changed. Saddam now let the disgruntled read into him what they wished. He offered himself to the imagination of the thwarted. He was a second Nasser, it was said, but a Nasser with teeth.

There was something in Saddam's conquest of Kuwait for practically all spectators. For the Yemenis sitting at the edge of the oil wealth, he provided the vicarious satisfaction of seeing the wealthy stumble and fall. Beirutis—East Beirutis, that is, in the Christian sector of the city, whom Saddam had supported against Syria—

celebrated his deed: The ruin of their city had spread to a city in the Gulf that had been orderly and precious. For the young semi-Westernized Algerians and Tunisians living in close proximity to Europe, Saddam acted out their rage against the West, a rage born of dependence and the failure of the postcolonial state to stand on its own and keep its people at home. Saddam had warred against Ayatollah Khomeini for nearly a decade; he had insisted that religion and politics did not mix, he had prided himself on the secularism of the Ba'th party. He now paid his old Iranian nemesis a curious compliment by falling back on Khomeini's language of fire and brimstone. Although he had a Christian foreign minister, Saddam summoned believers to a jihad, a holy war: "Arabs, Muslims, believers in God wherever you are, it is your duty to jump up and defend Mecca, hostage to the Americans."

With the Palestinians Saddam Hussein forged an instant bond. He was a revisionist leader assaulting the status quo, and they were the quintessential revisionists. In the West Bank and Gaza, they had been waiting for an Arab cavalry, and Saddam was the "Knight of Arabism" riding to their rescue, the "Second Saladin." The Palestinian press under Israeli occupation paid tribute to him. In April Saddam threatened to hit Israel with a "binary-chemical weapon," to torch "half of the country" if it attacked Iraq. The crowd on the West Bank and Gaza did not know exactly what the binary chemical weapon was, but they assumed it was a weapon of wonder that would bring the invincible Israelis to heel.

A DISTINCTION IS made in the lands of the Gulf littoral between *Arab al-Shimal,* the Arabs of the north, and *Arab al-Khalij,* the Arabs of the Gulf. The Arabs of the north had been content to spare the lands of the Gulf their deadly political feuds. Utopias of all kinds were unleashed in the lands of the north: currents of radical nationalism, flings with socialist politics, absolutist temptations of every kind. It was a simpler world among the Arabs of the Peninsula and the Gulf. Few thought that the world of princes and merchants could be remade. Authority was paternalistic, but ruler and ruled lived in a social and political world held together by bonds that men generally did not break.

In the summer of 1990, Iraq, the borderland between the Arabs of the north and the Gulf Arabs, served a warrant on the old order in the Gulf. The failed lands in the north—the ruinous politics, the burdened state-run economies, a demographic explosion that provided young foot soldiers for the politics of despair and banditry—spilled southward. The precarious peace between the Arabs of the Peninsula and Gulf (constituting about 8 percent of all Arabs) and their more impoverished neighbors had broken down.

By one interpretation put forth by the keeper of the Nasserite flame, the Egyptian journalist Mohamed Heikal, the crisis of the summer of 1990 was just another round in the struggle between "desert people and city people." The struggle for national independence, Heikal wrote, was conducted in the cities—Cairo, Damascus, Baghdad, and Beirut. The "tribal leaders" got the oil, and the cities were "deprived of the fruits of their struggle." A contract of sorts had been concluded between the city people and the tribal leaders, but a new generation grew up in the oil states "believing that they had the right to rule"; the royal households grew in size and transformed a "tribal system into a regal one." The Saudi royal family alone, Heikal observed, now numbered 6,500–7,000 people. The contract with the cities was broken. In Heikal's formulation, Arab history—the writ of that "Arab national movement" in the cities—now warred with geography, the location of oil.

For the oil states this kind of political logic, which glided past their sovereignty and legitimacy, was a throwback to an unhappy past. The rallying cry of "Arab oil for the Arab people" had been the stuff of politics in the 1950s and 1960s, the high tide of Nasserism. In those perilous times, the oil states had walked a tightrope between some fidelity to the wider Arab world and self-preservation. There were insurance policies from afar—a British guarantee for Kuwait, a more durable American guarantee for Saudi Arabia. It was still a time, though, when local predators were easily held in check by outside powers. Days after the British terminated their treaty of protection of Kuwait in 1961, the Iraqis moved their army across the border, staking a claim. The British then returned to the scene and the Iraqis retreated. Not long afterward Nasser went into Yemen. He did not head straight to the oil fields of Saudi Arabia; he was a more cautious player. Nasser may have been a revisionist, but he was no outlaw. He knew the balance of forces and the logic of things that can and cannot be. The Yemen War pitted Saudi Arabia against Egypt, and Egypt lost.

Saddam's bid closed a circle; the pan-Arab arguments and radical sensibility of the 1950s returned. The new bid, though, had behind it the cruelty of the man at the helm of the Iraqi state, its weapons of mass destruction, and Saddam's conviction that he lived in a political world shorn of all restraints and scruples. Saddam had implicated much of his world (Gulf Arabs, Egyptians) and powers beyond (Americans, French) in his anti-Iranian and anti-Shia drive, in the cruelty of what he did at home. No wonder he was impervious to judgment and acted as though he himself had been betrayed by the furious response to his invasion of Kuwait. A decade earlier Saddam had dispatched his cowed countrymen eastward in a campaign against the "fire-worshipping Persians." Back then he had banned grief and public funerals for the war dead. This time around, the expedition southward, to Kuwait, held out the promise of Kuwait's treasure and the heady illusion of a crusade to expel the West from the Peninsula and the Gulf. For this threat, the Gulf Arabs and their benign societies had no ready deterrent.

We should not read into that desert world more purity than its history warrants. The Arabs of the Peninsula and the Gulf littoral are the products of a pragmatic world. No bloody anticolonial struggles have been waged in the region. The people of the inlands of central Arabia were spared the trauma of coming to terms with foreign rule. No conquering power had bothered with central Arabia. The injuries inflicted on the more exposed lands of Morocco, Tunisia, Egypt, and Algeria in the age of colonialism were not visited on the desert. Even the nominal sovereignty of the Turks had remained a hollow claim. In the lands of the littoral, the foreigner was a more familiar figure. Britons had ruled Aden since 1839; they were the de facto rulers and protectors of the waters and the coastal lands of the Gulf. On the whole, though, the presence of the foreigner had been benign and benevolent.

The Arabs of the Gulf had dealt with the West for a long time, but from within their own world. They were more fortunate than the semi-Westernized Arabs who made themselves over in the image of the West, only to be rebuffed and patronized. The Arabs of the desert told no great tales of betrayal by Western powers. These were Palestinian, Lebanese, and North African tales, told in those parts of the Arab world where the West had made promises and where people convinced themselves that they had been let down and betrayed. The lands of the Gulf carried on a vast commercial traffic with the West, but on their own terms. Foreigners—Americans— came to Arabia in the 1930s and 1940s, but they arrived after the age of empire had passed. And they came to Dhahran, on the Persian Gulf, to soften the life of the desert and take it beyond its history of desolation and scarcity. On the whole, they were careful not to offend the cultural sensibilities of their hosts and to conform to the decorum and style of the place.

A man who had risen in the isolation of Iraqi politics, Saddam Hussein had misjudged the American state of affairs. There was that anxiety about America's role in the world that came with the great changes of the *annus mirabilis* of 1989. As Robert Tucker and David Hendrickson have put it in *The Imperial Temptation,* that brief period between the fall of the Berlin Wall and the outbreak of the crisis in the Persian Gulf was a time of great confusion over America's world role:

> The events of 1989 put an end to containment. . . . The result was to leave the United States without a military or ideological challenge. A long period in the nation's history had apparently come to an end. But if this was indeed the case, what then was the justification for persisting in the global role America had

played since World War II? And if this role no longer seemed appropriate, given the recession of threats to the nation's security, what is America's new role to be?"

The expedition to check Saddam Hussein's bid rolled together longstanding American commitments in the Gulf and a new definition of America's role in the aftermath of the Cold War. A local despot had risen, but there was no local deterrent worth the name, so the deterrent had to be supplied by American power.

There were American doubts about the Arab lands to be rescued and the regimes to be shored up. There were worries that the Saudis might accept a puppet regime in Kuwait and settle for the Iraqi dictator's terms. There was a risk of rushing to distant shores—with a load of moral arguments—only to find a neighborhood squabble. It was "invariably the case in the east," George Orwell once wrote, that a "story always sounds clear at a distance, but the nearer you get to the scene of events the vaguer it becomes." Only three or four years earlier, America had been taken to the cleaners by the Iranians over its hostages in Beirut, and the American straightman had walked out of the twisted alleyways of the local bazaar with his pockets picked and his pride battered. A foreign savior assembling a vast expedition had a lot to worry about. Bob Woodward's "first draft" of the historical material in his book *The Commanders* (1991) sketches the mood of an August 4th meeting (two days after the Iraqi invasion of Kuwait) that brought together President Bush and his principal lieutenants. "Among those gathered, there was a pessimism about the Arabs in general. Everyone heaped blame on them. They could not be relied on; they could pay off the thief at their throat . . . the United States after all, had limited power and could not help those who didn't want to help themselves."

But the Rubicon was crossed in a hurry: from deterrence at the Saudi–Kuwaiti border to rollback in Kuwait. If anything, the doubts about the ways of the Arab states steeled the American will that the matter had to be concluded in a decisive fashion. The great power could not afford to be snookered or conned. The Iraqi leader had thrown down the gauntlet in broad daylight; he would not be granted a way out. There would be no French exit, no last-minute Soviet guide taking him past trouble, no fraternal "Arab solution" saving the Iraqi from the folly of his ways.

Because this was "the East," it became doubly important to be clear. The ambiguity was set aside. That structure of rhetoric was to be American through and through. It wasn't a "small country" that was at stake but the "big idea" of a "New World Order" and a world free of aggression. (Kuwait's record could not bear the weight of a major war; this was a country whose minister for foreign affairs had dismissed the Carter Doctrine a decade earlier because the people of the region were "perfectly capable of preserving their own security and stability.") The endeavor was to be a moral crusade. It was impossible to convince the majority of Arabs outside the Gulf that America had come into their midst to repel aggression; there was no use trying. The moral language was for the audience that mattered most: the American public, which was being invited to sustain a vast, new expedition in an Arab-Muslim setting this public neither knew nor trusted.

A whole edifice was pushed out of the way of Operation Desert Storm: Arab nationalism, the belief that a war against Iraq would become an "American–Arab war," that the "Arab street" would rise in rebellion against the outside power and threaten its regional interests. George Bush broke with received wisdom about the Arab world. The course of battle was going to determine this conflict. That fabled "Arab street" (we should give that street a decent burial) could field no divisions on Saddam's behalf or cushion him in defeat. The Arab world was divided, it was easy to see. No undue homage was paid to the protesters in Amman, Nablus, and Tunis. The direct beneficiaries of the American expedition were a minority of Arabs, the Gulf and Peninsula Arabs, less than 8–10 percent of that large Arab world. But what of it? The lands of the Gulf were the Arab lands that mattered the most. The flanks of the Gulf states were covered by pressing Egypt and accepting Syria into the anti-Saddam coalition. The distinction between Arab "haves" and "have-nots" was thus blurred. Those who hitched a ride with the Iraqi claimant were to be written off. Back doors were left open to some of them (the Jordanian monarch, in particular). After the dust settled, the penitents could be rehabilitated.

It should have taken no great literacy in strategic matters to know that Saddam's bid for mastery over the Gulf would end in defeat and ruin. When the Iraqi despot's bluff was called, he couldn't back it up. In a flash of lightning we saw the kind of world he had built: the officers who deserted their men; the elite Republican Guard, the "golden children" who were kept away from the front lines; the intelligence operatives who fled Kuwait at the earliest sign of trouble, leaving behind those who were not in the know. The despot's frightened men walked out of the desert to surrender to anyone who would have them. The Iraqis kissed the hands of their captors. After all, the despot had trained them in this sort of thing. They had to grovel before him whenever he triumphantly toured the front.

War is the cruelest and most honest of tests. Saddam Hussein broke his countrymen. Ruled by the whip, his soldiers gave up on their leader's campaign. Caught between the enemy in the front and the execution squads at their backs, his soldiers made a run for it. "Angels of mercy will be at your shoulders," the armies of Iraq were told by the Maximum Leader. This was, presumably, to compensate for the air cover they lost so early in the war.

Saddam Hussein promised his soldiers angels, and he promised the Arabs who rallied to his banners a bright new world, a world without the old weakness, free of the old and familiar taste of defeat, but in the end it was all a swindle. Saddam Hussein's performance recalled the devastating Arab defeat in the Six Day War of 1967: the Egyptian rockets that didn't fire; the air force that was destroyed on the ground; the promised demolition of Tel Aviv that turned into a monumental Arab defeat; the barefoot Egyptian soldiers lost in the Sinai Desert; the officers who swaggered at home and hoarded the society's goods and honors fleeing to save their skins. And above all there was Gamal Abdul Nasser, the leader who had asked only for obedience, offering that incredible explanation of the defeat: Israel had attacked from the west when he had expected the attack to come from the east and the north. A society that had lived through that ordeal should have been immune to another pretender, but in a culture susceptible to legend and the promise of the strongman, there were takers of what Saddam Hussein had to peddle.

Operation Desert Storm and the American victory over Iraq closed a circle in the Gulf. Whereas the peace of the Persian Gulf had been a Pax Britannica, Saddam Hussein's audacious bid for mastery in the Gulf legitimized a Pax Americana. In retrospect, that time between Britain's withdrawal from "east of Suez" in 1971 and the new American role in the Gulf was but an interlude between two orders of power, an interregnum. British power had protected the smaller realms in the Gulf. Left to their own devices, the Wahhabi zealots of the second Saudi state (1824–1891) would have overrun Oman and Bahrain in the 1850s and 1860s. From the 1860s onward, the small sheikhdom in Bahrain was sheltered by the British against the claims of the Persian state as well. Ibn Saud, too, had to be checked as he consolidated and expanded his realm. The temptation of that great desert warrior to claim the "land of his ancestors"—in Qatar, Oman, and the states of the Trucial Coast—was discarded in favor of a live-and-let-live strategy with British imperial power. Ibn Saud knew the balance of forces and the might available to the British. The zealots among his followers, the *Ikhwan* (religious bands of warriors), who had served as his shock troops in the 1920s, wanted permanent warfare against the "infidel" regimes in Iraq and Transjordan and the conquest of Bahrain, Oman, and Qatar. The unbridled enthusiasm of the *Ikhwan* was reined in, and of course it was the British who as late as 1961 defended the independence of Kuwait in the face of Iraqi claims. This kind of task now fell to the Gulf's American protectors.

The local order of power—successive bids for dominion by the Shah, by the Iranian revolutionary state, and then by Saddam Hussein—had not produced a workable balance. Two decades of drift thus served as the basis for a new American writ in the Gulf. In truth, it must be recalled, the rulers of the small Gulf states had looked with dread on Britain's withdrawal a generation earlier. Radical nationalist ideas were blowing their way. The rulers saw these ideological assertions for what they were—a threat to their autonomy, their rule, and their riches. Pax Britannica's wards even offered to pay the costs of an imperial presence, but the British were determined to "untie the knot" and release themselves. The new dependence on America was simply a return to that older sensibility.

This was to be a circumscribed American imperial role, order its principal concern. No messianic impulse was to be unleashed on the lands of the Gulf and the Peninsula, no great theories of reform let loose on these societies. The shape of things to come—the power and then the limits to be drawn on the exercise of that power—was foreshadowed in the prosecution of the campaign against Iraq. After the swift victory, the moral crusade was brought to a halt.

Iraq's American conquerors were the most reticent of conquerors. They had no taste for an imperial role that would take America deep into the thicket of Iraqi politics. Old-fashioned imperialism (and the responsibility that went with it) has been banished from today's order of states. Matters were of course quite different in the age of empire. In a memorable essay on the imperial age, "A Few Words on Non-Intervention," John Stuart Mill expressed the consensus of his contemporaries on the kinds of responsibilities that came with a great power's intervention. "A despotic government only exists by its military power," he wrote. If an outsider destroys that military power, he is forced "by the necessity of the case" to offer the vanquished society a new order in place of the old despotism. American power broke the Iraqi claimant but would not come to the aid of the Shia and Kurdish rebellions America had all but called for. Bush had called upon the Iraqi leaders and people to "take matters into their own hands" and topple Saddam Hussein. These words were taken to heart by the Iraqi populace waiting for deliverance. As soon as the ground war against Iraq came to an end, on February 28, 1991, popular frenzy broke out in the southern city of Basra, then spread to the Shia holy cities of Najaf and Karbala, and northward to Kurdish towns. The pent-up resentments of a population eager to be rid of the dreaded despot clashed with the wounded fury of the remnants of a defeated Iraqi army determined to keep its world and power intact. Because the despot had leveled the political life of the land, the leaderless rebellion of the Shia relied on the opportunity of the moment. Civilians were joined by army men straggling in from the front; the prisons were emptied, the loyalists of the regime, and the men of the intelligence service, and of the ruling party, were overrun, many of them dealt swift retribution. Mastery of the regime, it appeared for a moment, had cracked.

The insurgents had no script to follow. They had risen in the hope that an Iraqi opposition based in Iran would ride to the rescue, in the hope that the foreign armies that had defeated the dictator's forces would impose a new order of things. The despot's eldest son, Udday, a merciless hothead, dismissed the rebellion as "nothing but stray dogs barking." The divisions of the Republican Guard spared by the American-led coalition rallied to the defense of the regime; the rulers were in a fight for their lives and their dominion. The insurgencies would be put down in a welter of blood. The divisions of the Republican Guard may have been helpless against the high-tech weapons of a Western army, but their helicopter gunships (allowed them by the cease-fire that the Americans had dictated) and their artillery were more than they needed to snuff out the rebellions. The expectation that the Persian state would step in to pick up the fragments of Iraq and install a regime in its image turned out to be a scarecrow. The insurgents had risen and fought alone. The cruelty with which the insurgency was put down was true to the dictator's history. The most merciless of the dictator's lieutenants was assigned the task of snuffing out the rebellion, his cousin Ali Hassan al-Majid, who had earned his reputation for cruelty in the regime's war against the Kurds a few years earlier. In that earlier genocidal campaign, al-Majid had ordered the use of nerve gas in Kurdistan and been dubbed "the hammer of the Kurds." He would bring to this new campaign the panic of the regime, the knowledge of its inner circle that it was now "rule or die" for them. In a terrified land with a history of cruel rule, the heartlessness with which the rebellion was put down made an impression even on the servants of the regime. "It was all blood, blood, blood," an organ of the regime, its newspaper, *al-Jumhuriyah,* told its readers after the tide had turned against the insurgents. "Blood was painted on the streets and the walls of Karbala."

Rid of its problems in the south, the regime then turned to the Kurds and put them to flight. Those rebellions (to borrow John Stuart Mill's words again) had demonstrated that there were people in Iraq "willing to brave labor and danger for their liberation." A strong case could have been made for remaking the Iraqi state. It is as sure as anything that the people of Iraq—the great majority of them—would have been grateful for the chance to be rid of the despot and the chance after years of living on their nerves for something approximating normalcy. But from that kind of responsibility the victors drew back.

The victory had been swift, American and allied casualties surprisingly light. There was a desire to let well enough alone. The British wanted the military campaign to continue. They wanted to "close the loop" on the fleeing Iraqis. But they were overruled by Washington and told that it was not in the American military tradition to shoot a fleeing enemy in the back. Men use and misuse history and analogy. The specter of the "Lebanonization of Iraq" stayed America's hand. The Bush administration did not trust its knowledge of Iraq and its distant ways and sects. America was haunted by the memory of Lebanon—the warring sects, the deadly fault lines—and convinced that the Shia of Iraq were destined to fall under Iran's sway. The Shia were the majority of Iraq's population, a people of that country, the Shia faith having spread in the nineteenth century (the tale has been told in an exemplary work of scholarship, *The Shi'is of Iraq,* by Brandeis University historian Yitzhak Nakash) because the nomadic tribes of Iraq had taken to it when they settled near the Shia shrine towns of Najaf and Karbala in search of water for their agricultural work. There had been no "racial" divide, no clear-cut distinctions between the Sunnis and Shias of Iraq. All this was unknown to those who had waged the war against Iraq. America had seen the terrible harvest of aggrieved Shi'ism in Teheran and Beirut. No one wanted a replay of the past. Hard as the Shia leaders of Iraq would insist that they had no "sister republic" of the Iranian theocracy in mind, they could get no hearing for their case.

Nor did the Kurds, in the northern hill country of Kurdistan, fare any better: the Kurds had always been friendless in the world. Arab nationalism had never taken them in; nor was Turkey ready to countenance a Kurdish separatist regime in northern Iraq. It was easy for the American imperial expedition to walk away from the Iraqi rebels. Some key players in the Bush administration—the chairman of the Joint Chiefs of Staff, General Colin Powell, who never wanted to resort to arms to begin with, Secretary of State James Baker, who had hedged his bets all along about the war— were eager for a "clean break" from that war. "Neither revolt had a chance," Powell would later write of the Kurdish and Shia rebellions. "Nor, frankly, was their success a goal of our policy." It was an odd, heartless ending for a moral crusade. The war would be called off; the conquerors would fall back on the incantations of the "balance of power." We needed Iraq, it was asserted, as a balance to the threat from Iran. A political handler of the American president, it later came to light, counseled a sudden end to the military campaign because a "hundred-hour ground war" had a nice symmetry to it and would be a boon in the presidential campaign to come.

America had kicked the "Vietnam syndrome" in the Gulf, it was said. There was no need for greater exertion and no desire to look deeper into the burden (and the possibilities) that came with the victory. More than half a million Kurds were driven into their desolate hills and overflowed the borders of Iran and Turkey; their ordeal sullied and nearly overwhelmed the American-led victory, but the reticence of the victors held. A sense of the moral abdication that followed the brilliant campaign is revealed in James Baker's memoirs, *The Politics of Diplomacy,* where the secretary of state of the victorious power comes to witness firsthand the terrible scenes of Kurdish suffering in the snow-capped mountains of southeastern Turkey and northwestern Iraq shortly after the Iraqi rebellions were crushed. A man who had endured a six-day march from the city of Kirkuk broke through the Turkish security detail and pleaded with Baker for the children suffering from exposure and hunger. A Kurdish delegation presented him with a respectful petition: "All Iraqis were waiting for freedom and a democratic regime in Iraq. But the mistakes and wrong decisions that allowed the Iraqi regime to use tanks and helicopters caused this tragedy." Baker witnessed all this, and on the helicopter ride back to Diyarbakir in Turkey he reflected to himself that "the people I had just seen were living examples of the will to be free." The spinmaster never rests. He had just seen not only a "true humanitarian emergency" but the consequences of an American decision. For the man in the loop, for a witness to events that mattered, he was oddly disengaged. He had seen the consequences of terrible doings, but he shook off what he saw and offered up the familiar banalities: We did not want to see the "Lebanonization of Iraq," we did not want to turn Saddam into a nationalist hero, the "Arab street" would have never forgiven us a march on Baghdad, and so on. No one bothered with the matter of Iraq's liberty; the war was about more unsentimental issues.

IN THE END, that war in the Arabian Peninsula and the Gulf was a battle between a local predator and a foreign savior. Rescue came from afar; there was no assurance that the lessons of this conflict would sink in and endure. On pain of extinction, cultures often stubbornly refuse to look into themselves. They retreat into the nooks and crannies of their history, fall back on the consolations they know. In the scheme of such things, the war had been quick and (outside Iraq) decisive. This left open all sorts of escapes. Those who fell for Kuwait's conqueror were free to claim that they had been misunderstood, that they were only patriots responding to the coming to the Arab world of yet another Western army, that they had only wanted to be heard because there had been no place for them in the "New World Order" the foreigner came to uphold. This was a world with endless escapes. The defeat of the Iraqi predator provided no guarantee that the political sensibilities which had sustained him were vanquished once and for all.

My favorite example of the kind of ambiguity that awaited the new order in the Gulf and the foreign power's victory is Souad al-Sabah, the cheerleader for Saddam in the 1980s who experienced a change of heart after the Iraqi ruler sacked her birthplace.

The defect of her vision was given away in what she wrote as she and her country awaited the onset of the military campaign against Saddam Hussein. She hectored the foreign power, doubted its will to fight, described the standoff between Iraq and the United States (a mere nine or ten days before the air campaign against Iraq was launched) as a "struggle between Rambo and Nebuchadnezzar, King of Babylon." The Iraqi "brother" had been banished from the clan, turned into a man of Babylon. A terrible punishment was being readied for Iraq, but Souad al-Sabah was impatient with America and its soldiers: "Some want to fight in the winter, some in the fall, some do not want to fight in any season of the year. Some want to go home quickly for some fast food at McDonald's." All Rambo wanted, she warned, was the lion's share of the land's wealth.

The poetess was back at it in early February 1991, deep into the air campaign against Iraq. She now wrote of the Scud missiles that the Iraqis had launched into Israel and Saudi Arabia. Those were "mindless rockets," she wrote, for such rockets treated "the Arabs and the Zionist entity" as equals, made no distinction "between places that worshipped God and places that worshipped the devil." She had no problems with Arab rockets, she said, "so long as such rockets were part of an Arab arsenal made ready for the big battle against Israel." Saddam's rockets were, in her eyes, only a measure of the dictator's narcissism, his inability to understand who the "true enemy" of the Arab future was; these rockets were only "fireworks" that gave Israel a pretext to "extort" greater concessions from powers the world over.

Souad al-Sabah could not step out of her skin. The rescue of her land had been a foreigner's gift, but after their ordeal the Kuwaitis were to conceive a deep attachment to American power. It was a sudden romance and a break with the emirate's political climate of the preceding quarter-century. Virtually all of Kuwait's hopes were projected onto the distant power: the rulers' hopes for protection against Iraq, and the oppositionists' hopes that American power would buttress their campaign for greater democracy in their land. Kuwait had been betrayed by the very deities it had sought to propitiate—Arab nationalism, the Palestine cause, the cause of Iraq against Iran. To see the country again for the first time after its calamity—I went there three months after its liberation—was to come face to face with the bitterness of that betrayal. The old headquarters of the PLO—what was once the center of a state within a state—was gutted. The graffiti on the walls damned Yasser Arafat and Saddam Hussein as "traitors." The building that housed the Palestinian Federation of Women was boarded up. The Hawali district, the Palestinian quarter in Kuwait City, seemed like a marked place. Among Kuwaitis of every stripe, the bonds with the Palestinians had been shattered. In place of the old pan-Arabism there was an attachment to American power and an American presence. American missionaries had once built a hospital in Kuwait City, when Kuwait's most celebrated and skilled emir, Mubarak al-Sabah (ruled 1896–1915) permitted them access to his domain in 1911. The building was run down and decayed. There had been plans to bulldoze it. "This will stay now," a Kuwaiti friend guiding me through the city said. "It might yet be restored."

There had once been an old skill in Kuwait: the art of political survival and independence courtesy of the "balance of power." The Kuwaitis had to relearn that skill. In its purest form, the game was played by that ablest of al-Sabahs, Mubarak, who must be reckoned the founder of the modern polity of Kuwait. In the early years of the twentieth century, Mubarak made his way among the powers that impinged on his domain. He made his country (with its port facilities) a ward of Pax Britannica and used British power as a counter to Ottoman authority. The British did not want responsibility for Kuwait, but they did not want any other power dominant over Kuwait. They obliged Mubarak, and that relationship served him and his inheritors for decades to come. The Ottomans were kept at bay, and so were the Wahhabi zealots of the Saudi realm, who wanted the conquest of the lax principality on the Gulf. That old skill of Mubarak was now needed to ward off a standing Iraqi claim to Kuwait and to commit Pax Americana to Kuwait's defense. There was no need for excessive romance for the foreign protector; the kind of enthusiasm that surrounded the Americans in the aftermath of Kuwait's liberation could not last. Kuwait needed a foreign protector even as its people wrestled with, and resented, the facts of their dependence. The presence of the foreign power became a contested matter, but the disputations were carried on in the expectation that foreign protection would be there when needed in the face of another threat from Baghdad.

Vulnerable and destined to live in the shadow of larger powers, Kuwait had to tread carefully. A gap had opened between those who had fled the Iraqi occupation and those who had stayed in the country. A spirit of defiance seized the latter. They wanted their rulers brought to account; they pressed for a genuine parliamentary life; they were no longer bullied or awed by their rulers. But Kuwait could not be reinvented. The truth of this small principality has always been its commerce. The play between prince and merchants is an old and time-honored art in the place. Favors could be given or denied; men grumble but they make their peace. In the time of oil, *fi Zaman al-Naft,* the ruler's purse has been more important than his sword in this benign place. Another source of dynastic power has been the divided sectarian and ethnic composition of the population. There is a Sunni majority and a Shia minority; the latter is itself divided into Shia who came to Kuwait from Bahrain, others who trace their descent and ancestral culture to Iran, and still others who migrated here from Hasa, the eastern province of Saudi Arabia. There is, as well, a substantial population, perhaps 150,000, who were stateless, the *Bidoon,* mostly nomads, who claim no other citizenship but have been denied the prerogatives of Kuwaiti citizenship. A careful dynasty making its way through the divisions of the place, granting what treasure was available to it, could ride out many a storm. Congenitally cautious, the Sabah ruling family were not merciless autocrats; nor were their opponents, who spoke the language of parliamentary rule and hectored the rulers about the costs of the American presence, devoted democrats. The dynasty had suspended parliamentary life in 1986; it restored it under duress in the aftermath of the war because the people pressed for it, and because the Americans pressed for it as well. The two parliaments elected in 1992 and 1996 were a fair reflection of the population: a mix of "constitutionalists," Muslim (Sunni) fundamentalists, Shia representatives, leading men of the tribes beyond the urban population of Kuwait City, and loyalists of the regime. It was a tribute to the openness of this principality that a young Shia cleric, trained in the seminaries of Iran, sat in its 1996 parliament, with his clerical garb and the black turban of a *sayyid,* a descendant of the Prophet Muhammad. There was a delicate mix here between the facts of dynastic and tribal rule and the yearnings for participatory politics. The elections could not alter the distribution of power or dictate a new course for the principality. The durable truths of Kuwaiti political life had outlived the Iraqi invasion and the aftermath of the war.

A different kind of play was to unfold in the Saudi realm. Two terrorist attacks—one in Riyadh in November 1995 that targeted an American training facility of the Saudi National Guard and killed five Americans, and a more devastating deed of terror in June 1996 in the oil town of Dhahran against a housing complex for American military personnel that took the lives of nineteen Americans—brought home to the dynasty and to the foreign power the hazards of their "special relationship." Saudi Arabia was not about to be convulsed by revolution, but the simplicity of that American–Saudi encounter had become a thing of the past. The car bomb, the terrorist weapon of choice of the 1980s, had turned up in Saudi Arabia. The sphere of influence staked out for American power by Franklin Delano Roosevelt was now visited by some of the furies at play in the wider world of Islam. It was fitting perhaps that Dhahran was the setting of the more devastating deed of terror. Dhahran was a creature of the American presence in Arabia. It was there that American prospectors turned up in the late 1930s and American oil companies built a suburban sprawl in the American image, bringing to the Arabian lands the skills and magic of an alien, benevolent civilization. The culture of an America that now belongs to a simpler past—the culture of the 1950s, with its rhythm and diet and certainties—still lingers in Dhahran in an oil complex set apart from the world around it. It was from Dhahran that U.S. armed forces monitored the restrictions that had been placed on the Iraqi military in the aftermath of the Gulf War. The perpetrators of this deed were brutally effective in the target they chose. Whereas the bombing in Riyadh was a homespun affair, early evidence indicated that the terror in Dhahran might have been the work of Shia underground plotters from the eastern province with Iranian links.

"EACH STRANGER MADE his own poor bed among them," T. E. Lawrence wrote of the companions who rode with him in the "Arab revolt." His words could be borrowed to describe the way America's Desert Storm must have looked through Arab and Muslim eyes. General Allenby's guns were pounding the Turks, and "the intervening hollows of the Dead Sea" drummed up the echoes of the big guns. "The Arabs whispered 'They are nearer; the English are advancing; God deliver the men under the rain.' They were thinking compassionately of the passing Turks, so long their weak oppressors; whom, for their weakness though oppressors, they loved more than the strong foreigner with his blind indiscriminate justice."

The authority that America won in its high-tech campaign in 1991 was not destined to last. A terrible retribution had been administered against Iraq, but there had been no excessive gratitude for the distant power. (Even in Kuwait the revisionists and the doubters were also heard in time.) These were kinsmen who were devastated in that merciless hundred-hour ground campaign and reduced to poverty in the years to come with harsh economic sanctions that stayed in place only because American power decreed it so. Egyptians had taken part in that campaign against Saddam; a good deal of their foreign debt had been forgiven (no less than $25 billion of debt was written off) for having made the correct call against Iraq. They had sustained no casualties; it had been a good ride for them. But when the military campaign came to an end, there surfaced in Egypt sympathy for Iraq. The rivalry between these two centers of Arab political power was, for all appearances, buried and forgotten.

The region had worked its will on the foreign power's victory. Five years later, America's Arab allies in that campaign had gone their separate ways; an Islamist government was in power at the time in Turkey, and Desert Storm had become a distant memory. A small crisis in August–September 1996 laid bare the difficulties of administering an imperium in a world that both beckoned American power and recoiled from it. This crisis was triggered by the Iraqi ruler; in a pattern that had become something of a personal signature, Saddam Hussein dispatched his army, and his squads of assassins, north into Kurdistan, into the "safe haven" that American power had marked for the Kurds after Desert Storm. This time around, America was on its own when it sought to punish Saddam for his deed. The two volleys of Tomahawk missiles that were fired against Iraqi air defense installations had to be launched from American ships in the Persian Gulf and B-52 bombers that flew in from Guam. Those two volleys of missiles were fired in the hope that America would hear no more from its nemesis in Baghdad. No nation in the region wanted to associate itself with this timid American response. The earth had shifted again. Two of the dynastic states of the Gulf—Qatar and the United Arab Emirates—were now expressing open sympathy for Iraq and speaking of it as a victim of Iranian and Turkish designs. There was no rustling up a posse for an effort of this kind. The dictator in Baghdad was a shadow of his former self. No one (save for Kuwaitis) believed in his menace, and no one believed that the American leader himself was in this affair to stay.

America brought to this endeavor against Saddam Hussein that enduring American contradiction between interests and turf that American power claims and reluctance to pay the price of imperial authority. There was in place a neat symmetrical doctrine for securing American interests in the Gulf: "dual containment" of Iran and Iraq. But this was more pretense than reality. The foreign guarantor of order was reluctant to walk the beat and had a dread of being drawn deeper into an unfamiliar world. Those missiles could not do the trick. The people of the earth and the hills there have a knack for knowing when strangers fire their guns as a cover for their retreat back to their own world.

The foreign power could ward off a local predator, but it was hard to embrace that power and its interests and ways. Between the foreign power and its allies in the Gulf and the Peninsula lay reciprocal need and reciprocal caution. The depths of these societies were inaccessible to their American protectors. The rulers wanted it this way; the larger society as well. For its part, America could feign no enthusiasm for those lands, no great curiosity about them. There were markets to be protected and imperial turf to be secured. America wanted to sell its planes, telephones, and weapons. This was a fair price, it was thought, for the military protection. These lands needed the protection even as they grumbled about its terms and the presumption that came with it. No greater intimacy could be had between these worlds.

In the age of the "trading state," empire must pay for itself if it is to be sustained. There had never been an American calling for empire in the Middle East to begin with. Those vast, pristine deserts that had bewitched the likes of Sir Richard Burton, Gifford Palgrave, Charles Doughty, Gertrude Bell, and T. E. Lawrence had not ensnared Americans. That romance had cracked in Britain's own imperial venture. As early as 1920, a great debate was waged in England about the costs of an imperial presence in the Middle East and about the treasure poured into those "thankless deserts" at a time of economic retrenchment at home. The Pax Britannica of the inter-war years had to be secured on the cheap. Fleet Street made the costs of empire one of its principal causes; the custodians of empire accommodated the popular demand for economy. These kinds of pressures operate in greater force in the case of America's new imperium in the Middle East. Trade must follow the flag; production lines must remain open in Missouri and California, or the whole edifice of imperial authority is called into question. The new realities of empire were captured by an episode in February 1994. When the national carrier of Saudi Arabia put in an order for $6 billion in U.S. civilian aircraft, the announcement was made by the American president himself. He let it be known that he had lobbied for the contract for several months, that the deal was a victory for "America's businesses and workers" against the European consortium, Airbus Industrie, which had competed for the same contract. What worries the Americans had been expressing about budgetary deficits and budgetary discipline in Saudi Arabia were forgotten; the contracts for Boeing Company and McDonnell Douglas Corporation were the spoils of Desert Storm.

Although no great debate materialized in the United States about the costs of playing international gendarme in the Gulf, the elements of such a debate were in place. The large Fifth Fleet patrolled the sea lanes in the Gulf—twenty-one ships manned by fifteen thousand sailors and twelve more ships with equipment for ground troops. In addition, there were ten thousand American soldiers on the ground in the Gulf states. The costs of this American presence were estimated at $50 billion a year. Americans were being snookered, the critics could claim. They were paying the cost of imperial authority when a "free ride" was being had by Europe and Japan. Empire, it was asserted, was a bad habit, an atavism, that had lingered from the days of containment and the Cold War, a role a debtor nation could not afford. The critics of this presence in the Gulf had not carried the day, but those who bet on American protection were fated to live with a healthy measure of insecurity about

CHAPTER FOUR

IN THE LAND OF EGYPT:

THE SAINTS AND THE WORLDLINESS

———◆———

A GENERATION AFTER THAT day of October 6, 1981, when Anwar al-Sadat was struck down, a strange bond had been forged between Sadat and his assassin, Khalid Istanbuli. A place had been made in the country's narrative for both men. The history of Egypt, her very identity, was fluid enough to claim the wily ruler who swallowed his pride to deal with Israel and the United States and also the assassin appalled by the cultural price paid in the bargain. In a sense, Sadat and Istanbuli are twins, their lives and deeds one great tale of the country's enduring dilemmas and her resilience amid great troubles, about the kind of political men Egypt's history brought forth when her revolutionary experiment of the 1950s and 1960s ran aground.

It was not hard for Egyptians to recognize much of themselves and their recent history in Istanbuli, the young lieutenant who proclaimed with pride that he had shot the pharaoh. He was in every way a son of the Free Officer revolution of Gamal Abdul Nasser, of July 23, 1952, when Egypt cast aside her kings and set out on a new, nonaligned path. Istanbuli was born in 1957, a year after the Suez

War, during what seemed to be a moment of promise in the life of Egypt. He was named after Nasser's oldest son. His father was a lawyer in a public-sector company that was a product of the new, expanding government. He was ten years old when calamity struck Egypt in the Six Day War and the Nasser revolution was shown to be full of sound and fury and illusion. The country had been through a whirlwind, and Istanbuli's life mirrored the gains and the setbacks.

Istanbuli had not been particularly religious; he had attended a Christian missionary school in his town in Middle Egypt. Political Islam entered his life late in the hour, not long before he was to commit his dramatic deed of tyrannicide. An older brother of his, a religious activist, had been picked up in a massive wave of arrests that Sadat ordered in September 1981. All sorts of political men and women had been hauled off to prison: noted men and women of the elite, from the law, journalism, the universities, former ministers, Muslims and Copts alike. The wave of arrests had been a desperate throw of the dice by Sadat and it had backfired. It broke the moral contract between Sadat and his country. In taking revenge, Istanbuli did what normal society could not do for itself. "Khalid," an admiring author wrote in tribute to the assassin, "I spoke and you did, I wished, and others wished, and you fulfilled our wishes."

But Sadat too has a place, and an increasingly special one, in the country's memory. Sadat, it is true, died a loner's death. Presumably victorious in October 1973 in the war against Israel, he was yet judged a lesser figure than his predecessor, who was defeated in 1967. But a certain measure of vindication has come Sadat's way. He broke with Arab radicalism, and the years were to show that Arab radicalism's harvest was ruin and bankruptcy. He opted for peace with Israel; the Palestinians and other Arabs, so many of them shouting treason and betrayal, followed in his footsteps. The crafty ruler, to his fingertips a wily man of the countryside with a peasant's instinctive shrewdness and wisdom, was able to see before it was evident to others that the Soviet Union was no match for American power.

It was not lost on his people that Sadat foresaw American primacy and placed his bets on American power, making the sort of accommodation with America that his proud predecessor would have never been able to pull off. Then there is the gift he bequeathed his country: the liberation of the land that his legendary predecessor lost in 1967. Indeed, ten days after Istanbuli was put to death with four of his fellow conspirators, in April 1982, Israel returned the Sinai Peninsula to Egyptian sovereignty.

Sadat had to wait for his vindication. The trial of his assassins, the great body of writings about them, became a trial of Sadat himself. He had imprisoned men and women of formidable talents, and they had come out of prison to have their say about him. From the feminist-physician Nawal el-Saadawi came *Memoirs from the Women's Prison;* from Mohamed Heikal, *The Autumn of Fury.* A book about the Sadat assassins was given the provocative title, *The Assassination of a Nation.* Every day there was a new revelation about the man, his wife, Jihan, or the corruption of his family. Egypt took what Sadat had secured—the aid from America, the land liberated from Israel, the end of her ruinous wars with Israel—but there was no kind word to be heard about the man or his legacy.

It was said that his wife had not really grieved for him, that she had gone back to the university and her social life before a decent interval of mourning. It was whispered that even the "caterpillars of the realm" who had done well by his regime and had devoured the gains of the new order were glad to be rid of him. The detractors wrote that a *"Khawaga* complex" (a foreigner's complex, a deference to the white man) ate at him, that he had been tormented by his dark pigmentation, that he worshipped all things and people American. The men and women of the universities and the professional world mocked his pretensions and those of his wife. The tale of his wife defending her M.A. thesis in literature on national television and passing with distinction became the quintessential tale of the Sadats: the newcomers hoarding what was there to be had, claiming for themselves honors and distinctions they had not earned. Egypt had tired of living on its nerves and was eager for a time of normalcy. Sadat was in perpetual need of adulation. Convinced that his countrymen—the intellectuals among them, the pretentious ones whom he suspected of looking down on him—had given his predecessor a place in their hearts that they denied him, Sadat seemed like a man out of control toward the end. The weary land sought a repose from the man and his torments.

The years and the distance from that time of living on edge did their work. One of the country's acclaimed commentators and establishment journalists, Ahmad Baha al-Din, came forth with an appreciation of the ruler, *Muhawarati ma' al-Sadat* (My Conversations with Sadat). It was an unassuming work, published six years after Sadat's assassination. Baha al-Din had been reasonably close to Sadat; he had served as editor-in-chief of two of the country's dailies (including the preeminent *al-Ahram*) as head of the syndicate of journalists. He had left his country to live in Kuwait, where he edited a cultural monthly, but was in and out of Egypt, a respected man of the craft who enjoyed official access but was never smothered by it.

It is a wily and complex ruler who emerges in Baha al-Din's rendition, a man who very much wanted to lay down the foundations of democratic rule but dreaded any criticism of himself, a ruler who gloried in his love of homeland but hated Cairo and its intellectual classes and spent as much time away from his troubled capital as he could. The love of the West that gripped—and burned—Sadat was there in him right from the start. On a journey back from Guinea in 1960, Baha al-Din recalled, Sadat broke his trip for a vacation in Vienna. He wanted to be in a beautiful place where he would not hear the words "colonialism" or "imperialism." Vienna, the future ruler said, was one of the prettiest places in the world, "dearest to my heart." He had nothing but contempt for the whole nonaligned world. He revered the Shah of Iran way back then, when Egypt and Iran were the bitterest of enemies. He admired the Shah, for the latter understood that there was only imperial authority in the world, Pax Americana, and that the Soviet Union was nothing but a fraudulent pretense.

Sadat now belonged to history. True, said Baha al-Din, he had fallen under the spell of America and exaggerated his ties to the great American personages he knew: David Rockefeller, Henry Kissinger, and Jimmy Carter. But he had done what he could for his country. Quick to anger, he was never really brutal toward the opposition. He banished Baha al-Din only to forgive and rehabilitate him. He imprisoned his opponents, but his was a benign form of autocracy. He ridiculed other Arab leaders—he dismissed his rival in Damascus, Hafez al-Assad, as a grocer who negotiated as though he were haggling over the price of cheese and mocked the Gulf Arabs—but he did so because he and Egypt were caught in mighty winds. He and his wife may have had their pretensions, but they were, on the whole, decent people eager to open up the life of the country and to bring to a close its ruinous ideological wars and its enmity toward the West.

Five years later, it was another writer, the sociologist and political commentator Saad Eddin Ibrahim (a dual national, an Egyptian and an American citizen who teaches at the American University in Cairo), who provided yet another reassessment in *The Vindication of Sadat*. Ibrahim had both courted the Sadats—husband and wife—and angered them. A master of the sound bite at home in pan-Arab circles and in the universities and official institutions of the West, Ibrahim had a stormy meeting with Sadat in the summer of 1981, shortly before the ruler's murder. The sociologist had been summoned to Alexandria, to one of Sadat's many retreats outside Cairo. Sadat had bullied his visitor and fenced with him; he wanted to know the mood of the "chattering classes" in Cairo; he wanted to deliver, through him, a message to the oppositionists in the academy and the press. He had had his fill of their opposition to his peace with Israel and their charges that he had betrayed the Nasserist inheritance. It was a wrecked country that his predecessor had bequeathed him. The sooner the country's intelligentsia understood that, the better for all concerned. Nor was his visitor spared: He had belittled Egypt in his writings abroad, he was told, and he had smeared its president and his wife.

It did not end well, the sociologist's visit. Ibrahim was a self-styled Nasserist. But a decade later, he felt that Sadat was due a fuller appreciation. The echo of what Sadat told him during that encounter in the summer of 1981 could be heard in this summation: "Sadat came to power when Egypt was wounded and defeated, suffering the nightmare of an Israeli occupation, her ambitious development plans had ground to a halt. . . . Then came the decision in October 1973 to go to war and the astonishing Egyptian performance. The man felt that this accomplishment entitled him to his own independent source of legitimacy." Nasser and Sadat belonged to the same generation. The ideas that formed them had been right perhaps for Nasser, but Sadat had had to make adjustments of his own to a wholly different era. "Woe to a ruler who incurs the wrath of the intellectuals," the sociologist wrote. Sadat died isolated from the intellectual class; they had not been able to alter his policies; they had done what was within their grasp: They had stripped him of his legitimacy. He was now owed a new history and a second look.

The deepest and most sympathetic retrospective of Sadat, though, was to come from the great novelist Naguib Mahfuz in a pretty work that was as captivating as it was simple in its story line, *Amam al-Arsh* (Before the Throne). In this novella, the country's rulers, from the time of King Mina to Sadat, appear before a panel of judges drawn from their own ranks. The court is presided over by Osiris, chief deity in the Egyptian pantheon; he is flanked by his wife Isis on his right and their son Horus on his left. Each ruler gets a chance to tell of his time and his rule and is then questioned by his fellow rulers. Sadat's opening statement to the court depicts him as a simple Egyptian who held deep within himself the spirit of patriotism, who had known imprisonment as a young officer because he was caught up in plots against collaborators with British rule, and who inherited political power from Nasser when the country was in great agony. He had done what he could for *Misr* (Egypt), the immortals were told. He had liberated the land, opened up the economy, and experimented with democracy, but a "religious current" struck him down on the very day commemorating his great victory of October 6, 1973.

When the immortals have their say, the ambivalence toward Sadat—the ambivalence that his country has always felt for him—yields to a fuller assessment of what the man did for the tormented country. Akhenaton greets him as a kindred spirit who opted for peace in his time as Akhenaton had done. "I am not surprised," Akhenaton said, "that your enemies accused you of treason. They did the same thing to me for the same reasons." Amenhotep III sees in Sadat his own love of glory, splendor, and palaces but pities him because Sadat ruled during a time of poverty: "My own time allowed me to enjoy bliss without interruption, but yours was a bittersweet time. Let me tell you of my love and sympathy for you." For Horemheb, too, Sadat was a sympathetic though weak figure: "You ruled during circumstances that resembled mine when I ruled in the aftermath of the death of the old king Ay and there was chaos in the land. I grant you that you did great things, but you were negligent in punishing corruption until the corrupt elements turned your victories into setbacks." Mustafa al-Nahhas, a prime minister on the eve of the Free Officer revolution of 1952, gets his chance to remind Sadat of his conspiratorial past: "You tried to assassinate me, you almost succeeded had it not been for divine protection. You lost your life to an assassination. Do you still believe in such methods?" "We need several lifetimes, before we learn wisdom," Sadat answers.

Predictably the harshest audit is rendered by Gamal Abdul Nasser, who rails against Sadat's shameful peace with Israel, his betrayal of the poor, the rampant corruption of his regime, and his breach of faith with the revolution of 1952. "Just as my time was a time of security for the poor, yours was a time of security for the rich and for the thieves." Nor is Nasser impressed with Sadat's military performance or his accommodation with Israel and American power. "You gave up everything for a sullied peace, you stabbed the Arabs, and you condemned Egypt to isolation and alienation. You replaced one superpower that backed us with one that had been our enemy."

The judgment that matters, the final words on Sadat, though, belong to Isis and Osiris, who have before them the long life of the land and its people. Isis hails him as "a son who restored the full independence of Egypt as it was before the Persian invasion, who committed his share of errors but who accomplished more than other rulers." Osiris grants him a place of honor among the immortals.

THIS TENSION IN the psyche and politics of Egypt will persist: between Sadat's world, with its temptations and its window on modernity, and Istanbuli's world, with its rigors and furious determination to keep the West at bay. A fissure has opened right in the heart of Egypt's traditionally stoic and reliable middle class. A wing of this class has defected to theocratic politics. The state insisted that this theocratic wind blew in from Iran, and the men and women of the secular tradition explained it as a malady that came in from the Gulf and the Arabian Peninsula, but there was no wishing it away and no resolution in sight for this dilemma.

We misconstrue Egypt's reality and the nature of its malady if we see it as another Islamic domino destined to fall and if we lean too hard on the fight between the regime and the Islamist challengers. For all the prophecies of doom and the obituaries written of the Egyptian state, the custodians of political power have ridden out many storms. This is a country with a remarkable record of political stability. Only two regimes have governed modern Egypt over the last two centuries: the dynasty of the Albanian-born Muhammad Ali, the soldier of fortune who emerged in the aftermath of the chaos unleashed by Napoleon Bonaparte's invasion of the country in 1798, and the Free Officer regime of Nasser, Sadat, and their inheritors. The sorrow of Egypt is made of entirely different material: the steady decline of its public life, the inability of an autocratic regime and the middle class from which this regime issues to rid the country of its dependence on foreign handouts, to transmit to the vast underclass the skills needed for the economic competition of nations, to take the country beyond its endless alternation between false glory and self-pity.

We must not exaggerate the strength of the theocratic challenge or the magnitude of the middle class's defection. In our fixation on the Iranian revolution—the armed imam chasing Caesar out of power—we have looked for it everywhere and grafted its themes and outcomes onto societies possessed of vastly different traditions and temperaments. There never was a chance that Shaykh Omar Abdul Rahman, the blind Egyptian preaching fire and brimstone in Brooklyn and Jersey City, would return to his land, Khomeini-like, to banish the secular powers and inherit the realm. Even the men who gunned down Sadat were under no illusions about their own power in the face of the state. No fools, these men knew the weight of the state, the strength of all they were hurling themselves against. They sought only the punishment of "the tyrant," sparing the lives of his lieutenants (Hosni Mubarak included), who stood inches away on the reviewing stand. Sadat's inheritors, the assassins hoped, would be humbled by what they had seen; they would refrain from playing with fire and from the kinds of violations Sadat (and his wife Jihan) committed against the mores of the land.

Nor should we project Algeria's descent into hell onto Egypt. Look at Algeria, with its terror and counterterror: armed Islamic groups campaigning against all perceived Francophiles, secularists, and emancipated women; reprisals by the state and its "eradicationists," who pass off their violence as the defense of modernity itself; state-sponsored killer squads, the ninjas with their ski masks. This politics of zeal and cruelty, so reminiscent of Argentina and Chile in the 1970s, is alien to the temperament of Egypt. The chasm between the Francophiles and the Arab-Islamists at the root of the terror in Algeria has no parallel in the experience and the life of Egypt. The political and cultural continuity of the place has not ruptured. No great windfall was squandered by the Egyptian elite the way the nomenklatura in Algeria blew the oil revenue of the last three decades. Most of all, unlike the shallow roots of the Algerian state—a postcolonial entity that rose in the 1960s—central authority in Egypt reaches back millennia.

There was no denying the troubles that had come to Egypt, though. The four years from 1990 to 1993 were the bloodiest period of civil disorder this century. By the estimate of the Egyptian Organization for Human Rights, the death toll of political violence rose from 139 in 1991 and 1992, to 207 in 1993, then to 225 in 1994. Altogether, nearly 1,200 people—insurgents, policemen, civilian victims of terror, Copts targeted by the religious extremists—perished between 1992 and 1996. A small war had broken out between the state and the Gamaat Islamiyya, the Islamic groups, as the loosely organized underground of the forces of political Islam call themselves. The armed bands treated the country to a season of wrath and troubles, but the state fought back, showing little mercy toward the insurgents. It pushed their challenge to remote, marginal parts of the country, provincial towns in Middle and Upper Egypt, the country's poorest areas. There, beyond the modernity of Cairo and Alexandria, away from the glare of publicity, the running war between the police and the Islamists degenerated into the timeless politics of vengeance and vendettas, an endless cycle of killings and reprisals. The campaign of terror against foreign tourists, the targeting of men of letters, the killing in the summer of 1992 of Farag Foda, a brave secularist commentator, the attempt on the life of the venerated and aging Naguib Mahfouz two years later—all played into the hands of the state. Men of the regime were also targeted by the insurgents. In 1993, over the space of some six months, there were three separate attempts on the lives of the minister of information, the minister of the interior, and the prime minister.

Thus faced with a relentless campaign of subversion, the regime responded by showing no mercy. The state apparatus was given a green light to root out armed Islamic groups and to do so without the kinds of protections and restraints a society of laws honors and expects. The governors and police officers dispatched to Middle and Upper Egypt, the hotbeds of religious strife, were invariably men known for their willingness to use force. Massive searches and arrests became routine there, as they were, when deemed necessary, in the poorer and more radicalized parts of Cairo. The military tribunals were swift. Nearly seventy death sentences were decreed and carried out in the first two years of this running war.

Tough police work was one side of the response to the terror of the Islamists; the other was a discernible retreat on the part of the regime from secular politics and culture. Historically the agent of social change, the one great instrument for transforming this old land and pushing it along, the state now seemed to slip into a cynical bargain with some devoted enemies of the secular idea. It granted these preachers and activists cultural space as long as the more strictly political domain (the police power of the regime, its hegemony over defense and foreign affairs) was left to it.

The custodians of the state drew a line between the legitimate and moderate Islamic groups and the armed Islamists. While the regime hunted down the latter, it made its peace with the former. A regime anxious for religious credentials of its own and for religious cover bent with the wind. Preachers and religious activists drawn from the ranks of the old Muslim Brotherhood, an organization now sanitized and made respectable in comparison with the younger, more uncompromising members of the Gamaat, were given access to the airwaves and the print media and became icons of popular culture. They dabbled in incendiary material, these respectable sorts, careful to stay on the proper side of the line. They advocated an Islamic state but said they would seek it through legitimate means. They branded as heretics and apostates noted secular figures in politics and culture. They hounded the Copts and made no secret of their view that the best the Copts, a community of no fewer than six million people, could hope for in a would-be Islamic state was the protected but diminished status of a subordinate community. To all this the state turned a blind eye. (The demographic weight of the Copts is one of the great riddles of Egypt. "We count everything in Egypt: cups, shoes, books. The only thing we don't count are the Copts. They have been two million since 1945. No one has died; no one has been born," political historian Rifaat Said observed. The political Islamists prefer a low estimate of two million Copts. The lower figure was precisely the figure given to me by Adel Hussein, a noted figure in the Islamic political movement.)

The country's leading center of Islamic learning and jurisprudence, al-Azhar University, was given greater leeway and authority than it has possessed at any time this century. Where al-Azhar had been on the defensive during the Nasser years as an institution that had to be modernized and reformed, it now speaks with self-confidence on the social and cultural issues of the day. A wide swath of the country's cultural life is now open to the authorities of al-Azhar. The theological alternative has seeped into the educational curriculum. By the time the state caught on and set out to reclaim some of this lost ground, whole schools had been ceded to the Islamists. There the advocates of political Islam, their apparent zeal and devotion a marked contrast to the abdication all around, had gone to work, weaning the young from the dominant symbols and outlook of the secular political order. In schools captured by the Islamists the national anthem and the Egyptian flag were banned, for they were, to the religious radicals, the symbols of an un-Islamic state. "Political Islam had been checked in its bid for power," the shrewd analyst and observer Tahseen Basheer said, "but the Islamization of society has gained ground."

It did not come on the cheap, this victory of the state over the political Islamists. The country felt trapped, cheated, and short-changed in the battle between an authoritarian state and a theocratic fringe. The state's tough response did its work, but important segments of the population in the intellectual, political, and business classes drew back in horror at the tactics. Some of the very men and women sheltered by the regime against the fury of the Islamists were taken aback by the number of executions ordered and the speed with which they were carried out. "Mubarak orders the executions but loses no sleep over them," a prominent figure of the opposition said to me. It had come down to this because the regime had little else in its bag. It was no consolation to Egyptians that they were spared the terror visited on less fortunate places like Syria,

Iraq, and the Sudan. This is a country where lawyers and the rule of law had an early footing, a society with a rich syndicalist tradition and associational life and an independent judiciary with pride in its legacy. The terror gave Mubarak a splendid alibi and an escape from the demands put forth by segments of the middle class and its organizations in the professional syndicates—the lawyers, engineers, and journalists—for a measure of political participation. Mubarak had done order's work; it became easy for him to wave off the tangled issues of economic and political reform.

Symbolically, the siege of the secularists began in the summer of 1992, on June 8, when Farag Foda, an agronomist whose passion for modernity and secular culture had taken him into public commentary, was assassinated by the Islamists. Foda was forty-seven years of age when he was killed by two masked men on motorcycles, in front of his teenage son and a close friend, who were both injured in the attack. Foda had neither bent to the will of the theocrats nor hidden. Although he had received countless death threats, he had petitioned the authorities to call off his police protection so he could get on with his normal life.

Foda harked back to the secularists of the 1920s, who insisted on the separation of religion from politics, who wrote as Muslims but consigned the faith to personal matters and religious rituals. Above all, the damning sin that marked him in the eyes of the Islamists was a book he had written in 1985, *Qabl al-Suqut* (Before the Fall), which elaborated a thorough and uncompromising secular interpretation of political life. The "just city," Foda had written, was not of this world. Those who held out to the young a theocratic utopia as a "paradise on earth" were peddlers of false dreams. Brave, perhaps foolhardy, Foda offered an unsentimental view of early Islamic history (the sacred utopia of the political Islamists). Three of the first four "Guided Caliphs," the successors of the Prophet, had been murdered, he reminded his readers. There was no "golden age" in some remote past; the "Muslim sword" that the theocrats yearn for had beheaded more Muslims than nonbelievers.

Place and time, Foda said, dictated everything. Men and women had to be awake to their own world. He rejected the notion of an Islamic community; he wrote as an Egyptian and mocked the claim that an Iranian Muslim could be closer to him than his Coptic neighbors and compatriots. He wrote that the doctrine of *takfir* (declaring others apostate) had become the "curse of the land," taking in everything the theocrats did not like—women in the national assembly, music, philosophy, coeducation at the nation's universities.

You could see the scientist at work in Foda's book. He approached this theocratic phenomenon, the rise of political Islamism, in his country with precision. It had arisen, he wrote, because there was no rival national project in the land, because Sadat had encouraged it and given it legitimacy out of his desire to give himself and the new order he had launched religious sanction. Sadat, he wrote, had let a genie out of a bottle, and the genie had struck him down. A space had been opened for the theocrats that had not been opened for their secular rivals; the theocrats had filled that space, and their ideas had taken root among the poorer classes, the newly urbanized, and the gullible. What Egyptians had to do was nothing less than restore the secular project. This will not be easy, he said, for this theocratic idea blows with vengeance. There was the Islam of the state and politics, and there was the Islam of the faith and the heart. One should bow to the latter and acknowledge that the former was a matter of interpretation and debate, he was to write in his book, *Before the Fall*. "Gentlemen, I vow to you I will never retreat from facing up to these questions as long as I live, and I will not abandon my cause as long as life throbs in my veins. I will always believe that all this new phenomenon [political Islam] is merely politics in the garb of religion and not the other way around. I will never tire of reminding you that this is all sedition, *fitna,* and may God spare Egypt the dangers of this sedition."

The reference to *fitna* was clearly a reference to the national unity of the land, to the place and fate of the Copts. Foda had taken up a great and urgent public cause. Shortly before his murder, he and a small band of secularists, Copts and Muslims, had launched a civic-political project, the Egyptian Committee for National

Unity. The recognition that the political Islamists and the theocrats were slowly remolding the culture of the land had galvanized the secular intellectuals. Foda had given every indication that he would not relent. "We had to kill him," one of his two murderers said, "because he attacked our beliefs."

> "Farag, these bullets that struck you were only instruments of murder," a fellow secularist, Rifaat Said, a man of no less courage and eagerness for combat than Foda, wrote in memorium to his old friend in the leftist paper *al-Ahali:*

The bullets that struck you in the chest were the product of a dark atmosphere that the real killers had fashioned—the television that gives the crows of darkness every chance to speed up the destruction of our homeland, the national newspapers that provide ample space to those writers who praise the extremists and call on everyone to follow their opinions. The bullets came from official circles and official deeds that have fed this climate of sedition.

Rifaat Said, a historian, a prolific writer, a man of the left born in 1932 who spent fourteen years in prison under the monarchy and under Nasser and Sadat, situated the deed of murder in the wider struggle for the country's modernity. Day after day, Rifaat Said propounded the same themes: the abdication of the state, the falseness of the distinction between "moderate" Islamists and "extremists," the steady erosion in the status and life-chances of the Copts. His columns in *al-Ahali*, which he assembled into widely read books, sounded the alarm bells that the national unity of the country was becoming a thing of the past. Copts from everywhere wrote him telling of discriminations and fears endured in daily life. Hundreds of letters (some signed, mostly unsigned) reached him. A tireless researcher who wrote of every facet of contemporary Egyptian history, he published the letters, and his columns became a sounding board for a country in the throes of an unmistakable assault on its secular political norms.

In the letters, physicians, professors of medicine, wrote of promotions that Copts could not have, of the emergence of a culture of discrimination and bigotry that was engendering among the Copts a feeling that they were "second-class citizens in a country at the gates of the twenty-first century." The correspondents of Rifaat Said bared their souls. The Copts of Upper Egypt wrote of armed Islamists terrorizing them at will, murdering pharmacists and goldsmiths and looting their property and money. (The militant cleric Omar Abdul Rahman, from his base in the country and then from America, where he went in 1990, declared the wealth of the Copts *halal*, forfeit and permissible to the diehards.) From Rifaat Said's hometown of Mansura in the Delta, a childhood friend wrote nostalgically of "a time we knew no distinction between a Muslim and a Copt." He reported that a Coptic priest was being harassed because he had built a room in the courtyard of his church without permission. "I don't want to compare," the friend had written, "how our Muslim brothers build places of prayer and worship everywhere, in any location. We don't question that right, we only want some of this accommodation for ourselves, so that we can feel we are truly brothers, in deed and not only in words." An old Coptic correspondent from Tanta laid a fair measure of the blame at the doorstep of the state:

> The government plays a significant role in the spread of extremism among its people. The television and the radio broadcast messages of incitement, and the preachers who play to the extreme find great popularity. Sir, look anywhere for a Copt who is a provincial governor and you will not find him. Among the ambassadors you will find only a Copt or two. . . . Is this the Egypt that we knew down through the ages? Is this the country that the Prophet Muhammad, peace be upon him, had spoken of its Copts with appreciation and had instructed that they be treated with kindness?

Educators and schoolteachers and parents wrote of school textbooks (in government schools) heaping derision upon the Copts and upon Christianity as a whole. A reader from Jersey City, one of the thousands of Egyptians in New York and its surroundings, sent a copy of an article that the influential preacher Shaykh Muhammad Ghazali, an astute and wily figure of the Muslim Brotherhood who had one foot in the religious establishment and one in the camp of the religious extremists, had written in a London-based Arabic magazine attacking Christianity and its adherents. Samir, an accountant who supplied only his first name, wrote that every Friday he heard insults in Friday sermons that made him quiver, "preachers who call us infidels, who call upon the worshippers to avoid our company, to refrain from eating with us. In the school where my wife teaches, it is unapologetically and openly stated that it is *haram*, forbidden, to take private lessons from Christian teachers. Do you know that there is an unwritten pact, in private companies and in the government, to limit the employment of Christians?"

The historian had opened the floodgates. He was never without material; the mail brought him the complaints, the worries, and the grievances. And he was never without examples plucked from Egypt's history—more generous times, more tolerant times. He shamed and challenged his readers; he found greater indifference to religious identity in presumably darker times in centuries past. Naturally, he looked back to the bourgeois era—the time of his own childhood—and had no trouble demonstrating the greater openness of that era. A contemporary of the historian, a man of like-minded politics, the engineer Milad Hanna, a Copt, wrote him a commentary about that time when both of them came of age: "We the generation of the 1940s lived with all our senses a rich and fertile period of Egypt's history. We never imagined that Egypt would regress and would come to know a time of religious strife."

The courage displayed by Farag Foda did not die with him. If anything, Rifaat Said would outdo Foda in his eagerness to do battle with the Islamists. No surprise, he quickly became a marked man; the Islamists vowed to cut him down. I had known Rifaat Said for more than a dozen years, and although his politics were not mine, his door had always remained open to me. I came to see him three or four times after Foda's murder. In a great, ironic twist, the man who had known the political prisons of his country was now under police protection. He moved about with police escort, a plainclothes policeman with a machine gun checked the visitors to his office. With a gesture of resignation he lifted a sweater to reveal a hand gun tucked into his belt, the first time I had come to see him during this season of terror. He savored the irony of his new relation to the security forces. It had not been easy for him, he said, to take to this new situation.

There is a "black atmosphere" in the country, he observed. "We accumulated democratic space, did it the hard way, paid for it. Now that space is disappearing." The Copts, the liberals, the secular intellectuals, he said, had been frightened into the bosom of the state. The terror on one side, the authoritarian regime on the other. It was not a pretty spectacle, and this thoroughly political man accepted the protection of the state and all that came with it as the lesser of two evils. He knew even without admitting it that the agenda of a leftist party of which he was a leading figure, and the agenda of all the other opposition parties, had no chance of being aired in the midst of this deadly fight.

In October 1994, the terror that struck down Foda and hovered around Rifaat Said struck at an icon of the country's cultural life: the aged novelist Naguib Mahfuz. A twenty-one-year-old appliance repairman who had never read any of Mahfuz's novels, together with an accomplice, stabbed the writer in the neck, severing his artery. Mahfuz survived, but his writing hand was paralyzed. Born in 1911, awarded the Nobel Prize in 1988, Mahfuz held a special place in the country's image of itself. This was the son of Cairo, and of *Misr,* Egypt, who had chronicled its modern condition, who had never bothered with the world outside Egypt (he had not even gone to Stockholm for the Nobel ceremonies), who had remained himself amid all the great changes that had blown through the country. A creature of habit and routine, he frequented the same coffeehouses, hung around the same friends. He was free of affectations. Ideologies came and went, Arabism gave way to a fling with America and the West, the great struggle against Israel yielded to a time of uneasy peace, but Mahfuz stayed at his craft for sixty years, and the country loved what it saw in the mirror that Mahfuz's life and fiction held up. He wrote his first novel in 1932; forty-five short stories and countless essays later, he gave his country an inheritance destined to endure the test of time. He beheld the land and its people, listened to and rendered his country's moods and great concerns.

Mahfuz had had his troubles with the keepers of religious truth. A novel he had published in 1960, *Awlad Haratina* (The Children of Our Quarter), had been banned by the authorities of al-Azhar University for its secular tone and the liberties it took with religious symbolism. He had endorsed the peace that Sadat had made with Israel. But he was a man of enormous gentility, and there was no indication that the Islamists bore any particular animus toward him. His age, it was natural to think, afforded him protection. But Mahfuz had turned up in the rantings and pronouncements of Shaykh Omar Abul Rahman, who had emerged since 1981 and the assassination of Sadat as the clerical tribune of the younger Islamists. Mahfuz was then the perfect target. The very reverence in which he was held, his fame abroad, the great prize he had been awarded by judges in the infidel world, all marked him for a terrorist-theocratic movement bent on remolding the culture of the country.

The men of the regime and of the secular world of letters rushed to Mahfuz's bedside. The theocrats had struck at a national symbol, and the country had seen the wages of this new time of terror. A writer who knew the ways of his land, Mahfuz understood the storm that swirled around him and the uses to which the ruling order was putting the attack against him. In the midst of this great turmoil, he kept his head about him and handled it all with a dignity worthy of any of his best characters. He wanted none of the adulation of the national media; he would not take part in the barrage of words aimed at the terrorists. He was stoic and resigned in the midst of this ordeal. Because of his failing and sensitive eyes, he had not seen his assailant. The prosecutors who tried his case before a military tribunal granted him his wish to stay away from the trial of the men charged in the attack against him.

For all the cruelty and senselessness of the Mahfuz episode, it was a different case that caught the agony of the secular men and women of letters: that of a writer and academic at Cairo University, Nasr Hamid Abu Zeid, and his wife, Ibtihal Younis, a professor of French literature. Here no shot was fired; the weapon of choice was a lawsuit, and the matter played itself out between 1992 and 1996. The charge against Nasr Abu Zeid was apostasy, and the theocrats who hounded him at the university and through the courts sought to dissolve his marriage on the grounds that the marriage of a Muslim woman to an apostate was null and void.

Before Nasr Abu Zeid and his wife made a run for it and quit their country for the Netherlands (he got an academic appointment at Leiden University), the theocrats had unearthed a powerful, new weapon: a doctrine, the *hisba,* which they claimed gave any interested Muslim the right to obtain a ruling from a judge to stop actions deemed harmful to the society of Muslims. The principle of *hisba,* used by Muslim jurists centuries ago, had no standing in Egyptian courts. The courts of the land had been thoroughly secularized in the latter years of the nineteenth century (the foundations of the mixed courts system were laid in 1876, then came the codification of the civil and commercial codes in the early 1880s). It was in this spirit that a personal status court threw out the challenge to the marriage of Abu Zeid and Ibtihal Younis in 1994. In a surprising turn of events, however, a court of appeals in June 1995 ruled in favor of the Islamists invoking the principle of *hisba.* Abu Zeid was declared an apostate and his marriage was dissolved.

Other legal maneuvers were yet to come. A year later, the court of cassation upheld the judgment of the court of appeals and the charge of apostasy. Then another court, the court of urgent cases, issued a stay of the appeal court's decision. Through it all, the regime squirmed and hoped for the best. The secular elite watched the case with growing alarm. The bases of the legal profession and of an independent judiciary ran deep in the society; the bar association had been established in 1912. In the interim, lawyers had played a pivotal role in the country's modernization. Judges and lawyers became great public figures; in a litigious country, judicial proceedings and national courts were held in great esteem. The ability of the Islamists to subvert the legal process was a breach of a secular, modernist stronghold. With the capitulation of the courts, the official religious establishment, which had been hoping that the case would blow over, rushed to join in the condemnation of the embattled couple. The shaykh of al-Azhar, Muhammed Tantawi, called upon Abu Zeid to declare that he was "innocent of everything he had written, erroneous in everything he had written." Earlier in this crisis, Shaykh Tantawi, a religious scholar of reformist instincts, had spoken against the rush to judgment and had offered the opinion that Muslims could not be charged with apostasy for what they wrote. But the ground had shifted after the court battles, and the jurist had made his adjustment.

For Abu Zeid, a prolific and exacting scholar, the trouble began in 1992, when he was fifty, with virtually impenetrable books of scholarship. An erudite, irrepressible man, Abu Zeid had taken into religious studies, and into interpretations of the Quran, modern literary-philosophical techniques that located texts in their time and in the time and needs of their readers. Muslims had fought among themselves, the scholar wrote, and "Quranic interpretation was one of the tools used in intellectual, social and political struggles." Religious texts were, in his view, "ultimately linguistic texts that belong to a particular cultural edifice and to the language of a particular tradition." A text can only be understood if situated in the world, in the push and pull of social and political forces, in the dominant ideas of a given time and place.

Abu Zeid's books came to public attention in the unlikeliest of ways: a review of the matter of his promotion in the Arabic department at his university. A member of the review committee, Shaykh Abdul Sabbur Shahin, took the case beyond the confines of the university. Shahin was a figure of this era of politicized religion and of the new power—and wealth—of political Islam. He was an empire builder who straddled the worlds of finance, religion, politics, and the academy. He was a prayer leader of one of Cairo's great mosques, the Amr Ibn al-As Mosque; he was an advisor to one of those Islamic management funds that had emerged in the 1980s to compete with the nation's banks (many of these funds failed and were nothing but pyramid schemes). Shahin had seen in the scholar's work nothing but heresy, and he took it upon himself to bring the apostate to justice. It was his hope, he said, that God would make a place for him in paradise because of his good work against the academic who had lost his way.

The tranquil academic life behind them—they had a home on the outskirts of Cairo, in one of the quiet satellite towns—Nasr Abu Zeid and Ibtihal Younis departed their country in the summer of 1995. Life under police protection had become unbearable. The teaching at the university was awkward and forced, painful at times. A former student of Abu Zeid, now a colleague, was agitating against him; there were other torments. The prayer leader, the imam of the local mosque in his village, whom he had known in his childhood—they had studied the Quran together as children—was busy denouncing him from the pulpit. And then came the decision to leave. The release, Abu Zeid later called, came when he and his wife arrived in Spain on a mercilessly hot day in August 1995. The joy of throwing their bags in the hotel and rushing outside to the streets without police escort underlined the hell they had endured. There was work for him outside Egypt; there were universities that knew his talent and output. But now in exile he spoke of his *hanin* (yearning) for his country and vowed to return.

Professors in the land had become entrepreneurs; university appointments were vehicles for political and social ambitions. The work in the Egyptian academy had responded to the temptations held out by the philanthropic foundations of America and Europe. Abu Zeid had done serious, methodical work. He did write one polemical work, *Naqd al-Khitab al-Dini* (Criticism of Religious Discourse), which demolished the distinction between "moderate"

Islamists and "extremists" and took apart the way religious texts and the Islamic discourse had been used in the political marketplace of the Sadat era and beyond. A writer at home with the methods and language of Michel Foucault and Antonio Gramsci, he subjected the dominant ways of religious interpretation to a precise autopsy.

That old battle over religious texts between "mythology and legend in the guise of religion" and the forces of secularism had not ended, he wrote. He warned that those who tried to battle orthodoxy with its weapons—deferring to it, borrowing its techniques in the hope of subverting it—were destined to come out second best in that struggle. He distinguished between religion and religious thought; in painstaking detail he traced how theological ideas of politics and the political-moral order had crossed over from the theocratic fringe to the religious establishment. Ideas such as *hakimiyya* (sovereignty belonging to God) and *takfir* (declaring secular thinkers apostates) had made their way, he said, from the fringe groups to the mainstream of the country's life. An influential religious preacher, a "star" of the government-owned television, one Shaykh Muhammad Shaarawi, who had been favored during the Sadat years, had said that he had prayed in gratitude when the forces of the Egyptian secular state were defeated in the Six Day War of 1967. It was time, Abu Zeid observed, to recognize that the religious weapons and ideas introduced by terrorists and extremists were fast closing up the political world and undermining the prospects for the rule of reason and secularism.

The cornerstone of Abu Zeid's work and his most problematic book for the Islamists, though, was probably a more difficult work, *al-Itijah al-Aqli fi al-Tafsir* (The Rational Approach to Interpretation). In that book he gave a brilliant exposition of an early Islamic philosophical movement, the Mu'tazilah, whose philosophers had, in their time of ascendancy and flowering in the ninth century, let loose a great philosophical battle between orthodoxy and reason, over the very soul of Islam and the nature of the faith. Rationalists to the core, the Mu'tazilah applied to the Quran the canons of

Greek philosophy; they insisted on the rationality of God's ways and made ample space for unaided reason in the evolution of the world. Careful to stay on the proper side of the faith, they argued for the capacity of man to act freely in the world. Most importantly, though, they denied the eternity of God's word and declared it to be a created accident. The centerpiece of their philosophy—the human creation of the Quran—was rejected and turned back by the orthodox jurists and by the masses who followed these jurists in the latter years of the ninth century. That battle was a fierce war, rather resembling the Inquisition in Christian Europe.

That great inheritance was there, and Nasr Abu Zeid had written of it. He had seen that movement and the forces that snuffed it out as they were: protagonists in a great sociopolitical struggle. It was natural, he said, in a battle of that kind that the Mu'tazilah philosophers picked the verses of the Quran that "supported their point and belief in reason," and equally so for their opponents to adopt the same means. Muslims had been doing so ever since, Abu Zeid said. What had come to them was the faith as transmitted and reworked and fought over since the dawn of Islam: The divine revelation had merged with *al-Khitab al-Insani,* the human discourse.

Abu Zeid delivered his message in the most respectable—and academically unimpeachable—manner. There were hundreds of footnotes, the scholarly apparatus was in place, there had been no intention to inflame or to play with fire. There was nothing here of the irreverence that marked a Salman Rushdie. If anything, the scholar remained in the background. He told the tale of the rationalists and described the techniques they and their opponents had deployed. To be sure, he sided with the rationalists, he had a message to deliver, he was marking out philosophical space for reason in the face of orthodoxy. But the implications of what he wrote had to be teased out, someone had to bell the cat, for the stuff of his book was not streetcorner reading.

In yet another book, *Falsafat al-Ta'wil* (The Philosophy of Interpretation), Abu Zeid went back to one of the great mystic philosophers of medieval Islam, Ibn Arabi (1165–1240). A wanderer and traveler born in Murcia, Spain, who spent his final years in Damascus, Ibn Arabi roamed the expanses of Islam. He lived in Mecca and Cairo, in the heart of Anatolia; he reached the borders of Iran. He attracted and spurned fame and patronage. He left a huge body of writings that posited the central argument that divinity and humanity were not two distinct natures but merely two aspects present in every creation. Divinity was that which was hidden, humanity the external or outward manifestation of things.

Abu Zeid went back to Ibn Arabi, he said, because, that great controversial philosopher had an "elaborate philosophical approach" to the religious text. No philosopher, Abu Zeid wrote, had been as controversial as Ibn Arabi. For some he was a "saint" who had intuited and known God's truth, for others he was a "heretic and an apostate" who had conformed to the outward requirements of the faith but was a rationalist deep down and an agnostic. It was the inventiveness and creativity of Ibn Arabi in his approach to the divine text that had made him the center of an endless controversy, and it was the very same inventiveness that drew Abu Zeid to the Andalusian.

Author and subject are never haphazard combinations. A subject begets and beckons an author, and an author in Cairo of the late years of the twentieth century, at a time of new religious disputation, had gravitated toward a time of turmoil in a distant Muslim setting and had picked a philosopher of great genius and humanity for his hero. Of his hero, he wrote:

In his first *watan* [homeland], Ibn Arabi lived through the peak of the struggle between Christianity and Islam, and of all the intra-Muslim disputes between Sunnis and Shia, Sufis and *ulama,* philosophers and jurists. When he left his homeland for the eastern domains of Islam, he found the same spectacle. . . . Turmoil was rampant, the unity of the Muslim state was torn asunder. In the shadow of this dark time, Ibn Arabi lived and arrived at his philosophy of the world and of the universe. In truth, his travels, save for a lengthy period of time in Mecca, imbued him with a permanent sense of anxiety and restlessness.

Abu Zeid had found his literary and philosophical vehicle. Amid the tumult of his world and of the battle over Islam between "literalists" and modernizers, he had found the perfect ancestor. So many elements had gone into the eclectic and forgiving outlook of Ibn Arabi—Jewish and Christian ideas, Sunni and Shia doctrines, neo-Platonic concepts—and Abu Zeid hammered home his themes. *His* Ibn Arabi was a man for this time: a "foot in every camp" (he endorsed this view of Ibn Arabi that an earlier writer had used), and a man at home in a messy world of rival social and philosophical truths. In Abu Zeid's portrait of the philosopher, Ibn Arabi had built an "interior world as a substitute for the real world he had roamed and of which he had despaired. He found his final refuge in God's all-encompassing mercy, which took in the Muslim and the non-Muslim, the believer and the apostate."

Out of the Andalusian philosopher and his subtle way in the face of religious truth, and of the scripture, the Cairene was fashioning his own interior world. Just as Ibn Arabi had been hard to decipher, Abu Zeid, too, was no easy read. He deconstructed the working method of Ibn Arabi and wrote with obvious awe and relish of the Andalusian's skill with exegesis, his dexterity with religious texts. It is often hard, Abu Zeid wrote, to separate the text of the Quran from the words of Ibn Arabi. Ibn Arabi had read the whole world into the Quran. For both the Andalusian and his chronicler, human language was an echo of divine language, and the text was a medium into which the perplexed and the seekers read their own times and queries.

In the chronicler's admiring summation, Ibn Arabi soars over his time:

Ibn Arabi tried to resolve the great struggles of his time, in particular the matter of interpreting the text, on a philosophical and intellectual level. He ended up with a doctrine of absolute love, universal faith, and divine mercy that human existence started and to which it must return. But all the solutions of Ibn Arabi took the shape of one big dream from which you wake up to discover the ugliness of the world and the fierceness of the struggles of mankind on all levels. Ibn Arabi had tried to lead and guide the world, but he turned his back to it and built for himself an altogether different world, harmonious and complete, ruled by a perfect man who was but the shadow and the reflection of God with all His laws of justice, mercy, and love.

The Cairene had written an epilogue of his own tale into the Andalusian's. The sort of enforcers who had driven Ibn Arabi on his wanderings were still around. That timeless battle for forgiveness within the faith had not yet come to an end.

Innocence and a commitment to the primacy of reason come together in the Cairene's work. To the French scholar Gilles Kepel, who came to visit him in his new home in the Netherlands in early 1997, he restated his creed: He had only wanted to pose, and to read into the faith and the scripture, "the questions of our time." There was no contradiction, he maintained, between the "divinity" of the Quran and the view of it as a "historic text" revealed in a "specific place and time, in a specific language, a cultural product." He reflected on his own experience to make the broader point about the worldly struggle over religion and religious texts. Born in the 1940s, he was old enough to have seen Islam depicted as a "religion of socialism and of the workers and of Arab nationalism in the 1950s and 1960s, and of private property and of peace with Israel in the 1970s." What he sought was the freedom to interpret the faith and the text. He saw nothing in his quest to separate him from his faith or his inheritance.

It had happened before in Cairo, seven decades earlier, when another writer, Taha Hussein (1889–1973), his generation's most influential modernist, provoked the enforcers of religious orthodoxy with a daring book, *Fi al-Shi'r al-Jahili* (On Pre-Islamic Poetry). A poor son of the land, a village boy from Upper Egypt who lost his eyesight in early childhood, Taha Hussein made his own way through a traditional religious education to the Egyptian university and then to the Sorbonne. He rose to the deanship of the college of letters at the university. Fearless and headstrong, a prolific writer, he carved a place for himself as the standard-bearer of his country's secularism. He pulled no punches in that book, which put him at the center of a great national controversy when it was published in 1926. He relished the combat, ridiculed the traditional jurists, and called for the ascendancy of "scientific investigation" heedless of the restraints of nationality and religion. For the traditional jurists and interpreters, pre-Islamic poetry was a reference source for interpreting the Quran; Taha Hussein dismissed that method of interpretation and exegesis. The jurists, he wrote, had been able to prove what they wanted to prove. More reckless still, he took the sacred tradition head on, arguing that the Quranic narrative about Abraham (Ibrahim) and Ishmael (Ismael) was only myth and allegory.

It took years for this affair to blow over. The traditionalists charged Taha Hussein with apostasy—it was no help to him that he had married a French woman. A campaign was launched to expel him from the university. His colleagues stood by him; he sought a respite from this storm and traveled to Europe, where he stayed for a year. He came back to the university and to his deanship, only to be hounded out of his position by a dictatorial prime minister, Ismael Sidqi, in 1932. But the tide shifted again in his favor: Two years later, he was back at the university. A huge rally was held to celebrate his return, and the students carried him on their shoulders to his office.

Taha Hussein, and his cause, prevailed. He was minister of education in the last *ancien régime* cabinet between 1950 and 1952. He was mourned as a great figure of his country's modernity when he died in 1973. The crowd carried his coffin on the same route the students had carried him decades earlier.

Abu Zeid knew the tale of Taha Hussein, of course. He saw in his own ordeal a bleaker time and a harsher verdict. "Taha was accused of apostasy by people from outside the university and the university defended him. I was accused of apostasy inside the university, and some people from the outside are defending me. Taha Hussein was never called a *kafir* [idolatrous]. What's most telling is how the conception of apostasy has now been transplanted into the university."

AT THE HEART of Egyptian life there lies a terrible sense of disappointment. The pride of modern Egypt has been far greater than its accomplishments. For all the graces of this land and for all the long struggle of its modernizers, that gap between Egypt's sense of itself and its performance is impossible to ignore: the poverty of the underclass; the bleak political landscape that allows a military officer to monopolize political power and diminish all would-be rivals in civil society; the sectarian strife between Muslim and Copt; the state of its cultural and educational life.

A country of sixty million people, the weekly magazine *al-Mussawar* recently revealed, now produces a mere 375 books a year. Contrast this with Israel's 4,000 titles, as the magazine did, and it is easy to understand the laments heard all around. *Al-Ahram,* the country's leading daily—launched in 1876 and possessed of a distinguished history—is unreadable. There is no trace of investigative journalism or thoughtful analysis on its pages, only the banal utterances of political power. No less a figure than Naguib Mahfuz, spoke with sorrow and resignation about this state of affairs. "Egypt's culture is declining fast," he wrote. "The state of education in our country is in crisis. Classrooms are more like warehouses to cram children in for a few hours than places of education. The arts and literature are barely taught in these institutions, which are run more like army barracks than places where cultural awareness and appreciation can be nurtured." In more apocalyptic terms, the commentator Karim Alrawi warned that the modernizing imperative that has dominated and driven Egypt since the early 1800s after its encounter with Europe is being reversed.

It is out of this disappointment that a powerful wave of nostalgia has emerged for the liberal interlude in Egyptian politics (the 1920s through the revolution of 1952), for its vibrant political life, for the lively press of the time, for the elite culture with its literati and artists, for its outspoken, emancipated women, who carved a place for themselves in the country's politics, culture, and journalism. Some of this is the standard nostalgia of a crowded, burdened society for a time of lost innocence and splendor; some, though, is the legitimate expression of discontent over the mediocrity of public life. Egypt produced better, freer cinema in the 1930s than it does today. Its leading intellectual figures were giants who slugged out the great issues of the day and gave Egyptian and Arabic letters a moment of undisputed brilliance. When the critic and writer Louis Awad, a Copt, a prolific and independent man of letters born in 1915, died in 1990, an age seemed to come to a close. The Egypt of the military and the culture of hypernationalism was hard pressed to point to literary men and women of his like.

A pugnacious man of enormous curiosity and energy, Awad was born in a small village in Upper Egypt; his father was a clerk in the Anglo-Egyptian civil service. He was educated in English literature at the Egyptian University in the years 1933–1937. (This university has had names to fit all seasons. It was later named King Fuad University; today it goes by the name of Cairo University.) A modernist, an irreverent, irreligious man, he went on a government scholarship to Cambridge University in 1938, then took a Ph.D. at Princeton in comparative literature. A scholar and critic of eclectic interests, he translated Aeschylus, Shelley, Hardy, Joyce, and Eliot. He wrote on the theme of Prometheus in English and French literature; he wrote large, serious volumes about modern Egyptian thought. A fearless man, he ventured into explosive terrain with a study of comparative linguistics which argued that Arabic was related to Indo-European languages. That particular work ignited a controversy, and the religious authorities of al-Azhar suppressed it in 1980. Awad had known the risks: To the faithful, Arabic, the language of the Quran, was antecedent to history and was not to be subjected to this kind of scholarly, materialist analysis. Awad, a Copt at that, had been particularly brazen, an intellectual against the power of custom and orthodoxy.

Awad's willingness to go against the current, his eagerness to push the intellectual and cultural frontiers of his society, were life-long commitments. He stood up to his father in his choice of his studies. (The father had wanted a practical course in law; the son had insisted on literature.) He was the only student at the university to attend classes without a fez at a time when the fez was the official head cover in the land. He was zealous in his love of European letters and culture. He claimed Europe as a spiritual home. It came to him, he once wrote, when he first crossed the Mediterranean to Europe, that he was a man of Europe kidnapped by gypsies and delivered to Egypt during his childhood. He was no mimic man: That yarn about gypsies was rendered in Egyptian dialect. He loved his country and its history; he was part of its search for enlightenment and a workable order of things. He worked at his research and was a guide for younger scholars and literati; he served as an arts and cultural editor for two of the leading dailies in the aftermath of the Free Officer revolt. He gave the new order his loyalty but was brave and forthright enough to dissent from it. He paid for his politics with a period of imprisonment and exile, when the Nasser regime turned against the independent intellectuals and the Left. Always he worked and wrote, never at a loss for subjects, and always his own man. He was awake to the details of his country's politics, but he never groveled and never obeyed the powers. The great political and cultural themes of interest to him—reform of the language, cultural renewal, the independence of the educational system, the life of the theater, the development of an unfettered secular culture—sustained him. One of his last enduring contributions was an autobiography, *Awraq al-Umr* (Notes of a Lifetime), which he completed shortly before his death. It was at once the tale of his life and a forthright, intimate recapitulation of the politics and life of his generation.

Awad's talent was obviously his own, but he had not come out of a void. His genius and daring and the large, universal themes that moved him sprang out of a specific age and its temper and sensibility. It was not some fabled age that formed Awad and his contemporaries. The liberal, progressive impulse that moved Awad did not grip a whole generation. A war (and Awad's memoirs are exquisite in depicting that struggle) erupted in the nation's universities, literary salons, and streets between modernists and religious reactionaries who wanted to keep women out of the universities. The modern world would not be held back. Women entered the university in the year 1929–1930: Four of them, Awad tells us, made it into the college of letters that year, eight in the next year, and sixteen a year later. They were there to stay. When religious reactionaries sought to drive them out of the university a few years later, their male colleagues confronted the reactionaries and scattered the ranks of demonstrators who had stormed the college. The preeminent educator and writer of that time, Taha Hussein, assembled the students and called upon them to defend the cause of women's education. That cause, he said, was a "raging sea" and could not be held back by "throwing pebbles into it." Taha Hussein gave a rousing speech more befitting a military commander addressing his troops before battle. This was a "just cause," he said as he exhorted the students to attack the reactionaries before the reactionaries struck. Louis Awad, himself a child of the countryside of Upper (southern) Egypt who witnessed that episode, saw in the passion of Taha Hussein on that day not only the passion of a modernizer but the anger of an *ibn balad* (a son of the countryside) that outsiders were intruding into the domain of women. The southern countryside, *al-Sa'id,* was a land where the code of male honor ruled. In the reactionaries' assault on the campus and on the women of his college, Taha Hussein saw a breach of the moral code of the land.

It was not an unbroken journey, that struggle for modernity. A deadly fight played out between those generally liberal and leftist sorts who rode with the Wafd party and fascist bands of Young Egypt (Misr al-fatat), a party that drew its inspiration and tactics from the fascist world in Europe: the "blue shirts" of the Wafd boys against the "green shirts" of Young Egypt. Bloody battles were fought between the "blue shirts" and the "green shirts." Some men of culture and letters began as modernists only to yield to custom, orthodoxy, and reaction as the liberal wave lost its force. The liberalism was frightened and tentative, superimposed on a society burdened with enormous poverty and ignorance below. For every admirer of Locke and liberal thought, there was someone on the other side of the divide who was thrilled by the example of Mussolini and his "black shirts." (There were seventy thousand Italians in Egypt at the time; the cult of Il Duce drew in those dissatisfied with British rule.) But the noise of the hucksters, the demands of political nationalism, and the pressures of mass education had not yet leveled the intellectual landscape.

"We sat in the coffeehouses late into the night and discussed the world," the peerless Mahfuz told American journalist Mary Anne Weaver shortly after his close brush with death, recalling the society of his and Awad's youth. "We did not have to worry about what life would bring us the following day. Our economic situation was far better, and we had more democratic rights. We could choose any political party, and we could choose our government. . . . We had the hope to rule, and to have a chance. But the young men of today don't have our hopes, or our opportunities. They also don't have our dreams."

This nostalgia became a Mahfuzian trademark, and there was more to it than an old man's yearning for his youth. Mahfuz had been a modernist and innovator all his life, and his characters had invariably embraced and assimilated the thrill of what was new and different. In his later fiction, there emerged a painful yearning, *hanin,* for what was lost of the Egypt during the interwar years. "The land, the land is full of bigotry," an older character laments in Mahfuz's 1985 novella, *Yawm Qutala al-Za'im* (The Day the Leader Was Killed), a fictionalized account of Anwar al-Sadat's assassination. "They wish to drag us back fourteen centuries." In the same novella, an aged man, Mahtashami Zayyed, sees his shrunken house by the Nile, amid the high-rise buildings, a "pygmy of a house, by a river which itself had changed, and which had lost its splendor and glory and seasons and is no longer capable of anger. Oh how numerous are the cars, how large the fortunes, how bitter the poverty, and how many beloved ones have departed from this world."

In a bewitching work of vignettes stitched together out of personal impressions and remembrances, entitled *Asda' al-Sira al-Dhatiyya* (Echoes of an Autobiography), the author's double, a wanderer, happens onto a man alone—a miracle it must be in the crowded world of Mahfuz's Cairo—playing a flute in homage to the beauty of the world. "It would be great if the people got to hear your melodies," the wanderer tells the flutist. But the flutist knows better: "They are busy quarreling and weeping," he says. A flicker of optimism persists in the man wandering about his land and circling his past: "Every person has a time where he yearns for solitude."

The wanderer—Abd Rabbo, servant of his God is the name he goes by—accepts the cycles of life and its great diversity: faith and play, the meandering, forgiving ways of the world:

> I knew a man through two stages of his life. In his youth he was devoted to worship and prayer, he was always at the mosque, he was enchanted with the blessed Quran. In his old age, fate took this man to the tavern, where he became addicted to drink, forgetting all the things that no longer mattered to him. He would return to his home, drunken in the late hours of the night, singing the songs of his youth, fumbling through darkness. When he was warned against walking through darkness, he brushed the warnings aside and said, "Angels of mercy are looking after me, and a light around my head illuminates the place."

And here is the wanderer, sly and dismissive of the utopias and the cult of the ancestors that the theocrats had turned into a narcotic: "I was walking along the road by the cemetery on my way back from the tavern. A voice came to me from the grave and asked me, 'Why have you stopped visiting us and talking with us?' I answered, 'You only love talking of death and the dead and I have wearied of all that.'"

The easy passage back and forth between faith and worldliness.

It was a Mahfuzian theme, but it was also an inheritance of a time when the world was more accommodating and the faith was not a weapon.

Curiosity about this bourgeois past and its contemporary relevance led me to the home of Fuad Pasha Serageddin, a nearly legendary figure of that era, born in 1908, a man of the *ancien régime* who was the boy wonder of his time, rising to become a minister at age thirty-two. On the eve of the Free Officer revolution, he was the *ancien régime's* largest landholder, secretary-general of the Wafd party, the repository of bourgeois Egyptian nationalism from 1919 until the military revolt of 1952. The Free Officer regime imprisoned and then exiled him; he returned in the 1970s, when Sadat opened up the life of the country, and in no time his political party under its revered old name, the Wafd, became a force to reckon with. It was in many ways a natural home for the professionals, the Copts, and the men and women of private industry and commerce. Sadat had derided the Pasha, calling him Louis XVI, but this figure from the prerevolutionary past made a place for himself in the new political order.

The Pasha—the country knew him by no other name—lived in a palace in Garden City, one of Cairo's neighborhoods that still has patches of what the city was in more quaint and less crowded times a half-century ago: villas once grand but now shabby and covered with dust; homes with gardens where the great bourgeois families once lived, secure in their sense of place and order. The Pasha's palace, built by his father in 1929, speaks of bygone splendor. Dark and decaying inside, with the threadbare furniture of the era, it has the grand entrance and the marble columns of its time. The staff and servants, too, old and bent by the years, must have been with the Pasha's household since better times.

A scent of old Egypt, the Egypt of the grand tour, the country celebrated by Lawrence Durrell in his *Alexandria Quartet,* blows in with the Pasha when he enters the reception room. He has spanned decades and worlds of Egypt's contemporary history. Nostalgia and a scathing judgment of the military regime drive the Pasha's vision.

He ridicules the government-controlled press; he now reads *al-Ahram*, he says, for the obituaries of his old friends; there is nothing else to read in the subservient press. He has a jaundiced view of the American role in Egypt. The Americans, he believes, feel quite comfortable with authoritarianism. The American fear of a fundamentalist takeover, he observes, plays into the hands of Mubarak's regime.

The Pasha's world, the world of his Wafd party, has deep roots in this conservative land, but after a moment of genuine enthusiasm, the Wafd lost much of its lure. A bargain it made to contest the parliamentary elections back in 1984 in alliance with the Muslim Brotherhood seemed like a betrayal of the party's secular heritage. The Pasha's age was another handicap. The memories his presence evoked were increasingly his alone. He reintroduced into the political world a measure of courage in the face of the state and launched a daily paper infinitely better than the official organs of the regime, but Egypt's troubles seemed beyond his scope. Sixteen million people were added to the population between 1981 (the beginning of Mubarak's rule) and 1996. This increase alone is more than the combined total populations of Jordan, Israel, Lebanon, and the Palestinians of the West Bank and Gaza. The facts of Egypt's poverty and need are so well known that one hardly need state them. One set of figures reveals the trouble: four hundred thousand people enter the job market every year; 75 percent of the new entrants are unemployed; 90 percent of these people have intermediate or higher education diplomas. That is why some of Mubarak's critics concede the burden the regime has to carry. The task of keeping the place afloat and intact is like plowing the sea. This crowded land has gone beyond that pleasant bourgeois age and its houses with gardens.

This yearning for the past was given a cold assessment by a defender of liberal secularism, Hussein Ahmad Amin (a writer and diplomat born in 1932; his father, Ahmad Amin, was a prolific historian and advocate of reason and liberalism in social and political affairs in the interwar years). It was in the nature of man everywhere and in all ages, he observed, to locate order and meaning in some lost, beloved past. A surviving pharaonic text lamented that youth had once been more deferential to age than was the case in its writer's time. Virgil and Homer grieved, in their time, for a fabled, heroic age. The celebrated tenth-century Arab poet al-Mutanabbi had wept for a golden age. In Egypt today, the cult of the past, he concedes, has "spread like a plague." The 1920s, 1930s, and 1940s have become

> the most cherished periods in our history—a time when the means of transportation were fit for human beings, and the streets free of crowds, and the skies were not darkened with pollution, and the signs of "apartment for rent" could be located on every streetcorner. . . . What is this Alexandria of today with its polluted sea, with rust and decay everywhere, when compared to the Alexandria of yesterday with its clean beaches and its Greek restaurants? Everyone is convinced that we have no writers of the stature of Taha Hussein and Ahmad Amin, that even the sky of Cairo was clearer and more blue than it is today.

This yearning, Amin wrote, issues from Egyptians' disillusionment with all that they have experimented with in their recent history:

> We tried liberalism and military dictatorship, a multiparty system and one-party rule, capitalism and socialism, an alliance with the East followed by an alliance with the West, Egyptian nationalism and pan-Arabism. . . . Our writers and journalists have turned their coats a thousand times; we sang the praises of our rulers then we damned them, we built statues to these rulers and then tore them down, we named streets after them, then changed these names. We fought Israel then made peace with it, we resisted American influence, then succumbed to it; we signed a friendship treaty with the Russians then tore it up. What

haven't we tried yet? What remains to us other than plunging deep into a past that we have adorned, from which we have deleted all that was painful and problematic and retained what was bright and worthwhile?

IN ONE OF the country's best recent works of fiction, *al-Harb fi Barr Misr* (War in the Land of Egypt), Yusuf al-Qaid, a novelist of the younger generation, expresses the sense of siege and failure among his contemporaries:

> Every generation has a particular fate, and our fate, we the sons of Egypt, is that our ambitions were greater than our possibilities. We stepped forward but we found no ground underneath us; we lifted our heads to touch the clouds and the sky disappeared from above us. And at the very moment we divined the truth of our time our leader [Nasser] deserted us with his death right when we needed him. Let us look carefully at our land and our country. It is a strange place, at once dangerous and safe, hard and accommodating, harmonious and full of envy, satiated and hungry. The age of wars has ended; in Egypt today it is the age of words, and because words feed off one another the land of Egypt will only know the reign of words.

Qaid's 1979 novel was one of those rare, blessed works that catch a time and a place: title, plot, and a voice resigned, ironic, and knowing came together to narrate what had befallen the land after the dream of Nasserism and of remaking the place ended in frustration. Where Mahfuz had worked the quarters of Cairo, Qaid went for his material to the countryside. A warrant is served on a village watchman, a *ghafir*, informing him that land he had been given by the government in the days of agrarian reform was being returned to the *Umdah*, the head man of the village. The *ghafir's* son, Misri (meaning "Egyptian") swears that the land will not be returned, that the family will "pay with its blood" to keep what it was given in that moment of hope and enthusiasm. The government's day is a year, the old *ghafir* said; it would take time for the government representatives to show up in the village. But a crafty woman of the village says that the matter is decided, that the *Umdah* will get what he wants, for "water never runs upstream" and the masters of the realm never lose to the downtrodden.

An official of the state, a police officer, soon turns up in the village to confiscate the land. He had come along with his men, the officer said, because he was an Egyptian and the old watchman's family were his family; he did not want them to receive the dreaded news from others. Although the land had to go back to the *Umdah*, Egypt was still, in the officer's words, a "merciful place that would never leave its sons without land and work." Egypt was kind to the strangers let alone to its sons. Egypt was now in the age of sovereign laws, the officer added, and no voice was higher than the voice of the law.

"They took from him who did not have and they gave to him who has the entire world," the grief-stricken *ghafir* says of a world that looked like the old, timeless life the village had always known. Villagers watching the spectacle vowed to quit the land of Egypt now that oppression and inequality had returned. In the midst of his sorrow, the *ghafir* is invited to have tea with the *Umdah*. A sycophant of the *Umdah* tells him that the master of the village has a favor to ask of him, and the *Umdah* had always thought that the *ghafir* was of one mold and the entire village of another, that the *Umdah* had always had a soft spot in his heart for the old watchman.

The *Umdah* had a scheme to propose: he wanted Misri, the watchman's only son, to do the military service of the *Umdah*'s son and to assume his identity. Son number 7 being spared, his military duty redeemed, by an only son needed to help with farming and with the work of the land. It would not be that great a burden, the *Umdah* said. Three years would pass like the "blink of an eye," and Misri would have all sorts of choices before him: stay in the army, work for the government, or return to the village and the *Umdah* would look after him. Yes, it would be one of those noble deeds that bear witness to the love Egypt's sons had for one another. Blood would be one, the *Umdah*'s clerk said, a "tax of blood" would be paid by one son of Egypt for another.

Misri had had big plans for himself; he had dreamed of going to the university. He was a young man who had in him "all the contradictions of our country: love of the world mixed with abstinence, courage and hesitation, fear and bravery, outward submission combined with inner rebellion." He submitted to his fate and went into the military. "We all love Egypt," the narrator says, "but everyone loves her in his own special way. Which Egypt do we love: the Egypt of those who suffer hunger, or the Egypt of those who are satiated with indulgence?"

Misri falls in battle; he pays the "tax of blood" for the beloved land, for the *Umdah*'s son. But the *Umdah* presses for more: He now wants Misri's pension and the honor that a son of his had fallen in battle. A well-intentioned man of the government looks into the matter but is told to stay out of harm's way and refrain from playing with fire. "The *Umdah* is powerful, and he always insists that his power derives from God. This would appear to be true. It would seem that God had chosen the side of the rich while the poor are left looking for divine mercy. Perhaps they will find it. I learned today that our country has become like cats which devour their kittens without mercy, and that its sons have become like fish, the big fish devouring the little ones."

THIS IS A jaded country that has known many false starts and faded dawns. Modern Egyptian history telescopes easily: from the time Napoleon Bonaparte's armada turned up off the coast of Alexandria in the summer of 1798, Egypt's history has in the main been its Sisyphean quest for modernity and national power. The ease with which the modern artillery of the French shredded the Mamluk soldiers who had conquered and possessed Egypt was the great dividing line in Egypt's history and the great spur of its political class. A quintessential romantic who knew texts and understood the power of memory, Bonaparte evoked Egypt's former splendor and greatness: "The first town we shall come to was built by Alexander.

At every step we shall meet with grand recollections worthy of exciting the emulation of Frenchmen," he told his soldiers. From Cairo, in a later dispatch, the great conqueror noted a paradox: "Egypt is richer than any country in the world in corn, rice, vegetables, and cattle. But the people are in a state of utter backwardness."

The paradox the outsider saw may have been the self-serving justification of a commander who happened onto a foreign adventure that went badly for him and was seeking a way out, but it would be fair to say that this paradox has engaged Egyptians over the last two centuries. Egypt has thrashed about in every direction, flirted with ideologies of all kinds—liberal ways, Marxism, fascist movements, Islamic utopias—but the urge for national progress, and the grief at being so near and yet so far, have defined the Egyptian experience in the modern world.

Dreams of national power and deliverance have visited Egypt no less than four times in its recent history, and they all ended in frustration. Muhammad Ali (who ruled 1805–1848) made a bid of his own, a classic case of revolution from above, but he overreached and ran afoul of his nominal Ottoman masters and of Pax Britannica; his attempt to build a powerful state and a national manufacturing base came to naught. His descendant, the vainglorious Ismael Pasha (who ruled 1863–1879) gave it another try when cotton was king and a windfall came Egypt's way. Ismael built boulevards, railways, and an opera house; he declared on one occasion, "My country is now in Europe; it is no longer in Africa." But Ismael's dream ended in bankruptcy and ruin and led to the British occupation of Egypt in 1882.

The liberals of the 1920s and 1930s had their moment, flirting with a native capitalist path and parliamentary politics of sorts, but theirs was a fragile liberalism, prone to corruption, outflanked by collectivist ideologies (it was in this period, in 1928, that the Muslim Brotherhood was formed), a liberalism in the shadow of an occupying foreign power. In the end, that bourgeois era issued in frustration. It could not resolve the country's economic weakness. (Even the fez, the headgear of the time, was imported from Austria.)

The culture of the bourgeoisie needed adequate material bases, and these did not develop. Then came Nasser's bid, perhaps Egypt's most heartbreaking moment of false promise: import substitution, pan-Arabism, a place in the nonaligned world, a national army that looked imposing and fierce before the whole edifice of Nasserism came crashing down.

Egyptians who know this narrative by heart see all these bids as brushes with success. This is part of the country's self-image. To rule Egypt is to rule against the background of these expectations and disappointments. Egyptians are not blind to what has befallen their country. They can see the booming lands in Asia, countries that were once poorer than Egypt, digging out of the poverty of the past. No way out ever materialized for Egypt. The dreams of liberal reform, the hopes for revolution from above, the socialist bid of Nasser all withered away. A decade after Mubarak inherited power, the country was adrift. No Lee Kuan Yew arose here to make the place orderly and efficient even at the price of political and cultural freedom. The economy was a hybrid. It combined a wild form of laissez-faire capitalism for the sharks and fat cats who raid the place with subsidies for the poorer classes. There had been endless talk of economic reform, but the state had chosen the path of least resistance and stayed with the status quo. The push for privatization that raised the share of the private sector from 23 percent of industrial output in 1974 to 30 percent a decade later stalled. Four decades of positioning the country for foreign assistance from the Soviet Union, the Arab oil states, and the United States and the World Bank inflicted terrible damage to Egypt. A political economy and a mentality of dependence set in.

Mubarak was no great reformer bent on remaking the economic landscape. To begin with, he labored against the background of an adverse set of changes in the economic domain. The 1980s proved to be a difficult decade for Egypt's economy. The rate of annual growth plummeted; in the years 1989–1990 the economy grew a mere 2 percent, less than the growth in the population. Egypt dropped from the World Bank's group of lower middle-income countries to its lower-income category; inflation rose and the real income of industrial workers eroded. A regime unable to reverse this decline fell back on its powers of coercion when the Islamists took on the state.

The Mubarak years, it often seemed, were an endless struggle between the regime and the International Monetary Fund. The familiar morass—the debt burden, a budget deficit as high as 20 percent of the gross domestic product, a foreign reserve crisis—crippled the economy. No sooner did the regime catch its breath from the insurgency of the Islamists in 1994 and 1995 than it appeared ready to take the stiff medicine of the creditors and the International Monetary Fund. The break with the public sector of the Nasser years, and with the regime of subsidies, was now under way.

There was no miraculous deliverance for Egypt, but the new push for economic reform yielded some tangible benefits. The inflation rate, 22 percent in 1990, was down to 7 percent in 1995. Foreign reserves rose from $600 million to $16 billion, and the budget deficit shrank to a mere 1.3 percent of gross domestic product. And in a significant break for the country, the rate in population growth went down from 2.8 percent in 1985 to 2 percent a decade later. Egypt had not found a bright new world—its economic growth remained virtually stagnant, its literacy rate was still around 50 percent, and it had a foreign debt of $33 billion—but the ruling order understood it could no longer stay with the path of least resistance it had adopted in the 1980s. Egypt had lived off the balance of power then, trading on its political assets and its importance to Pax Americana and regional peace to dodge economic reform. That choice was no longer an option in the mid-1990s. The state had tipped its hand: it was willing to launch economic reform while keeping political power as its own privileged domain. Markets and political autocracy, a variant (Egyptian-style) of the East Asian political economy.

Two deities, it seemed, had descended on the land: privatization and globalization. They had come courtesy of the International Monetary Fund, and they had behind them the authority and prestige and sanction of the United States. And the president of the republic had thrown the weight of the regime on the side of the new political economy. All the reverence that had once been heaped upon socialism and the public sector now belonged to these new deities. There were, suddenly, cellular phones aplenty in the land; there were glossy new magazines and trendy restaurants and nightclubs; there for an outsider to see was a new bounce in the country, a new hipness in the style of the children of the wealthy. Undeniably a break had come the country's way. It was too early for restraint and circumspection: Those with money were eager to flaunt what they had. Hot money had come into the country, public companies were being privatized, the stock market had become a subject of conversation, and a few had made a killing in the early stock offerings when the best of the public companies had been sold off. A new publication that tracked the stock market, *al-Borsa,* had become popular reading. Egypt had had its fill of deprivation. The new monied classes would not be denied: They were sure that this new path—anything for that matter—was better than what had befallen Egypt under the political economy of the public sector and of austerity.

"We are being Lebanonized from above and Iranized from below," an articulate physician with an unerring instinct for the political trends in the country said to me. He was thinking of the Lebanon of old: the glamorous women, the money, the fancy homes and cars, and he was thinking of the theocratic politics of Iran. He was too bleak, the physician, but there were reasons for the bleakness: the country had known too much heartbreak and was given to premature celebrations. A day or two after the physician offered that insight, some sobering facts turned up: the country's imports had risen by 8 percent in 1996, her exports had declined by 8 percent as well. There were fears that this boom may have been a false recovery and worries that this boom, which had not made much of a dent in unemployment, was a break for the monied few but offered no new hope for the underclasses.

"Go see for yourself the new golf course at Qatamiya," the physician had said. He had picked the new golf course on Cairo's outskirts on the road to Suez as an emblem of the new gilded classes; he had picked it to illustrate the follies of this economic change, this seeming panacea that had come with the bravado of a conquering ideology. The golf course had been put up in close proximity to a massive run-down public housing project, which was home to 20,000 victims of an earlier earthquake. No expense had been spared: the barren desert had been turned into lush fairways in record speed. *Cairo Times,* a feisty English-language magazine, had reported that the sprigs of grass had been flown in in refrigerated crates from Tifton, Georgia, in the United States. The developers were not a discreet lot: their brochures had described the venture as "a lifestyle for the privileged few." Nearly three hundred villas were planned near the golf course, and two-thirds of them had already been sold.

It was too easy a target, this golf course, on the other side of the squalor. The country had been suffocated by an economy of *etatisme* and regulation. It had had to bite the bullet and bow to the new realities. There was no escaping the abuses in this change of direction. The country was to pay for the dismantling of the public sector and of the economy of regulation and protection. Egypt was at a watershed, and she could not be spared the pains and horror stories that came with so massive an adjustment. That cynical hybrid creature, bureaucratic capitalism—where the enforcers of the old system of controls and protection and their privileged children make the leap into the market economy—was working its way through the land. There were worries that this bureaucratic capitalism would help itself to the fat and the goods of the land without really putting in place a genuine, workable capitalist order.

"If my memory does not betray me," the novelist Sonallah Ibrahim wrote in a scathing new work of fiction, *Sharaf* (1997), "you and your likes are quick to respond to every new opportunity. . . . You are totally loyal to the master you serve. You are the stars of every age." Ibrahim was describing the beneficiaries of the new economy, who had made a seamless transition from the public sector that had given them their start.

We saw you bravely proclaiming your love of homeland, praising our unique socialism, chairing our national companies,
dominating politics and economics and the media, claiming for
yourselves the good things of the earth—the loveliest homes and
cars, the most expensive fashions, the most beautiful women,
the best chances for your children. And, then, at precisely the
right moment there you were at the head of the new foreign
companies, agents for the giant corporations of the West, deal-
makers in the big bargains, making sure you had guaranteed for
yourselves splendor and plenty in a country where half of its
people live below the poverty line, and nearly half a million people inhabit the graveyards of the dead.

These were not "businessmen," native capitalists, who had
risen, but "agents" of outsiders. Sonallah Ibrahim added in an echo
of widely spread worry in the country. "Were you truly businessmen," a skeptic in *Sharaf* tells this class,

> you would have built industries, repaired the land, trained work-
> ers, financed research, as your foreign masters had done in their
> lands, but you are imitating your fathers and grandfathers, who
> were always followers, servants to the Persians, and the Greeks
> and the Romans and the Arabs and the Turks and the Italians
> and the Armenians and the French and the British, and most re-
> cently the Americans and the sons of Israel.

This is not a country that trusts its ability to compete and stay
with the world outside. It had to feel and argue its way into this
global economic order of things. This was a radical, new departure
for the regime. Markets and ballots were not to come together in
Egypt. The economy was to be opened up, but the political power
was not to be delegated or shared.

Chroniclers of the Mubarak regime may look back on his rule
as ten good years of modesty followed by the usual tendency of
power to want to organize the political space on its own terms. By
his own early accounts and self-portrayal an unassuming man with

no claims to greatness, Mubarak appeared to heed the fate of his predecessor. A cautious man, he drew back from the precipice, stitching back together as best he knew how the fault-line between the state and the mainstream opposition. He rebuilt bridges to the Arab world burned by Sadat; he gave every indication that the fling with America and the West that had carried Sadat away would be reined in and that a sense of proportion and restraint would be restored to Egyptian politics. He presented himself as a man with clean hands who would put an end to the crony capitalism and economic pillage of the Sadat era.

In retrospect, the choice that mattered was made by Mubarak with his coronation for a third term in 1993. A modest man (a civil servant with the rank of president, a retired army general of Mubarak's generation described him to me) had become president for life. Mubarak had broken a pledge that he would limit himself to two terms in office. Although outsiders may have a romantic view of Egyptians as patient *fellaheen* (peasants) tilling the soil under an eternal sky, in veritable awe of their rulers, in fact a strong sense of skepticism and a keen eye for the foibles of rulers pervade Egyptian political culture. No one had the means to contest Mubarak's verdict; a brave soul or two quibbled about the decision, but autocracy would have none of it.

Tahseen Basheer, one of the country's most thoughtful and temperate public figures, sent an open letter to Mubarak questioning the wisdom of a third term. A man of the state—he had been an aide to Presidents Nasser and Sadat, a press spokesman for the latter—Basheer was a public figure of uncompromising integrity. Retired from public service, outspoken in and out of office, Basheer raised in his open letter virtually all the tangled issues of succession and political participation:

> I still remember the day Sadat chose you for vice-president. He said to me, "I will not leave Egypt's ship of state at the mercy of the winds when God wills the end of my journey. Whoever succeeds me will have to come from the armed forces until we arrive

at that day when there is full convergence between popular will and the armed forces. I have chosen Mubarak because I see in him the ability to preserve the stability of the country." The wisdom of the late president was revealed after that day on the reviewing stand when Sadat was assassinated. I was grateful for Sadat's foresight, for his determination to preserve the continuity of political power at a time of enormous stress. I then followed with great admiration your early and careful steps, your avoidance of the limelight and of political rhetoric. . . . But I have come to fear for Egypt of late.

Like a searchlight, the Basheer letter, published in the opposition newspaper *al-Wafd,* illuminated all the political issues of consequence: the lack of an orderly process of succession; the cult of personality that had come to surround the once modest air force officer; the political culture of supplication; the spectacle of public sector companies taking up advertisements to proclaim their loyalty to Mubarak, of sycophants in the universities, students and faculty alike, interrupting academic gatherings to chant for the ruler. The outcome is certain, Basheer said, a third term was inevitable. But the logic of the third term was the logic of an "imperial presidency," a presidency-for-life unworthy of a country with democratic aspirations.

A healthy measure of the regime's legitimacy seemed to vanish overnight in the aftermath of that third presidential term. That keen eye for the ruler's foibles now saw all Mubarak's defects. He had hung around too long. An inarticulate man, he had never bonded with the country. The national elections he presided over became increasingly irrelevant. Worse still, Mubarak ran afoul of his country's sense of propriety by refusing to designate a successor or help develop a process of orderly succession. His two predecessors, much larger historic figures with far greater claims to political legitimacy, their personal histories deeply intertwined with their country's, never dared go that far. Supreme in the political domain, Nasser always ruled with a designated successor in place, and Sadat had chosen Mubarak in homage to generational change. Mubarak had no claim to inheritance when Sadat picked him from a large officer corps; it was Sadat's will that made him. In contrast, Mubarak ruled alone: the glory (what little of it there had been of late) and the burdens were his. He stood sentry against the armed Islamists, but the expectations of the 1980s—modernizing the polity, giving it freer institutions, taking it beyond the power of the army—had been betrayed. At heart he was a gendarme determined to keep intact the ruler's imperative. Was it any wonder that those rescued from the wrath and the reign of virtue promised by the Islamists had no affection for the forces of order and felt no great sense of deliverance?

The defects of a political system without an orderly succession in place and reliant on the armed forces as a last arbiter were laid bare in June 1995, when Mubarak, in Addis Ababa to attend a meeting of the Organization of African Unity, escaped unhurt from an armed attack on his motorcade. He rushed back home full of fury against the Sudanese, whom he accused of masterminding the attempt on his life. He was eager, as well, to tell of his cool under fire, the man of the armed forces who had known greater dangers. The play of things was given away in the scripted celebrations of Mubarak's safety. The men of the religious establishment hailed Mubarak as a just ruler who kept the faith. The military officers renewed their pledge of allegiance and warned that they were there to ward off the dangers to the regime. The minister for municipalities said that the crowds from the provinces who had wanted to come to Cairo would have covered the "face of the sun." The one obvious lesson that was not drawn, the danger that went unexamined and unstated, was the vacuum, the uncertainty, that would have been left behind had Mubarak been struck down in Ethiopia. Egyptians were no doubt relieved to have Mubarak back: That is not the kind of tragedy they would want for him or for themselves. But no staged celebrations or display of bravado on the Egypt–Sudan frontier could hide the stalemate of the Egyptian political order.

A year later, that episode in Addis Ababa would become part of the hagiography of the regime and the ruler: the sovereign delivered from danger and returned safely to his grateful land. "A year ago, on June 26 to be exact, the heart of Egypt pounded when bats of the night tried to engulf with their darkness the leader of Egypt and the builder of its renaissance and its faithful son," the editorialist of *al-Ahram* wrote on June 27. "Today Egypt is full of happiness while it embraces the great Mubarak as he leads her day after day on its journey toward freedom, liberty, progress." The modest officer had followed the arc of his predecessors; he had survived at the helm, and with the years the ruler's cult had grown, and he had taken to it. The secular parties had been frustrated, wealth had not yet come into its own as a contender for power, the army (the black box of the society, the silent force, as an able Egyptian interpreter described it to me) was content to be out of the limelight, and parliament was for all practical purposes an empty shell and a pretense. The cult of the ruler had spread at the expense of all other competing centers of power. Egypt had not yet found a way out of the authoritarian trap; it had not created a political order worthy of its self-image. The national bourgeoisie had tried and tried, but it was still reliant on the protection and power of a final arbiter—a military class and the officer at the helm of the state.

IN A CHARACTERISTICALLY penetrating survey of his country's quest for modernity, Louis Awad depicted the seesaw battle between renovation and regression that has been at the heart of Egypt's life:

> The force of renewal has always been more vital to Egypt than the force of old things. It is noteworthy that the forces of reaction always gain in the aftermath of defeats and national setbacks. . . . The state in Egypt is invariably on the side of renewal in periods of success and cultural flowering, and on the side of what is old in times of defeat and setbacks. But the spark of renewal is never extinguished and smolders beneath the ashes until it errupts again. Such is the rhythm of Egypt's history. This does not mean that the forces of reaction visit our country from

the outside: such forces live dormant in the depths of Egyptian society like a heavy beast stirred up by cultural decline.

Egyptians who know their country well have a way of reciting its troubles, then insisting that the old resilient country shall prevail. As an outsider who has followed the twists of the country's history and who approaches the place with nothing but awe for its civility amid great troubles, I suspect they are right. The country is too wise, too knowing, too tolerant to succumb to a reign of theocratic zeal. Competing truths, whole civilizations, have been assimilated and brokered here; it is hard to see Cairo, possessed of the culture that comes to great, knowing cities, turning its back on all that. The danger here is not sudden, cataclysmic upheaval but a steady descent into deeper levels of pauperization, a lapse of the country's best into apathy and despair, Egypt falling yet again through the trap door of its history of disappointment.

Egyptians love the thesis of their own pluralism and eclectic history. Milad Hanna—a Copt, by training an engineer, by vocation a public housing advocate and a man of the secular Left who served in the country's parliament—gave this thesis a new elaboration in a recent book, *al-Amida al-Sabaa fi al-Shakhsiyya al-Misriyya* (The Seven Pillars of Egyptian Personality). In his brief book Hanna sees his country as the sum of its unique history and location. Egypt's personality, he observes, is the product of four historic pillars and three geographic ones. The historic pillars are pharaonic, Greco-Roman, Coptic, then Islamic. The three pillars of geography are the links to Europe through the Mediterranean, to Africa, and to the Arab world. Hanna echoes a recurrent theme in this land: Egypt as a crossroads civilization, with Europe beginning at Alexandria, Asia at Cairo, Africa at Aswan. It is against this cultural eclecticism, this old, saving ambiguity, that the Islamists hurl themselves and their simple doctrine.

Part analysis and historical narrative, part hope and exhortation, Hanna's book is an affirmation of the unity of his land and its people. No Islamist was going to read this man out of home and national tradition. The Copts, he writes, belong to the soil of Egypt; they have in them the psychological attributes of the Egyptians, patience, goodness, and an aversion to violence. They are spread everywhere in Egypt, in the cities and in the remote countryside. Unlike the Maronites of Lebanon with their attachment to Mount Lebanon, the Copts were everywhere in Egypt, "like air and water," in all walks of life. They have no specific quarters of their own in the towns; and though they excelled at particular trades—pharmacy, goldsmithing, accounting, tanning, the building trade—they partake of practically all the work and trades of the country.

Muslims needn't worry about the political aspirations of the Copts. In the history Hanna sketches, the Coptic church never sought political power, never shared it, and "never had any other loyalty except for its devotion to the soil of Egypt." Persecution at the hands of the Romans and then under Byzantine rule convinced the Copts of the follies and cruelties of political power. It was that history which led the Copts to welcome the Islamic conquest in the seventh century. Unlike Catholicism in Europe, Judaism, and Islam, which had organized their own states and were both state and religion, the Coptic church never had that kind of political drive and so was the ideal church for a ruler. It stayed out of the way and gave the state its loyalty.

In the narrative of this thoughtful work, the "hydraulic society" and its history, the land and the centralized state that governed it, take precedence over religious affiliation. Egypt changes its religion and its language three times but remains a unique place that can never be remade in the image of any other land. There was no Lebanon in Egypt's future, and no Iran. Islam conquered Egypt in the seventh century, but there is a consensus that it was sometime in the fourteenth century the country acquired a Muslim majority. The faith put down roots, but the two religions had lived side by side for centuries. The conversion to Islam was slow and peaceful. Families often split right down the middle between those who stayed with the old Coptic faith and others who took to Islam. Those ancient rites and rituals of life and death of the land of Egypt were carried over to the new Islamic faith as they had been to the Coptic church before.

There is no "purity" in Milad Hanna's Egypt. The country appropriated all that had come its way. Its permanent truth has been the land and the powerful state and the cult of the ruler. "From the time of Alexander until the rule of Abdul Nasser, Egyptians lived on the dream of change and improvement. Whenever they heard of the death of an emperor or a caliph or a governor, they would expect more just rule and better circumstances. In the end they resigned themselves to the state of things." It was an old, weary land, a place exposed to all that was around it. This was Milad Hanna's Egypt. Its Copts had known the "sweet and bitter" times that history had brought her. Its two religious communities knew better than to run after wild schemes. For an epigraph to his book, the author chose a maxim from the Book of Proverbs: "Wisdom has built her house, she has set up her seven pillars" (9:1).

Hanna gave me his book after a discussion at one of Cairo's genteel gathering places, the Diplomatic Club. We had been joined by one the country's well-known "moderate" political Islamists. The Islamist, an acquaintance of Hanna of many years, had insisted that his utopia, a state moved and organized by the faith, was no threat to the Copts. Hanna had not said much. I suspect that the gift of his book was his answer to what he had heard. For him, a man of a secular outlook who was at odds with the clerical establishment in his church, the pluralism of his country was an unquestioned article of faith. He knew no other home and had no other ideology.

The recognition that a historic tradition at home was being undermined must account, in part, for the resurgence of the country's pan-Arab vocation. This is an old temptation in this land: to escape from repairing the country into ventures beyond. It is the return of an old consolation that brought Egypt failure and bitterness. From her pundits and intellectuals can now be heard a warmed-over version of the pan-Arab arguments of the 1960s, a disquiet over the country's place in the region. And for all the vast aid the United

States has poured into Egypt over the last two decades, nearly $40 billion in military assistance and economic help, there is in the air as well a curious free-floating hostility to American ideals and interests, a conviction that the United States wishes Egypt permanent dependency and helplessness, a reflexive tendency to take up, against America's wishes, the cause of renegade states like Libya and Iraq, a belief that the United States is somehow engaged with Israel in an attempt to diminish and hem in Egypt's power and influence. The peace with Israel, we know, stands, but it is unclaimed and disowned by the professional and intellectual class in the country, the pharaoh's peace, concluded by Sadat a generation ago and kept to a minimum by his inheritors.

This new version of pan-Arabism, we are told, will be pragmatic, whereas the old movement led by Nasser was romantic, loud, and strident. Egypt will lead other Arabs, help defend the security of the Persian Gulf states (against Iran), and set the terms of accommodation with Israel, but without shrillness, without triggering a new ideological war in the Arab world. Egypt will use its skills and vast bureaucratic apparatus to balance the power of Israel.

In truth, the pan-Arabism that the Egyptian state (and the intellectual class) wishes to revive is a mirage. Egypt's primacy in Arab politics is a thing of the past. Arabs have gone their own separate ways. Egypt was the last to proclaim the pan-Arab idea, the first to desert it. If Egypt succumbs again to that temptation as a way of getting out of its troubles, the detour will end in futility. To borrow an old expression, pan-Arabism will have visited twice: the first time as tragedy, the second as farce. Egypt cannot set the terms or the pace of the accommodation in the Fertile Crescent between Israel and each of its neighbors. These terms will be decided by the protagonists. The irony was not lost on the Jordanians when the Egyptians began to deride them for their forthcoming peace with Israel. It was under Egyptian command during those fateful six days in 1967 that Jordan lost the West Bank and East Jerusalem. Jordan then had to wait on the sidelines for an entire generation after the

Camp David accords, as Egypt garnered the wages of peace and the vast American aid that came with it.

Egypt cannot render services that are no longer in demand. Its doomed and quixotic campaign, waged in 1995, against the extension of the Nonproliferation Treaty and the attempt to hold the treaty hostage to new controls over Israel's nuclear capabilities offers a cautionary tale. The campaign rolled together Egypt's panic about its place in the region, its need to demonstrate some distance from American power, and its desire to reassert Egypt's primacy in Arab politics. The regime threw everything it had into the fight. For months it was high drama: Egypt against the elements. But it was to no avail. There were no Arab riders anxious to join the Egyptian posse.

Nor is there a special assignment for Egypt in securing the sea-lanes of the Persian Gulf or defending the Arabian Peninsula. To balance the two potential revisionist states, Iran and Iraq, the conservative states of the Gulf will rely on American power and protection. This is an assignment for an imperial power; it is now America's, as it had been Britain's. In that kind of work Egypt has a minor role, as it did in Desert Storm, providing an Arab cover for American power. There could be gains for Egypt here, but they are at best marginal ones.

In one of those consoling statements Egyptians make about their world—part truth, part pride, and in part a way of coping with material circumstances that fall short of the country's self-image—the influential journalist Mohamed Heikal, Nasser's main publicist, set out to explain to Henry Kissinger in the aftermath of the October War of 1973 that Egypt was more than a state on the banks of the Nile, that it was an idea and a historical movement. Yet this is all that remains. Both the Mediterranean temptation of Egypt being a piece of Europe and the pan-Arab illusion have run aground. To rule Egypt today is to rule a burdened state on the banks of the Nile and to rule it without the great consolations and escapes of the past.

Egypt's gift to other Arabs is the gift of its civility and its example. The subtlety of Egypt's history and identity, that relentless and heroic quest for modernity in the face of such difficult odds, are what Egypt can offer Arabs who look to it. Egypt is "deeper" than the rest of the states around it, and its history is more forgiving. Egyptians needn't trade on their animus toward Israel, and they needn't rail against Pax Americana to get a hearing in Arab and Muslim lands. They didn't trade in that kind of material when their liberal culture was the lodestar of other Arabs in the 1920s and 1930s. A society that could produce the life of letters that Egypt did in freer times needn't be shrill or loud. There is a special kind of primacy in Arab lands that is Egypt's natural possession. It needn't be asserted by the tedious functionaries who run the Cairo-based (now moribund) League of Arab States or by the "security experts" conjuring up threats to the "Arab security order" that only the Egyptian state could ward off.

A small political-literary storm that broke out in early 1995 and a Syrian-born poet's "open letter" to the Egyptian General Association of the Book come close to capturing that unique Egyptian role in Arab cultural life. At the center of this controversy was the celebrated poet Nizar Qabbani. A furor broke out over a poem he had written, "When Will They Declare the Death of the Arabs?" and a campaign was launched to rescind an invitation that the General Association of the Book had issued him to visit Cairo. The literary and political elite stood their ground: The great poet was free to write what he wished, and Egypt's doors would always be open to him. As it turned out, Qabanni had not been able to come. He sent instead an "open letter" from his new home in London, an unabashed letter of gratitude and devotion to the country. It was published in a new, vibrant magazine, *al-Qahira,* sponsored by the association:

My dear friends in the land of Egypt:
    I can't write of Egypt with neutrality or love her with neutrality. Egypt is my mother: from her I was fed, I drank from her

wellsprings, from her I learned how to walk, how to utter my first words. When I arrived in Cairo in the mid-1940s I was but a boy looking for a mother, for a cultural womb. I want to acknowledge that Egypt nursed me, sang over my bed, until I learned how to compose my verse, until I was able in 1948 to publish my first daring poetic collection. . . . I want to say that Egypt never made a distinction between me and its native sons: Often she took my side and the side of my poems paying no heed to my Damascus ancestry and my Syrian dialect. Egypt had embraced my ancestor, my grandfather, Abu Khalil Qabbani, welcomed him as a pioneer in theater in the final years of the nineteenth century. And here it is embracing my poetry in the final years of this century. This is but a confirmation of its heritage as a defender of freedom, creativity, and the creative spirit.

The invitation I received from the General Egyptian Association of the Book is not just an ordinary invitation. It is an invitation that carries the scent of Egypt, and the tenderness of Egypt and her eternal devotion to her progeny: I am one of Egypt's children who was not abandoned in the midst of a storm, left to face wind, rain, and the cold of exile. In the midst of the flood stirred up by my recent poem Egypt extended her hand to me from under the water. . . . Such is the destiny of Egypt since it has been Egypt. It has not been Egypt's way, at any time in its history, to be with the killer against his victim, with the oppressor against the oppressed, with the jailer against the prisoner, with the illiterate against the letters of the alphabet. My dear friends this annual celebration of the book held in Cairo is a victory for those who read over those who kill, for those who know over those who don't, for those who compose beautiful poems over those who make coffins.

The genius of Egypt lies in her artistic and cultural sensibility: the skill of its men and women of letters with narrative, a way with cultural creation in film, soap operas, theater, political and philosophical argument, and the song. On a recent visit there, in the famed Cairo bookshop Madbuli, where a publishing firm displays and sells its recent titles, in Talaat Harb Square, I saw that indispensable Egyptian role in Arab and Muslim life. A young man from the Gulf was pleading for a book he wanted that was temporarily (so the publisher said) out of stock. It was the young man's last day in Cairo; he was desperate for the book; he had been told that new copies would be available on that day, but the books had not arrived. He offered endless deals for Madbuli's manager. He would pay to have it delivered to his hotel, he would pay in advance, and he would throw in a generous tip, if one of the boys at Madbuli would meet him at the airport with the book. The young Gulfie was from a place of wealth, but he was leaving a city where the gift of writing and the culture of books had not yet died. (On that very day, there had been a run on every title that the embattled academic and philosopher Nasr Abu Zeid had written.)

There was a cultural siege (of sorts) in Egypt, but the life of letters had deep roots here. It was in Cairo, in the mid-1870s, that two brothers, Salim and Bishara Taqla, Christian emigrés from Lebanon, established the daily paper *al-Ahram*. And it was Egypt that gave two great figures of Arab modernity, Faris Nimr and Yaqub Sarruf, a second chance in the 1880s, after the American missionaries at the Syrian Protestant College (the AUB) dismissed them for their enthusiasm for Darwin and the theory of evolution. The first of these two men rose to become one of the great, wealthy personages of Egypt, the powerful editor of a paper of his own. Faris Nimr lived a long, full, and productive life; he worked at the intersection of politics and journalism until his death in 1951, on the eve of the Free Officers revolt, at the age of ninety-five. He never bothered to hide his devotion to the ways of the West, and the virtues and discipline of Anglo-Saxon culture, which he wanted to graft onto "the east." It was the Egyptian theater, and the social rhythm that sustained the theater, that gave the Syrian, Ahmad Abu Khalil Qabbani, the chance to pursue his craft and art in the latter years of the nineteenth century. When a remarkable pair, Farid al-Atrash and his sister Amal, children of the ruling princely family in Jabal Druze in

Syria, yearned for a world beyond their confining ancestral land and for careers in music, film, and song, they left their home for Cairo in the 1930s. Farid al-Atrash became one of the most successful crooners and film stars. His sister Amal, using the single stage name of Asmahan and whose career was cut short by a premature death, was one of the great beauties of the age. Her talent with the song fused Arabic and European aesthetics, and her films were huge hits. The public could never get enough of her or of the gossip about the men in her life, who included the head of the king's administrative council, a noted film director, and the ex-husband of her closest friend.

The (Western) novel came to Egypt in 1911; the first Egyptian film was made in 1926, and it was made by a woman filmmaker and actress, Aziza al-Amir, who had been raised fatherless and poor. Women's magazines made their appearance in the 1900s. By 1914, there were more than twenty women's periodicals. To come to a possession of a cultural sensibility in the Arab world was to assimilate the artifacts and products of Egyptian creativity. Arabs have not always known what to make of Egypt. The very same men and women from other Arab lands who have been known to be crushed and surprised by Egypt's poverty and squalor on their first encounter with a land that had come to them in film and fiction touched by glamour and magic have been known to recover their poise as they went out again to savor the graces of that surprising place.

A COUNTRY'S MYTH can console and knit together men and women of different needs, carry them through difficult times, explain sorrow and defeat, locate them in the world. But the myth can also hide a country from itself, hide it from scrutiny. There is a myth of Egypt—the gentle soil, the steady river, the patient folk at peace with itself and with its world. Much history had gone into that idea of Egypt, the hydraulic society of great stability. But blood has been spilled of late and patience has worn thin. The very balance between man and the soil has been altered. Peasants now buy their eggs from the city, boutiques have penetrated the remotest of villages, and farm land is now claimed by squatters and builders who need it for a growing population. The passion of an angry religious scribe, Shaykh Omar Abdul Rahman, who once preached his sermons in the tranquil oasis town of Fayoum, on the edge of the Western Desert of Egypt, made itself felt as far away as New York City in 1993, where the preacher found new recruits and new material.

In the mythology of the Nile—the sanguine river of memory and longevity is the way Simon Schama described it in his book, *Landscape and Memory*—the Nile, a life-giver, a steady stream moving upward, promised and sustained regularity. Where the rivers in Greek mythology, or in the hills of Lebanon, crashed down from mountainous heights and were rivers of fits and starts, the Nile was the quintessential river of civility and continuity.

But the steady river could betray. The Nilometer gauges on its banks, which measure the level of the water, bear witness to that. Too little water and the earth is scorched, the crops and the livestock perish, and civic order is overwhelmed. Too much water and havoc ensues; the granaries are destroyed, disease comes to the land, and the people suffer. The Egyptians, we are told, had their own measure of the relationship between the water level and the human condition on the banks of the river: twelve cubits meant famine, thirteen hunger, fourteen cheerfulness, fifteen security, and sixteen social bliss and delight.

There is no law of social peace, no fated happiness or civility in any land. There had been lamentations on the banks of the Nile and times of celebration. There is a decisive role here for the human will monitoring the cycle of life and all it brings by way of seasons. It is not enough consolation to pay tribute to the good soil and the patient river. Those gauges on the banks will have to be read and watched with care.

CHAPTER FIVE

THE ORPHANED PEACE

I N EARLY 1995, the Union of Arab Writers, based in Damascus, expelled the Syrian-Lebanese poet and literary critic Adonis from its ranks. Two years earlier the poet had gone to Granada for a meeting sponsored by UNESCO that brought Israeli and Arab writers together. The meeting was attended by Israeli Foreign Minister Shimon Peres and the Palestinian leader Yasser Arafat. A great storm had broken out in Arab intellectual circles over normalization, *tatbi*, and cultural traffic with Israel. No sooner had the peace of Oslo between Israel and the Palestinians been announced in Washington in September 1993 than the new battle began, the fear of Israeli military supremacy now yielding to the specter of Israeli cultural hegemony.

Adonis, in Paris since 1986, said little in his own defense. The episode was a sideshow, he was to tell one interviewer. Adonis knew and could handle ostracism and charges of betrayal. He was an old hand at that sort of thing, and he was good at standing alone. He had been in the line of fire for more than three decades. Years earlier, in a collection of his writings, *Zaman al-Shi'r* (The Time of Poetry), he had derided the "literature of authority" and the writers who do the bidding of political power. He had divided the literary class into writers who settle for "servitude," writers who prefer isolation and solitude, and writers who take to the road and settle for exile in order to have the space to work and write. "Tell me, o political regime, what your policy is and I can tell you what your literature and culture are."

Adonis and writers of his temperament and standing knew the defects of the literary union and its bureaucracy. A distinguished Egyptian critic, Ghali Shukri, spoke for the free spirits in the intellectual class when he dismissed this union as a body of functionaries that had never issued a list of writers imprisoned throughout the Arab world or books banned by the ruling regimes. Its meetings had not shut down a prison or provided bread to the needy or returned an exiled writer to his home, Shukri had written. A union based in a city ruled by a merciless military autocracy was hardly the right party to a debate on cultural matters. The campaign of the writers' union against what it called "the culture of peace" was, for all practical purposes, an intellectual cover for the policy and preferences of the Syrian regime.

Adonis found a handful of independent supporters. A couple of writers quit the union in solidarity. A leading Syrian novelist, Hani al-Raheb, took Adonis's side and took apart the way in which Israel had been depicted in Arabic culture and letters. He was scornful of the ignorance of Israel's institutions and language and literature, the taboo on dealing with it, the negation of its statehood and accomplishments. A decade earlier, Hani al-Raheb had lost his academic position at Damascus University for speaking out against official corruption. A serious scholar of English, he had written a book about the depiction of the Jews in English literature. He had had his share of troubles with the writers' union. Back in the mid-1980s, he had labeled its leaders "report writers"—hack informers of the regime and propagators of its truth. For more than four decades, Hani al-Raheb wrote, Israel was busy translating and mastering the best of Arabic literature and culture, while "we continued to banish and deny Zionist culture." It was time, he said, to cease looking at Israelis who live among the Arabs as though they were "extraterrestrial beings" who had descended on the region from an alien world. Israel had remarkable achievements to its record but should not be feared. Israel and the Arab world had fought each other to a draw and were both in need of a reprieve.

Another Syrian writer, Saadallah Wannous, spoke in roughly the same vein. In the attack against normalization, Wannous saw nothing but an extension of the old ways of doing things, which had visited on the Arabs a "succession of defeats and led us to the diplomacy of surrender." Wannous had no patience for those who feared Israel's cultural hegemony and the "contagious" effect of her thought. "I can assure my Arab brethren that Israel does not have a culture richer than ours and intellectual achievements deeper than ours." It was wrong, he wrote, to assume that Israel's edge on the battlefield will carry over into the domain of thought and culture. At any rate, that military edge was the product of Arab political weakness and the bankruptcy of Arab regimes. Arabs cannot bury their heads in the sand or be frightened by their political setbacks:

> I have faith in our history and our people, in the enormous re-sourcefulness of our national culture, I have faith that the future is still open, that we can change this cruel, sterile landscape. When a full encounter with Israeli culture materializes, I doubt if anyone will take pride in unions of writers. I am sure they will point with pride to the works of Naguib Mahfuz, and Adonis and other innovators among the Arabs.

Adonis, Hani al-Raheb, and Saadallah Wannous were part of a distinct minority (Wannous died at the early age of fifty-six in 1997.) It fell to the Arab world's most popular poet, Nizar Qabbani, to catch the widespread opposition to the peace. Qabbani had always risen to great, memorable occasions (the Six Day War of 1967, the death of Nasser in 1970, the descent of the world of Beirut, which was then his home, into barbarism), and he was to do so again in a fierce prose poem, "al-Muharwiluun" (The Hurried Ones), which he wrote from his new home in London and which was published in the daily *al-Hayat* in October 1995. All the anger with the new peace, all the yearning for what was once true and revered, were poured into this poem (here is my rough, truncated translation):

The last walls of embarrassment have fallen
We were delighted
and we danced
and we blessed ourselves
for signing the peace of the cowards
Nothing frightens us anymore
Nothing shames us anymore
The veins of pride in us have dried up.

We stood in columns
like sheep before slaughter
we ran, breathless
We scrambled to kiss
the shoes of the killers.

They starved our children
for fifty days
And at the end of the fasting
they threw us an onion.

Granada has fallen for the fiftieth time
from the hands of the Arabs
History has fallen
from the hands of the Arabs.
All the folk songs of heroism have fallen.

We no longer in our hands
have a single Andalus
They stole the walls, the wives, the children
the olives and the oil
and the stones of the street.

They stole Jesus the son of Mary
while he was an infant still.
They stole from us the memory of the orange trees
and the apricots and the mint
and the candles in the mosques.

In our hands they left
a sardine can called Gaza
and a dry bone called Jericho.
They left us a body with no bones
A hand with no fingers.

After this secret romance in Oslo
we came out barren.
They gave us a homeland
smaller than a single grain of wheat
a homeland to swallow without water
like aspirin pills.

Oh, we dreamed of a green peace
and a white crescent
and a blue sea.
Now we find ourselves
on a dung-heap.

Who could ask the rulers
about the peace of the cowards
about the peace of selling in installments
and renting in installments
about the peace of the merchants
and the exploiters?
Who could ask them
about the peace of the dead?
They have silenced the street
and murdered all the questions
and those who question.

There was to be no Arab dancing
at the wedding.
Or Arab food, Arab songs
or Arab embarrassment
The sons of the land
were not to be there
at the wedding.

*   * * *

The dowry was in dollars.
The diamond ring was in dollars.
the fee for the judge
was in dollars.

The cake was a gift from America
and the wedding veil
the flowers, the candles
and the music of the marines
were all made in America.

And the wedding came to an end
And Palestine was not to be found
at the ceremony.

Palestine saw its picture
carried on the airwaves,
she saw her tears
crossing the waves of the ocean
toward Chicago, New Jersey, Miami.

Like a wounded bird
Palestine shouted:
This wedding is not my wedding!
This dress is not my dress!
This shame is not my shame!

The Qabbani poem became an overnight sensation. Political
power was in the hands of kings and dictators, businessmen were

coming and going to economic conferences and "summits" in Casablanca, Amman, and Cairo, trumpeting the advent of a new Middle Eastern economy, but this poet had his own kingdom. As he himself so defiantly put it, poetry was "written on the forehead of every Arab from his birth until his death." The Arab was the "quintessential poetic being." Poetry had its own dominion; *sultat al-shi'r* (the dominion of poetry), and was nobler and truer than the authority of "patriarchy and the authorities of marriage, and politics, and the military." These later dominions were mere "soap bubbles." Poetry was at the heart of the *turath* (heritage), and this *turath* is "our identity, our passport, our blood type; without it we will become bastard-children."

The Qabbani poem triggered an exchange between the poet and the venerable Naguib Mahfuz, which took place in the pages of the newspaper *al-Hayat*. The great novelist, the Cairene, was recovering from the physical and emotional trauma of the attempt on his life by radical Islamists a few months earlier. A supporter of the peace since the early 1970s, his response had the calm and reason of the man. He praised the beauty of the poem while noting its political weakness:

> There are those who reject the peace while falling short of calling for war. They offer no third option. . . . The other party [Israel] is not waiting for anyone and goes on with its conquest of the land. There is no peace without negotiations; since the option of war is not available to the Arabs there is no justification for this attack against the pragmatic Arab negotiators of the peace. . . . It is idle to berate the leaders and the negotiators, to tell them that they lost Granada and Seville and Antioch. There is no doubt that Nizar Qabbani is sincere in his opinions. This is his view; he has every right to it. There are many adherents to this view in the Arab world, those who reject the peace, even if we gained from it. It is their right to maintain such a view.

Qabbani took refuge in poetic license. He was under no compulsion to offer an alternative to this defective peace, he was to write

in response to Mahfuz. He was not a general planning wars or calling a halt to wars. The poet, he said, composes the *Qasida,* the ode,
and does not make political decisions. "Poetry is not governed by
daily habit or routine. She is an angry woman who says what she
wants with her fingernails and her teeth. She is a watchful wolf
ready to pounce day and night on the thieves and the mercenaries
and the pirates of politics and the merchants of the temple." Naguib
Mahfuz, Qabbani wrote, is not used to reading "enraged *Qasidas*
that spread their *abayas* (cloaks) on the ground to rail like furious
cats against this night of Arab decline, heedless of what people say,
heedless of scandals."

The difference between the two of them, the poet said, is in part
the difference between the novel and the poem. The first is deliber-
ate; the novelist arranges all the elements of his fiction and probes
the psychology of his characters without the pressure of time. But
the poet works with "highly combustible material." He cannot
postpone or control his work, for "poetry is a comet," whereas the
novel is a "workshop open twenty-four hours a day." The poem in
this Arab world was a

siren that goes off in hours of danger. It asks people to go down
to their shelters, to put on masks that protect them against fear,
and repression and dictatorship. Naguib Mahfuz is a product of
the Sadat school, which believed in the genius of Sadat and in his
prophesies and in his vision of the future. I am a student of the
school of Nasserism, with all its madness and pride and patriotic deeds and victories and defeats, with all its weddings, and
sorrows. Naguib Mahfuz's fingers were soaking in water while
mine are turning over a fire. As a poet, I am constitutionally of
the party of peace, for poetry cannot be written in the shadow
of death and desolation. But what we are offered here is not
peace but a pacifier made of rubber with no milk in it, a bottle
of wine with no bottom, a love letter written in invisible ink.
What we are offered takes from us what is above us and what is

under our feet, and leaves us on a mat. . . . Nothing remains for us of Palestine in the shadow of this ruinous peace.

Between Yasser Arafat's and Yitzhak Rabin's celebrated handshake on the south lawn of the White House, on September 13, 1993, and the Israeli election on May 29, 1996, which ended in the defeat of Shimon Peres and Labor Zionism, lay a period of difficulty for the Arab intellectual class. A stealth peace had been made that took away from them every cherished illusion. The purists had lived on the idle hope that Egypt's peace with Israel—made a generation earlier—was destined to fall of its own weight, that it had all been the whim of Anwar Sadat, a man who had been seduced away from his world by American treasure and American acceptance. That peace was written off as the "pharaoh's peace." A measure of consolation was derived from the grudging peace Egypt had granted Israel, from the opposition of that country's intellectual and literary elite to their country's accommodation with Israel.

The peace of Oslo was a wholly different matter. A Palestinian, Yasser Arafat, had made that peace. He was Mr. Palestine; he had held the deed to the land. In Tunis, his base after his expulsion from Lebanon in 1982, at considerable remove from the land he claimed, Arafat had survived as a figure of continuity with an Arab political tradition that reached back to the 1950s and the 1960s, the high-water mark of Arab nationalism. He may have blundered along the way, the Old Man of the Palestinian movement, but he had remained *of* his world. He brought ruin to the Lebanese when he made his base among them for more than a decade, from 1970 to 1982, but he had not forced himself on the place, he and his supporters could claim with some justification. Beirut was an "Arab city," a "garden without fences"; Arafat had walked in and given this city and its youth, its Muslims and those among the Christians who rallied to him, a moment in the sun. He had turned West Beirut into an "Arab commune," giving a city known among other Arabs for its frivolity, "lightness," and red light district a great political undertaking. He had taken a ride with the Iraqi conqueror of Kuwait in 1990, but he was hardly alone in that choice.

For Arafat, the peace of Oslo was an expedition into uncharted waters. He was now going where the likes of King Abdullah of Jordan and Sadat had gone before him. He had reinvented himself. The leader of the Palestinians who had taken to the road in 1948—the refugee communities in Jordan, Syria, Lebanon, and the Gulf—had given himself a new task. He would set out to build, with Israel's help, a small political world in the West Bank and Gaza. There would be new respectability for him in odd places: a Nobel Prize for Peace; a photo op in the Oval Office with Bill Clinton in May 1996; a visit to the World Bank to discuss with its president, James D. Wolfensohn, the matter of finances and aid for his Gaza-based regime. But in his new incarnation, Arafat seemed to be a man alone. His solitude bore an eerie resemblance to the solitude of those other two men who had dared break with the ways of the crowd: Abdullah and Sadat. The man who had run the affairs of the Palestinian national movement from his back pocket for a quarter-century was now second-guessed at every turn, his peace dismissed as a deed of surrender. A Palestinian Versailles was the way Palestinian-American author Edward Said labeled it. It was an ironic twist of fate for Arafat. He had lived to be dismissed by those who had hitherto followed him through thick and thin as a "collaborator" of Yitzhak Rabin and Shimon Peres, a local cover for a new Israeli bid for hegemony over the region. To the opponents of accommodation with Israel, Arafat was a *muhallil*: He would make it *halal* (permissible) for those who were waiting to arrive at their own compromise with Israel—the Hashemites east of the Jordan River, the dynastic rulers in Qatar and Oman, the Tunisians, the Moroccans, and so forth.

The idea of Palestine had been far grander than the squalor of Gaza and the oasis town of Jericho where Palestinian self-rule began. "Once it was a noble city," the chroniclers always wrote of Jericho, its splendor beyond it in some remote, irretrievable past. "The water of Jericho is held to be the best, the lightest of all Islam," the renowned tenth-century Jerusalemite historian al-

Muqadisi wrote of the town where travelers paused before their final push into Jerusalem in the hills above. "Bananas are plentiful, also dates and fragrant flowers. . . . There grows in these parts much indigo and many plants." There was not much for the historian to add. History happened elsewhere. The small verdant town, with its unkempt gardens and orchards of bananas, could not bear the weight of a large nationalist dream.

In exile and loss, Palestine grew and grew. The orange groves in the narrative of the refugee camp dwellers became lands of bliss, shade, and *khayr* (well-being). The men and women who had taken to the road from Jaffa and Haifa in 1948 had turned these cities into places of splendor where everything was pristine and good and whole. "To Haifa, the bride of Mount Carmel: She has been in captivity far too long," a refugee from Haifa, Abdul-latif Kanafani, writes in a typical work of remembrance, *Bourg Street: Haifa,* published in 1995. Kanafani was nearly seventy years old when he wrote of Haifa. He had had a good measure of professional success. He knew the world of finance; he had pursued a career in Kuwait, Saudi Arabia, Oman, and Lebanon. Every detail of Haifa is preserved in Kanafani's account: the teachers at the Islamic school he first attended; the soccer rivalry between Haifa's al-Shabab al-Arabi and Jaffa's al-Nadi al-Riyadi al-Islami, a particularly thrilling match in 1947 that ended with a score of 3 to 1 in favor of Haifa; the peerless Abu Salim, the exemplary and skilled taxi driver on the Haifa–Beirut run; the commercial competition between Haifa and its rival, the city of Acre. In the remembrance, Haifa is the "lighthouse of the Mediterranean in culture and art," a port city second only to Marseilles in the waters of the Mediterranean. In the remembrance, Haifa is a worldly, secular place where religious differences were of little consequence. "Religion is in our hearts, and the light of progress is in our eyes" was the anthem of its youth.

Such memories and yearnings had sustained the national movement that Yasser Arafat had led. They had been held by the Palestinian upper orders and refugee camp dwellers alike. "On cold winter days we would gather around the brazier to hear grandmother tell us stories about how half the land in Irak al-Manshiyeh belonged to our family," Fatima Abu Warda told a foreign reporter. The reporter was there, with the Abu Warda clan, after Fatima's cousin, Majdi, a boy of eighteen, blew himself up on a Jerusalem bus on February 25, 1996, killing twenty-five passengers. "We always regretted the loss. She would tell us about the oranges, about the cows, how no butter ever tasted as sweet, and about the grapes." Fatima Abu Warda and the extended family now lived in the refugee camp of Al Fawwar, on the West Bank, in a four-room concrete bunker. These memories, and the expectations that came with them, were there stalking the practical peace Arafat had settled for.

Fawaz Turki, a Palestinian writer born in Haifa, a political renegade who had made his own way without the support of official dogma, without the sustenance of nationalism, had the daring to travel back from his home in the United States into the city of his boyhood after an absence of more than forty years. In *Exile's Return*, a book of political and personal memoirs (1993), he records a traumatic passage, searching out and finding his old house at the corner of Miknass and Talal streets. An old man, an Israeli in his late sixties, opens the door for him. The encounter ends badly. "But the man wants me out of his house. His House. My House. Our House." He had come looking for home to discover that he was "a stranger in a strange city. These people live here now. This is their city, their dawn." Fawaz Turki had always been a man on the fringe of things. His willingness to travel back into his claim and to let go of it were his alone. The refugees of 1948 had been shipwrecked by the peace, robbed of the idea of "return." Reality was prosaic and circumscribed. The Palestinian political enterprise Arafat put together could never match the grand expectations.

It was Zionism, confident of itself but eager to be done with the burden of occupation, that had thrown a life-line to Yasser Arafat and his lieutenants in exile in Tunis. Israel had outgrown the "tower and stockade" Zionism of its youth and yearned for a new life beyond the siege. It had wearied of the occupation. In a landmark election in June 1992, a quarter-century after Israel's conquest of the West Bank, the country closed a circle, bringing to power Yitzhak Rabin, the commander who had led it to victory in the Six Day War. Not a man of words, when he prevailed at the polls Rabin had not said much about how the great enmity with the Palestinians would be resolved. He had promised only to "get Gaza out of Tel Aviv." He had offered his country the promise of "separation" from the Palestinians. A majority of Israelis cast their fate with him, trusted that the gruff soldier, the boy of the Palmach (the elite strike force of the Jewish underground), the dutiful son of Zionist pioneers, would do right by his country as he had done all along. Instinctively, Israelis understood what Rabin had in mind: The "green line" separating Israel from the West Bank would be redrawn, and Israel would find a safe, new world after the siege. The River Jordan and the mountain slopes along the Jordan rift would mark Israel's "security border," and the demographic and political lines within the West Bank would provide a border between Israelis and Palestinians.

It was peace without illusions. To pull it off, Rabin and his foreign minister, Shimon Peres, found a new role for Yasser Arafat. They rescued the Palestinian leader precisely at a time when the world Arafat had mastered (inter-Arab politics and the game in the councils of Arab power) had been blown out from under his feet by the Gulf War of 1990–1991 and by the ride he had taken with the Iraqi conqueror of Kuwait. In the end, the man who had taken every wrong turn was the only Palestinian who could return his people to the principle of partitioning the land. He had wanted it all—*min al-nahr ila al-bahr* (from the river to the sea)—but Arafat now settled for what he could get. By one measure of things, Arafat had nowhere else to go, no other choice to make, and he capitulated to the logic of brute, irreversible facts. But this ignores the ruinous temptations of nationalism. Arafat could have chosen to remain in the wilderness; he could have persisted with the politics of the past. He could easily have settled for the fate of that other leader of the Palestine Arabs, Hajj Amin al-Husayni, the mufti of Jerusalem

(1893–1974), who took his followers on a disastrous ride—a trail of assassinations and terror, a fling with the Axis powers in the Second World War—and never doubted the wisdom of what he had done. Hajj Amin died in Beirut, unrepentant. The faithful continued to honor him, and thousands of young men and women, a biographer tells us, came to see him over the years "to pay their respects and to receive the advice of an old warrior." Arafat could have opted for that large Palestine of the imagination and the unambiguous legacy of the old warrior. No wonder he took his time (nearly a year) to go to Gaza to claim his earthly turf. He knew what had befallen King Abdullah and Sadat. No doubt he knew that his political life would have been easier had he chosen to remain in the impossible (and un-sullied) world of political maximalism.

Arafat had done well by Oslo; history had given him that rarest of gifts—a second chance. Palestinian nationalism had been res-cued, but Arafat had gone into the situation alone, it seemed. Few among the Palestinian intellectual and political class were there for him. He was deserted by some of the very figures of note who had been the standard-bearers of Palestinian nationalism in the preced-ing three decades. The poet laureate of the Palestinian national movement, Mahmoud Darwish (born in 1942), now living in Paris, gave voice to the disenchantment with the peace in an interview he gave on a visit to Gaza in 1995, when he said that he had felt as though he had returned to Palestine and had not returned, that he had arrived and not arrived, that his exile had not come to an end. The language, he said, had to be modest in the face of this kind of misery. In less poetic terms, the Palestinian-American author Ed-ward Said, a former member of the Palestine National Council and a writer who must be considered the preeminent public intellectual among the Palestinians, condemned the peace of Oslo as an Amer-ican peace and dismissed Arafat as an enforcer of Israeli rule. The great day on the south lawn of the White House, the celebrated handshake between Yasser Arafat and Yitzhak Rabin, ought to be a "day of mourning" for all Palestinians, Said wrote. The Arafat regime in Gaza, the Palestine National Authority, was, in Said's view, a security apparatus working in tandem with the Israeli intelligence services. "People have been tortured to death. Newspapers have been closed. His [Arafat's] opponents are being rounded up. And still he rules, and most of his people either endure that rule silently or try to get a position in it." A "quisling" Palestinian regime had arisen in Gaza; the Palestinians had come out empty-handed from this "Israeli-American peace."

Arafat had recast himself. He was in his mid-sixties when history gave him his new assignment in 1993. He rode two seemingly irreconcilable forces into his new domain. One was the power of Israel and its desperate need to separate from the Palestinians. The other was the force of the Palestinian underground and its "children of the stones." There was no denying that Arafat put behind him the Palestinians of Syria, Lebanon, Jordan, Detroit, New York, and Australia to lead those still on the land. In a different political world, when the idea of a Jewish state was still an audacious bet, the Zionist leader Chaim Weizmann had said he would accept a state the size of a tablecloth. That was the kind of choice Arafat had to make when the political culture and the international order that had sustained his old maximalism were swept away. A metaphysical "right of return" was held out for the refugees of 1948, but no one was fooled. No one foresaw a Palestinian return to Acre, Jaffa, and Haifa. Opting for the possible, Arafat bid farewell to an entire legacy. Ghada Karmi, a Palestinian researcher in London, captured the view of those disappointed by the peace:

> It is as if the PLO's acceptance of the Oslo Accords in 1993 had canceled a sixty-year history and set of agreed principles which had been the core of the Palestine cause. At one stroke, it apparently became acceptable to settle someone else's country, expel its inhabitants and ensure by all possible means that they never return. By the same token, it became unacceptable—in bad taste even—to mention that these things had actually hap-

pened. Anyone who still uses the rhetoric of injustice, dispossession, the Palestinian right of return, etc., is now regarded as
being hopelessly out of touch or politically naive.

Hisham Sharabi, whom we already met as a young follower of
Anton Saadah, now in his late sixties and an American academic of
genuine authority in the Palestinian dispersion, spoke of the peace
with unrelieved bitterness. He had wanted very much to believe in
this peace, he says. After Oslo he put his "reservations" aside and
journeyed to Israel with the novelist Amos Oz to probe the possibilities of reconciliation. For a fleeting moment he felt that reconciliation between the two peoples might stand a chance. But three years
into the enterprise, he became convinced that the peace was but
a way of forcing the Palestinians into "shameful surrender." The
regime of Arafat, his Palestine National Authority, was not the
"democratic independent Palestine" that many Palestinians had
worked for but a "Bantustan" set up to do Israel's bidding. A man
of the 1948 refugees, Sharabi saw nothing for his own kind in the
peace Arafat accepted. Those outside the "historic land of Palestine" now find themselves, he observed, "legally cut off from their
people and from the land of their ancestors, deprived of all their national and human claims." Though helpless to overturn the balance
of power and reject this unjust peace, the "Palestinians of dispersion" owed it to themselves to persevere in their opposition to what
Arafat had accepted. Instead of Arafat's peace, Sharabi called on his
compatriots "inside and outside of Palestine" to stick to the cause
of "real peace," which would guarantee the refugees the "right of
return" and give birth to an "independent Palestinian state with a
capital in Jerusalem."

At the root of this bitter politics lies, no doubt, a measure of
personal guilt and a search for absolution. Sharabi had been a child
of privilege. In his 1975 memoirs, *al-Jamr wa al-Ramad* (Embers
and Ashes), he acknowledged as no one in his class has been able to
do the responsibility of his social class for what had befallen Palestine. He was in his formative years during the Arab Rebellion of

1936–1939, and he renders that period and the world of the well-off of Palestine with great candor. Consider this portrait of his father and his father's friend, Omar al-Baytar, a major landowner and a mayor of Jaffa who incurred the wrath of the rebels by his land sales to the Jews and his support for British rule:

> We lacked for nothing during the revolt of 1936. Danger was far away from the privileged classes. Only the *fellaheen* and the poorer classes fought and suffered and paid the price for the revolt. The educated people and the *Effendis* followed the revolution through the newspapers *Filastin* and *al-Difa'a*. We used to hear that a house was demolished, that a rebel was executed and we would curse the British. But our lives would continue in the same manner. In the summer of 1938, an incident which came to have a great effect on my life took place. Someone tried to assassinate Omar al-Baytar, a close friend of my father. . . . When my mother heard the news she began to pack our bags. "We must leave immediately," she said, "your father's turn is next." In the morning Abu Zaki [Omar al-Baytar] and his wife left for Lebanon. The next day, my father, my mother and I followed them. In the town of Alayh, Abu Zaki and my father donned their red fezzes and marched to the coffee house overlooking the hills, sat around a small table, puffed on their water-pipes with enjoyment and contentment as though they were saying that the world is blessed with a thousand blessings, *al-alam bi alf khayr*. At the end of the summer, we went down to Beirut and rented a small apartment. . . . My father enrolled me in the preparatory school of the American University. The next year he and my mother returned to Jaffa and I went to boarding school. I remained in Beirut throughout the war years until my graduation from the American University in 1947. During this period, I did not return to Palestine except to spend some holidays.

His last memory of the Palestine of his youth was in December 1947, when he came to bid farewell to his family before leaving for the University of Chicago. On a cold day he makes the crossing from

Lebanon to Palestine, through Ras al-Naqura. In the fading light of dusk, he sees the walls of Acre—for him the most magical of cities—and the minaret of al-Jazzar Mosque, and behind it Haifa and Mount Carmel, descending to the sea. The roads are empty save for two (Jewish) buses of the Egged Bus Company on their way to Nahariya, the only Jewish settlement in western Galilee. He bids farewell to two childhood friends, one of whom assures him that all of Palestine will be liberated by the time he is back from America.

It did not take long for the final play for the land to unfold. Through the dispatches of the *New York Times* he followed the events from Chicago—he notes that young men (and women) his age were fighting in the Haganah while he was far away. April 1948, he records, was a catastrophic month. On April 6 the Jews broke the siege of Jerusalem. On April 8, Abdul Qadir al-Husayni, the able Palestinian commander, was killed in the battle of Kastel on the out-skirts of Jerusalem. On April 19 the town of Tiberias fell to the Jews. Three days later, it was Haifa's turn. Then came the fall of his city of Jaffa. A dispatch in the *New York Times* of May 2 reported that the forces of the Irgun had turned over control of the city to the Haganah: "I remember the sea of Jaffa well. It was the sea of my childhood. I can still smell it, taste its salt, feel its wind on my face."

Memory stood in the way of accommodation. An apparition, the Old Palestine rebuked this practical peace. Memory sanctified all that had been there before the loss and the defeat. "The Palestine I left in 1947 as a young man was a small and beautiful land on the cusp of modernity," Sharabi told an audience in Munich in Decem-ber 1996. Like a genie, the Old Palestine had been summoned and released by this new accommodation; the memorialist could not take to this new land. It was time, he said, to acknowledge the force of that old claim:

At the end of the Second World War, Palestine was the most pro-gressive of Arab lands. . . . Its daily papers were the most vi-brant, most daring in the Arab world. Unlike most surrounding countries, Palestine enjoyed a great deal of freedom from feudal

rule. The villagers were emancipated, most of them owned their
own land. In the cities there was a rising educated middle class.
In Jaffa, most of the women had given up the traditional veil. It
was the normal practice then to send young girls to school. The
Palestinian teachers and managers and physicians and engineers
were the vanguard of modernity in the Arab homeland.

Forty-six years after his flight from his birthplace, Sharabi traveled into his past with Amos Oz and a BBC camera crew, which
came along to record this occasion. It was a journey into a dream:
"Everything had changed in Jaffa and nothing had changed." He
walked the main street of Jaffa. There were the same low, old buildings, even the shops he had known. "I heard the horns of cars and
the voices of the vendors and the conversations in the street. But
these were not the people I knew, and they were not speaking Arabic." The Clock Square was the same, only the old town hall was
gone that the Irgun had blown up in 1947:

> With the BBC crew we visited my old home in the Ajami district,
> which is now an Arab ghetto. The garden, in the front of the
> house, was the same, and the jasmine plant from which my fa-
> ther used to pluck a little flower every time he left the house was
> in bloom over the same old wall. I learned that a Jewish family
> from Romania now lived there. When the producer suggested
> that perhaps I should go inside the house I declined, I could not
> bear seeing the hall as I had known it, the dining room, the other
> rooms.

A fidelity was owed this past. Over the horizon, Sharabi could
not see anything but strife, violence, and a breakdown of this illegitimate peace. He did not fear for the failure of the peace; his
dread, he said, was the success of this peace on Israel's and America's terms and the betrayal of that sacred past.

There was a powerful Palestinian national narrative of dispossession. It had given the Palestinians sustenance and a disproportionate place and role in Arab courts and political movements alike.

The narrative had to yield to a concrete political enterprise. Like travelers arriving at a diminished version of what they had wanted and pined for, the Palestinian political class were robbed of their great expectations. Purists noted that Arafat had secured only a one-sentence recognition of the Palestine Liberation Organization from Yitzhak Rabin in September 1993. Other disappointments were still to come. When Arafat arrived on his new political turf in Gaza in July 1, 1994, nearly a year after his handshake with Rabin in Washington, he arrived by land from Egypt in a convoy that could only fall short of the dream of return. The foreign press had wearied of waiting for him; only a small contingent had stayed on. The speech he delivered was embarrassingly flat. He spoke to a small audience under a scorching sun. People began to depart before he was through with his speech. For more than four decades the imagination had burdened the dream with messianic expectations. The man himself and the speech he gave were bound to be less exalted than the expectations.

Arafat had come with his lieutenants to a place he was yet to know. Dissent was quick to follow. There were charges that the Arafat regime had nine security services, that opponents had been tortured, that his jails were filled with twelve thousand people, that the press had been muzzled, that two pro-Jordanian publications, *an-Nahar* and *Abna al-Balad,* had been bullied, and that the latter had ceased to exist. There were petty blunders on Arafat's part. He banned the books of Edward Said, once his principal advocate in Western intellectual circles. Arafat had made the career of Hanan Ashrawi, a literature professor who had become a media icon after the Madrid Peace Conference of 1991, but she emerged as a figure of the opposition. (Arafat responded by taking her into his cabinet in June 1996.) The man had not changed. In exile he had monopolized power and controlled the finances of the Palestine Liberation Organization. He had done all that but had remained the undisputed leader of the Palestinian National Movement, the "Old Man" at the helm, a revolutionary among revolutionaries and a man of

Arab courts and official circles. He was to be subjected to a kind of scrutiny he had not known before Oslo and the peace.

In reinventing himself, Arafat had made his way into unexpected places. On May 1, 1996, he had his first meeting in the Oval Office with Bill Clinton. This was his reward, secured him by Shimon Peres. A fortnight earlier, Arafat and his parliament, the Palestine National Council, were reported to have amended the Palestine National Covenant. A document of the 1960s, the covenant had claimed all of Palestine as the patrimony of the people and rejected Israel's statehood. The annulment of the covenant had long been one of Israel's principal demands. Arafat had obliged, or so it seemed. True to his past, he was to be in this episode all things to all men. He left enough ambiguity in what he had done to give himself plenty of cover. The diehards were given the assurance that the amendment of the covenant had been put off, that the process had only begun and that they themselves would be given yet another chance to consider a new political charter. But there was enough there for Shimon Peres to claim a great accomplishment, to hail the change as "the greatest revolution that the Middle East had known in the last hundred years."

This ambiguity aside, the deliberations of the Palestine National Council occurred in the midst of a military campaign that Israel had launched against Hizbollah forces in Lebanon. The Lebanese had given Arafat more than a dozen years of indulgence. Their country had been his base from the time of his expulsion from Jordan in 1970 until his forces were routed by Israel in 1982. Arafat paid scant attention to that Israeli campaign into Lebanon in April 1996, meeting with Prime Minister Shimon Peres in the middle of the campaign. Arafat had switched arenas. He was playing for the sympathy of Israel and Washington. He was eager to secure the election of Prime Minister Shimon Peres in his battle with Likud challenger Benjamin Netanyahu. The meeting in the Oval Office was Arafat's political reward, but there was other business to transact. The self-styled president of Palestine called on a new friend in town, James D. Wolfensohn, president of the World Bank, to work out the details of a World Bank loan for his regime. A Palestinian state, the political chameleon said, was on the way. Arafat made the rounds in Washington. He engaged in that city's favorite vocation, political punditry; he turned up with Larry King on CNN. He foresaw a victory for Shimon Peres. The Israeli election would be close, he said, but Shimon Peres would prevail.

No fantasist in Beirut of the 1970s, when the Palestinian pamphleteers and the Palestinian revolutionaries had the run of the place, could have foreseen this turn of events. Back then, Arafat had not overrun or conquered Lebanon. He had sold enough of its Muslims and some of its Christians on the idea of a shared destiny; he had found a niche for himself in Lebanon's fractured politics. He operated in Lebanon with a warrant granted him by weightier Arab players: the Egyptian state and the states of the Persian Gulf. In the intervening years, he had traveled far. Realpolitik and skill in the eyes of some, "treason" and "surrender" in the eyes of others, had led him to Washington in the midst of Lebanon's ordeal. He had looked with a cold eye on the scales of power. He must have reasoned that there was little the Arab world could do for—or to— him. He was in a race with Jordan, which had begun to thicken its own peace with Israel. He was loathed in Damascus and locked into a conflict with Palestinian organizations sheltered by the Syrian regime. There was no center for Arab political life. The place had fragmented. No one could decree what was *halal* (permissible) and what was *haram* (impermissible) in this new order of things.

This peace of Oslo could not win over the Arab intellectual elite. It was not their peace but the rulers' peace, they insisted, made at a time of Arab disarray and weakness, in the aftermath of a season of discord in the Arab world. In the Persian Gulf War of 1990–1991, Arab had fought Arab and an Iraqi state that had presented itself to the intellectual class as the new bearer of their political truth had been stripped of its delusions and made a pariah in the world of nations. There was no honor in this unequal peace, the true believers said. The language, the preserve of the intellectual class, came to the

aid of the opponents of the peace. In a play on words, normalization, *tatbi* was dismissed as *tatwi* (domestication) and peace, *salam*,
as nothing other than surrender, *istislam*.

Per capita income in Israel was ten times what it was in Jordan
and nearly twenty times what it was in Egypt. The Zionist political
enterprise had been vindicated. By 1995, Israel's economy had
sprinted ahead of Spain and Portugal. Israel's success intersected
with the collapse of the Arab world's economic growth that oil rev-
enues had made possible. A period of growth had come to an end in
the Arab world. By the early 1990s, the time of Arab–Israeli peace,
the region provided a spectacle of economic failure. A World Bank
report, *Claiming the Future* (1995), put the economic dislocation of
the Muslim Middle East and North Africa in stark terms. These
lands, with a population of 260 million people, exported fewer
manufactured goods than Finland with its 5 million people. Capital, what there was of it, had sought shelter abroad. Some $350 bil-
lion of the region's private wealth was in assets held abroad. The
region had become truly marginal to the world economy, attracting
less than 1 percent of the total capital flows to the developing world.
East Asia had dug out of poverty; Latin America was beginning to
reap the dividends of privatization and economic reform. Alone, it
seemed, the lands of the Muslim Middle East and North Africa
were in dire economic distress. (Africa had a dismal performance
as well, but this is not the sort of yardstick by which the Arabs in
the 1970s and 1980s had measured themselves and their world.) By
the early 1990s, even the lands of El Dorado, the oil states, were
on the ropes. The six Arab states of the Gulf had behind them a
decade of deficits and had begun to run down the foreign assets and
reserves they had accumulated during the boom era (1973–1983).

The populations of these oil lands had more than doubled in
twenty years, entitlements had grown, and an increasingly younger
population no longer knew or retained memories of austere times.
To give one telling example, the foreign assets of Kuwait, some $113
billion in the year 1989–1990, were down to $46 billion by 1996.
Poverty had not come to the lands of the Peninsula, but the pros-

perity these oil lands had brought to countries on their periphery was a thing of the past. There had once been ambitious ideas about the economic renovation of the Arab world, talk of a grand public project that would secure the place a better future. The dreams had come to naught. The talk of an "Arab economy" belied the dependence of that world on links to the industrial economies and the astonishing lack of trade among the Arabs themselves.

It was no help to this peace of Oslo that its Israeli architect, Shimon Peres, promoted the peace as a dawn of a new age for the region, heralding the birth of a "New Middle East." Millennial in its expectations, Peres's vision was a world of markets, ballots, and open borders. The deserts of the Middle East would be made to bloom, conquest would yield to commerce, and nationalism would lose its hold. "In the past, a nation's identity was molded from its people's special characteristics, the geography of its land, the unique properties of its language and culture. Today, science has no national identity, technology no homeland, information no passport," Peres said in one of his standard utterances. Peres had walked in— exuberant, wordy, and hopeful—during a funeral. Arab intellectuals were mourning the loss of their world. Everywhere around them there was evidence of terrible political and economic weakness; military despotism in the age of democracy's (alleged) triumph in new, unexpected places in Latin America and Eastern Europe; an emboldened theocratic alternative in Lebanon and Egypt and among the Palestinians; the end of the ride that oil wealth had made possible. Peres, this new bearer of cosmopolitanism and modernity, arrived trumpeting a world that held out nothing but the promise of cultural alienation. Instead of an Arab world that was whole and true, the popular Syrian poet, Nizar Qabbani, lamented, "we now get a supermarket with an Israeli chairman of the board." It was easier for the true believers in Arab nationalism to deal with Yitzhak Rabin. The gruff soldier offered a soldier's peace: the hesitant handshake he extended to Yasser Arafat on the lawn of the White House was true to the man and true to the situation. Peres's challenge was different. To the keepers of the Arab flame, Peres was the great seducer. He would take his truth, his technocratic vision, to the un-suspecting in Doha, Oman, Tunis, and Rabat. There, and in other citadels to fall, he was sure to find the gullible, willing, and faint-hearted. He would divide the ranks of the Arabs and impose on them his new era of Israeli primacy. In Peres's world, the truth that generations of Arab nationalists had nurtured would be scattered to the wind.

It was no surprise, then, that the defeat of Shimon Peres in May 1996 was to the Arab intellectual class a gift of political deliverance. They were off the hook. They had not bought the man's vision, and now the prophet of this new technocratic age was rejected by his own. The rejection of Peres and his vision was made easier by the military campaign he had launched into Lebanon, Operation Grapes of Wrath, six weeks before his defeat at the polls. That dis-astrous operation was Peres's response to a grim wave of terror, four suicide operations over the course of eight days in Ashkelon, Jerusalem, and Tel Aviv, which took a heavy toll of fifty-nine lives and called into question the entire logic of the peace with the Pales-tinians. The peace had promised separation between Israel and the Palestinians, but the terror launched by the forces of the Islamist movement, Hamas, underlined the entanglement of the two peo-ples. The last of these suicide attacks had hit Dizengoff Street, the main shopping and entertainment center in Tel Aviv, on the eve of Purim. With this deed of terror in Tel Aviv, "the sky fell," Israeli historian and author Meron Benvenisti wrote. The attacks on Jerusalem had occurred on the fault line between Arab and Jew, in a city "saturated with violence." Tel Aviv was a different matter. This was, in Benvenisti's apt description, the "hedonistic underbelly of Israel, where Israelis feel more removed from the bloody con-flict." Peres struck into Lebanon to absorb the anger of his country, but his incursion boomeranged. On April 18 a makeshift refugee compound at a United Nations post in the town of Qana in south-ern Lebanon, a few miles south of the city of Tyre, was hit by Israeli artillery shells. More than a hundred civilians perished in Qana. The old enmity had been given a new lease on life. The past and its

feuds and passions seemed more true and lasting than the technocratic peace and the businessmen's deals.

A political regime in the small principality of Qatar had struck
out on its own, deepening political and commercial traffic with Israel. When Peres turned up in Qatar, the Hatikvah, the Israeli national anthem, was played on the tarmac of Qatar's airport in his
honor. The Qataris had sought an Israeli market for their natural
gas, and a counterweight, no doubt, to the power and influence of
their large neighbor, the Saudi state. It had been a brave policy for a
small principality, which had gone beyond the old prohibitions,
and it was attacked at home. A popular preacher, one Dr. Yusuf
Qardawi, imam, religious leader of Doha's Omar ibn al-Khattab
Mosque, agitated against the policy in his sermons. He stigmatized
those who would shake Peres's hand, said that the hand that would
shake Peres's would be made impure and had to be "washed seven
times, one time with dirt," to remove the stain. And the Qatari policy was met with the opposition of larger Arab states. The Qatari
rulers had taken all they could; with the defeat of Peres, a greater
caution was forced on them.

Farewell to the new Middle East, the purists proclaimed. Ed-
ward Said was not alone when he welcomed the victory of Benjamin
Netanyahu: "Better a crude and brutal Netanyahu than a posturing
but also crude and brutal . . . Peres." In the immediate future, in
Said's view, there would be "dark and confusing days" for Arabs and
Jews. Over the long haul, there would come, though, a "reciprocal
peace." Muhammad Rimawi, a Palestinian analyst writing in the
London-based Arabic daily *al-Hayat,* came closer to the heart of the
Arab intellectual consensus. Peres, he said, had "draped himself
with his New Middle East projects and with his vision of economic
cooperation; Netanyahu will be naked, a crude warrior roaming the
streets of a modern city." Netanyahu's victory was the return to a
world the Arab intellectual class trusted and understood. There was
no hope that the pan-Arab political order could be put back together again. But the return to the old enmity, the drawing of lines
that Peres—and Arafat—had blurred, was a consolation all the

same. There had been an Arab political game with discernible rules and rituals: summit meetings that promised to put an end to the rivalries of Arab states; endless plans for repairing the imbalance between Israel and the Palestinians. That political world had been emptied of whatever content it once had. The Gulf War of 1990–1991 had made a mockery of that old political style. But that game was given a new lease on life in the aftermath of the defeat of Labor Zionism. "Today we are torn apart," said Egyptian president Hosni Mubarak as he convened an Arab summit in Cairo in June 1996. The Egyptian state was now determined to reconstitute the old order of Arab states under its leadership.

An open letter from the poet Nizar Qabbani to the rulers assembled in Cairo captured this sense of relief that the Israeli peacemakers were gone. Beyond the satire and bitterness of Qabbani's text, there was the hope that this "treasonous peace" and its illusions were a thing of the past:

> I am delighted that you have announced your marriage which has been delayed for centuries, even though you have agreed to marriage after you have reached the age of despair, and your bones have wearied and your powers have waned. We are delighted if you can live under the same roof for three days.
>
> If Benjamin Netanyahu has been able to raise your blood pressure, to light fire in your nervous system, to change your blood type, a thousand thanks to him.
>
> If Benjamin Netanyahu has been able to convince you of the virtues of marriage, to gather your heads on one pillow, to convince you to sit at one table, to eat from one plate, to drink from one glass, how beautiful it is what he has done.
>
> If this man has been able to remind you of your identity, of the place and the date of your birth, to restore you to your Arab nationality, how beautiful it is what he has done.
>
> If this man has been able to restore the Arabs their Arabism, and the children of the stones to their childhood,

If he has been able to remind us of the names of our fathers, and
the names of our children,
A thousand welcomes to his arrival.
Gentlemen, this is the last occasion of love open to you before
you become extinct.

The peace of Oslo had been on the ropes, an unwanted and
unloved peace. For three years, Arabs had engaged in a wrenching
debate about "normalization." In speaking of Israel, they had, as
has been their way since this Zionist project came into their world,
spoken of themselves. The play was given away in 1995, when the
Jordanian minister of culture said that the peace treaty with Israel
would be honored by the government but that "associations and
people" were free to decide for themselves on the traffic with Israel.
This had laid bare the rules of the game between the state and the
intellectual class. No other Arab ruler had been as openly support-
ive of the peace as the Hashemite ruler, but political power and
official writ had their limits. Normalization—its speed and its
depth—was left to make its own way. The rulers who opted for the
peace had not embraced it in public. They gave every hint that theirs
had been a grudging choice, dictated by the balance of power, or by
the abandonment by other Arabs of what should have been a collective Arab fight, or by the end of the Cold War, and so forth. This
gave the intellectuals the space they needed to go at the peace. It was
not lost on the intellectual class in Egypt that Sadat's successor,
Hosni Mubarak, had been in office for fourteen years without making a single voyage to Israel. (He was to go for the funeral of Yitzhak
Rabin in November 1995, but he explained this passage as a courtesy owed to the dead; this was not an official visit, his handlers were
to say.) In his discomfort with the peace, in his subtle hints that he
was only honoring a peace his predecessor had bequeathed him, in
his frequent reminders to the critics of the peace that the accommodation with Israel was a precondition of American goodwill and
American patronage, Mubarak left ample space for the opposition-

ists to the peace. They could rail with abandon against an unloved peace.

The Egyptian state had reached an accommodation with Israel, but the influential head of its syndicate of artists and performers and literati, Saad Eddin Wahbe, prided himself on his hostility to Israel and on the resistance he put up to "normalization" of cultural traffic with Israel. Wahbe was a powerful figure in the movie and theater industry, and his enmity toward Israel was undisguised and unadorned. He made no apologies for it. Normalization was the "sole card" in the hands of the Arabs, he believed. They should not "throw it away even if all the Arab rulers signed peace agreements with Israel." He hounded artists and performers who dared cross the line by traveling to Israel or dealing with Israeli artists. There was no culture in Israel worth bothering with, he believed. Hazem Saghieh, a skilled reporter traveling in Amman in April 1996, found himself in the presence of Wahbe, in the office of the Jordanian head of the union of writers, and recorded this remarkable performance by the man. Wahbe was looking for new books to take back with him to Cairo. He waved off the Protocols of the Elders of Zion with a triumphant smile: "We have plenty of copies of this work; I myself saw to its publication four times." Another book sparked his interest, one he had not heard of before on the Freemasons and their relation to Judaism and Zionism. Wahbe could not conceive of screening an Arabic film in Israel, "not even in Gaza and Jericho," he told the reporter.

Wahbe stood at the gates, a keeper of an older trust, an upholder of a deep historic enmity. The army ruled the state, a coalition of businessmen and bureaucrats ran the economy, the Islamists claimed what opposition there was. Wahbe was left as a centurion of culture. He presided over an international film festival in Cairo in 1994 that banned *Schindler's List* for "nudity and violence" while giving pride of place to Oliver Stone's *Natural Born Killers*. Israeli filmmakers and films were kept out of the film festival. Wahbe was formed in an earlier era, a simpler one, the culture of Nasserism and

Arab nationalism. He could not topple the state or hurl it into a new military conflict with Israel, but he denied his sanction and support to the peace his country made with Israel. No "visitors of dawn" were going to haul him off to prison for his opposition to the peace. He knew the limits drawn by the Egyptian state for his dissent, and he knew as well the power of the symbols he claimed for himself. Normalization, Wahbe said, was a state of mind. It was inconceivable that he would enjoy an Israeli song, for he had stored in his mind "tens of scenes of Israeli massacres. . . . The Arab psyche shall remain shut before everything that comes from Israel."

There were deficits in the oil states, there was hunger and failure in Iraq, and the men of the Palestine Liberation Organization were aging revolutionaries without treasure to dispose of or international backers. A peace concluded in stealth in Oslo in 1993 could not be an equal peace, the pundits insisted. The principal tribune of Nasserism and Arab nationalism, the Egyptian journalist Mohamed Heikal, put the peace with Israel in dramatic terms familiar to Arabs who had been reading him for four decades: Just as the 1950s and 1960s had been an "Egyptian era" of nationalism and political struggle, and the 1970s and 1980s a "Saudi era" of wealth and petro dollars, the 1990s had turned into an "Israeli era." The peace concluded in the 1990s was sure to reflect the facts of Israel's power. Egypt had defected from the "Arab system" and left it defenseless. The peace that Arafat accepted was the best a leader on the ropes could do. Abandoned by an Arab world in disarray, a Palestinian leadership formed in "exile and siege" that partook of a culture of "guns and bombs" knew no other way than a stealth deal with an Israeli government that held all the cards.

It was pointless, Heikal wrote, to blame the Palestinians for their acceptance of a truncated peace. The Palestinians were at the end of their tether, and the world had wearied of them. The Arabs had given up the cause and were pushing the Palestinians toward that unequal peace. There had been chances for a better peace for the Arabs in the decade that followed the October 1973 war, a time when they could have secured better terms, but the chances had been squandered. A new map was being drawn for the region, "one more dangerous perhaps than the map drawn by the Sykes-Picot accords" in the aftermath of the First World War. Where that old map merely divided up the inheritance of the Ottoman empire, the Sick Man of Europe, the new map was a "birth certificate" for a new order destined to subjugate the Arab world. Heikal dreaded what the new dispensation had in store for the Arabs. Their world was "penetrated" and dependent, their states ill equipped to deal with the new balance of power, and they themselves "kept in the dark" in this time of "satellites and mass information."

A whole world had slipped through the fingers of two generations of Arabs who had come into their own in the 1950s and 1960s. A city that had once been their collective cultural home, Beirut, had been lost to them. A political culture of Arab nationalism, which had nurtured them, which had come to them sure of itself and had been accepted whole and unexamined, had led down a blind alley and had been made an instrument and cover for despotism and a plaything of dictators. No ship of sorrow could take these two generations back to the verities of their world. This campaign against the new peace would give the men and women of the pan-Arab tradition a chance to reclaim lost ground.

A POLITICAL WORLD had gone beyond its own legends and discarded its old fidelities. The intellectual class had only itself to blame. It had not looked reality in the face; it had not sought to describe the political world as it was. Its pronouncements had never incorporated the cold logic of power. Its world was a cocoon that a cruel decade had torn asunder. It was of little use saying that the Palestine National Council was a pliant body of Arafat sycophants who had done their leader's bidding and that the "substantial" figures of the Palestinian world had been struck down over the preceding decade. It mattered little to Arafat that the pundits took him to task in the columns of the Arabic press. He took the charges leveled at him in stride: He had a political regime to keep intact. He also had going for him the fact that he had carried the Palestinians from that "country of words" to some concrete political gains.

The Arab political imagination had never really probed in a serious way Israel's place in a region at peace. It had never felt the need to do so. As the Moroccan scholar Abdallah Laroui so hauntingly put it, it was widely believed that "on a certain day everything would be obliterated and instantaneously reconstructed and the new inhabitants would leave, as if by magic, the land they had despoiled; in this way will justice be dispensed to the victims, on that day when the presence of God shall again make itself felt." There had been no intellectual or psychological preparation for the peace. Muhammad Sid Ahmad, a figure of the Left in Egypt and a commentator possessed of an independent temperament and mind, had gone into uncharted territory in the early 1970s with a brave work, *After the Guns Fall Silent.* He had tried to sketch a futuristic, provocative assessment (and he had done it in Arabic) of what peace would entail for Israelis and Arabs: He had made a place in his scheme of things for a "normal" Israeli state in the region. Nearly twenty years later, a younger academic and activist from Jerusalem, Sari Nusseibah, took the unusual step of coauthoring a book with Mark Heller, an Israeli researcher, *No Trumpets, No Drums,* which advocated and divined the tentative workings of a normal order of states, with Israel and Palestine side by side. Nusseibah hailed from an aristocratic background. His family's roots in Jerusalem go back centuries; his father, Anwar Nusseibah, had been a member of the Jordanian cabinet. A courageous man, inquisitive and knowing of the terms of the encounter on the ground between Israel and the Palestinians, Sari Nusseibah wanted to go beyond the prohibitions of an intellectual tradition. He put down on paper a rudimentary outline of a Palestinian state that accepted Israel's legitimacy in return for reciprocal recognition. He broke with the orthodoxy, but the book was written in English and, thus, was easy to ignore.

There the matter remained. The custodians of political power in the Arab states set out on their own in pursuit of accommodation,

and the intellectual class was left to carry on the old fight. Faith saw
the intellectual class through all kinds of disappointments. Anwar
al-Sadat rode out many storms. His "illegitimate" peace survived.
Yasser Arafat and the Jordanian state picked up Sadat's trail. The
men who pulled the levers of power were "born masters of statisti-
cal science" (to borrow Jacob Burckhardt's exquisite description
of the rulers of the Italian city-states in the Renaissance). The intellectuals were keepers of a sacred legacy; an understanding was
reached. Diplomatic accommodation would be the order of the day,
but the intellectual class was given a green light to agitate against the
peace. No one who reads the Egyptian daily *al-Ahram* would think
that Israel and Egypt were at peace. Its columnists and contributors
wage a steady campaign against normalization. No discernible lines
are drawn for them—Islamists, Arab nationalists, and military pundits alike. In a newspaper with strict limits on all other political and
cultural discussions, writings on Israel are a free-for-all. Cumula-
tively, the writers of *al-Ahram* drive home a message that harks back
to the time before the peace. They conjure up the specter of Israel as
an enforcer of Pax Americana, a power bent on diminishing the role
and the place of Egypt, severing Egypt from its natural hinterland
in the Fertile Crescent and the Persian Gulf.

The intellectual class did not govern, but it structured a moral
universe that hemmed in the rulers and limited their options. We
must not overdo the separation between the intellectual class and
the powers-that-be. The custodians of political power did not de-
scend from the sky; they partook of prevailing norms and could
read the political wind. The foreign policy of the Egyptian state
over the last several years—its campaign against Israel's nuclear
weapons, its eagerness to display its independence from America, its
determination to check the power of Israel in the region, and its den-
igration of Jordan's embrace of Israel—offered evidence that the
opponents of normalization had not labored in vain. The "cold
peace" with Israel emerged out of a subtle pact between the state
and the civil society. This was what the traffic would bear.

Sly and skilled in the ways of the world, confident that Israel and the United States feared the bogeyman of a theocratic revolution in Egypt, the Mubarak regime had ample room for maneuver. Israel was kept at arm's length, but the Egyptian regime could count on Israel's and America's indulgence. A generation after the Camp David accords, Egyptian statecraft had emerged with the best of all possible worlds: Egypt was at peace with Israel; it had been rid of her pan-Arab vocation; and it had garnered the wages of the peace and the American aid that came with it, but had offered few ideological and diplomatic concessions in return. The state had remained within the bounds of expediency. It had not undertaken an intellectual battle on behalf of the peace. Egypt has always been a society of tumult and words, its state remarkably good at manufacturing consent and symbols, multitudes of intellectuals and pundits at the ready to do the bidding of the state. The silent peace with Israel was an olive branch held out by the regime to its critics in the professional syndicates and the universities. The regime's hostility to Israel was a safety valve for a political order that has been in the grip of a long season of troubles. The towering intellectuals who were there for Sadat in the 1970s, an older generation of writers and thinkers who wanted an end to the conflict with Israel, were gone now or quite old. Of the generation of giants—the likes of the critic Louis Awad, the playwright Tawfic al-Hakim, the historical writer Hussein Fawzi, the novelist and short story writer Yusuf Idris—only Naguib Mahfuz remained. All born and formed under the monarchy, these men had known a tradition of dissent and relative tolerance. They were individuals of large horizons and wide-ranging interests. They had no love for Israel but wanted release for their homeland from the ruin of its wars with Israel and from the authoritarian political culture that the wars had justified. All (with the possible exception of Yusuf Idris, who was a good deal younger than the rest) were unabashed Westernizers who thought that Egypt's natural home was across the Mediterranean in a European tradition. Tawfic al-Hakim, Naguib Mahfuz, Louis Awad, and Hussein Fawzi had all seen the pan-Arab vocation of the Nasserite state and the wars that came with it as an unmitigated disaster for Egypt, a betrayal of its promise and a warrant for despotism. For these men, peace with Israel was a precondition of modernity and an open society. Five or six years before Sadat made his daring visit to Jerusalem, Hakim, Mahfuz, and Fawzi told the head of state that it was time to put an end to the fight with Israel. A decade before the Egyptian state opted for peace, both Yusuf Idris and Naguib Mahfuz had probed and given voice in their fiction to an illicit yearning for normalcy and peace.

Tawfic al-Hakim, the eldest of this unusual group of writers, born in 1898, was a fearless man at home with controversy. He had gone to Paris in the mid-1920s and returned with what became his trademark, a French blue beret, at a time when the fez was the standard head cover. He had practically invented the modern play in Arabic. More important, he had been President Nasser's favorite writer. The ruler, who was a generation younger than the playwright, had paid homage to the author, credited him, his books, and his ideas with having been sources of inspiration for him as a young officer and political dreamer. In his youth Nasser had tried his hand at writing; an abortive novel bore the distinct mark of Tawfic al-Hakim. In 1957 Nasser bestowed on Hakim one of the country's highest honors, the Order of the Republic. The two men had a parting of the ways in the 1960s, when Hakim's plays began to express an unmistakable disillusionment with the regime and the culture of military dictatorship and populist nationalism, but Hakim had become a political and cultural icon. His advocacy of reconciliation with Israel when he was in his seventies was of a piece with the man's entire life and true to his sense of Egypt's calling. His age, his place in the country's development, the inspiration he gave three generations of Egyptians, and the awe in which he was once held by Nasser, made him politically invulnerable. When Hakim said that "unlike the British and the Dutch who had colonized Southern Africa without having any historic links with that region, the Zionist who settled Palestine was returning to a homeland he had inhabited in the past," his audience took that heretical view as yet another display of this writer's independence. There was no way of reading Tawfic al-Hakim out of the fold of home and country. He and the small group of writers around him were immune to the easy charges of "treason" that were routinely hurled at lesser figures who dared question the prevailing political orthodoxy. Two of these writers, Louis Awad and Yusuf Idris, paid for their politics, doing time in prison when Nasser's military regime sought to snuff out the independent power of the labor unions, leftist intellectuals, and communists.

When Hakim died at a ripe old age in 1987, he was mourned as a national hero, a beloved son of the land who had brightened up the life of Misr (Egypt) and whose life had mirrored the Egyptian quest in this century. He was given a grand state funeral, and tens of thousands turned out for the funeral procession. More than a hundred of his colleagues eulogized him in a book of farewell and homage; not a single writer saw fit to call up the matter of his support for the peace with Israel or to question his love of homeland. He had lived and died a fearless man and a patriot. In the era of the "open door" economy, when the literary class was on the lookout for new money and opportunities, he remained incorruptible and indifferent to the temptations of the time. His support for the peace with Israel was true to a man who had led a life of his own choice.

"We can't belittle these people," the writer Ghali Shukri, a prolific and passionate man of the Left and an uncompromising critic of Sadat and his peace with Israel, said of Tawfic al-Hakim, Naguib Mahfuz, Hussein Fawzi, and Louis Awad. Shukri had gone into exile in Beirut and Paris in the 1970s and had been stripped of his citizenship by the Sadat regime, but he still honored his elders, the pioneers of modern Egyptian thought and letters, and understood why they had backed peace with Israel: "Palestine and Arab nationalism were not issues that mattered to their generation." These men had been "raised on liberal Egyptian nationalism." They were well off; they wanted nothing from Sadat. "There was nothing that Sadat could do to Tawfic al-Hakim. . . . These men were truthful to themselves. . . . Long after the political positions of Hakim and Fawzi and Mahfuz are forgotten, what they gave in fiction and literature shall remain the heritage of every Egyptian and every Arab."

A special history and undisputed genius had functioned like a charm for this group of doves. (The attempt on Mahfuz's life in October 1994 by radical Islamists tells of the coarsening of the country's political culture.) Their authority had shored up the peace. But the younger breed of intellectuals were of a different sensibility. Neither the Nasserites nor the Islamists took to the peace and normalization. A distinguished playwright, Ali Salem, ran afoul of the consensus of his peers by traveling to Israel in 1994. There was to be no end to the charges leveled at the man. It was said that he was bought off by Israel, that he was paid hundreds of thousands of dollars for his deed and his views. It was rumored that entrepreneurs and tycoons with ties to Israel had financed his passage there. Ali Salem had no apologies to make to his detractors. He went to Israel as a man of letters and culture and a supporter of peace, he said in his defense. He saw no alternative to the peace. He saw no threat to Egypt or the Arabs from Israel, "none at all, now or in the distant future." He saw himself as a person who "belonged to the Mediterranean, to the pharaohs, Egypt and the Arabs." It was out of this complex identity and out of his commitment to a "civic, free and democratic society" that he had embraced the peace. "Let me say to you that the Egyptians and the Jews are the two closest people in the region," he told one interviewer. "In the depths of the Jew there is a feeling that he belongs to a tribe that had come out of Egypt. Culturally, the Jew thinks that he and the Egyptians complement one another, and it is because of this that the Jew hates to be an enemy of the Egyptians."

Ali Salem did not retreat under fire. In a book that chronicled his visit, *Rihla ila Israeel* (A Passage to Israel), he wrote that the campaign against cultural traffic with Israel was the product of a "demagogic politics," born of a feeling of "inadequacy and an ignorance of Egyptian culture and thought." He had faith in the innate wisdom, special genius, and culture of Egypt and did not fear that Egyptian culture would be overwhelmed by Israel; his brother had been killed in one of Egypt's wars with Israel, and he was eager to have this border of his country become a normal border. Those who warned of an "Israeli cultural invasion of Egypt" were peddling myths, holding up a *ghool* (a man-monster) to frighten the young, who were still searching for truth and who were owed the chance to make their own choice with courage and curiosity. A satirist who never lacked for a clever turn of phrase, Salem wrote that the cultural invasion, when it comes, would be a "pincer movement" led by General Ariel Sharon, that Israel's novels would be propelled over Egypt's skies by rockets that would demolish the works of Naguib Mahfuz, Taha Hussein, Tawfic al-Hakim, and all the rest. For Egypt's "long history," Israel would substitute its "brief, abbreviated history," and this brief history would hold Egyptians in thrall. In the eyes of her enemies, Israel had become a temptress from the Thousand and One Nights, "a clever seductress with an enchanting voice that will lure you away and pull you to the bottom of the Nile."

Men and women fear the unknown. Salem had gone to Israel, and he had seen a normal country with all its warts. He meant his chronicle, as witty, irreverent, and rambunctious as all his popular plays and works of satire, to strip the society across the border of its mythic, demonic quality. He had haggled over the price of his hotel room in Tel Aviv, flirted with the receptionist, bonded with many of Israel's Sephardis, drawn from the Arab lands, whom he found as *baladi* (sons of the village) as all the villagers of the Egyptian countryside. They were *baladi*, he said, and Arabs to the core even in their hatred for the Arab governments under whose rule they and their elders had once lived. He was not frightened by the enmity of the Sephardis to the Arab world. He recognized in it, and in their yearning for the music, culture, and cuisine of their old Arab homelands, a fidelity to the culture that had been theirs.

I saw Ali Salem in Cairo three years after his passage. A very tall and large man, talkative and irrepressible and disheveled, he looked as though he was a character straight out of one of his own plays. Right away it was clear that this was a man who had endured a bruising drawn-out battle. He needed very little prompting to delve into what he had been through. A Cairo literary newsletter had published a photograph of him with Israeli leader Shimon Peres; in the picture, Ali Salem had the same bag he carried to our luncheon. Under the photograph the newsletter had printed the following words: "Ali Salem and Shimon Peres, Between them an open handbag." It was the style of that kind of journalism, and it was a crude suggestion that the passage to Israel by Ali Salem had been a mercenary endeavor. This was his world and his city: he had taken such malice in stride, but it had taken its toll on him. It had become harder for him to make his way in his guild and his work.

For all he had endured, the playwright insisted that he would have it no other way. I had pressed him on the promptings of his trip to Israel and on the sources of his politics. He did not hesitate: he located them in his childhood (born in 1936, in the "liberal" interlude) and in Damietta, the city of his birth, on the seacoast of Egypt, where the Nile flows into the Mediterranean. A city of trade open onto the world—silk of splendor had once been woven there; in more recent times furniture of exquisite quality had been made in that city—ships from all Mediterranean ports docked in Damietta's harbor. The city had stamped him, Salem said, with its worldliness and gentle breeze. He had been free all his life; he had taken to the laboring life as a boy, he had made his own way, and he had seen this new endeavor of his (support for the peace with Israel) as something true to the daring literary work he had been doing all along.

Ali Salem represented a continuity with the old, confident spirit of Egypt's cosmopolitanism that had moved Tawfic al-Hakim, Louis Awad, and Hussein Fawzi. He knew the strength of the current he was swimming against. Of a large syndicate of Egyptian artists (some thirteen thousand in all), only a small contingent shared his outlook. Fewer than a dozen mavericks from the world of culture, arts, cinema, and letters had violated the unwritten taboo on travel to Israel. The writer Muhammad Sid Ahmad has given a fair assessment of the Egyptian intellectual scene: "The Egyptian intelligentsia in its bulk is deeply resentful of any normalization.

The diplomats and military men have to follow rules and talk to Israel. But with the intellectuals nothing has changed. It's even become more radical than before."

In a haunting short story written in 1972, Yusuf Idris foresaw both the Egyptian–Israeli peace and the recoiling from it, the daring voyage to Jerusalem by Sadat in 1977 and his assassination four years later. Spare and dark, "Innocence," is written in the first person. An Egyptian (clearly Sadat) is visited by a temptation to see the world of his enemies on the other shore. A general with a black eye patch (obviously the Israeli commander, Moshe Dayan) turns up on an old dock. "The general's smile, the boat, and the invitation." A vast crowd watches on the wooden dock, silent, "the silence of Judgment Day." The general's smile is friendly, his teeth are stained, but "he had no fangs, no fangs." On a whim, the storyteller accepts the invitation, crosses to the other shore on "water like silk, or silk made of water." The general does not seek to embarrass his guest, does not stretch his hand for a handshake. "I just want to watch. . . . How can I shake their hands when their hands are full of snakes and scorpions? I am sure that had I held out my hand and shook one of theirs it would stick to it forever. . . . I have just come to watch. I had been watching from the other shore and now here I am. What harm is there in this, what harm?"

A whole world was there on this other shore, "cities big and small, beaches, brothels, factories for secret weapons." The general is discreet, he leaves the guest to wander on his own, but he hovers nearby, a smile on his lips, a baton under his arm. A long line of women, older ones and maidens thirteen years of age, turn up. "Pick what you want, point with your finger, the line is very, very long, and the women many and different. . . . There is no sin in watching, my heart is clean and pure like cotton, and the desire in my breast is repressed and shackled. I am afraid that were I to begin to express myself I would collapse. . . . I was no longer able to stay and to watch."

The general's smile of farewell has in it pity; it is a little mocking. The visitor returns: "I had passed a difficult test, my conscience at ease. . . . I did not touch, I did not defile myself." The crowd is there, where he left it, on the dock; the visitor returns to this "great silence." An unexpected sight materializes on the dock: "My son, barefoot, in his nightshirt, standing there, shaking off sleep, looking toward me. . . . This is my son, my flesh and blood." The look in the son's eyes is severe and steady, "a look that froze me in my place, a look with no trace of a son's feeling in it." The son reaches into the pocket of his nightshirt, pulls out a pistol, a real pistol, not a children's toy. "I did not touch, my son, like all these people here I was just watching and looking." The plea fell on deaf ears; the look in the son's eyes was the look of an executioner. "A bullet in my shoulder; I could see tears in his eyes. The second bullet hits me in the chest, I could hear its echo. The third bullet, I no longer heard."

Made from above, by autocratic regimes, and made in stealth, the peace found its most determined opponents in the pockets of the "civil society" that the Arab regimes did not fully control: the professional syndicates, the assemblies of engineers, physicians, and journalists, the literary guilds, and so forth. The freest and most independent, as it were, took up the cause of the old enmity. In the romance with "civil society" that sprang up in the twilight of communism and the triumph of democratic capitalism, we have come to see the institutions of "civil society" as instruments of redemption, the building blocks of a new democratic order of nations at peace. This was a view that the landscape of Eastern European lands under communist regimes spawned. However, we cannot extend this kind of confidence in "civil society" to the Arab political and intellectual class and its encounter with Israel. (We cannot extend it to many postcommunist societies either, but that is another discussion.) It is among the most articulate sections of the society, among the professionals and the enlightened, that the resistance to normalization is most tenacious and uncompromising. There, among the writers, physicians, lawyers, engineers, and journalists, the old flags are unfurled and the sense of betrayal is most acutely felt, that a conflict so vital could be waved off at the rulers' behest. In part this is due to the disproportionate influence of the Islamists in the professional associations, but the opposition to the peace bridges the secular–theocratic divide. It is hard to know with any precision where opposition to the rulers per se ends and animus toward Israel begins. The rulers governed alone, monopolizing the public space and the great decisions of war and peace. An intellectual class diminished by its powerlessness and resentful at its subjugation, but unable to do much about its condition, did what came naturally to it. It took the rulers' peace and the dividends of that peace while damning the rulers' work all the same.

The dominant political tradition had led to ruin but had not been fully abandoned. Peace had come across the Jordan (a better peace, a fuller peace than that which obtains between Egypt and Israel), but even here, in a tempered, stable polity, the political and intellectual class remained surly and unconvinced of the new course. By the objective measure of things, the founder of the Jordanian realm, King Abdullah, the great realist who had sought an early accommodation with the Zionist project, had been made to look wise and prescient. Abdullah had been struck down for "treason" by a Palestinian assassin in the summer of 1951, but history had vindicated him. His courage was remembered by Bill Clinton in the summer of 1994, when Jordan and Israel signed a peace treaty in Washington. "Today, forty-three years later, Abdullah's grandson has fulfilled his legacy," the American leader had said of King Hussein. Abdullah was invoked yet again on November 6, 1995, at the Israeli military cemetery on Mount Herzl, by the gravesite of Yitzhak Rabin, when Abdullah's grandson and political heir came to mourn Yitzhak Rabin. A great stylist, the king fully understood the poignancy of the moment: He was in Jerusalem for the first time since 1967, there to honor the commander who had led Israel's forces in the Six Day War of 1967: "We are not ashamed nor are we afraid, nor are we anything but determined to continue the legacy for which my friend fell, as did my grandfather in this city when I was with him and but a boy." He never thought that his first visit to Jerusalem since the Six Day War of 1967 "would be on such an occasion." When his time came, he said, "I hope it will be like my grandfather's and like Yitzhak Rabin's." This was a moment loaded with meaning; the monarch had gone far, and he would soon hear from the purists.

The memory of his grandfather had always stalked King Hussein. And the dead were to be remembered with vengeance a day after King Hussein's oration, in the town of Irbid near the Syrian border, when an Islamist leader, head of the engineers' syndicate, turned up for a political speech on the anniversary of the Balfour Declaration. The speaker, Laith Shubaylat, hailed from the apex of Jordanian society, the aristocracy of the realm. His father, Farhan Shubaylat, had been King Abdullah's minister of court and had served as King Hussein's minister of defense. The son, born in 1949, was his own man, an oppositionist with a history of anti-regime activism behind him. Elected to the Jordanian Parliament in 1989, where he served until 1993, he had been charged in 1992 with conspiring against the regime. A court had sentenced him to twenty years in prison, but his sentence had been commuted by King Hussein. Unrepentant, Shubaylat had persisted in his politics. He brought to this remembrance of the Balfour Declaration the rage of a man convinced that a culture had dismantled all its defenses, had taken the enemy unto itself. "It passes without notice, this anniversary of the Balfour Declaration, where it had once been an occasion for the masses to be mobilized against those who betrayed it and who sold its land." The popular will, he said, was being deceived and led astray. Where once there were bonds of Arab solidarity, there was now talk of the brotherhood of the "sons of Abraham." The Jews, "accursed by God," were now partners, whereas Iraqis not so far away were "dying like flies" because of their faith and because of who they are as Arabs. History has been disfigured in this new peace: "Yitzhak Rabin was mourned, God forbid, as a martyr of peace," the government media in Jordan treated the matter as a "national calamity," and the Queen of Jordan grieved for the "head of the Zionist tribe." A bond had been forged, said Shubaylat, between "the rulers and the builders of the Third Temple."

This "treason," so apparent today, has deep roots in the polity, Shubaylat observed. He made his way through the testimonies of nationalist historians to sketch the familiar portrait of the Hashemites: dependence on the British; betrayal of the Arabs of Palestine; land sales to the Zionists. He dredged up an old remark of Abdullah to the Zionist leadership in 1926: "We are poor and you are rich. Please come to Transjordan. I guarantee your safety." He used it as definitive proof of Abdullah's complicity in the calamity that had befallen the Palestinians. The grandson, he says of Hussein, has been true to the grandfather's ways: Zionist chronicles, says Shubaylat, reveal the close ties between King Hussein and the Zionist enemies. How else could one explain the reference "to my brother Rabin and my sister Leah"? (The reference is to Rabin's widow, Leah.) The "devil's work" is being committed in our time, but the "faithful few" will triumph with God's will and sustenance. (Laith Shubaylat crossed a line with his ridicule of King Hussein and his wife. This brought him a three-year prison sentence in March 1996; he was released in November of that year. True to the spirit of a monarch who had rehabilitated many of his would-be assassins, King Hussein himself drove Shubaylat from prison to his family home.)

A culture's respect and approval can be strange. There is no justice in the way they are given or withheld. In an Arab political history littered with thwarted dreams, little honor would be extended to pragmatists who knew the limits of what could and could not be done. The political culture of nationalism reserved its approval for those who led ruinous campaigns in pursuit of impossible quests. It was futile to expect a grand apology for Abdullah, some public warrant for what he did long ago. The tracts of nationalism will not be rewritten. The likes of Laith Shubaylat will not be appeased. A foul wind, and a spirit that bordered on nihilism, greeted this peace. In the time of the Americans, the Arab intellectual world had become militantly illiberal (as though to compensate for the political hegemony of Pax Americana). In their opposition to the peace, writers and activists marked out an intellectual tradition beyond America's power and beyond America's judgment.

IN THE LATTER part of the nineteenth century there had been *al-Mahjar*, the lands of emigration, in Europe (Paris in the main) and the New World where intellectual exiles from the Arab domains of the Ottoman empire fled political oppression. It was there and in Cairo that Arabic liberal thought had its early footing. A century later, a circle was closed: Arab political discourse and Arabic political journalism put down roots in London and Paris (and America, to a lesser extent). The great sheltering truth of Arab nationalism found refuge in the West. (This is why novelist Abdelrahman Munif described Paris as the capital of the Arabs.) The pan-Arab papers—*al-Hayat, Asharq al-Awsat, al-Quds al-Arabi*, the magazines *al-Wasat, al-Watan al-Arabi*, and so forth,—were published outside the borders of the Arab world. The intellectual luminaries were abroad: Qabbani in London, Adonis in Paris, Edward Said and Hisham Sharabi in the United States. Where the Palestinian scholar Walid Khalidi had once had a base at the American University of Beirut, he had now moved to Cambridge, Massachusetts. From Beirut, via Amman, the political analyst Ghassan Salame had settled in Paris; the Iraqi Ja'far Hadi al-Hassan was in England. There were countless others: Iraqis on the run from Saddam Hussein; Syrians looking for air; Lebanese looking for a reprieve from their country's ordeal.

Beirut had once offered the Arab intellectuals and the written, oppositional word a home, but Beirut had been lost first to violence and then to Syrian hegemony. Another center of pan-Arab intellectual life, a different one to be sure, had been lost in 1990: Kuwait. In its own way that merchant principality had given sustenance to the pan-Arab enterprise. Its national university and newspapers had been staffed by expatriate Arabs. There was, of course, that large Palestinian community in Kuwait; the presence of some three hundred thousand Palestinians in that small city-state had left its mark on that principality's politics. There were generous funds for writers and conferences and magazines when money was plentiful in Kuwait. In the shadow of their calamity of 1990, the Kuwaitis were left nursing their own wounds.

From the safety—and alienation—of exile, the Arab world could be whatever the emigré intellectuals wished it to be. The one cause that had been the cause of their early years was the matter of Palestine. This was the trail back to the past. In exile, fidelity had to be extreme and unbending. The great nineteenth-century Russian writer, Alexander Herzen, who spent his adult life in exile from his homeland (he went to Paris in 1847 at the age of thirty-five and never returned) chronicled emigré politics in Geneva, Paris, and London and left us a portrait of intellectual exiles in *My Past and Thoughts,* which comes close to the politics of the Arab emigrés:

> I do say even now that exile, not undertaken with any definite object, but forced upon men by the triumph of the opposing party, checks development and draws men away from the activities of life into the domain of phantasy. Leaving their native land with concealed anger, with the continual thought of going back to it once more on the morrow, men do not move forwards but are continually thrown back upon the past; . . . Irritation and trivial but exasperated disputes prevent their escaping from the familiar circle of questions, thoughts and memories which make up an oppressive, binding tradition. . . .
>
> All *emigrés,* cut off from the living environment to which they have belonged, shut their eyes to avoid seeing bitter truths, and grow more and more acclimatized to a closed, fantastic circle consisting of inert memories and hopes that can never be realized.

The late years of the twentieth century became a time of migration for the Arabs. It was not just the Palestinians who had been uprooted. The Egyptians, since time immemorial a people of the land loath to leave their country, began to emigrate in droves in the aftermath of the 1967 war. The awe about distant lands had been shed (witness the unexamined irony of Shaykh Omar Abdul Rahman, the zealous cleric convicted in the bombing of the World Trade Center in 1993, leaving Egypt, through the Sudan, and ending up in Jersey City to preach fire and brimstone against the rulers of his country and their American benefactors). The wars of Lebanon uprooted a whole class of people. With the Lebanese who left, there had scrambled out of the country the countless exiles from other Arab lands who had found a second home in Beirut. The tyrannies of Baghdad and Damascus had banished their share of emigrés, as did the cultural (and generational) wars of Algeria that erupted with fury in the late 1980s.

Exile hardened the emigrés, as it was bound to. Robbed of so many great truths, they were in no mood to give up the one struggle that had formed so many of them. In the way of emigrés, they filled the past—and the lost country—with wonder and gave it their loyalty. Even when exile was good to them—prestigious appointments in Western universities, a new life in the professions—the new lands were not fully theirs. It was natural for them to cling to the old lands.

"A lost homeland is like the corpse of a near relative; bury it with respect and believe in eternal life," a character in the gifted Lebanese-French writer Amin Maalouf's novel, *Leo Africanus,* observes. Maalouf wrote that magical work, set in Granada and the Mediterranean world in the late fifteenth century, as an allegory of the modern Arab condition. Granada falls to the *Reconquista* and a native son of it, Hassan al-Wazzan, takes to the road in search of a new home. He makes his way through Fez, Timbuktu, and Cairo; Sicilian pirates kidnap him and take him to Rome as a present to the Pope Leo X, who gives his own name, Leo, in friendship and appreciation for the "Moor" of travel and education. It is a voyage of forty years' wandering and much heartbreak: "Is it misfortune which calls out to me, or do I call out to misfortune?"

Hassan the Granadan became a "son of the road" and accepted

his condition. "Never hesitate to go far away, beyond all seas, all frontiers, all countries, all beliefs." In Leo's odyssey, Maalouf expressed his own ease with his life in France: from journalism in Lebanon to the writing of fiction in French, which earned him France's highest literary honor, the Goncourt Prize. Maalouf had no desire to fight the old battles. He made his peace with France and with French as a medium of his work. He carried with him the literary material of his birthplace and his generation. The themes were there for him—the history of the Crusades, the recurring times of war and discord in Lebanon, the courage and skill required to pack up and leave for a new home. These themes seeded his work, and the French language proved a blessed medium.

The great exemplar of this choice that Maalouf made was, of course, Joseph Conrad, who put Poland and the Polish past at a safe distance because he always felt (the words are his) the shadows crowding upon him, obscuring his vision. Born to a heartbreaking legacy of Polish patriotism and defeat—his father, Apollo Korzeniowski, was a reckless revolutionary exiled to northern Russia when young Conrad was not yet four years of age, and his mother died when he was seven—Conrad left Poland at age seventeen, boarding a train for France "as a man might get into a dream." Conrad roamed the world as a "castaway"—one of his favorite terms—before he settled for the life of a writer in England. The "fatal brand" of Poland always haunted him, hovering over his fiction; the Polish exiles in London charged him with betrayal of the Korzeniowski inheritance. He returned to Poland in 1914 after an absence of thirty years only to be trapped there by the outbreak of the First World War. A fan of his, the American ambassador in Austria, had to intervene to facilitate his escape back to the safety of England. The autobiography is unmistakable as one of his characters in the novel *Under Western Eyes* considers the matter of betrayal.

Betray: A great word. What is betrayal? They talk of a man betraying his country, his friends, his sweetheart.... All a man can betray is his conscience. And how is my conscience engaged here; by what bond of common faith, of common conviction, am I obliged to let that fanatical idiot drag me down with him? On the contrary—every obligation of true courage is the other way.

The solitude Conrad chose is loathed by politicized men and women. So is the equanimity of *Leo Africanus* about roaming God's "broad lands" and living beyond creed and dogma. The old world had been lost to the Arab emigrés, but they were not released from its grip. The shadow of the power of the West (America in the lands of the Gulf and the Levant; France in the affairs of North Africa; Britain in its old zone of primacy in the Gulf) lay over the Arab lands. This gave the emigrés a warrant for political activism on distant shores.

The distance from home showed in the Arab press produced in foreign cities. A daily paper is first and foremost a creature of its city. It must mirror its place, which must sustain and nurture it. An Arabic paper in London or Paris has to call up its own world. The angry patriotism, the anti-Americanism, the rage against Israel—all these, on some subliminal level, make up for a lost home. You could exalt the freedom of exile, you could insist that London or Paris was a temporary home until Beirut was rebuilt or Damascus and Cairo made more liberal and appropriate for a free press, but there was no getting around the alienation of exile, no way that a "normal" journalistic craft could be pursued away from the earth and the world that the journalism covered. The craft in exile was disconnected and strident at the same time. It could not have been otherwise.

The sorrow and anger of the regular contributors to the exile publications ran deep. A large number of these contributors wrote from Paris, London, Geneva, and New York. There would have been Arab unity, and there would have been home, and houses with gardens and cities of grace, had it not been for America, the distant power, which had tempted and then betrayed a whole culture, and had it not been for the garrison Israeli state that the distant power nurtured. The grief was bottomless. It had in it the yearning for home and for simplicity, and for the uncomplicated politics of youth and nationalism. In their imagination, the writers could recall a time of innocence, a time when a great political inheritance had been the unexamined possession of a whole generation. It took no powers of remembrance on the part of the writers to recall the exuberance they had known when the Egyptian Gamal Abdul Nasser nationalized the Suez Canal in 1956 and a world awakened to a new sense of political will. Two generations had owned that moment of exuberance, as they had owned the thrill of the war against French rule on the other side of the Arab world, in Algeria. No one could have foreseen what nemesis lay in store for Algeria, the terrible failure awaiting that land after independence, the bloodletting between Islamists and Francophiles. There were collection boxes in the schools for contributions for the fighters for Algeria and there were demonstrations against the French. The political world was whole and intact; the certainties of nationalism had not yet ruptured.

This grief and yearning for home easily spilled into and merged with maximalist politics. It was but a short journey from wailing for what was lost in Damascus and Beirut to an unbending politics of opposition to peace with Israel and normal traffic with America. It was easy to make that leap, easier, to be sure, than acknowledging that a social and political world was irretrievable, that demography, urban sprawl, and coarse, unrelenting politics had blown it away. A book of free verse and prose published in 1995, *Dimashq Nizar Qabbani* (Nizar Qabbani's Damascus) had the poet's memory of his city, his home, and his childhood:

> My childhood I spent in the shadow of our old house. That house marked, to me, the borders of the world; it was my companion, it was an oasis, a place for winter and summer alike. I could close my eyes now and count the nails in its gate, summon back the verses of the Quran carved on the wood of its hallways. I can count the floor-tiles one by one, its marble stairs one by one. I can close my eyes and call up, thirty years later, my father sitting in its courtyard, his coffee in front of him, and his brazier

and his can of tobacco and his newspaper. On the newspaper would fall, in intervals of five minutes, white jasmine flowers, as though they were love letters falling from the sky. On the Persian carpet rolled out in the house I did my schoolwork; I memorized the great poets. That house has left its mark and its fingerprints on my poetry the same way Granada and Cordoba and Seville left their mark on Andalusian poetry. The Arabic poem was covered with a thick layer of desert dust when it arrived in Spain and entered the mountains of the Sierra Nevada and the banks of Guadalquivir River and the olive groves and vineyards in the plains of Cordoba. There the Arabic *Qasida,* the ode, removed its clothes and plunged into the water. From this historical encounter between thirst and water there was born Andalusian poetry. . . . The same thing happened to my childhood and to my poetry and my alphabet in that house in Damascus.

The road to that childhood bliss and to that city of grace with its gardens and courtyards was blocked. Qabbani had quit Damascus for Beirut long ago; he had quit Beirut for London. He loved Cairo but could not make it his home. He had carried his notebooks and his anger to Europe. That anger could not be stilled or reasoned away. In the peace with Israel that the rulers pursued, he saw the scattering to the wind of his links to his own past and to the political truths he had been bequeathed.

All Qabbani had left was his "kingdom of poetry." The gods had given him a rare ability to hear and render his culture's inner voice; he had been granted a special dispensation, a mastery over a literary form that occupied a special place in Arab culture. He and his poetry were part of much of what had come to pass in recent Arab political life; he had been at his craft since the late 1940s. He had been frivolous and carefree when the world of the Arabs needed and treasured his frivolity and irreverence. He had then taken into his poetry the sorrows of his world when defeats and disillusionment had set in. There had, of course, been the loss of his wife, Balqees, in that bombing in Beirut. He had left for London when countless Arabs quit their lands for Paris, London, Germany, and America in a great migration. No wonder he could wield his poetry like a sword. His *Qasidas,* he said, would not "wear bullet-proof jackets or carry insurance policies." No regime, he taunted the rulers, "could arrest my poems for they are dipped in the oil of freedom. I have never dined at the table of any sultan or any general or any emir or minister. My sixth sense always warned me that to dine with such company would be my last supper."

THE PROMISE OF peace came in the year 1992–1993, and with it the call of modernity. For a moment, it seemed, the great enmity between Arab and Jew had become a thing of the past. The protagonists had closed a circle. In an earlier time, in the aftermath of the 1948 war, Israeli leaders had toyed with the idea of sponsoring some form of Palestinian autonomy west of the Jordan River. Advocates of the scheme thought that a mini-state sure to slip into their orbit was preferable to a larger Arab state on both banks of the Jordan, but nothing was to come of this. There would be no "Palestinian option" for Israel. Palestinian society disintegrated under the pressure of war; King Abdullah of Transjordan, the Arab leader who had crossed into Palestine to claim the West Bank as his own, would not be denied. He was a great realist; his forces were on the ground and the cause of the Palestinians would vanish into the wind.

Different kinds of diplomatic choices presented themselves to the Jewish state's leaders after they had fended off the Arab armies. There were "Transjordan firsters," who placed their faith in the Hashemite ruler King Abdullah, whom they knew and had long dealt with. There were "Egypt firsters," David Ben-Gurion among them, who loathed the British patrons of King Abdullah and instead sought an accommodation with the largest Arab state, which had emerged from the war with the dubious gift of the Gaza Strip.

Then there were the adherents to the Palestinian option. They were an imaginative band who knew the weakness of the Palestinians. They sought to revive their Arab neighbors, help them build a political world of their own, and thus shut out the larger Arab powers from the affairs of the West Bank. Some Palestinians stepped forth and claimed they could rally their people to a deal with the Jewish state, but they were timid men. It was not in them to make such a daring leap. A Palestinian option was not in the cards: nationalism was not a gift that one people could bestow upon another.

Nearly half a century later Labor Zionism returned to the "Palestinian option." The peace Israel made in 1993 rested on the shoulders of the unlikeliest of instruments: the soldier-statesman Yitzhak Rabin. He presented the peace as the most unromantic of things—a dream of separation between Israelis and Palestinians. He held out to his country a chance, even under siege, for a normalcy it had not known. "The east is my stranger," the controversial ideologue Vladimir Jabotinsky (1880–1940), founding father of revisionist, militant Zionism once observed. It was with this conception of the relation between Arab and Jew that the peacemakers broke in Oslo and Washington. Whether he admitted it or not, Rabin had given the green light to the emergence of a Palestinian state west of the Jordan River. In a supreme piece of historical irony, the great reconciliation between Zionism and Palestinian nationalism was launched by the first Israeli prime minister to be born on the land, a son of Zionist pioneers, a man whose own personal history mirrored that of his country's evolution. Rabin had given up his first vocation—agriculture and a scholarship to study hydraulic engineering at the University of California—to take up arms for his country in the forces of the Jewish underground in Palestine in 1941. For the agrarian frontier society of his youth, there was in place now a country of considerable economic, scientific, and military power. Rabin had accepted the burden—and possibilities—that power had opened up for Israel. A dutiful son of the founding generation of Zionist pioneers—his generation had been the obedient, silent generation that consolidated the gains of their revolutionary parents—Rabin set out to lay the foundations of a new Zionist project. Timing was to give his assassination, three years into his work, a measure of tragic artistry. Rabin's Canaan was just over the horizon: "For you shall see the land before you, but you shall not go there" (Deuteronomy 32:52)

Rabin's assassination was a deed of patricide, the killing of a father. Rabin's great gift to his people had been the victory in the Six Day War of 1967; his assassin, Yigal Amir, a young messianic Zionist, twenty-five years of age and a law student, was born after that time of peril had passed; he had incorporated the conquered land into his psyche and made it his own. With the victory in the Six Day War and the acquisition of biblical land, Israel had been placed in the way of a great temptation. "For a month, for a year, or for a full generation, we will have to sit as occupiers in places that touch our hearts with their history," the novelist Amos Oz wrote in his chronicle, *In the Land of Israel*. "We have not liberated Hebron and Ramallah, nor have we redeemed their inhabitants. We have conquered them and we are going to rule over them only until our peace is secured." This would not do for the religious nationalists. That strand of Zionism, which made the conquered land the measure of all things, broke with the secular, pragmatic Zionism of Israel's mainstream. The victory in 1967 that the methodical Rabin had won became to the messianic fringe a sign of divine favor and a permanent deed to the land.

Rabin himself saw no "miracle" at work in that victory. It had been a prosaic, worldly affair. He had done the commander's work. He had worried about the soldiers he led and about the Egyptian air force. Excess nicotine, fatigue, and worry had nearly broken him on the eve of the war. He had delivered his countrymen a stunning victory, but he gave an understated account of that war, a soldier's rendition of a professional campaign fought and won. "For me personally, the Six Day War was a high point of a military career," he wrote in his memoirs. He was not the sort of man to see "the finger of God" in a historical-worldly event. He had led the military campaign in 1967, and he was ready to trade the land for peace a quarter-century later. He was a secularist formed in the thoroughly irreligious world of Labor Zionism. The messianic temptation that blew in on "the seventh day of the Six Day War" (the arresting imagery of Meron Benvenisti) was alien to Rabin and to the whole secular tradition of mainstream Zionism. If anything, Rabin had not fully grasped the power of the religious/messianic reaction his pursuit of peace had stirred up.

Like all tentative new histories, the "new Middle East" was made of several parts: Israel's desire to be done with military rule over the Palestinians; Arafat's recognition that his past had led him down a blind alley; and the politics of that "plastic" moment in Arab life which followed the great crisis in the Gulf, when the pieties of Arab politics gave way. Five young men—the assassin of Rabin and the four suicide bombers of Hamas who struck in Ashkelon, Jerusalem, and Tel Aviv in the winter of 1996—then went out and put this new history to a great, cruel test. The terror frightened enough of Israel's population to tip the scales in favor of Likud and its religious-nationalist coalition.

Men love the troubles they know. The victory of Likud was the sort of outcome that the Arab intellectual class that had agitated against the peace could live with. It was easier this way. The sirens and alarm bells would go off when the psychological border between Arab and Israeli was crossed. There was no nostalgia for Yitzhak Rabin or Shimon Peres. True, the men of political power—some of them who had bet on the peace—mourned the passing of Rabin and the defeat of Peres. But in the main, and among the writers and thinkers in the Arab world, no tears were shed for a breakthrough they had never trusted and had never wanted in the first place.

The truth of Israeli politics was lost on the Arab opponents of the peace. The center of Israeli political life had opted for accommodation with Palestinian nationalism. Benjamin Netanyahu was carried to power by two differing camps: the religious nationalists, who wanted no accommodation with the Palestinians; and a larger stream that fell in with Likud's call for a reciprocal peace. Israel had outgrown the "tower and stockade" Zionism of its early years; there was no desire to stay in the towns of the West Bank and Gaza. The moment of truth came in the winter of 1997, when Netanyahu accepted Israel's withdrawal from Hebron only months after he came to power. A stark choice could not be deferred: a complicated, messy peace, or a return to the old enmity. In a democratic polity, the numbers told the story. The vote in the country's parliament in favor of withdrawal from Hebron in January 1997 was a lopsided affirmation of normalcy and accommodation—87 to 17, with one abstention and 15 absent. The military equipment in Hebron was hauled off, the Israeli flag was lowered, and the keys to the old British military headquarters were turned over to the Palestinian authority just after dawn on January 16. Reason had not come to Hebron. The volatile mix of religion and nationalism was not banished, but a principal component of the peace made in 1993 had been honored.

A Palestinian political enterprise had arisen between the River Jordan and the Mediterranean. In a break with one of the tenets of Zionism, a Palestinian armed presence had been introduced west of the River Jordan. A complicated history was in the making, but its force and meaning—and legitimacy—was lost on the centurions of the Arab political orthodoxy. The braver in the Arab world were the rulers who dared break with the culture's prohibitions and the few traders eager for a new order of things.

In January 1997 there was a crack in the intellectual consensus, a brave departure from the great prohibition. In a benign European city, Copenhagen, a meeting took place between Israeli and Arab intellectuals and pundits from Jordan and Egypt and from among the Palestinians. The Arabs who made it to Copenhagen were a brave lot. Led by an Egyptian figure of the Left, the journalist Lotfi al-Khuli, they included a man of the Jordanian establishment, a former minister, Adnan Abu-Odeh, the Jordanian columnist Rami Khouri, and the Palestinian academic and activist Sari Nusseibah. By the standards of dissent in open societies, the Copenhagen undertaking would have been a very modest affair. A band of individuals from the political world and from journalism and letters launched what they described as an "international alliance for

Arab–Israeli peace." Peace, the Copenhagen group said, was too "precious and war too abhorrent for us to sit idly by while a deterioration takes place." They pledged their support for the peace of Oslo, upheld the rights of the Palestinians to a state of their own, and called on Israel to put a halt to the building of new settlements in the West Bank. But the "Copenhagen Arabs"—this was a handy label doubling up as a convenient way of identifying them and a way of political and cultural banishment at the same time—were, according to the commentaries, either collaborators or fools who did the enemy's bidding. They had given in to the enemy; they were publicity seekers or worse. They had given Israel what was not theirs to claim or grant.

To his credit, Lotfi al-Khuli fought back and did not squirm or hide. He had been in the political arena for many years, and he knew his world. He had opposed the peace of Camp David and the diplomacy of Sadat, and he was now ready to travel a different path. The peace of Oslo had changed him. He had access to the pages of *al-Ahram* and to the Arabic press in Europe. The motive behind the Copenhagen undertaking, he argued in repeated appearances in the press, was his recognition that the Arab–Israeli conflict had been "transformed," that it was not some "eternal, primordial fight" to the finish between Arab and Jew. He was a realist, he wrote, and wanted realism to prevail among the Arabs. The dream of "Greater Israel" and the Arab dream of liberating "all of Palestine, from the river to the sea" had both been thwarted. It was time—a century after the first Zionist Congress in Basel in 1897—to acknowledge the great changes that had taken place on the land, the rise of a Palestinian authority west of the Jordan River with thirty-five thousand armed policemen, and the emergence of a genuine yearning for peace among the Israelis. A maximalist tradition among the Arabs had led to endless defeats, and in Lotfi al-Khuli's view, it was time to break out of the stagnant ways of the past.

The old Arab world with its truths could not be reconstituted. The exiles could not find the way back to their old homes and their lost cities. The one truth that could not be bartered or betrayed, the one sure way back to the old fidelities, was this enmity with Israel that harked back to the past. This was the one domain that the rulers could not hand over to their American patrons and protectors, their inner space and sanctum, which would remain inviolable and intact.

The full sense of the bitter opposition to the peace was dramatized in 1997 when a Jordanian soldier, Ahmad Musa Daqamsa, twenty-six years of age, opened fire on a group of Israeli schoolgirls, seventh- and eighth-graders visiting a shared patch of land in the Jordan valley on March 13, killing seven of them before his rifle jammed. Daqamsa and the debate about him put on display the inability of the Arab rulers to sustain the peace, and the mix of rancor and nihilism that attended the accommodation with Israel.

Three days after that terrible episode the king of Jordan turned up in Israel to offer his condolences to the bereaved families. He brought with him two of his children and called on all seven families. He knelt by the parents of the children as they sat on the ground in the custom of Jewish mourning. He told them of his sorrow and grief; he offered deep apologies for the tragedy that befell them. He said to each family that he felt as though he had lost one of his own children, pledged that he would do all he could to spare Arabs and Jews further calamities of this kind. But Daqamsa became, to the Arab opponents to the peace, a figure to rally around. Laith Shubaylat, recently released from prison and now a former head of the engineers' syndicate, it was reported, put a sticker on his car proclaiming, "We love you Ahmad Musa Daqamsa." A legal defense team that took up Daqamsa's case was headed by the leader of the Jordanian lawyers' syndicate. There were lawyers from other Arab lands, Lebanese and others, who volunteered to join Daqamsa's defense effort. It was claimed, on his behalf, that he had been sexually provoked and taunted by the young girls while he was praying. It was said by his defense team that he was but a soldier in an "eternal war" between Arab and Jew and that he could not be held responsible for what he did in that war. When a court sentenced him to a term of twenty-five years, more than a thousand university students in

Amman demonstrated in his support. The monarch who embraced the peace, the civil society that honored the old enmity: by now this had become a familiar spectacle.

Hazem Saghieh, a Lebanese journalist and a man who marches to his own drummer, who is never afraid to dissent from the prevailing political orthodoxy, saw the matter of Daqamsa for what it was: a window onto the culture, a way of reading its mood. In a short book published in Beirut in mid-1997 by Lebanon's best publishing house, Dar an-Nahar, entitled *In Defense of Peace,* Saghieh wrote that "the enthusiasm for Daqamsa revealed that a deep ailment afflicts Arab culture. This is a matter deeper than politics and it renders irrelevant who wins or loses in politics." The debate had been joined: from Ali Salem to Adonis to Hazem Saghieh, the break with the dominant Arab legacy was under way. True, the Arab advocates of accommodation were a distinct minority, but in a culture of nationalism where dissent from the prevailing norms had not been easy, many had found their courage and their voice.

Unloved and unclaimed, this great accommodation between Israel and Palestinian nationalism had a force all its own. It was bigger than the political players caught up in it. It had going for it the fatigue of the protagonists, their recognition of the entanglement of their destinies. The truth of this entanglement was captured in a dazzling work of fiction written in the mid-1980s, *Arabesques* by Anton Shammas, an Israeli Arab novelist of the finest literary sensibility—that the work was written in Hebrew by a Christian Arab from Galilee was a commentary all its own on the layers of this deadly, intimate conflict. In that work that summoned the fight for Palestine in 1948, Shammas produced one of the most memorable of metaphors for that conflict. The Palestinian narrator's Galilean village is about to fall to the Jewish forces, and from somewhere a flute is whipped out and to its strains, the villagers break out into a "dance which had in it something of the joy of those who had been passed over by a fatal decree, and something of the pleasure of submission by the weak, and something of fawning before the stranger, and something of the canniness of the villager who draws the most unexpected weapon at the most unexpected moment. . . . One way or the other by the time the feet tired of the dance and the capriciousness of the defeated had cooled down, all those present at the ceremony were covered with a thin layer of dust, and as is the way of all dust, it did not distinguish between the conquering soldier and the conquered villager." A swirl of dust had covered everyone there, and a nemesis overtook the victor's triumph. Vanquished, the Palestinians had hitched a ride on the coattails of a successful Zionist enterprise. As the world batters the modern Arab inheritance, the rhetorical need for anti-Zionism grows. But there rises, too, the recognition that it is time for the imagination to steal away from Israel and to look at the Arab reality, to behold its own view of the kind of world the Arabs want for themselves.

SOURCE NOTES

1. Prologue: The Inheritance

For the story of the poet Buland Haidari, I drew on his book *Ila Beirut* (To Beirut), London, Dar Al Saqi, 1989. There was a good eulogy of him, with his parting testimony, in the London-based magazine, *al-Majalla,* August 24, 1996. Hazem Nusseibah's testimony can be found in his essay "Arab Nationalism: Decades of Innocence and Challenge" in a book of essays, Patrick Seale, editor, *The Shaping of an Arab Statesman,* London, Quartet Books, 1983. There are many descriptions by foreign reporters of the Beirut hotel, the Commodore. The one I used was John Kifner's in the *New York Times,* February 20, 1987. Thomas Friedman's book, *From Beirut to Jerusalem,* New York, Doubleday, 1990, has an exquisite description of the Commodore as well. Nazira Zayn al-Din's book, *al-Sufur wa al-Hijab* (Unveiling and the Veil) was published in Beirut, 1928. For the narrative of the Salam family, I drew on Anbara Salam al-Khalidi's memoirs, *Jawla fi al-Dhikrayat bayna Lubnan wa-Filastin* (Recollections Between Lebanon and Palestine), Beirut, 1983, and the memoirs of her father, Salim Ali Salam, *Mudhakkirat Salim Ali Salam,* Beirut, 1982. For the history of the small fragment of Lebanon where I grew up (the southern hinterland), the best source is a multi-volume grab-bag by the religious scholar, Muhsin al-Amin, *A'yan al-Sh'ia,* Beirut, 1960–1963.

For George Antonius I drew on the archives of the Institute for Current World Affairs in Hanover, New Hampshire, and on the Antonius files in the Israel State Archives in Jerusalem, and the Public Record Office in London. For the life of Charles Crane, I read

Crane's papers and letters in Hanover. I also consulted a Ph. D. dissertation by Leo J. Bocage, *The Public Career of Charles R. Crane,* Fordham University, 1962.

2. *The Suicide of Khalil Hawi: Requiem for a Generation*

I read widely around and about Khalil Hawi: For his poetry the best place to begin is a work of interpretation and translation, *Naked in Exile: Khalil Hawi's The Threshing Floors of Hunger* by Adnan Haydar and Michael Beard, Washington, D.C., The Three Continents Press, 1984. For the translation of the poem "The Bridge" I use here Issa Boulatta's *Modern Arab Poets,* London, Heinemann, 1976. Tahar Ben Jalloun's eulogy was in *Le Monde des Livres,* July 9, 1982. Mahmoud Darwish's view of Hawi is in his book *Memory for Forgetfulness,* Beirut, August, 1982, Berkeley, University of California Press, 1995. Other eulogies, including one by his classmate, Munah al-Sulh, can be found in a special issue on Hawi by the literary journal *al-Fikr al-Arabi al-Muasir,* June–July 1983. This issue also contains a penetrating remembrance by the Iraqi writer, Daisy al-Amir, which is summed up in the text.

By far the most rewarding and the fullest source is the biography of the poet by his brother, Iliya Hawi, *Ma' Khalil Hawi: fi Masirat Hayatihi wa-Shi'rih* (With Khalil Hawi: On His Life and Poetry), Beirut, 1986.

There are countless portraits of Beirut and of Mount Lebanon at the end of the nineteenth century and in the early years of the twentieth century. Historians would find Engin Akarli, *The Long Peace: Ottoman Lebanon, 1861–1920,* Berkeley, University of California Press, 1993, quite useful. For my purposes and for reconstructing Hawi's own time and place and the world of his childhood, I draw on the following sources: Grace Dodge Guthrie, *Legacy to Lebanon,* (private printing, Richmond, Virginia, 1984) was exquisite. On her paternal side, Grace Dodge was the daughter of a president of the American University of Beirut; on her maternal side, the granddaughter of yet another president. She knew that world and that time—Lebanon in the First World War and in the 1920s. Her father's portrait of that time is drawn from her book. Another useful source is Ethel Stefana Drower, *Cedars, Saints and Sinners in Syria,* London, Hurst & Blackett, 1926.

Khalil Hawi's own perspective on Lebanon—the country, the mountain, the ways of its people—is fully elaborated in his Cambridge dissertation on his early literary hero, the poet Kahlil Gibran, *Khalil Gibran: His Background, Character and Works,* Beirut, 1972. Another helpful source for reconstructing the background of the American University of Beirut and the years of Anton Saadah in Lebanon is a charming account by Hawi's professor at the AUB, Anis Frayha, *Qabl An Ansa* (Before I Forget), Beirut, 1979. The essay by Leon Wieseltier quoted in the text, "Against Identity," was originally published in *The New Republic* but reprinted and expanded as a short book published by William Drenttel in New York, 1996.

Hisham Sharabi's memoirs, *al-Jamr wa al-Ramad* (Embers and Ashes), Beirut, 1975, is the most authoritative narrative of Saadah and of the politics of the mid-1940s in Beirut. Saadah's book, *al-Sira' al-Fikri fi al-Adab al-Suri* (The Intellectual Struggle in Syrian Literature), first published in Buenos Aires in 1943, then in Beirut in 1947 and 1953, is the most illuminating view we have of Saadah's "metaphysics" on Syrian social and cultural life.

There are several portraits of the American University of Beirut. I drew my narrative from Stephen Penrose, *That They May Have Life,* Beirut, Lebanon, 1970, and John Munro, *A Mutual Concern: The Story of the American University of Beirut,* Delmar, New York, Caravan Press, 1977. Charles Malik's depiction of the Greek Orthodox can be found in A. Wessels, *Arab and Christian/Christians in the Middle East,* Kampen, The Netherlands, Pharos Books, 1984.

The passage from Nietzsche is from *Thus Spoke Zarathustra* (translated by R. J. Hollingdale), Penguin Books, 1961.

Hawi's letters to Daisy al-Amir and his Cambridge interlude are in a book, Khalil Hawi, *Rasail al-Hubb wa al-Hayat* (Letters of Love and Life), Beirut, 1987. Also useful for this period of his life that I drew on and cited is Jamil Jabr, *Khalil Hawi,* Beirut, 1991.

Hawi's relation to the Arabic language, his eagerness as a Christian to proclaim the Arabic heritage as his own was best conveyed in an interview with him printed in the special issue on him of *al-Fikr al-Arabi al-Muasir,* already cited (June–July 1983). Iliya Hawi's novel, *Nabhan,* Beirut, 1986, afforded me a different insight into Khalil Hawi's life. Ihsan Abbas, *Ghurbat al-Ra'i* (The Shepherd's Exile), Amman, 1996, provides a good account of the decline of Beirut's intellectual life and of the troubles of the AUB in the late 1970s. I used and cited two essays from the latter years of Hawi as a measure of his disillusionment with the Arab "awakening" in culture: "Reason and Faith in Arab Culture," in *al-Fikr al-Arabi al-Muasir,* June 1980, and "The Awakening and the Search for Identity," December 1981–January 1982, of the same journal.

The poem by Bayati, written in Madrid, which was cited in the text appeared in the special issue of *al-Fikr al-Arabi al-Muasir,* June–July, 1983, dedicated to Hawi. Mahmoud Shurayh, *Khalil Hawi wa Anton Saadah* (Khalil Hawi and Anton Saadah), Sweden, 1995, retells the final days of Hawi and has a sophisticated understanding of the meaning of Saadah's life for Hawi.

Postscript: The Murder of Malcolm Kerr

For the life of Malcolm Kerr, and the narrative built around it, I drew on Stanley Kerr's *The Lions of Marash,* Albany, N.Y., State University of New York Press, 1973. Ann Zwicker Kerr's *Come with Me from Lebanon,* Syracuse, N.Y., Syracuse University Press, 1994, was invaluable. Two of Malcolm Kerr's essays cited in the text were "Arab Society and the West," in Patrick Seale, editor, *The Shaping of an Arab Statesman,* London, Quartet, 1983; and "Rich and Poor in the Arab Order," *Journal of Arab Affairs* I:1 (October 1981).

There are countless missionary narratives of the period and portraits of Beirut. The best is David Finnie, *Pioneers East: The Early American Experience in the Middle East,* Cambridge, Mass., Harvard University Press, 1967. W. M. Thomson's *The Land and the Book,* London, T. Nelson and Sons, 1872, is unrivaled in its beauty and detail and illustrations.

3. In the Shape of the Ancestors

Nizar Qabbani's reflections on Beirut were in the Kuwaiti daily, *al-Siyasa*, May 9, 1985. The poem "Balqees," one of the signal poems of Arab life in the 1980s, was widely available, in handwritten form by Qabbani. My former student Lisa Buttenheim translated it in 1986. I used her translation, with her permission, in my essay, "The Silence in Arab Culture," April 6, 1987. Adonis's book, *al-Shi'riyya al-Arabiyya* (Arabic Poetics), was published in Beirut in 1985. For the life and craft of Adonis, I drew on his literary autobiography, *Ha Anta Ayyuha al-Waqt* (Here You Are Time), Beirut, 1993. The translation of the Adonis poem, "Lamentations for Our Present Time," is mine. The Adonis poem, "The Desert," translated by Abdullah al-'Udhari, was published in an anthology of the works of Samih al-Qasim, Adonis, and Mahmoud Darwish, entitled *Victims of a Map*, London, Al Saqi Books, 1984. Abdelrahman Munif's reflections on Arabic literature and Arab political life and political exile can be found in his book *al-Kateb wa al-Manfa* (The Writer and Exile), Lebanon, 1992. His cycle of novels, *Cities of Salt*, has been translated and superbly so, by Peter Theroux, and published by Pantheon Books. The passages I quote are from the Theroux translation. Wilfred Thesiger was one of the great travel and desert chroniclers; his book, quoted in the text, *Arabian Sands*, published by Penguin Books in 1964, was his best and most memorable work.

Adonis's four-volume work, originally written in 1979, *al-Thabit wa al-Mutahawwil* (The Fixed and The Changing), to which he appended his reflections on Iran, was published by Dar Al Saqi, in London in 1994. Sadiq al-Azm's critique of Adonis was published in the Beirut journal *Dirasat Arabiyya*, February 1982.

The "open letter" to Khomeini by Mehdi Bazargan was circulated and published in 1986 by Maktab Publications, Houston, Texas.

The Trilogy of the Children of the Stones was published in 1988 by Nizar Qabbani Publications, Beirut, Lebanon, 1988.

"Passing Between Passing Words" was published in a Paris-based Arabic magazine, *The Seventh Day*. An English version of it was published in *The New Republic,* April 25, 1988. It was a joint effort by myself and Leon Wieseltier (who worked with a Hebrew translation!).

The Adonis poem about a people bewitched with a history written with chalks of illusion was published in *al-Hayat,* March 6, 1997. A big, creative book by Adonis, entitled *al-Kitab* (The Book), appeared in London and was published by Dar Al Saqi in 1995.

A report in *The Economist,* "When History Passes By," May 12, 1990, caught the Arab bewilderment in that "springtime of nations" in Europe—just before the Iraqi conquest of Kuwait. Mohamed Heikal's, "Out with the Americans, In With a New Arab Order," appeared in *The Times,* London, September 12, 1990. Robert W. Tucker and David C. Hendrickson, *The Imperial Temptation,* New York, Council on Foreign Relations Press, 1992, have an interesting depiction of the American mood prior to the Gulf War. John Stuart Mills' essay "A Few Words on Non-Intervention" appeared in *Dissertations and Discussions, Political, Philosophical, and Historical,* vol. 3, Boston, Mass., William Spencer, 1964–1967.

Three standard works on the Gulf War quoted in the text are Bob Woodward, *The Commanders,* New York, Simon & Schuster, 1991; James Baker III, *The Politics of Diplomacy,* New York, Putnam, 1995; and Colin Powell, *My American Journey,* New York, Random House, 1995.

Souad al-Sabah's writings on Kuwait appeared in *al-Hayat,* December 4, 1990, January 6, 1991, and February 6, 1991.

The passage from T. E. Lawrence on the reaction of the Arabs to the pounding the Turks received from General Allenby is from *Seven Pillars of Wisdom,* Penguin Classics, 1962.

4. In the Land of Egypt: The Saints and the Worldliness

Egyptian fiction remains unique in its ability to render the life of Egypt. From Naguib Mahfuz, I read and drew on *Amam al-Arsh* (Before the Throne), Cairo, 1983; *Yawm Outala al-Za'im* (The Day the Leader Was Killed), Cairo, 1985. And *Asda' al-Sira al-Dhatiyya*

(Echoes of an Autobiography), Cairo, 1997. Yusuf al-Qaid's *al-Harb fi Barr Misr* (War in the Land of Egypt), Cairo, 1979, has a superb portrait of the mind and the condition of Egypt in the 1970s. Sonallah Ibrahim's *Sharaf*, Cairo, 1997, also quoted in the text at some length, is incomparable for its sharp sense of realism about Egypt in the mid-1990s. Myral al-Tahhaoui's *al-Khiba* (The Tent), Cairo, 1996, has a feminist critique of the Islamic movement.

Ahmad Baha al-Din's *Muhawarati ma' al-Sadat* (My Conversations with Sadat), Cairo, 1987, is a fair and balanced retrospect of the Egyptian leader. Saad Eddin Ibrahim's *The Vindication of Sadat* was published in Arabic in Cairo in 1992, and in English (a shorter version) by the Washington Institute for Near East Policy, Washington, D.C., 1993. I used the fuller Arabic version. Farag Foda's *Qabl al-Suqut* (Before the Fall), Cairo, 1985, has the essentials of that secularist's views. Rifaat Said is an enormously prolific writer. In this text I used his works *Misr: Muslimin wa Aqbat* (Egypt: Muslims and Copts), Cairo, 1993; *Madha Jara li-Misr?* (What Happened to Egypt?), Cairo, 1991, and *Wa al-Samat La* (And No to Silence), Cairo, 1995.

For Nasr Hamid abu Zeid, I read his works *Naqd al-Khitab al-Dini* (The Criticism of Religious Discourse), Cairo, 1994; *al-Itijah al-Aqli fi al-Tafsir* (The Rational Approach to Interpretation), Cairo, 1993; and *Falsfat al-Ta'wil* (The Philosophy of Interpretation), Cairo, 1993. The daily *al-Hayat,* September 16, 1996, had an excellent interview, which I used, with the philosopher, conducted by Mahmoud Wardani, on his departure from Egypt.

Louis Awad, as my text makes clear, I think, stood out as one of the most distinguished figures in the world of Egyptian letters. His volume of memoirs, *Awraq al-Umr* (Notes of a Lifetime), published in 1989, quoted at considerable length in these pages, is a seminal work on university and cultural life in Egypt in the 1930s and 1940s. I also drew on his work *Tarikh al-Fikr al-Misri al-Hadith* (The History of Modern Egyptian Thought), Cairo, 1986.

The passage from Naguib Mahfuz in a conversation with the

American reporter Mary Anne Weaver is from *The New Yorker,* January 30, 1995; Hussein Ahmad Amin's reflections on the yearning for Egypt's past is from an article in *al-Hayat,* June 20, 1996. The passage from Louis Awad on the force of the renewal in Egyptian culture is from his book *Tarikh al-Fikr al-Misri al-Hadith* (The History of Modern Egyptian Thought), Cairo, 1986. A good and elegant statement of Egypt's pluralism is provided by Milad Hanna in his book *al-Amida al-Sabaa fi al-Shakhsiyya al-Misriyya* (The Seven Pillars of Egyptian Personality), Cairo, 1993.

Nizar Qabbani's "open letter" to Egypt was published in the magazine *al-Qahira,* February 1995.

Simon Schama's *Landscape and Memory,* New York, Vintage, 1995, has an elegant statement on the culture and symbolism of the Nile. Two other books that elaborate on the politics of the Nile are Wyman Herendeen, *From Landscape to Literature: The River and the Myth of Geography,* Pittsburgh, Pa., Duquesne University Press, 1986, and Emil Ludwig's moving tribute to that river and to Egypt, *The Nile in Egypt,* London, George Allen and Unwin, 1937.

5. *The Orphaned Peace*

The episode of Adonis's suspension from the Union of Arab Writers draws on a report in the *New York Times,* March 7, 1995, by Youssef Ibrahim; the attitude of the literary union was conveyed in their monthly journal, *al-Mawqif al-Adabi,* April 1995; the writer Saadallah Wannous's defense of Adonis can be found in the Lebanese daily, *al-Safir,* April 19, 1995; Hani al-Raheb's in the Kuwaiti journal *al-Arabi,* March 1995.

The Qabbani poem *"al-Muharwiluun"* (The Hurried Ones) appeared in *al-Hayat,* October 2, 1995. Naguib Mahfuz's commentary on that poem appeared in the same paper on October 5, 1995. Eight days later, in the pages of *al-Hayat* still, Qabbani gave his own defense of his poem and his view of the poet's craft, which is set out in the text.

The biography of Hajj Amin al-Husayni quoted in the text is by

Philip Mattar, *The Mufti of Jerusalem: Hajj Amin al-Husayni and The Palestinian National Movement,* New York, Columbia University Press, 1988.

Edward Said produced a very large body of writings in the aftermath of Oslo. He wrote regularly in *al-Hayat,* and his columns for that paper were then assembled and published in English in a book of essays, *Peace and Its Discontents,* New York, Vintage Books, 1995. Readers may want to consult as well his larger book, *The Politics of Dispossession,* New York, Pantheon Books, 1994. In his essay "The Mirage of Peace," *The Nation* (October 16, 1995), Said further elaborated the reasons for his opposition to the peace of Oslo.

Ghada Karmi's case that the Israeli-Palestinian accord of 1993 had wiped out the historic claims of the Palestinians was stated in her essay "What Role for the Palestinian Diaspora After Oslo?" in a collection entitled *Palestinian Elections and the Future of Palestine,* published by the Center for Policy Analysis on Palestine, Washington, D.C., 1996. For Hisham Sharabi's opposition to the peace of Oslo, see his reflections and remembrance of pre-1948 Palestine in *al-Hayat,* February 14, 1997; see also his article in the same paper, July 16, 1996, spelling out the case of the Diaspora Palestinians against the peace.

Meron Benvenisti's remarks on the terror that hit Israel in February–March 1996 are taken from his essay "The Twilight War," *The New Yorker,* March 18, 1996.

Edward Said's views on the Israeli elections, welcoming Benjamin Netanyahu's victory, can be found in *Time,* June 10, 1996. Mahmoud Rimawi's similar view was put forth in *al-Hayat,* June 10, 1996. Nizar Qabbani's words to an Arab summit that convened in June 1996 appeared in *al-Hayat,* June 21, 1996. Hazem Saghieh's report on "normalization" and the resistance to it is drawn from *al-Hayat,* April 9, 1996.

For Mohamed Heikal's views, I drew on the text of a lecture, available to me, which he gave to the students of the American University in Cairo, October 19, 1993. See also his *Misr wa al-Qarn al-Wahid wa al-Ishrin* (Egypt and the Twenty-First Century), Cairo, 1994.

Abdullah Laroui's remarks on Israel are from his book *The Crisis of the Arab Intellectual*, Berkeley, University of California Press, 1976.

The Egyptian critic and author Ghali Shukri is one of the brightest of the literary stars of Egypt. I have drawn on his *Balagh ila al Ra'i al-Amm* (A Declaration to Public Opinion), Cairo, 1988; and his *Mara'at al-Manfa* (The Mirror of Exile), London, Riad El-Rayyes Books, 1989.

The playwright Ali Salem's trip to Israel in early 1994 marked him among his peers in the artistic world of Egypt. His record of that journey, *Rihla ila Israeel* (A Passage to Israel), was published in Cairo in 1994.

The writer Muhammad Sid Ahmad's perspective on "normalization" with Israel is stated in *al-Ahram,* June 27, 1996.

Yusuf Idris's enchanting short story, "Innocence," was first published in *al-Adab,* June 1972. It was reprinted in his collection *Ana Sultan Qanun al-Wujud* (I am Lord of the Laws of the Universe), Cairo, 1980.

Amin Maalouf's beautiful novel, *Leo Africanus,* has been translated into English by Peter Sluglett and published by New Amsterdam Books, New York, 1992.

The options available to Israel in 1948 and sketched in my text were elaborated on by Avi Shlaim in his book *Collusion Across the Jordan,* New York, Columbia University Press, 1988. And for a different perspective, see Itamar Rabinovich, *The Road Not Taken,* Oxford and New York, Oxford University Press, 1991.

Lotfi al-Khuli's defense of the gathering at Copenhagen is best elaborated on in an essay by him in *al-Ahram,* April 29, 1997.

ACKNOWLEDGMENTS

———❦———

MANY PEOPLE SAW me through this endeavor: Three assistants at the Johns Hopkins School of Advanced International Studies were there for me. Laila al-Hamad looked everywhere for obscure Arabic sources, retrieved for me much of the trail of Khalil Hawi. Camille Pecastaing, a young scholar of endless curiosity, picked up where Laila left off; he tracked down sources and fiddled with the meter and style of the poems.

Megan Ring was a gift all her own. She did all but write this book, editing and re-editing draft after draft. In the Library of Congress and elsewhere, she found all kinds of fragments of the tale I tell here. For this exuberant woman from California, this Arab tale was oddly bleak, but she never wavered. For what she did for this book, for her dedication and friendship, she will always have my deep gratitude and affection.

Several friends took interest in this work and read parts or all of it: Tahseen Basheer, Leslie Gelb, Richard Ullman, Robert W. Tucker, Meron Benvenisti, Mark Danner, Stephen Szabo. No author could have had a better group of readers. The political philosopher Michael Sandel was a unique source of support, although he insisted that this subject lay beyond his expertise. Nevertheless, he illuminated many things for me along the way. Leon Wieseltier has been a friend, a critic, and a collaborator for many years. Some of what I have written bears his mark. For a long time now, he and Martin Peretz have given me access to *The New Republic*. I am grateful to them.

The filmmaker Tawfic Saleh, the playwright Ali Salem, Mahmoud Abaza, Abu Zeid Rageh, and Kamal El-Ebrashi taught me many things about Egypt. Their feel for their birthplace, their wonder at its ways and subtlety, were humbling. Michelle Ajami read or heard all of this—and more. Like Michael Sandel, she loves to proclaim her superficial knowledge of these matters. And like him, she knows more than she lets on.

James F. Hoge, Jr., and Fareed Zakaria, editor and managing editor of *Foreign Affairs,* gave me two assignments—particularly one on Egypt—that helped me research and rethink Egypt. I have been lucky to have them as collaborators and readers of my work. Mortimer Zuckerman, editor-in-chief of *U.S. News & World Report,* and his colleagues at the magazine have provided me a forum for several years now. I owe to *U.S. News* a trip to Egypt when I needed it.

I was blessed to have Linda Healey as editor. Years ago, I began an earlier book for her, but I faltered. Her faith never wavered. She returned with an assignment, and it was thanks to her that I had written a short book (with photographer Eli Reed) *Beirut: City of Regrets.* She came back to me yet again for this new endeavor. And in the midst of her own grief, in the summer of 1997, when she lost her beloved husband, the gifted journalist and writer Tony Lukas, to a premature and tragic death, she still had time for my own speck of small worries. What merit this book has is in no small measure owing to her belief in me.

SHEILA RENTAS AND Helen Haislmaier at Johns Hopkins helped with all sorts of support and administrative work.

INDEX

Abbas, Ihsan, 80, 90

Abd al-Wahhab, Muhammad ibn, 153

Abdullah, King of Jordan, 71, 262, 266, 294, 295, 296, 304

Abdul Rahman, Shaykh Omar, xv, 201, 208, 211, 252, 299

Abna al-Balad, 272

Abu-Odeh, Adnan, 308

Abu Warda, Fatima, 264

Abu Warda, Majdi, 264

Abu Zeid, Nasr Hamid, 212–21, 250

Acre, 13, 263, 267, 270

al-Adab, 80

Addis Ababa, 241–42

Adonis (Ali Ahmad Said), xii–xiii, 79, 80, 81, 111–12, 114–23, 297

  childhood and education of, 117, 119–20, 144

  criticism of, 143–44, 253–55

  Iranian revolution supported by, 142–46

  poetry and literary criticism of, 114–16, 120–23, 144–46, 164–65

  political sympathies of, 117, 121, 142–46

  Shia ancestry of, 119–20

Adonis, cult of, 118

Adonis River, 34, 118

Aflaq, Michel, 34

Afrika Korps, 58

After the Guns Fall Silent (Ahmad), 284

"Against Identity" (Wieseltier), 54

al-Ahali, 207

al-Ahram, 196, 221, 242, 250, 285, 309

Ajami, Dahir (Dahir the Persian), 14

Alawi sect, 134

Aleppo, 66, 101, 109

Alexander II, Tsar of Russia, 33

Alexander III, Tsar of Russia, 33

Alexander the Great, 245

Alexandria, 16–17, 19, 197, 202, 243

Alexandria: A History and a Guide (Forster), 16–17

Algeria, 171, 173, 201–2, 302

Ali, Caliph, 150, 151

Allenby, General, 188

Alrawi, Karim, 221

Amam al-Arsh (Before the Throne) (Mahfuz), 198–200

American Board of Commissioners for Foreign Missions, 101

American University of Beirut
   (AUB), 15, 17, 22, 26, 29, 30,
   34, 37, 53–54, 84, 100–105,
   120, 140, 143, 164
   Arabic department of, 71, 72,
      89, 90
   campus and gardens of, 60, 78,
      91, 98–99, 102
   "Darwin affair" rebellion at, 89,
      250
   founding of, 60, 102, 108
   Hawi as student and professor
      at, 26, 47, 57, 59–62, 63,
      67–69, 71, 77–78, 86–91, 96,
      98–99
   Lebanese and Palestinian rivalry
      at, 90
   library of, 44, 91
   medical school of, 89
   student rebellion at, 89
American University in Cairo, 101,
   197
al-Amida al-Sabaa fi al-
   Shakhsiyya al-Misriyya (The
   Seven Pillars of Egyptian
   Personality) (Hanna), 243–45
Amin, Ahmad, 228–29
Amin, Hussein Ahmad, 228–30
al-Amir, Aziza, 251
al-Amir, Daisy, 31–32, 71, 72–73,
   78, 94–95
Amir, Yigal, 306
Amman, 19, 65, 71, 176, 281,
   311
Amr Ibn al-As Mosque, 214
Anatolia, 57, 217
Andover Theological Seminary,
   106
Anglican Church, 33, 44, 71
Anglo-Saxon culture, 143, 250

annus mirabilis of 1989, 170,
   174–75
Antioch, 65–66
anti-Semitism, 17
Antonius, George, 16–24, 34, 103
Antonius, Katy Nimr, 17, 18, 22,
   23
Arab Awakening, The (Antonius),
   16, 17, 19, 23, 24, 34, 103
Arab culture:
   breakdown of, 3, 9, 27, 29, 30,
      103–4, 109, 123–24
   city Arabs vs. desert Arabs and,
      125–25, 172
   emphasis on family, clan, and
      religion in, 28, 30, 71, 74, 78,
      92, 111, 144, 148, 155
   Gulf Arabs vs. Arabs of the
      north in, 171–72
   impact of oil wealth on, 123–30,
      133, 169
   modernity in, xiv–xvi, 16, 92,
      97, 106, 114–15, 119, 123–24,
      148, 157, 164
   poetic tradition in, 45, 54–55,
      67, 76–81, 111–13, 117, 260,
      303, 304
   postcolonial age and, 76–77,
      117–18, 171
   social classes in, 30, 46–48, 49,
      55, 57, 59, 60–62, 74, 87–89,
      104, 108, 123–24, 131, 133–34
   traditional moral order of, 124
   Western thought vs. Islamic
      tradition in, 61–62, 114–16,
      140, 141, 165, 171
Arabesques (Shammas), 311
Arabian Peninsula, 19, 27, 55, 80,
   81, 118–19, 123, 124, 130, 145
Arabian Sands (Thesiger), 128–29

Arabic language, xix, 6, 20, 23, 24,
    29, 45, 57, 103, 116, 117
  impact of Christian secular
    writers on, 42–43
  poetry and literature of, 27, 29,
    62, 67–68, 72, 76–77, 79–81,
    92
Arabism, 76, 87, 100, 101, 102,
    146, 155, 156
Arab nationalism, xi, 4, 5, 7–9,
    11–14, 16, 20, 27, 29, 30, 32,
    51, 83–84, 120, 158
  chauvinism in, 8, 124
  collectivist assertions in, 55, 123
  declining colonial powers and,
    76–77, 117–18
  Germanic theories on, 137
  Greek Orthodox Church and,
    32–34, 64, 66
  impact of Six Day War on, 7,
    27, 83–84, 121, 123, 124, 130,
    143
  intellectuals support of, 123,
    131, 164
  radicalism in, 14, 105, 121, 123,
    125, 131–40, 171, 194
  secular tradition in, xi–xiii, 3, 6,
    30, 111, 133, 144, 157, 158,
    164
  see also pan-Arabism; specific
    states
Arab Predicament, The (Ajami),
    24
Arab Rebellion (1936–1939), 162,
    268–69
"Arab renaissance," xii–xvii, 5–6,
    9, 11, 14–15, 18–19, 24, 61,
    67, 76–81, 90–92, 119, 144
  decline of, 90, 103, 111–14,
    122–24

"Arab street," 176, 183
Arafat, Yasser, 62, 139, 185, 253,
    261–62, 265–68, 272–73, 276,
    283, 285
Arberry, A. J., 72
Argentina, 44, 51, 63, 65, 201
Arizona, University of, 104, 109
Armenia, 56–57
Armenian massacres, 102
Armenian refugees, 56–57, 101–2,
    109–10, 142
Arnoun, 25
Asda' al-Sira al-Dhatiyya (Echoes
    of an Autobiography)
    (Mahfuz), 226–27
al-Assad, Hafez, 139, 197
Assassination of a Nation, The,
    195
Assyrians, 57, 137
Ataya, Salima, 39–40, 48–49, 73,
    78, 79, 81, 91, 96, 97, 99–100
Ataya, Shafiq, 99
al-Atrash, Amal, 250–51
al-Atrash, Farid, 250–51
al-Atrash, Sultan Pasha, 46
Autumn of Fury, The (Heikal),
    195
Awad, Louis, 222–24, 225, 242–43,
    286–87, 288, 291
Awlad Haratina (The Children of
    Our Quarter) (Mahfuz), 211
Awraq al-Umr (Notes of a
    Lifetime) (Awad), 223
al-Azhar University, 204, 211, 213,
    222
al-Azm, Sadiq, xii–xiii, 143

Babylon, 184
Baghdad, xi, xiii, 3, 4, 125, 131,
    156, 167, 168, 172

Baghdadi, 157–58

Baha al-Din, Ahmad, 196–97

Bahrain, 153, 156, 178, 186

Baker, James, 182–83

Balfour, Lord, 52

Balfour Declaration, 295

"Balqees" (Qabbani), 113–14

Basheer, Tahseen, 204, 239–40

Basra, 168–69, 180

Ba'th party, 34, 69, 130, 139, 149, 171

Baudelaire, Charles Pierre, 117

Bayadir al-Ju' (The Threshing Floors of Hunger) (Hawi), 48

al-Bayati, Abdul al-Wahhab, 5, 79–80, 81, 85, 93–94

Baytar, Omar al-, 269

Bazargan, Mehdi, 147, 151–52

Beard, Michael, 48, 98

Beaufort Castle, 10–11, 107

Bedouins, 128, 168

Beirut, xi, xii, 3, 5–6, 7, 11–12, 18–21, 27, 28, 32, 41, 47, 49, 56, 60, 101–2, 131

    American mission in, 20, 21, 101

    bombing of Iraqi embassy in, 112

    fall of, 164

    intellectual and literary life of, 79–81, 85–86, 88–89, 94–95, 113, 119–20, 121, 164

    Martyrs' Square in, 38–39

    modernity in, 14–15, 113, 135

    nineteenth century, 35, 106–8

    violence and death in, 103, 112–13, 116, 121–22, 123, 136–37

    Western schools in, 14, 15, 17, 22

    see also East Beirut; West Beirut

Bekaa Valley, 37, 57, 104, 135, 141

Bell, Gertrude, 128, 190

Ben-Gurion, David, 304

Ben Jalloun, Tahar, 28

Benvenisti, Meron, 23–24, 277, 307

Berlin, Isaiah, 162–63

Berlin Wall, fall of, 174

Bible, 35, 43, 82, 106

Bidoon, 187

Bisharri, 74

Bliss, Daniel, 60, 102, 108

Bolshevik revolution, 33, 42, 66

Bonaparte, Napoleon, 200, 232–33

al-Borsa, 236

Boulatta, Issa, 27–28

Bourg Street: Haifa (Kanafani), 263

Bourj Hammoud, 56, 57

Braudel, Fernand, 49

"Bridge, The" (Hawi), xii, 27–28, 32, 77, 83, 94, 97

British army, 47, 58–59, 68

British Council (Beirut), 62

Browne, E. G., 148

Burckhardt, Jacob, 285

Burton, Sir Richard, 190

Bush, George, 175, 176, 179, 181, 182

al-Bustani, Butrus, 43

Buttenheim, Lisa, 113–14

Byblos, 34, 118

Byzantine Institute, 20

Byzantium, 33, 65–66

Cairo, xi, xvi, 8, 19–23, 101, 104, 119, 125, 131–32, 172, 196–97, 202–3

Cairo Times, 237

Cairo University, 212, 220, 222

Cambridge University, 16, 26, 50,
    71–73, 76, 77, 91, 96, 222

Camp David accords, 247, 286,
    309

Carter, Jimmy, 197

Carter Doctrine, 176

Catroux, Georges, 59

Cedars, Saints and Sinners in Syria
    (Drower), 41–42

Cénacle Libanais (al-Nadwa al-
    Lubnaniyya), 119

Central and Eastern Arabia
    (Palgrave), 154

Chaldeans, 57

Chicago, University of, 53, 269

Chicago Bulls, 109–10

China, 17–18

Chrara, Waddah, 140

Christianity, 32–34, 37–39, 41–43,
    65–66, 120, 131
    see also specific sects

Cities of Salt (Munif), 125–28,
    129–30

Claiming the Future, 275

Clinton, Bill, 262, 273

CNN, 274

Cold War, 175, 191, 280

Come with Me from Lebanon
    (Kerr), 102

Commanders, The (Woodward),
    175

Conrad, Joseph, vii, 300–301

Constantinople, 33, 36, 38, 66

Copts, 194, 202, 203–4, 206–10,
    221, 222, 243–45

Crane, Charles R., 17–18, 19, 20,
    22

Crane, John, 22–23

creationism, 89

Criticism of Religious Thought
    (Azm), 143

Crusades, 10–11, 66, 151

Da Vinci, Leonardo, 75

Damascus, xi, 10, 11, 19, 34–36,
    59, 63, 66, 69, 108, 126,
    131–34, 139, 143, 150–54,
    172, 197

Damascus University, 117, 254

Damiri, Adnan, 162

Daqamsa, Ahmad Musa,
    310–11

Dar an-Nahar, 311

Darwin, Charles, 89, 250

Darwish, Mahmoud, 28, 84,
    161–62, 266

Dawra, 56, 57

Dayan, Moshe, 292–93

Dayr al-Qamar, 16

Dead Sea, 188

de Gaulle, Charles, 59

democracy, 169, 170, 171

"Desert, The" (Adonis), 122

De Tott, Baron, 49

Dhahran, 174, 187–88, 192

Dickson, Harold, 154

al-Difa'a, 269

Dimashq Nizar Qabbani (Nizar
    Qabbani's Damascus)
    (Qabbani), 302–3

Diplomatic Club (Cairo), 245

Dodge, Bayard, 37, 41, 53, 60

Dodge, David, 102–3, 105

Dog River, 34

Dormition abbey, 24

Doughty, Charles, 190

Drower, Ethel Stefana, 41–42

Druze, 46, 54, 56, 105, 139

Duhur al-Shweir, 49

East Beirut, 14, 120, 170–71
East Jerusalem, 246
Egypt, xiii–xvi, 12, 17, 20, 51, 55,
        79, 118, 149, 168, 189,
        193–252
    American primacy in, 131,
        194–95, 197, 228, 234–35,
        245–46, 247
    civil disorder and terrorism in,
        202–12
    cult of the past in, 227–30
    economic conditions in, 234–38
    English campaign against, 7, 11,
        73, 76, 117, 123, 193–94
    Israeli peace agreement with,
        xv, 27, 123, 194, 197, 199,
        211, 247, 261, 281
    middle class in, 200–201
    military regime in, 118, 119,
        193–94, 199, 200
    myth of, 251–52
    Napoleon's invasion of, 200,
        232–33
    secularism and modernity in,
        xiv–xvi, 16, 55, 118, 200, 205,
        211, 221
    Sinai Peninsula returned to, 195
    Six Day War defeat of, 121,
        177–78, 194, 195, 215, 246
    theocratic politics in, xiv,
        200–221
    Yemen War of, 173
Egyptian Committee for National
        Unity, 206–7
Egyptian General Association of
        the Book, 248–49
Egyptian Organization for Human
        Rights, 202
Eisenhower, Dwight D., 13–14
ESPN, 109

ethnicity, 4, 6, 8–9, 155
Euphrates River, 52, 90, 151, 169
Exile's Return (Turki), 264

Faisal II, King of Iraq, 5, 14
al-Fajr, 162
Falsafat al-Ta'wil (The Philosophy
        of Interpretation) (Zeid),
        216–19
al-faqih al-askari (armed jurist),
        142, 145–46
fascism, 51, 73, 224–25
"Fathers and Children: Turgenev
        and the Liberal Predicament"
        (Berlin), 162–63
Fathers and Sons (Turgenev),
        162–63
Al Fawwar refugee camp, 264
Fawzi, Hussein, 286–88, 291
"Few Words on Non-Intervention,
        A" (Mill), 179
Fi al-Shi'r al-Jahili (On Pre-Islamic
        Poetry) (Hussein), 219–20
Filastin, 269
Fisk, Pliny, 106
Flaubert, Gustave, 58
Foda, Farag, 202, 205–7, 209–10
Forrestal, James, 61
Forster, E. M., 16–17
Foucault, Michel, 215
France, 14, 16, 32, 35–36, 37, 38,
        56, 66, 98, 116
    colonial decline of, 55, 58,
        117–18
    colonial power of, 16, 18, 21, 46,
        52, 53, 55, 75, 117, 120
    literature and culture of, 58,
        117, 120, 143
Franciscans, 56
Frayha, Anis, 53, 54, 72, 90

Free French, 59
Freemasons, 281
French revolution, 147
Freud, Sigmund, 68, 88

Galilee, 10, 13, 270
Gamaat Islamiyya, 202–4
Gaza Strip, 59, 158–61, 163–64,
    171, 262, 265, 266–67
German language, 53, 58, 69–70
Germany, Federal Republic of, 170
Germany, Imperial, 36
Germany, Nazi, 55, 58
Ghazali, Shaykh Muhammad, 209
Gibran, Kahlil, 58, 74–77, 93, 96
Glasgow, University of, 42
Golan Heights, 47
Goncourt Prize, 300
Goodell, William, 106
Gramsci, Antonio, 215
Great Britain, 17, 56, 58, 66, 71–73
    anticolonial movement in, 73,
        76, 190–91
    colonial power of, 4, 5, 21, 47,
        58–59, 75, 168–69
    Kuwaiti interests of, 172–73,
        178, 186
    Suez role of, 38, 73, 178, 179
Greco-Roman civilization, 118,
    120, 243
Greek Orthodox Church, 16, 23,
    26, 41–42, 44–45, 50, 54, 62,
    87, 142
    Arab nationalism and, 32–34,
        64, 66
Greek philosophy, 80, 216
Guthrie, Grace Dodge, 41, 60

Habash, George, 62
Habboub, Saniyya, 15

Haganah, 270
Haidari, Buland, 3–9, 79
Haidari, Daud Pasha, 4
Haifa, 161, 263, 264, 267
al-Hakim, Tawfic, 286–88, 290,
    291
Hama, 139
Hamas movement, 164, 277, 307
Hammam, Nasib, 82
Hanna, Milad, 243–45
al-Harb fi Barr Misr (War in the
    Land of Egypt) (Qaid),
    230–32
Hassan, Imam, 150, 153
al-Hassan, Ja'far Hadi, 297
Hawi, Iliya, 30–31, 38, 78–79, 85,
    90–91, 93, 96
Hawi, Khalil, 26–36, 56–60
    Anton Saadah and, 50–51, 56,
        58, 66–67, 73, 81, 83, 86, 92
    Arab nationalist fervor of, 27,
        29, 30, 32, 34, 51, 56, 62,
        67–68, 77, 81–82, 83–84, 96,
        97, 111
    birth and village boyhood of,
        xii, 27, 29–30, 31, 32, 35,
        40–41, 42, 44–50
    British army job of, 47, 58–59,
        68
    education of, 26, 29, 30, 42,
        44–45, 47, 50, 58, 59–60, 62,
        63, 67–69, 71–77
    eulogies for, 28–29, 30, 94, 96,
        97
    fame and success of, xii, 77, 83,
        94–95
    Gibran dissertation of, 74,
        75–77, 93, 96
    Greek Orthodox faith of, 26,
        32, 34, 44–45, 50, 87

Hawi, Khalil *(continued)*
    poetry and intellectual life of,
        26–29, 30, 32, 45, 47, 48,
        49–50, 58, 62, 63, 67–76, 78,
        82–83, 90, 94–95
    political development of, 50–51,
        56, 62–63, 67, 81–82, 83–84
    poverty and manual labor of,
        xii, 30, 40–41, 45, 47–49, 50,
        56–58, 60, 63, 75, 77, 92, 96
    professorship of, 26, 47, 57, 71,
        77–78, 89–91, 96, 98–99
    suicide of, xi–xii, 26, 27, 28, 30,
        31, 32, 84, 93–94, 95–96,
        99–100, 111, 164
    troubled and solitary personal
        life of, xii, 26–27, 29, 30,
        31–32, 47–49, 71–72, 78–79,
        86–87, 89–99
Hawi, Salim, 40, 43, 45–47, 48–49,
    78, 79, 97
Hawi, Salima Ataya, *see* Ataya,
    Salima
Hawi, Sami, 79
Hawran, 37, 39, 46
al-Hayat (London), 256, 259, 278,
    297
Haydar, Adnan, 48, 97–98
Hebron, 308
Heikal, Mohamed, 130, 172, 195,
    247, 282–83
Heller, Mark, 284
Hendrickson, David, 174–75
Herzen, Alexander, 142, 298
hisba doctrine, 212
Hitler, Adolf, 53, 58
Hizbollah, *see* Party of God
Hofuf, 154–55
Holy Land, 106–7
Holy See, 32

Holy Trinity Church, 33
Hourani, Albert, 114
Hugo, Victor, 58, 140
Huleh Lake, 13
humanism, 120
al-Husayni, Abdul Qadir, 270
al-Husayni, Hajj Amin, 265–66
Hussein, Adel, 204
Hussein, Imam, 137, 150–51,
    152–53, 154, 155
Hussein, King of Jordan, 177,
    294–96
Hussein, Saddam, xiii, 137–39,
    149, 150, 156, 165–85
    Arab states in coalition against,
        176–77, 180, 189
    chemical weapons of, 8, 171,
        173, 180
    despotism and terrorism of,
        167–68, 170, 173, 177,
        180–81, 189–90
    invasion of Kuwait by, 165–66,
        167–68, 170–71, 173–77, 262
    Iranian war launched by, 149,
        155, 166, 171
    see also Persian Gulf War
Hussein, Taha, 219–21, 224, 229,
    290
Hussein, Udday, 180

Ibn Arabi, 217–19
Ibn Saud, King of Saudi Arabia,
    178
Ibrahim, Saad Eddin, 197–98
Ibrahim, Sonallah, 237–38
Idris, Yusuf, 286–87, 288, 292–93
Ikwan zealots, 178
Imperial Temptation, The (Tucker
    and Hendrickson), 174–75
In Defense of Peace (Saghieh), 311

Institute for Current World Affairs
    (ICWA), 18–23
International Monetary Fund, 235
In the Land of Israel (Oz), 306
Intifada, 158–64, 167
Iran, 14, 103
    American hostages held by, iv,
        103, 105, 175
    despotism and rebellion in,
        148
    Khuzistan province in, 137–38
    national and cultural tradition
        in, 149
    oil prosperity in, xiii, 124, 133
    Shah overthrown in, 147–48
    Shia Muslims in, 142–43, 147,
        149, 150–51, 153, 170
    U.S. arms sales to, 167
Iranian revolution, xii, 133, 137,
        138–52, 155, 201
    Arab opposition to, 140,
        143–44, 147, 149–51, 158
    "armed jurist" in, 142, 145–46
    political goals of, 146, 148–49
    see also Islamic fundamentalism
Iran-Iraq War, 9, 137–38, 146–47,
        149, 155–56, 166, 167, 171
Iraq, 3–5, 52, 59, 79–80
    American sanctions against,
        188–89
    British power in, 4, 5, 168–69
    Iran war with, *see* Iran-Iraq War
    Kurdish campaigns of, 8,
        179–83, 189
    monarchy in, 3, 4–5, 13–14
    1958 revolution in, 4–5, 13–14
    Shia majority in, 134, 137–39,
        148–49, 169, 179–82
    specter of "Lebanization" of,
        181, 183

    see also Hussein, Saddam;
        Persian Gulf War
Iraqi Cultural Center (Beirut),
        94–95
Irgun, 270, 271
Islam, 11, 29, 43, 65–66, 118–19,
        244
    cultural norms of, 15, 16, 103,
        124
    mysticism of, 120
    philosophy of, 29, 73, 92
    seventh century rise of, 65, 66,
        137, 145, 157
    Western thought vs., 61–62,
        114–16, 140, 141, 165, 171
    see also specific Muslim sects
Islamic fundamentalism, 7–8,
        130–32
    Arab politics and, 133–34, 158,
        201
    millennium promise in, 133,
        140, 155
    oil wealth and rise of, 130, 133
    sectarian elements in, 133–35,
        139
    see also Gamaat Islamiyya;
        Iranian revolution; Shia
        Muslims
Ismael Pasha, 233
Israel, xvi–xvii, 157
    Egyptian peace agreement with,
        xv, 27, 123, 194, 197, 199,
        211, 247, 261, 281
    establishment of, xvi, 13
    immigration of Russian Jews to,
        170
    Lebanese territory occupied by,
        136
    Persian Gulf War and, 171,
        184–85

Israeli-Palestinian conflict,
    xvi–xvii, 13, 19, 29, 52, 60,
    62, 84–85, 87, 253–75
  in Lebanon, xi–xii, 10, 26,
    98–99, 100–101, 123, 135–36
Israeli War of Independence
    (1948), 13, 29, 60, 88, 270
Israel State Archives, 18
Istanbuli, Khalid, 193–94, 195,
    200
Italian Commission, 22
al-Itijah al-Aqli fi al-Tafsir (The
    Rational Approach to
    Interpretation) (Zeid),
    215–16

Jabal Amil, 135
Jabal Druze, 39–40, 41, 250–51
Jabalya, 159
Jabotinsky, Vladimir, 305
Jabr, Jamil, 73, 96
Ja'far al-Sadiq, Imam, 155
Jafet, Nami, 44
Jaffa, 33, 61, 263, 267, 269
Jamal Pasha, Ahmad (al-Saffah,
    the Bloodshedder), 38–39
al-Jamr wa al-Ramad (Embers and
    Ashes) (Sharabi), 61–62,
    64–65, 268–71
al-Jarida, 51
al-Jazzar Mosque, 270
Jericho, 262–63
Jerusalem, 17, 18, 19, 22–24, 33,
    66, 106
  Christian presence in, 23–24,
    33, 106
  pilgrimages to, 33
  terrorism in, 264, 277, 307
Jesuits, 42, 43, 44–45, 120
Jewett, James R., 89

jihad (holy war), 171
al-Jihad al-Islami (Islamic Holy
    War), 105
Jordan, 47, 52, 121, 125, 132, 138,
    246–47, 274, 285
Jordan, Michael, 109
Jordanian Parliament, 295
Jordan River, 262, 265
Judaism, 244, 281
al-Jumhuriyah, 181
Junblatt, Kamal, 105, 139–40
Junblatt, Walid, 105

Kanafani, Abdul-latif, 263
Karbala, 137, 138, 150–53, 155,
    180–82
Karmi, Ghada, 267–68
Kastel, battle of, 270
Kepel, Gilles, 219
Kerr, Ann Zwicker, 100, 102, 108,
    109
Kerr, Elsa, 100, 102, 108
Kerr, Malcolm, 100–106, 108–10
  as AUB president, 100–101,
    102–4
  murder of, 100, 102, 104, 105,
    109, 110
Kerr, Stanley, 100, 101–2, 108,
    109–10
Kerr, Steve, 109–10
al-Khal, Yusuf, 80, 121
Khalaf, Nadim, 89
Khalaf, Samir, 89
Khalidi, Ahmad, 88, 89
Khalidi, Walid, 297
Khalidi family, 88–89
Khalil, Ataya Salima, *see* Ataya,
    Salima
Kharj, 192
Khawaqa complex, 195

Khomeini, Ayatollah Ruhollah,
xii, 133, 137, 140–41, 142,
145–53, 167, 201
exile and return of, 142, 148
Iraqi campaign of, 137–38,
146–47, 150, 152, 155, 168,
171
liberal criticism of, 151–52
stern clerical ruling style of,
150–53, 171
see also Iranian revolution
Khouri, Rami, 308
Khouri, Samira, 97
al-Khuli, Lotfi, 308–9
King, Henry C., 18
King, Larry, 274
King-Crane Commission, 18
Kissinger, Henry, 197, 247
al-Kitab (The Book: Yesterday, the
Place, Now) (Adonis), 165
Korzeniowski, Apollo, 300
Kufa, 151, 152
Al Kulliyah al-Arabiyya (Arab
College), 88
Kurdistan, 8, 169, 180, 182–83, 189
Kurds, 4, 6, 8, 101, 137, 169,
179–81, 182–83
Kuwait, xiii, 155–58, 165–71, 184,
188–89, 196
American presence in, 184–87
British protection of, 172–73,
178, 186
emirate of, 168, 169, 170, 184,
185–86
history of, 169, 176, 185–87
1961 Iraqi invasion of, 173
1990 Iraqi invasion of, 165–66,
167–68, 170–71, 173–77, 262
oil prosperity in, 169, 186, 275
Kuwait City, 185, 187

Kuwait University, 156–57, 158

Labor Zionism, 305, 306
"Lamentations for Our Present
Time" (Adonis), 121–22
Land and the Book, The
(Thomson), 106–8
Landscape and Memory
(Schama), 252
Laroui, Abdallah, 284
Latakia, 117, 119, 120
Lawrence, T. E., xi, 188, 190
"Lazarus 1962" (Harvi), 97–98, 99
League of Arab States, 248
Lebanese University, 91
Lebanon, 5, 8, 9–18, 25, 62–64, 73
American presence in, 11,
13–14, 21, 78, 100–101, 103,
105–10, 141
attack on U.S. Marine
headquarters in, 101, 105, 141
British presence in, 21, 47,
58–59, 75
Christian presence in, 30,
32–33, 37, 41–43, 59, 60, 64,
66, 84, 85, 86, 87, 104, 106–8
1975–1976 civil war in, 84, 85,
86, 87, 90, 95, 100
failed 1961 coup d'etat against,
81
famine and hardship in, 36–38,
51, 85, 97, 101
French trusteeship of, 16, 18, 21,
55, 75
Greek Orthodox Church in, 32,
41–42, 44–45, 50, 64, 87, 142
hill country of, 34–35, 49–50,
54, 69, 72, 84, 101, 106, 108,
118, 252
history of, 102, 118

Lebanon *(continued)*
  indifference of Arab states to
    fate of, 27, 85, 138
  Israeli military campaign in, 277
  Israeli occupation of, southern
    territory in, 136
  Mediterranean identity of, 5,
    49, 80, 108
  multinational forces in, 100–101
  mythology of, 118
  1982 Israeli attack on, xi–xii,
    10, 26, 98–99, 100–101, 123,
    135–36
  Ottoman rule of, 15–16, 17, 18,
    36–39, 51, 89
  Palestinian sanctuary in, 26,
    56–57, 62, 67, 80, 84–85, 88,
    132, 135–37
  refugee settlements, 56–57, 62,
    88, 101–2, 132, 136–37, 142
  sectarianism of, 52, 53, 63, 86,
    101, 105
  Shia Muslims in, 133–37
  silk industry in, 35–36, 42
  Syrian campaign for, 139
  Vichy French expelled from, 47,
    58–59
  *see also specific Ottoman
    territories*
Legacy to Lebanon (Guthrie), 41
Leiden University, 212
Leo Africanus (Maalouf),
  299–300, 301
Leo X, Pope, 299
liberalism, xv, 114, 162, 224–25,
  228–29
Likud party, 307
Lions of Marash, The (Kerr), 102
Litani River, 10, 107
London, 3, 6, 9, 18, 73, 209

Ludwig, Emil, xiv
Luther, Martin, 41

Maalouf, Amin, 299–301
McGill University, 27
Madbuli bookshop, 250
Madrid Peace Conference (1991),
  272
Mahfuz, Naguib, xiv–xvi, 8,
  198–200, 202, 210–12, 221,
  225–27, 230, 255, 259–60,
  286–87, 288, 290
al-Majalla (Brazil), 51
al-Majalla (London), 9
al-Majid, Ali Hassan, 180–81
Malik, Charles, 66
Marash, 57, 101–2, 109
Mar Elias, 41–42
Marines, U.S., 11
  terrorist attacks on, 101, 105,
    192
Maronites, 14, 32, 41–42, 53, 54,
  64, 66, 84, 85, 87, 105,
  135–36, 244
Marxism, 233
Mary Magdalene, Church of, 33
Mawaqif, 121
Mecca, 171, 217
*Mediterranean and the
  Mediterranean World in the
  Age of Philip II, The*
  (Braudel), 49
Mediterranean Sea, 5, 34, 49, 52,
  55, 57, 65, 80, 102, 108, 118,
  192, 247, 263
Memoirs from the Women's Prison
  (El-Saadawi), 195
Mesopotamia, 168
Metullah, 13
Middle Ages, 149

Mill, John Stuart, 179, 181

Milton, John, 142

Morocco, 149, 173, 262

Moskobiyya School, 42

al-Mostaqbal, 113

Mount Hermon, 10

Mount Lebanon, xii, 14, 16, 26, 29, 35–37, 39, 40, 42–43, 49–51, 74, 76–77, 97, 244

Mount of Olives, 18, 33

Mount Sannin, 29, 34–35, 73

Mount Scopus, 18

Mount Zion, 23–24

Mubarak, Hosni, 131, 201, 204–5, 228, 234, 238–42, 279, 280–81, 286

Muhammad (Prophet), 134, 137, 147, 150, 151, 187, 205

Muhammad Ali, 200, 233

"al-Muharwiluun" (The Hurried Ones) (Qabbani), 255–61

Muhawarati ma' al-Sadat (My Conversations with Sadat) (Baha al-Din), 196–97

Munif, Abdelrahman, xii–xiii, 125–30, 297

al-Muqadisi, 261–62

Muslim Brotherhood, 139, 203, 209, 228, 233

al-Mussawar, 221

Mussolini, Benito, 55–56, 225

al-Mutanabbi, 229

Mu'tazilah movement, 215–16

My Past and Thoughts (Herzen), 298

Nabhan (Hawi), 31, 78–79, 90–91, 93, 96

an-Nahar (Beirut), 64, 272

al-Nahhas, Mustafa, 199

Nahr al-Ramad (River of Ashes) (Hawi), 27, 77, 82–83

Naimy, Mikhail, 75

Najaf, 138, 180, 181–82

Nakash, Yitzhak, 181–82

Naqd al-Khitab al-Dini (Criticism of Religious Discourse) (Zeid), 214–15

nasab (genealogy), 87

Nasser, Gamal Abdul, 11–12, 13, 88, 130, 131, 138, 146, 149, 158, 168, 170, 172, 177–78, 198, 204, 207, 234, 239, 240, 245

death of, 255

Free Officer revolution of, 193–94, 199, 200, 223, 227, 250

Suez Canal nationalized by, 302

Yemen invaded by, 173

nativism, xii, xiii, 90, 146

Natural Born Killers, 281

al-Nay wa al-Rih (The Flute and the Wind) (Hawi), 67–68

NBA basketball league, 109–10

Near East Relief, 101

neo-Wahhabism, 153

Netanyahu, Benjamin, 273, 278–79, 307–8

"new world order," 176, 184

New York, N.Y., 7, 74, 104, 108, 209, 252

New York Times, 270

Niebuhr, Carsten, 169

Nietzsche, Friedrich Wilhelm, 68, 69–70

"Night of Long Knives," 162

Nile in Egypt, The (Ludwig), xiv

Nile River, xiv, 90, 247, 252

Nimr, Faris Pasha, 17, 22, 23, 250

Nobel Prize, 210, 262

No Trumpets, No Drums
    (Nusseibah and Heller), 284

Nusseibah, Anwar, 284

Nusseibah, Hazem, 7

Nusseibah, Sari, 284, 308–9

October War of 1973, 123, 130,
    131–32, 194, 198, 247, 282–83

Odessa, 33

oil industry:
    Arab politics and, 172–74
    corruption of the "desert
        world" by, 124–29
    economic downturn in, xiii,
        124, 275–76
    intellectual distrust of, 124–30
    Western interests in, 125–26,
        130, 133, 155, 188
    "windfall society" spawned by,
        xiii, 123–24, 126, 130, 133,
        169

Oliver, Daniel, 42

Oman, 178, 262

Omar ibn al-Khattab Mosque, 278

Operation Desert Storm, 176, 188,
    247
    see also Persian Gulf War

Operation Grapes of Wrath, 277

Organization of African Unity,
    241

Oslo Accords, 253, 256–58,
    261–62, 266–67, 273, 274,
    276, 280, 282

Ottoman empire, 4, 131, 168–69,
    186, 233
    decline of, 36, 283
    Fourth Army of, 38
    German alliance with, 36
    Young Turks of, 36, 38, 56

*see also specific Ottoman
    territories*

Oz, Amos, 268, 271, 306

Pahlavi, Muhammad Reza, Shah
    of Iran, 12, 149, 178, 196
    fall of, 147–48

Palestine, 12–13, 17, 18, 51, 58, 59,
    106, 261
    Arab-Israeli struggle in,
        xvi–xvii, 13, 19, 29, 52, 60,
        62, 84–85, 87, 253–75
    British mandatory government
        in, 19
    Ottoman rule of, 28

Palestine Department of
    Education, 17

Palestine Liberation Organization
    (PLO), 26, 84, 139, 159, 185,
    272, 282

Palestine National Authority, 267,
    268

Palestine National Council, 266,
    273, 283

Palestine National Covenant, 273

Palestinian Federation of Women,
    185

Palestinian National Movement,
    51, 130, 131, 132, 161, 261–75

Palestinians:
    guerrilla warfare of, 132, 135,
        158–64, 167, 267
    in Lebanon, 26, 56–57, 62, 67,
        80, 84–85, 88, 132, 135–37
    leftist elements of, 84
    literati and upper classes of, 62,
        80, 143, 159, 263
    in refugee camps, 263, 264
    Saddam Hussein supported by,
        171, 265

Palestinian-Shia war, 136–37
Palgrave, William Gifford, 154,
    190
pan-Arabism, 67, 80, 83, 84, 96,
    102, 118, 120–21, 124, 130,
    131, 146, 169, 173, 234,
    245–46
Paradise Lost (Milton), 142
Paris, 6, 28, 126, 161, 253
    fall of, 58
Paris Peace Conference of 1919, 18
Parsons, Levi, 106
Parti Populaire Syrien, 51, 62, 81,
    83, 86
Party of God (Hizbollah), 139,
    140, 153, 273
"Passing between Passing Words"
    (Darwish), 161–62
paternalism, 61, 172
Pax Americana, xiii, 178, 186, 192,
    196, 285, 296
Pax Britannica, 154, 178, 179, 186,
    191, 233
peace movement, 161, 194
Penrose, Stephen, 61
Peres, Shimon, 253, 261, 262, 265,
    273–74, 276–78, 291
Persia, 80, 137, 149
Persian Gulf, 103, 104, 124–25,
    130–31, 156
    dynastic states of, 138, 147–48,
    153–54, 169, 170
Persian Gulf War, xiii, 173–83, 274
    air campaign in, 184
    American role in, 175–83, 188
    events leading to, 165–68,
    170–71, 173–75
    ground war in, 182
    Kurdish and Shia rebellion in
    aftermath of, 179–83, 189

Scud missiles launched against
    Israel and Saudi Arabia in,
    184
    see also Hussein, Saddam;
    Kuwait
Persian language, 17, 149
Peter, Saint, 65–66
petro era, 124, 132–33
Phalange Party, 105
Phoenicians, 37, 118, 120
Politics of Diplomacy, The
    (Baker), 183
Powell, Colin, 182
Prophet, The (Gibran), 74–75
Protestantism, 54
    missions and schools of, 30,
    32–33, 37, 41, 42, 43, 59, 60,
    66, 89, 106–8, 110
Protocols of the Elders of Zion,
    281

Qabbani, Ahmad Abu Khalil, 249,
    250
Qabbani, Balqees, 112–14
Qabbani, Nizar, xii–xiii, 27, 79,
    81, 111–14, 121, 159–61,
    248–49, 255–61, 276, 279–80,
    297, 302–4
Qabl al-Suqut (Before the Fall)
    (Foda), 205–6
Qaddafi, Muammar, 131
Qadisiyyat Saddam, 137–38, 155
al-Qahira, 248–49
Qaid, Yusaf al-, 230–32
Qardawi, Yusuf, 278
Qasida, 67, 81, 260, 303, 304
Qatar, 178, 189, 262, 278
Qatif, 155
Quakers, 54
Quincy School, 74

Quran, 120, 213, 214, 215–16, 218, 219, 222

Rabin, Leah, 296
Rabin, Yitzhak, 261, 262, 265, 266, 272, 276, 280, 294–95, 305–6
al-Ra'd al-Jarih (The Wounded Thunder) (Hawi), 86
al-Raheb, Hani, 254–55
Ras Beirut, 57, 77–78
Reagan, Ronald, 167
Red Cross, 16
Reginald of Sidon, 11
relief agencies, 57
Republican Guard, 177, 180
Reuters, 10
"Rich and Poor in the Arab Order" (Kerr), 103–4
Rihla ila Israeel (A Passage to Israel) (Salem), 289–90
Rilke, Rainer Maria, 117
Rimawi, Muhammad, 278
River Orantes, 65
Riyadh, 187, 192
Rockefeller, David, 197
Rogers, Walter, 19–20, 21–23
Roman Catholic Church, 32, 33, 41, 66, 244
    missions and schools of, 42, 44–45, 56, 66, 120
Roman empire, 65, 80, 98, 113, 244
Rushdie, Salman, xv, 216
Russia, 17, 33, 45, 162–63
Russian Orthodox church, 33, 42, 45
Rustum, Asad, 44

Saab, Najib, 95
Saad, Charles, 59
Saad, Taniyus, 59

Saadah, Anton, 50–56, 58, 63–67, 69, 86
    arrests and execution of, 51, 56, 64–65, 67, 71, 81, 83
    cult followers of, 50–51, 56, 58, 66–67, 73, 81, 83, 86, 92, 117, 120, 268
    intellectual pretensions of, 52, 53–54, 65
    revolutionary political philosophy of, 50–51, 52–53, 54–56, 62–64, 65, 71, 73
    South American years of, 50, 51–52, 54, 62, 63, 65
    Syrian nationalism and, 52–53, 55, 63–64, 65, 66, 67, 81, 83, 121
Saadah, Khalil, 44, 51–52
El-Saadawi, Nawal, 195
al-Sabah, Mubarak, 185–86
al-Sabah, Souad, 155–56, 166–67, 184–85
al-Sadat, Anwar, 131, 138, 193–201, 206, 207, 215, 227, 239–41, 285
    assassination of, xiii–xiv, 193, 194, 196, 197, 201, 211, 225, 240, 266, 292
    character and personality of, 195–97
    democratic principles of, 196
    fictional treatment of, 198–200
    Israeli peace agreement secured by, 194, 197, 199, 211, 261
    Jerusalem visit of, 292
    political opposition to, 194, 195–96, 197
    repressive arrests by, 194, 195, 197
    Western sympathies of, 196–97

al-Sadat, Jihan, 195, 197, 201
al-Sadr, Ayatollah Muhammad
    Baqir, 149
Safad, 13
Saghieh, Hazem, 281, 311
Said, Ali Ahmad, *see* Adonis
Said, Edward, 262, 266–67, 272, 297
Said, Rifaat, 203, 207–8, 209–10
Saint Sophia church, 33
Salam, Anbara, 16, 18, 88
Salam, Salim Ali, 15–16, 88
Salame, Ghassan, 297
Salam family, 15–16, 88–89
Salam Saeb, 16, 88–89
Saleh, Tawfic, xiv–xv
Salem, Ali, 289–91
Salibi, Kamal, 89
Sarruf, Yaqub, 250
Satanic Verses (Rushdie), xv
Saudi Arabia, 12, 104, 125, 138,
    147, 148, 167
    American role in, 174, 187–88,
        191
    dynastic rule in, 153–54
    oil fields of, 173, 188
    Shia Muslims in, 153–55
    Wahhabi zealots in, 178, 186
Sayigh, Tawfiq, 80
Schama, Simon, 252
Schiff, Ze'ev, 159
Schindler's List, 281
Scotland, 42
secular tradition, xi–xiii, 3, 6, 30,
    111, 133, 144, 157, 158, 164
    in Egypt, xiv–xvi, 16, 55, 118,
        200, 205, 211, 221
    theocratic politics and, xii, xv,
        7, 71, 77, 141–43, 171
Self-Criticism after the Defeat
    (Azm), 143

Serageddin, Fuad Pasha, 227–28
Seven Pillars of Wisdom
    (Lawrence), xi
Seventh Day, The, 161
Shaarawi, Shaykh Muhammad,
    215
Shahin, Shaykh Abdul Sabbur,
    213–14
Shammas, Anton, 311
Sharabi, Hisham, 61–62, 64–65,
    83, 268–71, 297
Sharaf (Ibrahim), 237–38
Sharon, Ariel, 132, 290
Shia Muslims, 9, 11, 12, 54, 57,
    104–5, 119–20, 131–43, 156,
    186–87
    cultural traditions of, 135,
        141–42, 149, 150–51, 155
    in Iran, 142–43, 147, 149,
        150–51, 153, 170
    in Iraq, 134, 137–39, 148–49,
        169, 179–82
    in Lebanon, 133–37
    mosques of, 12, 143
    Palestinian war with, 136–37
    radical militant revolt of, 105,
        131, 132, 133–40, 151,
        163–64, 168
    in Saudi Arabia, 153–55, 156
    suicide operations of, 136, 151,
        163–64, 188
    Sunni struggle against, 135, 139,
        149, 157, 165, 169, 182, 217
    underclass status of, 57, 133–34
Shi'is of Iraq, The (Nakash),
    181–82
Shi'r, 80, 121
al-Shi'riyya al-Arabiyya (Arabic
    Poetics) (Adonis), 114–16
Shubaylat, Laith, 295–96, 310

Shukri, Ghali, 254, 288

Shurayh, Mahmoud, 98, 99

Shu'ubiyya movement, 157

Shwayfat, 59

Shweir, 34, 36–37, 39, 40–45, 47, 49, 50, 53, 54, 56, 57, 72, 74, 81–82, 84, 91, 95

Sid Ahmad, Muhammad, 284, 291–92

Sidon, 10

Sidqi, Ismael, 220

Sinai Desert, 177

Sinai Peninsula, 52, 195

al-Sira' al-Fikri fi al-Adab al-Suri (The Intellectual Struggle in Syrian Literature) (Saadah), 55, 65

Sisyphus myth, xiv

Six Day War (1967), 7, 27, 83–84, 85, 121, 123, 124, 130, 131, 132, 143, 177–78, 194, 195, 215, 255, 265, 294

Smith, Eli, 43

socialism, 130, 139, 143, 171, 236

Song of Solomon, 34

Sorbonne, 120, 220

Soviet Union, 76, 194, 196, 234
    dissolution of, 170

Stark, Freya, 128

State Department, U.S., 18

St. Joseph University (East Beirut), 120

Stone, Oliver, 281

Sudan, 241

Suez Canal, 38, 302

Suez War (1956), 7, 11, 73, 76, 117, 123, 193–94

Sufi Muslims, 217

al-Sufur wa al-Hijab (Unveiling

and the Veil) (Zayn al-Din), 15, 16

Suleiman the Magnificent, 4

al-Sulh, Munah, 28–29

al-Sulh, Riad, 71

Sumerians, 118

Sunni Muslims, 53, 54, 64, 65, 87, 104, 131, 133, 135, 139, 142
    Shia struggle against, 135, 139, 149, 157, 165, 169, 182, 217

Suyyagh, Fayiz, 80

Sykes-Picot accords, 283

Syria, 5, 8, 14, 16, 18, 32–34, 35, 41, 59, 79, 103, 106, 108
    British campaign in, 22, 53, 58
    French rule of, 16, 52, 53, 55, 117, 120
    Great Rebellion in, 52
    history of, 65–66
    nationalist movement in, 50–53, 55, 62–67, 81, 83, 96, 121
    Ottoman rule of, 33, 37–38, 39, 66, 112
    sectarian struggles of, 8, 52–53, 65–66, 139
    seventh century Muslim conquest of, 65, 66
    volatile political climate of, 117

Syriac Orthodox Church, 57

Tabriz, 14

Taft, William Howard, 17

Tantawi, Shaykh Muhammed, 213

Taqla, Bishara, 250

Taqla, Salim, 250

Tartus, 117, 119, 120

Taurus Mountains, 52

Tel Aviv, 277, 290

Templars, 11

al-Thabit wa al-Mutahawwil (The

Fixed and the Changing)
(Adonis), 144–46
That They May Have Life
(Penrose), 61
theocratic politics, xii, xiii, xiv, xv,
7–9, 143, 150
see also Islamic fundamentalism
Theroux, Peter, 125, 127
Thesiger, Wilfred, 128–29
This Man from Lebanon (Young),
75
Thomson, W. M., 106–8
Thus Spake Zarathustra
(Nietzsche), 69–70
Tiberias, 13
Tigris River, 169
Toron, Castle of, 10
Transjordan, 58, 296, 304
tribalism, 8, 121, 137, 172
*Trilogy of the Children of the
Stones* (Qabbani), 159–61
Tripoli, 80, 131
Tucker, Robert, 174–75
Tunis, 125, 171, 173, 176, 261,
262
Turgenev, Ivan, 162–63
al-Turk, Jihad, 98–99
Turkey, 18, 57, 101–2, 108, 118,
173–74, 182–83
see also Ottoman empire
Turki, Fawaz, 264

al-'Udhari, Abdullah, 122
Umayyad dynasty, 150
Under Western Eyes (Conrad),
300–301
UNESCO, 253
Union of Arab Writers, 253
United Arab Emirates, 189
United States, 76

Arab oil interests of, 125–26,
130, 155, 188
foreign policy of, *see specific
states*
foreign terrorism against, 101,
105, 187, 192
popular culture of, 14
world role of, 174–75
al-Urwa al-Wuthqa (Close Bond),
29, 62

Van Dyck, Cornelius, 43
Vichy France, 22, 47, 58–59
"Vietnam syndrome," 182
Vindication of Sadat, The
(Ibrahim), 197–98

al-Wafd, 240
Wafd party, 224–25, 227, 228
Wahbe, Saad Eddin, 281–82
Wahhabi zealots, 178, 186
Walter Reed Hospital, 101
Wannous, Saadallah, 255
Weaver, Mary Anne, 225
Weizmann, Chaim, 267
West Bank, 158, 171, 246, 262,
264, 265
West Beirut, 9–10, 13–14, 26,
95–96, 139, 142
Arab commune in, 85, 261
politics and, 13, 15–16, 85, 86,
135
Shia dominance in, 135–37,
141–42
U.S. Embassy destroyed in, 101
"When Will They Declare the
Death of the Arabs?"
(Qabbani), 248
"Who Killed Kuwait?" (Sabah),
166

Wieseltier, Leon, 54
Wilson, Woodrow, 18
Wolfensohn, James D., 262, 274
women's rights, 6, 13, 15, 16, 88, 103
Woodward, Bob, 175
World Bank, 234–35, 274, 275
World Trade Center bombing, xv
World War I, 8, 16, 18, 36–39, 51, 55, 56, 57, 102, 168–69, 283, 300
World War II, xi, 20, 40, 47, 58–59, 175, 266
Wounded Thunder (Hawi), 97

Ya'ari, Ehud, 159
Yassin, Shaykh Ahmad, 164
Yawm Qutala al-Za'im (The Day the Leader was Killed) (Mahfuz), 225–26

Yazid, 151
al-Yaziji, Ibrahim, 24, 43
al-Yaziji, Nasif, 43
Yemen, 170, 173
Yemen War, 173
Young, Barbara, 75
Young Egypt (Misr al-fatat), 224–25
Younis, Ibtihal, 212, 214

al-Za'im, Husni, 63–64, 65, 71
Zaman al-Shi'r (The Time of Poetry) (Adonis), 253–54
Zayn al-Abidin, Imam, 155
Zayn al-Din, Nazira, 15, 16
Zayn al-Din, Said, 15
Zionism, xvi, 24, 62, 184, 264–65, 275, 281, 294
Zurayk, Constantine, 34